# Practical Clinical
# Supervision for Counselors

# About the Author

**Lisa Aasheim, PhD, NCC, ACS**, is the coordinator of the School Counseling Master's Program and the director of the Community Counseling Clinic at Portland State University. She also maintains a private practice offering counseling, clinical supervision, and agency and school consultation. She is a chapter author of numerous textbooks and has presented at ACES, ACA, and the Oregon Counselors Association. Dr. Aasheim has participated in the Oregon Board of Licensed Therapists and Counselors, the Teachers Standards and Practice Commission regarding social work licensure, and in clinical supervision revisions and standards.

# Practical Clinical Supervision for Counselors

## An Experiential Guide

*Lisa Aasheim, PhD, NCC, ACS*

SPRINGER PUBLISHING COMPANY

Springer Publishing Company, LLC
11 West 42nd Street
New York, NY 10036
www.springerpub.com

*Acquisitions Editor: Sheri W. Sussman*
*Composition: diacriTech*

ISBN: 978-0-8261-0786-2
E-book ISBN: 978-0-8261-0787-9

11 12 13/ 5 4 3 2 1

Library of Congress Cataloging-in-Publication Data

CIP data is available at the Library of Congress

Special discounts on bulk quantities of our books are available to corporations, professional associations, pharmaceutical companies, health care organizations, and other qualifying groups.

If you are interested in a custom book, including chapters from more than one of our titles, we can provide that service as well.

**For details, please contact:**
Special Sales Department, Springer Publishing Company, LLC
11 West 42nd Street, 15th Floor, New York, NY 10036-8002
Phone: 877-687-7476 or 212-431-4370; Fax: 212-941-7842
Email: sales@springerpub.com

Printed in the United States of America by Gasch Printing

*This book is dedicated to my lovely Madeline Rose,*

*whose empathic, warm, curious, and beautiful nature*

*inspires my work and play.*

# Contents

# Preface

My passion for clinical supervision was born one sunny afternoon on a park bench in Portland, Oregon. I had just left the university bookstore with Holloway's *Systems Approach to Supervision* in hand and, with an hour to spare before class, I decided to preview this required textbook while taking advantage of the early spring sunshine. Within a few moments, I was so deeply engrossed in the book that I, ironically, barely made it to the actual clinical supervision class on time.

It was on that park bench that I learned that supervision is not merely a task or duty assigned to a senior therapist. Instead, supervision is a field of study, complete with theories and models, practice standards, a code of ethics, credentialing, professional conferences, and professional organizations. It is a field of study and practice that is transdisciplinary and is relevant to many kinds of helpers in many helping professions. It was on that bench that I learned that the supervision relationship is core. Admittedly, that was not entirely new information; as a counselor, I already respected the critical importance of a strong, trusting relationship in any helping arrangement. I had also learned through experience that the relationship between a counselor and his or her supervisor was crucially important as well. I knew that my supervisors could directly impact my clinical work with clients through conversation, role modeling, demonstrations, and carefully guided discussion. I also knew my supervisors could directly impact my emotional and psychological experiences at work; the nurturance, guidance, and support afforded me in supervision somehow alleviated much of the frustration, helplessness, and isolation I felt as I did my best to help others live and function well. I did not understand, at the time, the mechanisms by which these supervisors could be so impactful. I just knew that my supervisors had the potential for great power in my professional (and personal) life; they had the power to influence and shape my relationships with my clients, my work setting, my colleagues, and my profession, for better or worse. I had certainly experienced both.

On that marvelously sunny afternoon, I first learned one approach to supervision; in the subsequent weeks and months, I learned the rest. Following that transformative hour on a park bench, I spent an evening and the following day listening with unswayable interest to my professor, Dr. Miars, share his knowledge and passion for this practice called "clinical supervision." I listened with great curiosity and mild skepticism as Dr. Miars insisted that with skill, practice, and forethought, we could all be effective supervisors. Then, at the end of less than ten hours, Dr. Miars sent the group of us off to provide supervision to Masters-level trainees and insisted, contrary to our insecure cries, that we would do alright. My profound disappointment at the brevity of the workshop was overshadowed by my excitement for what I had learned. Little did I realize that I, after consuming one book and a one-credit class, was actually more trained than many of my own supervisors had been.

Following that impactful experience, I used that one required book as a compass to direct my further investigation into this enigmatic practice called "clinical supervision." I used that initial book's reference section as a reading list and devoured every article and book I could find. I used each article to lead me to more articles, more information, until I could no longer find anything novel pertaining to the practice. Frustrated that the well of information had perhaps run dry, I attended every training and workshop I could find pertaining to the practice of clinical supervision. To my dismay, such workshops were few in number and far in distance. So, with a wide breadth of knowledge and a passion for the practice, I turned most of my professional attention to providing and practicing supervision so that I could learn experientially the many methods and approaches that I had merely read about. I offered supervision to Masters-level clinical mental health trainees, associate and bachelor-level addictions counselors, prelicensed and licensed counselors. I used individual, triadic, group, and classroom formats, all to gain a more intimate knowledge of the mechanisms and phenomenon that make supervision work. The hunger was mutual: I wanted to supervise as much as my counseling supervisees wanted supervision. We all longed for the powerful, formative experiences, and my supervisees and I looked forward to our time together and lamented at the end of each session that once again, time had flown by too quickly.

After completing a doctoral degree that focused on counselor education and supervision, then teaching counseling courses at two universities, I have finally landed at the very same university where I first learned about supervision. I teach alongside my dear colleague, Dr. Russell Miars, the very same professor who planted the "supervision seeds" many years ago. We and our colleagues take great delight in training supervisors for their future work with supervisees in a multitude of settings. It is for these supervisors that this book is written.

This book is for the supervisors who would like a practical guide to supervision, a framework that is applicable to any work context and most any situation; the supervisors who, like myself, wanted to learn supervision thoroughly so that it could be provided with the highest level of competence and effectiveness; the supervisors who also recognize that knowledge alone is not sufficient; our experiences, past and future, inform us as readily as the literature does. In reality, many supervisors have little time to gather vast amounts of information. Instead, this book brings that information directly to them in a way that integrates lived experiences with scholarly information.

My passion for clinical supervision continues as I teach classes for master's and doctoral level counselors who wish to provide supervision for licensure purposes. I conduct research to examine the quality and experiential aspects of counselor supervision in various settings, and I continue to practice, practice, practice. I direct a training clinic where I have the luxury of providing supervision and witnessing others provide supervision from behind a two-way mirror. I have a learning laboratory at my doorstep and take great pleasure in sharing my knowledge, experience, and enthusiasm with others both locally and nationally. You, as a reader of this book and an active participant in your learning process, will learn from my experiences as well as your own. This book is not didactic in nature; that is, it imparts information, but much of the learning will occur as you reflect, consider, and intentionally create your supervision experience.

Supervision is meant to be beneficial and fulfilling to all parties. While clinical supervision is an invariably challenging and, at times, distressing practice, it provides supervisors with the opportunity to impact thousands of clients by shaping and supporting their counselors. As you prepare to begin or continue your supervision practice, I invite you to find a spot on a lovely bench and dive into this book with the same curiosity, passion, and eagerness that drove your initial entry into the counseling field. Spend some time with this book and the opportunities therein; you will gain new knowledge, learn new concepts, and be introduced to new techniques and ideas. You will have the chance to reflect upon your own experiences, plan your future practices, and create your identity as a clinical supervisor. You may feel, at times, tempted to skip an exercise, section, or chapter. Resist the urge. Instead, allow yourself to be guided through the material and experiences therein. Your experiences, knowledge, and wisdom influence your learning and the meaning of this book's content. Engage fully in the activities and return to this book's material as often as needed so that you may make new sense of the information at a later time. From this point forward, read, learn, and supervise with intention. Enjoy.

# Acknowledgments

I am profoundly grateful for the support of my colleagues and mentors who listen to my endless musings about all-things-supervision: Susan Halverson-Westerberg and Russ Miars, who inspired my career with their support, wisdom, and guidance, and who have each provided me with countless opportunities to learn, grow, practice, and create; Deborah Rubel, who quite unintentionally inspired this book and quite intentionally taught me how to write, research, and write research; Cass Dykeman, who provided supervision-of-supervision and a myriad of opportunities to learn, teach, reflect, and practice; and Rick Johnson, a mentor who somehow knows just when to teach, support, guide, protect, praise, encourage, listen, and laugh. Additionally, I appreciate Kim Hattig for her tireless enthusiasm, relentless energy, and impeccable competence as a research assistant and colleague. I also thank Megan Scheminske and Tammy Schamuhn for their research assistance, and my dear colleagues Hanoch Livneh, Tina Anctil, Don Mihaloew, Kathy Lovrien, and David Capuzzi for their continued support and listening ears.

Additionally, I appreciate the scholars, researchers, and authors who influence my practice and feed my passion, including Holloway, Milne, Bernard, Ladany, Falendar, Goodyear, Borders, Stoltenberg, Delworth, Leddick, Lambert, Ellis, Nelson, Watkins, Wilcoxon, McNeill, Norem, and Magnuson (who has inspired me to write "60 by 60").

Finally, and most important, without the love and support of my family, I would not have the great fortune of sharing my work and passion with others. I am immensely grateful for my loved ones, who support me as I continue to live, work, and follow my passion.

# PART I

# PREPARING TO SUPERVISE

# ONE

# What is Clinical Supervision?

*F*ew aspects of the mental health profession are as illogical, inherently risky, and anxiety-provoking as clinical supervision. Ironically, the absence of clinical supervision is also illogical, inherently risky, and ought to be anxiety-provoking for all involved.

Clinical supervision at its finest protects client welfare and enhances the professional functioning and competence of mental health counselors (Holloway & Neufeldt, 1995). It has been shown to increase counselor skill levels, decrease risk to clients, and facilitate professional development and ethical functioning (Cormier & Bernard, 1982; Milne, 2009). It provides counselors with a venue for support, challenge, reflection, training, objective feedback, and professional discourse. When performed effectively, supervision is informative and transformative for all parties. When performed ineffectively, supervision is unimpactful in some cases, traumatic and hindering in others. Ineffective supervision may result in stagnation or a decrease in counselor skill development, potential ethical and legal violations, and, ultimately, increased risk of harm to clients (Ellis, 2001; Nelson & Friedlander, 2001). At its best, clinical supervision may be at once a counselor's best and seemingly worst professional experience. At its worst, clinical supervision is harmful to all involved, most notably the supervisee's clients.

## WHAT IS CLINICAL SUPERVISION?

Clinical supervision is not merely an activity specific to the counseling profession; rather, it is a distinct field of preparation and practice (Dye & Borders, 1990) that is interdisciplinary and maintains its own code of ethics, standards of practice, professional organization (The Association for Counselor Education and Supervision), national credential (the Approved Clinical Supervisor Credential, CCE Global), and scholarly journals (*Counselor Education and Supervision* and *The Clinical Supervisor*).

When one enters a new field of practice, it is reasonable to expect that additional field-specific training is needed to build competence in the new practice area. This is certainly the case with clinical supervision. Some believe that a highly competent, effective counselor will naturally become a skilled clinical supervisor. This is simply not the case. A skilled supervisor is not merely an experienced counselor. A skilled supervisor has received training specific to clinical supervision so that he has knowledge, skills, and disposition to meet the practice standards specific to the clinical supervision field (Borders & Leddick, 1987). Experience alone does not transform a counselor into a competent supervisor (Stevens, Goodyear, & Robertson, 1997); rather, experience as a counselor is simply one feature of the complete supervisor skillset.

## DEFINING CLINICAL SUPERVISION

Clinical supervision has been described as an essential, mutually advantageous, and impossible task (Borders & Brown, 2005; Zinkin, 1989). Further, defining *clinical supervision* has proven nearly as complicated as the practice itself. The literature presents a multitude of definitions, and the complexity of these definitions reminds supervisors of the complexity and multifaceted nature of the task itself.

In its simplest form, clinical supervision could be defined as "a controlling mechanism instituted to oversee directly the skills utilized in the treatment of patients" (Lyth, 2000, p.723) based on the literal meaning of the words *clinical* and *supervisor*. However, many would argue that the simple definition is inaccurate in that it omits most major defining variables of the practice. While it is agreed that the field lacks a strong, operational definition of the term clinical supervision, the term still carries strong implications for practice and tasks therein.

The most frequently cited definition, coined by Bernard and Goodyear (2009), defines clinical supervision as an intervention provided by a seasoned member of the field to less-experienced counselors in the course of an ongoing, evaluative relationship. That relationship aims to improve professional functioning of the newer counselor, monitor professional services rendered by the newer professional, and screen those who are attempting to enter the field (Bernard & Goodyear, 2009). Another notable researcher in the clinical supervision field notices some problems in operationalizing that definition for research purposes and presents the following definition as an alternative:

> The formal provision, by approved supervisors, of a relationship-based education and training that is work-focused and which manages, supports, develops, and evaluates the work of colleague/s. It therefore differs from related activities, such as mentoring and therapy, by incorporating an evaluative component and by being obligatory. The main methods that supervisors use are corrective feedback on the supervisee's performance, teaching, and collaborative goal-setting. The objectives of supervision are "normative" (e.g., case management and quality control issues), "restorative" (e.g., encouraging emotional

experiencing and processing), and "formative" (e.g., maintaining and facilitating the supervisees' competence, capability and general effectiveness). These objectives could be measured by current instruments (e.g., "Teachers PETS"; Milne et al., 2002) (Milne, 2009).

Supervision has additionally been defined as a "learning alliance that empowers the trainee to acquire skill and knowledge relevant to the profession and to experience interpersonal competence in the supervisory relationship" (Holloway, 1994). Drapela (1983) also focused on competence when he defined clinical supervision as a process of overseeing, guiding, and evaluating professional activities for the purpose of ensuring a high quality of counseling services for the clients served. Clinical supervision has also been defined as a practice in which a supervisor assists a counselor in working more effectively with clients to achieve successful outcomes (Herbert, 1997). Although readers are left to speculate about whether "successful" is defined by the supervisor, supervisee, or client, there is little doubt that the author is focusing on supervision as a tool for competence building.

The repeated cries for a unified definition is important on two levels: first, researchers who would like to conduct studies on the usefulness of supervision need a definition that lends itself to strong, empirical study. Second, clinical supervision as a practice is widely varied in the field. That is, the clinical supervision one counselor receives from one supervisor in one particular setting may be quite different from the clinical supervision another counselor receives from a different supervisor in another setting.

Clinical supervision is clinical in nature; that is, its focus is on the clinical services delivered to the client and the clinical skills of the counselor delivering such service. Often times, *administrative tasks* are necessarily intermingled with clinical tasks. Administrative tasks are tasks that necessarily accompany client care. These tasks are supplemental to direct service provision and include documentation and clinical communication (e.g., progress notes, case reviews, formal treatment plans). *Managerial tasks*, by contrast, center on meeting agency and bureaucratic needs (Haynes, Corey, & Moulton, 2003) and may include tasks that sustain agency operations and policies (e.g., budgeting, scheduling, systems coordination) (Spence et al., 2001). *Clinical tasks*, by contrast, focus more specifically on counselor and client needs (Kaiser, 1997) and include tasks such as case conceptualization, treatment planning, examination of the therapeutic relationship, and repairing alliance strains. Despite the inherent disparities, these clinical and managerial tasks often seem to exist within the same job description (Holloway, 1995; Powell, 2004).

In some cases, agency administrative needs (managerial tasks) may take precedence above clinical focus and supervisee development. This typically creates great role strain for the clinical supervisor, who attempts to balance clinical and managerial foci and typically creates dismay for the supervisees who would often rather attend to client care. Research reveals that supervisees prefer a clinical focus during supervision as opposed to an administrative one (Crimando, 2004; English, Oberle, & Byrne, 1979; Herbert & Trusty, 2006) and find great frustration with supervision sessions that do not adequately attend to client care needs. One study of rehabilitation counselors found that counselors who indicated their supervisor "always" took an administrative role (engaging in administrative tasks) were most dissatisfied with their "clinical" supervision experiences. This same study indicates that counselors who were much more satisfied with supervision when their supervisors "often, rarely, or never" engaged in administration roles and focused instead on clinical tasks (Herbert & Trusty, 2006, p.74).

Clinical supervision is intended to protect the welfare of the supervisee's clients above all else. Following that, supervision provides counselors with a means to improve their performance and build additional clinical and professional competence. Supervision welcomes counselors into the profession by providing developmental support from an objective, skilled, and experienced colleague who has the power to greatly influence the supervisee's experience of his clients, his clinical work, and his professional identity.

## THE PREVALENCE OF CLINICAL SUPERVISION

Virtually all counselors have some relationship with clinical supervision at some point in their careers. Clinical supervision is acknowledged as a critical and core function of counselor early training and development. The accreditation bodies who recognize counselor preparation and clinical psychology programs require ongoing and regular supervision of counselors in training (e.g., CACREP, AAMFT, APA). Clinical supervision is also recognized by state licensing boards as a critical and core function of prelicense counselor preparation (e.g., American Association of State Counseling Boards), and most states require prelicensed counselors to engage in clinical supervision while earning licensure (Pearson, 2000). Once licensed, most counselors are typically legally allowed to practice autonomously without additional clinical supervision. However, many of the recipients of effective, impactful supervision understand its value and prefer to continue to access supervision well into their professional career (Usher & Borders, 1993). Further, many employers and agencies require ongoing supervision of their counselors for the betterment of client care, oversight, and protection for all.

## THE PURPOSES OF CLINICAL SUPERVISION

Clinical supervision, above all else, is for the protection of client welfare. Every task and activity related to clinical supervision either directly or indirectly impacts client welfare. Supervisors help supervisees develop and maintain clinical competence so that clients will be more optimally served. Supervisors ensure that supervisees are practicing in an ethical manner so that clients are not harmed in the therapeutic process. Client welfare is at the core of all clinical supervision; supervisors help counselors gain and sustain clinical competence to that end.

### Developing and Maintaining Clinical Competence

Counselor supervision is essential in developing and maintaining clinical competence (Bernard & Goodyear, 2009; Borders & Leddick, 1988; Cross & Brown, 1983; Hansen, Pound, & Petro, 1976; Page & Wosket, 2001). The supervisor's job is primarily to create a relationship and environment in which the supervisee can learn essential skills that then transfer into the therapeutic exchange with clients (Holloway, 1995). Furthermore, supervisors help supervisees to connect the science and practice of counseling (Holloway & Wolleat, 1994), a task that is growing increasingly important with the strengthening emphasis on the utilization of evidence-based practices in agency settings (American Counseling Association (ACA) Code of Ethics, 2005; Blume, 2005). Supervision may additionally be used with counselors who need specialized or remedial training and guidance (Cobia & Pipes, 2002). In fact, increased clinical supervision is often required by state regulatory boards who find a counselor operating below acceptable practice standards. Finally, supervision by nature is evaluative: that is, supervisors are tasked with constantly evaluating the counselor's work in accordance with professional practice standards. This evaluation provides supervisees with necessary feedback about where their competence may be improved for optimal performance.

### Building and Sustaining Ethical Practice

Another key function of clinical supervision is to ensure that the supervisees are engaging in sound ethical practices. Clinical supervision affects the supervisee's level of ethical competence and, consequently, increases the quality of service delivery to the client (Cormier & Bernard, 1982; Herlihy, 2006). Counselor supervisors are ethically bound to ensure the well-being of the clients with whom the supervisee is working (Cormier & Bernard, 1982), while at the same time honoring the growth and continual development of the supervisee. So, supervisors take care to role model and provide ongoing evaluative feedback to supervisees with regard to optimal ethical practices (Borders & Brown, 2005; Cormier & Bernard, 1982).

Supervisees engaged in supervision will likely be encouraged to examine issues of informed consent, dual relationships, confidentiality, and ethical service provisions (Borders & Brown, 2005; Cormier & Bernard, 1982). Supervisors have the opportunity to provide training to supervisees and can engage in practice activities regarding ethical issues (Cormier & Bernard, 1982). Supervisors also serve as gatekeepers to the profession, meaning that they are responsible for keeping unethical practitioners away from the profession (and thus, away from clients) (Pearson & Piazza, 1997).

## HOW SHOULD CLINICAL SUPERVISION BE CONDUCTED?

The majority of this book provides supervisors with information so that they may make informed, well-considered decisions about how to practice clinical supervision in their particular practice setting. However, all clinical supervision practice should align with the practice standards and competencies specific to the supervision field.

The ethical guidelines for supervision were originated in the 1980s by the Association for Counselor Education and Supervision's (ACES) Supervision Interest Network (SINACES). This network created and recommended the Ethical Guidelines for Counseling Supervisors (Borders & Brown, 2005). The ACES Executive Council endorsed these guidelines and formally adopted them in March 1993 as a way to guide and inform supervisors in their practice (Borders & Brown, 2005; Hart, Borders, Nance, & Paradise, 1995). Currently, ethical guidelines for supervisors are embedded in the American Counseling Association's Code of Ethics (ACA, 2005).

The ethical guidelines clarify the responsible delivery of effective clinical supervision. The guidelines focus on client welfare and rights, the supervisory role, and the program administration role that is at times held by a supervisor (Supervision Interest Network/SINACES, 1993). The guidelines recommend that supervisors should utilize the following sequence when making decisions regarding supervision and supervisory tasks: relevant legal and ethical standards, client welfare, supervisee welfare, supervisor welfare, and program or agency service and administrative needs (Supervision Interest Network/SINACES, 1993). That is, clinical needs are the top priority, administrative tasks the lowest.

## SUPERVISOR DEVELOPMENT

Many new or untrained supervisors experience thoughts and feelings reminiscent of their days as novice counselors. They feel eager to perform well, are nervous that they will not know how to perform well, and wish they were beyond the point of being so concerned about their performance. Indeed, clinical supervisors move from novice to expert in a manner similar to that of most counselors and experience the same types of uncertainty, impatience, and at-times painful introspection along the way.

Watkins (1990; 1993) presents a supervisor development model that consists of four developmental stages. The first stage, *role shock*, involves a novice supervisor experiencing the "imposter phenomenon" so common of early counselors who worry that someone will notice that they are not actually a "real" counselor and quite probably have no idea what they are doing. This stage involves the struggle to build competence and a concern for "doing it right." Supervisors at this stage are concerned with learning and following the rules, and are eager to know concretely what the "rules" actually are so that supervision can be done "correctly."

The second stage is the *role recovery/transition* stage, in which supervisors begin to exercise some flexibility and relax a bit into the supervisor role. They have developed enough confidence at this point to tentatively address issues such as transference and countertransference but are not yet confident enough to effectively challenge a supervisee's performance deficits.

The third stage of the Watkins (1990) model is *role consolidation*. In this stage, the supervisor gains a greater understanding and confidence in his role and feels more ready to exert influence in the supervision process. This supervisor has adopted a theory or approach to supervision and is engaging in more flavorful practice as he tries new techniques and uses new tools.

The fourth and final stage is *role mastery*. This stage is typically a more comfortable one for the supervisor, as he has a clearer understanding of his competence as a supervisor. He uses a sense of humor and enjoys the intricacies of the supervision process. Further, he has integrated the supervisor role and operates comfortably from that position.

Many supervisors are excited to arrive at that final role mastery stage. However, they recall from their early days as counselors that there is work to be done before true mastery can be achieved. While enhancing their knowledge and skill base, supervisors learn to engage in ongoing *reflectivity* about their supervision practice so that they may move to optimal, autonomous functioning as supervisors. Concurrently, they will help their supervisees move toward optimal, autonomous functioning as reflective, self-monitoring counseling professionals.

## TOWARD REFLECTIVE PRACTICE

Reflectivity, or self-reflection, is a core tool in developing critical thinking, self-evaluation, insight, and autonomy in one's work (Orchowski, Evangelista, & Probst, 2010). Self-reflection refers to the cyclical process a supervisor uses to critically evaluate and examine his affective, behavioral, and cognitive experiences. This critical examination yields greater insight and understanding, which are then applied to one's conceptual framework and understanding. This greater insight and understanding leads to change (Orchowski, Evangelista, & Probst, 2010). Supervisors aim to become self-reflective supervisors who can autonomously engage in a critical analysis of the many complicated relationship dynamics, clinical phenomena, and stressors that are present in the supervision experience. There are innumerable factors to attend to, and supervisors, with practice, become increasingly skilled at efficiently making sense of voluminous amounts of information.

Supervisors engage in self-reflection for the betterment of their perform-ance as a supervisor; additionally, supervisors model reflectivity so that their supervisees may learn and develop the same self-reflective and analytic skills in their own clinical work. Ideally, a supervisee, with time and prac-tice, becomes readily able to self-monitor and manage his work with greater autonomy. Eventually, a supervisee becomes increasingly capable of self-supervision and is ready for fully autonomous clinical practice. Autonomous practice does not mean practicing alone or in isolation; rather, autonomous practice means having the skill and insight to be able to make in-the-moment corrections to one's work. Clinical autonomy means having the competence to recognize legal and ethical dilemmas as they occur and knowing how and when to access consultative assistance and support. Clinical autonomy means having an understanding of one's professional standards of practice, and being able to accurately evaluate one's performance in relation to those standards. For supervisors to move their supervisees to such proficiency in their clinical work, it is necessary for supervisors to move to proficiency in their competence as a clinical supervisor.

## COMPETENT SUPERVISION

Many of the major theorists and leaders in the supervision field have contributed to the collective understanding of what makes supervision "good" (e.g., Stoltenberg, McNeill, & Crethar, 1994; Worthen & McNeill, 1996). In that same spirit, many of these contributors have also examined what makes supervision "lousy" or ineffective (e.g., Magnuson, Norem, & Wilcoxon, 2000; Nelson & Friedlander, 2001; Wulf & Nelson, 2000). While the literature provides a fairly comprehensive and at times humorous account of the many features of good and bad supervision, supervisors must concern themselves first with providing *competent* supervision. Competent super-vision is supervision that aligns with the knowledge, skills, and attitudes described by the Standards for Counseling Supervisors (Supervision Inter-est Network/SINACES, 1993). A supervisor who aims to practice competent supervision builds his knowledge about supervision as a discrete field of practice, gains experience in providing supervision in a self-reflective man-ner, and actively works to identify as a member of the clinical supervision profession.

This book assists supervisors in these crucial tasks. While reading this book, supervisors will collect knowledge about the field and practice of clini-cal supervision. As they gather knowledge, supervisors will think critically and reflectively about their own experiences as a supervisee and, perhaps, as a supervisor. These recollections will help shape and inform current thinking about the supervision process and one's developing practice as a clinical supervisor. Finally, this book helps supervisors gain familiarity with the many key features of the clinical supervision profession: the methods and approaches, the standards and competencies, the code of ethics, the roles and functions, and the many interrelated tasks and features of the supervision process.

This book is an instrument to gain knowledge, develop skills, and form the habit of self-reflective practice. Supervisors should complete the readings and exercises in the order they are presented, as many of the components build upon prior experiences and reflections. Most importantly, supervisors should recognize that this book, while experiential and interactive, is only a book. It is not a substitute for the valuable learning and development that can be gained by supervisors who invite a more experienced and trained supervisor to oversee their work through supervision-of-supervision. Supervisors may use this book as a tool to develop knowledge and to form their professional plan and identity as a clinical supervisor; this book, combined with supervision-of-supervision, will assist supervisors in providing competent, effective, and impactful clinical supervision services.

# TWO

# Preparing for Effective Supervision

*E*ffective supervision serves several purposes: to protect client care, to develop and enhance counselor skill and functioning, and to provide self-governance for the profession by remediating or assisting compromised professionals (Bernard & Goodyear, 2009; Cormier & Bernard, 1982; Watkins, 1997). Ineffective supervision may result in stagnation or a decrease in counselor skill development, potential ethical and legal violations, and, ultimately, increased risk of harm to clients (Ellis, 2001; Nelson & Friedlander, 2001). To successfully carry out clinical supervision's many impactful responsibilities, supervisors must be fully prepared to operate with the highest levels of academic, ethical, psychological, multicultural, and professional functioning.

Supervisors must receive training and education specific to the practice of supervision (Falender & Shafranske, 2004), must understand the field standards of supervision practice (Borders & Brown, 2005), must be intimately familiar with all relevant ethical codes pertaining to both supervision and counseling practice (Knapp & Vandecreek, 1997), and should thoroughly examine the features of effective and ineffective supervision so as to practice with intention and forethought.

This chapter reviews relevant aspects of supervisor training and credentialing, standards of supervision practice, the qualities and characteristics of an effective supervisor, and features of effective and ineffective supervision experiences.

## SUPERVISOR CREDENTIALS AND TRAINING

Many supervisors find the practice of supervision to be somewhat complicated and challenging, especially in the absence of strong training, thorough preparation, and adequate support for such a complex professional endeavor. While many mental health professionals are likely to supervise at some point during their career (Bernard & Goodyear, 2009; Campbell, 2006), many supervisors simply have not received training specific to the practice of supervision and begin their practice without sufficient preparation

(Holloway, 1992; Little, et al., 2000; Watkins, 1992). However, in recent years, supervision is becoming more widely acknowledged as an essential and key function of the counseling professions (Scott, et al., 2000). As such, state licensing boards, credentialing bodies, professional organizations, and university training programs are paying increasing attention to the training and performance of clinical supervisors. The counselor-turned-overseers should no longer be operating without training and appropriate adherence to practice standards; instead, counselors who become supervisors recognize that they are embarking on a new enterprise with specific skills, dispositions, and regulatory aspects to adhere to.

## STATE LICENSING BOARDS

Although many supervisors begin their supervision practice without formal knowledge or training about how to supervise, many states now require that supervisors meet specific training and experience criteria in order to supervise prelicensure counselors. Some states have specific credential designations (such as a license for supervisors or a designation like "approved supervisor"), and others have just a list of requirements with no specific credential attached. A credential is simply proof of one's ability to perform the tasks of supervision, and state licensing boards are well positioned to make such determinations since supervision is considered an integral and necessary component of client care and professional development. The American Association of State Counseling Boards created an Approved Supervisor Model that states may adopt as their credentialing model, but many states have developed their own list of requirements. The Approved Supervisor Model states that approved supervisors

- have a current license in their jurisdiction
- have 3 years postlicensing clinical practice
- document 45 clock hours of graduate level supervision training, 30 hours professional level training, or 25 hours of supervision-of-supervision
- engage in continuing education about supervision; specifically, 3 hours per year
- stay current with codes and laws that pertain to supervision and other professional standards (e.g., ACES or ACA Code of Ethics)
- maintain liability insurance that specifically covers the supervision practice
- keep a current resume or vita on file with the state board (note that few, if any, state boards follow this guideline)
- have no disciplinary actions on their record against their license (AASCB, 2011).

Every state in the United States requires prelicensed counselors to practice under the supervision of an appropriately qualified supervisor (ACA, 2005). So, supervisors who wish to oversee the work of prelicensed supervisors need to become familiar with the requirements in their state before agreeing to supervise a prelicensed professional. Supervisors have an ethical responsibility to learn these rules and responsibilities prior to initiating supervision with a prelicensed supervisee so that the supervisee does not invest time, money, and hope in a supervisor whose credentials or preparation is not acceptable to the state licensing board (Table 2.1).

### TABLE 2.1
### Counselor Licensing Boards

| STATE | REGULATORY BOARD WEB ADDRESS |
| --- | --- |
| Alabama | http://www.abec.alabama.gov/ |
| Alaska | http://www.commerce.state.ak.us/occ/ppco.htm |
| Arizona | http://www.azbbhe.us/licensure%20apps.htm |
| Arkansas | http://www.state.ar.us/abec/ |
| California | http://www.bbs.ca.gov/ |
| Colorado | http://www.dora.state.co.us/mental-health/lpc/ |
| Connecticut | http://www.ct.gov/dph/cwp/view.<br>asp?a=3121&q=396902&dphNav_GID=1821 |
| Delaware | http://dpr.delaware.gov/boards/profcounselors/index.<br>shtml |
| Florida | http://www.doh.state.fl.us/mqa/491/ |
| Georgia | http://sos.georgia.gov/plb/counselors/ |
| Hawaii | http://hawaii.gov/dcca/areas/pvl/programs/mental/ |
| Idaho | https://secure.ibol.idaho.gov/IBOL/BoardPage.<br>aspx?Bureau=COU |
| Illinois | http://www.idfpr.com/dpr/who/prfcns.asp |
| Indiana | http://www.in.gov/pla/social.htm |
| Iowa | http://www.idph.state.ia.us/licensure/board_home.<br>asp?board=be |
| Kansas | http://www.ksbsrb.org/professionalcounselors.htm |
| Kentucky | http://lpc.ky.gov/ |
| Louisiana | http://www.lpcboard.org/ |
| Maine | http://www.maine.gov/pfr/professionallicensing/index.<br>shtml |
| Maryland | http://dhmh.maryland.gov/bopc/ |
| Massachusetts | www.mass.gov/dpl/boards/mh |

*(continued)*

**TABLE 2.1**
**Counselor Licensing Boards (*continued*)**

| STATE | REGULATORY BOARD WEB ADDRESS |
|---|---|
| Michigan | http://www.michigan.gov/lara/0,1607, 7-154-27417_27529_27536---,00.html |
| Minnesota | http://www.bbht.state.mn.us/ |
| Mississippi | http://www.lpc.state.ms.us/ |
| Missouri | http://pr.mo.gov/counselors.asp |
| Montana | http://bsd.dli.mt.gov/license/bsd_boards/swp_board/ board_page.asp |
| Nebraska | www.dhhs.ne.gov/crl/mhcs/mental/mentalindex.htm |
| Nevada | http://marriage.state.nv.us/ |
| New Hampshire | http://www.nh.gov/mhpb/ |
| New Jersey | http://www.njconsumeraffairs.gov/proc/ |
| New Mexico | http://www.rld.state.nm.us/counseling/ |
| New York | http://www.op.nysed.gov/prof/mhp/ |
| North Carolina | http://www.ncblpc.org/ |
| North Dakota | http://www.ndbce.org/ |
| Ohio | http://cswmft.ohio.gov/ |
| Oklahoma | http://pcl.health.ok.gov |
| Oregon | http://www.oregon.gov/OBLPCT/ |
| Pennsylvania | www.dos.state.pa.us/social |
| Rhode Island | www.health.ri.gov/hsr/professions/mf_counsel.php |
| South Carolina | http://www.llr.state.sc.us/pol/counselors/ |
| South Dakota | http://dhs.sd.gov/brd/counselor/ |
| Tennessee | http://health.state.tn.us/boards/PC_MFT&CPT/ |
| Texas | http://www.dshs.state.tx.us/counselor/ |
| Utah | http://dopl.utah.gov/licensing/professional_ counseling.html |
| Vermont | http://vtprofessionals.org/opr1/allied/ |
| Virginia | http://www.dhp.virginia.gov/counseling/ |
| Washington | http://www.doh.wa.gov/hsqa/professions/mentalhealth/ |
| West Virginia | http://www.wvbec.org/ |
| Wisconsin | http://drl.wi.gov/profession.asp?profid=43&locid=0 |
| Wyoming | http://plboards.state.wy.us/mentalhealth/index.asp |

*Activity:* What are the supervision requirements for prelicensed counselors in your state? Go to your state licensing board Web site to learn the most current requirements. As more state licensing boards pay increasing attention to supervisor *qualifications, the requirements may change quickly or may be in the process of changing, so be cautious not to assume you already know the requirements.*

*Answer the following:*

*What do I need to do to become a supervisor in this state?*

*Do I have the appropriate credentials to supervise?*

*With my credentials, who am I qualified to supervise? Which credentials can I supervise toward? (In many states, the requirements are very specific. For instance, if you are a licensed professional counselor, you may not be qualified to supervise someone who is working toward licensure in couples, marriage, and family therapy)*

*Have I held the appropriate credentials for a long enough amount of time? (Many states require that you have a certain number of years of postlicense experience prior to supervising)*

*Have I met the training requirements?*

*Am I required to get supervision of my supervision? If so, how can I access an appropriately qualified supervisor? (Hint: You can often check with the licensing board for assistance, or you can contact a local university that houses a counselor education, counseling psychology, or similar program)*

*Finally, examine the licensure requirements for your state so that you are familiar with the requirements your supervisees will need to follow. Have the supervision requirements changed since you were supervised? How? Familiarize yourself with relevant forms and documentation requirements, including evaluation procedures, so that you are well equipped to guide your supervisee through the process.*

## PROFESSIONAL ORGANIZATIONS AND ACCREDITATION

Several professional organizations and training program accrediting bodies have specific supervision guidelines and standards for the provision of supervision. The Council for Accreditation of Counseling and Related Educational Programs (CACREP) requires that students in counselor education doctoral programs receive formal instruction in clinical supervision (CACREP, 2001) and requires that those providing internship supervision are licensed professionals in a relevant field (CACREP, 2001). The American Association for Marriage and Family Therapy (AAMFT) holds a specific approved supervisor designation indicating that the supervisor has "obtained the educational, experiential, and supervisory training required for the competent supervision of marriage and family therapists and trainees" (AAMFT Approved Supervisor Designation standards & responsibilities handbook, p. 3). Candidates for this designation complete a specific supervision fundamentals course, provide and receive supervision, and receive supervision mentoring.

The Approved Clinical Supervisor (ACS) credential is a nationally issued credential that attempts to provide some standardization of qualified supervisor requirements. The ACS credential was initiated in 1997 and is intended to identify mental health professionals who meet professional supervision standards, promote the identity, visibility, and accountability of clinical supervisors, and encourage the professional growth and development of clinical supervisors (http://www.cce-global.org/ACS). Some states accept the ACS credential in lieu of their state licensing board's requirements for supervisor approval (e.g., South Dakota). This credential was initially overseen by the National Board for Certified Counselors and is now managed by CCE Global (www.cce-global.org).

*Activity: What professional organizations or accreditation bodies are you or your supervisees involved with? Examine their Web sites and/or manuals. Do they have specific supervision requirements or standards that must be met? What will you need to do to ensure their standards or requirements are being upheld?*

## STANDARDS OF SUPERVISION PRACTICE

A supervisor who meets the requirements to supervise is not necessarily supervising well. In fact, there are many examples in the literature of quite dreadful supervision performed by individuals who are quite well qualified (Gray, Ladany, Walker, & Ancis, 2001; Magnuson, Wilcoxon, & Norem, 2000). Since qualification to perform the job does not automatically correlate to quality, the field has developed standards of practice to guide ethical and behavioral functioning for supervision professionals.

The Association for Counselor Education and Supervision (ACES), in response to the known training and performance gaps in supervision practice, formed a committee entitled The Supervision Interest Network in the 1980s. This network created the ethical guidelines for counseling supervisors (Borders & Brown, 2005). The ACES Executive Council endorsed these standards and formally adopted them in March, 1993 as a way to guide and inform supervisors in their practice (Borders & Brown, 2005; Hart, Borders, Nance, & Paradise, 1995). The standards focus on 11 core domains that detail the knowledge, competencies, and traits of effective supervisors (Dye & Borders, 1990). These standards provide recommendations and guidance to supervisors intending to engage in professionally optimal supervision practices.

The standards focus on areas such as supervisor competence, the supervisory role, documentation, and the program administration role that is at times held by a supervisor (Supervision Interest Network/SINACES, 1993; Appendix A). The guidelines recommend that supervisors should follow this sequence-of-importance when making decisions regarding supervision and supervisory tasks: relevant legal and ethical standards, client welfare, supervisee welfare, supervisor welfare, and program or agency service and administrative needs (Supervision Interest Network/ SINACES, 1995). While the standards provide supervisors with an inclusive list of competencies, supervisors must additionally be familiar with various codes of ethics that adhere to their (and their supervisees') practice.

Supervisors adhere to several codes of ethics that align with each of their practice domains. First, supervisors follow the codes of ethics at a local and state level. A supervisor who holds a counseling license in his or her state will adhere to his or her state's code of ethics for both licensure and supervision. Further, that supervisor will follow the codes of ethics that pertain directly to his agency or work setting (some agencies have their own ethical codes that must be adhered to). Additionally, the supervisor adheres to his or her codes of ethics that relate to his practice area and credentialing body (e.g., the American Counseling Association's code of Ethics, the National Board for Certified Counselors code). The American Counseling Association incorporated the formerly separate supervision code of ethics into the 2005 revised ethical code (ACA, 2005), and many organizations have codes of ethics that include sections specific to supervision practice (e.g., AAMFT).

Supervisors must also be familiar with the codes of ethics that their supervisees must adhere to. Supervisors and supervisees should have ready access to all relevant codes of ethics, as they will often be incorporated into supervision sessions.

*Activity: Make a list of all codes of ethics that you must adhere to. List the codes that correspond to the following levels:*

- *Local or agency*
- *State (include supervisor codes and codes that govern your licenses or credentials)*
- *National (consider your national organizations and national credentials)*

*Examine copies of each of these codes. Notice any ethical guidelines that specifically relate to supervision and the responsibilities of a supervisor. Are these items fairly similar across codes? Are there any seemingly incongruent or opposing items?*

*Were any of the items surprising to you?*

*Do you believe you may have difficulty adhering to any of the items in any of the codes? What may cause the difficulty and what preventative measures can you take to ensure ethical compliance?*

Codes of ethics and standards of practice are not merely documents that should be learned for future reference. They are dynamic instruments that infiltrate and influence all areas of clinical practice. Supervisors should treat the codes as decision making and informative tools that will be integrated into supervision discussions and practice. Effective supervisors pay attention and adhere to ethical codes and optimal standards of practice, both as supervisors and as helping professionals (e.g., Ladany, Lehrman-Waterman, Molinaro, & Wolgast, 1999).

At this point, the focus shifts from a broader view of supervisor preparation to a more intimate analysis in an examination of the personal and professional characteristics of the ideal supervisor and effective and ineffective supervision practices.

## CHARACTERISTICS OF THE "IDEAL" SUPERVISOR

The ideal supervisor possesses many characteristics that align well with the traits and features of an effective counselor. However, the ideal supervisor is not necessarily someone who is or was an effective therapist. While it is important for a supervisor to be effective clinically, effective counseling skills do not automatically translate into good clinical supervision skills (Bernard & Goodyear, 2009). Instead, supervisors have the features of effective counselors plus some additional features that make them well suited for the unique responsibilities and demands of a supervision role. While the characteristics and features of "good" supervisors are considerably varied, Carifio and Hess (1987) describe the personal characteristics and behaviors of supervisors who appear to practice more optimally than others. Additional research in the field of supervision provides similar information (e.g., Borders, Cashwell, & Rotter (1995)), so the following section provides a comprehensive view of the characteristics and behaviors of supervisors who appear to provide more effective and beneficial supervision.

## THE SUPERVISORY ALLIANCE

The quality and effectiveness of any supervision experience largely depends on the relationship between the supervisor and supervisee, known as the supervisory alliance (Efstation, Patton, & Kardash, 1990). While the supervisor and supervisee both maintain multiple responsibilities in developing and sustaining a quality supervisory alliance, it is the supervisor's responsibility to create the space and container for the quality relationship to develop. The supervisory alliance is so central to effective supervision that an entire chapter is devoted to it later in this book. At this point, however, we focus on the ideal supervisor's ability to develop and maintain effective working relationships. Effective supervision cannot occur without an intact, well-formed professional relationship between the supervisor and supervisee (Bradley & Ladany, 2001; Holloway, 1995). Supervisors who maintain strong interpersonal skills are likely going to be able to engage in more effective supervision than supervisors who struggle in their relationships with others. We will now further examine some specific characteristics and behaviors that help supervisors develop and maintain effective and ideal working relationships.

## AVAILABILITY AND APPROACHABILITY

Ideal supervisors are available and approachable to their supervisees. A supervisee who perceives his or her supervisor as too busy, unwelcoming, or burdened by the supervisory relationship is unlikely to make effective use of supervision. The supervisor who maintains a welcoming and approachable attitude is inviting supervisees to share fully about their professional encounters and experiences. The approachable supervisor is warm and welcoming to a supervisee when that supervisee reaches out during nonsession times. Although it is very appropriate for a supervisor to set professional boundaries around the amount of contact a supervisee has outside of session, the responsible supervisor recalls the responsibility of oversight extends beyond the session itself. Further, a supervisor who welcomes contact is creating a space where the supervisee can fully inform and share vital information. In time, the supervisor's welcoming stance pays off in that the supervisee learns, through gentle direction, what information is appropriate to save and what must be shared more urgently. For instance, a supervisor may invite a supervisee to call anytime a need arises. That supervisor may find that the supervisee is calling frequently without obvious intention. The supervisor determines that the supervisee needs some assistance in knowing what clinical material needs immediate oversight and where he or she may exercise greater autonomy. The supervisor guides the supervisee in this discovery with comments such as "Let's put that on our list of items to discuss when we meet next" and "I'm glad you called to inform me about that mandated call to the department of child welfare. It sounds like you've covered what you needed to, including informing me, and I look forward to discussing your experience more when we meet on Friday."

Supervisors should be especially concerned with how they greet their supervisees. Is the welcome warm and inviting? Has the supervisor fully transitioned into the supervisor role? The initial greeting sends a clear message to the supervisee. It is the difference between "I'm glad to see you. Welcome." and "You are imposing on my busy schedule, so keep it brief!" If supervisors send the message that supervision should be kept brief, supervisees will likely take shortcuts and eliminate essential information and thorough processing. The supervisee will likely feel tense, anxious, and as if supervision is an imposition on the supervisor. Instead, supervisors should ensure their greeting and attention-giving behaviors role model what he or she would like to see his supervisees do in the therapeutic setting.

## CORE QUALITIES

The ideal supervisor possesses many of the same qualities and traits as the ideal therapist (Pierce, Carkhuff, & Berenson, 1967). However, the ideal supervisor maintains clarity about his or her role; that is, the ideal supervisor is not performing therapy but rather exhibiting some of the same qualities and skills that may have made him effective as a counselor. Ideal supervisors likely possess many of the facilitative features considered to be core conditions of a skilled counselor: empathy, positive regard, genuineness, and congruence (Rogers, 1957). Additionally, ideal supervisors often possess traits such as concern, flexibility, attention, investment, openness, and curiosity (Carifio & Hess, 1987). Further, empirical studies reflect that traits such as empathy, respect, genuineness, and concreteness are the "facilitative conditions" necessary for effective supervisor–supervisee interactions (Lambert, 1980).

### Appropriate Self-Disclosure

Self-disclosure may be a positive component of the supervisory process (Ladany, Walker, Melencoff, 2001). However, supervisors should maintain a professional and intentional stance with self-disclosure. That is, model appropriate self-disclosure to your supervisee so that your supervisee can best understand the usefulness and appropriateness of such disclosure at key intervention points in a helping process. Self-disclosure is helpful in supervision when the disclosure helps a supervisee develop a greater understanding or when it helps the supervisee convey empathy. For instance, a supervisor may recall a time when she felt an abundance of painful countertransference regarding a specific client. She may describe the situation in detail to the supervisee and then describe how she resolved the countertransference and used the experience to better her work with that and other clients. For instance, the supervisor may recall a time when she worked with a couple who were not able to reconcile their difficulties with one another and were contemplating divorce. The supervisor shares this anecdote with the supervisee, along with this disclosure: "You know, I felt so helpless on many levels, and a little bit like a failure as a therapist. Then I realized that my job isn't to help couples stay together. I hadn't failed in that regard. Instead, my job is to help couples get through their difficulties. They decided divorce was the solution, and I needed to accept that my role was to help through that. It was a painful time for everyone, and I ached right along with them. I think we all felt like failures for a little bit." This disclosure serves many purposes simultaneously: It helps the supervisee remember that the supervisor is human and has "human" experiences, it helps normalize the experience of countertransference in the therapeutic process, and it conveys deep empathy for the supervisee's plight. Further, it allows the supervisee to drop any defenses and share in a more intimate way that involves no punishment or shame.

The ideal supervisor is well boundaried and intentional with self-disclosure. The ideal supervisor understands that supervision is not an appropriate venue to discuss his or her own personal issues, therapeutic endeavors, or his or her own clients (except in select, well-considered instances when it is for the supervisee's developmental gain).

## ROLE CLARITY: SUPERVISOR OR THERAPIST?

Similarly, the ideal supervisor understands that supervision is not therapy and should not mirror a therapy session. While a supervisor utilizes similar skills and mannerisms as a therapist, supervisor and supervisee alike should be clear that supervision is not a place to discuss the supervisee's personal struggles except as they relate directly to client care (Carifio & Hess, 1987; Lambert, 1980). One study revealed that supervisees most disliked the work of supervisors who used therapeutic approaches to supervision (Rosenblatt & Mayer, 1975). Additional studies have detailed similar findings, and there is agreement in the literature that supervisees do not want their supervisors providing therapy as part of the supervision process (e.g., Magnuson et al., 2000). While supervisors may feel tempted to analyze or treat their supervisees, supervisors must consider the implications of therapeutic approaches. First, engaging in a therapeutic type relation with the supervisee creates (and stems from) role confusion. Recall that the supervisor's primary job is to oversee client care. The supervisor serves the client first, supervisee next. With these principles in mind, a supervision-as-therapy approach focuses on the supervisee's needs and leaves little room to focus on the client's care. Next, consider the objective, evaluative role a supervisor plays with the supervisee. Skilled therapists are often objective, nonevaluative, nonjudgmental neutral parties in a client's life. To be judgmental or evaluative may be damaging in many therapeutic relationships. On the converse, skilled supervisors must, by definition, be evaluative and hold power to influence the counselor's behavior and practice (Holloway, 1995). A supervisor can be effective with a supervisee, but cannot practice effective supervision from a therapist's role.

## ABILITY TO TOLERATE POWERFUL AFFECT

Supervisors provide a safe container in which supervisees can explore their reactions, responses, and feelings that emerge during the course of their work. Rak and Britton (1997) describe a situation where a counselor experiences anger and rage. The supervisor, in turn, allows the supervisee to explore these feelings in the context of her work with the client. The supervisee identifies a pattern of criticism then abandonment, which elicits anger and rage. By examining this pattern, the supervisee develops some therapeutic insight into her relationship with the client and the client's pattern of relating to others. The therapist brings this insight back into session with the client and utilizes this knowledge to further guide their work. The supervisor is able to tolerate the intensity of supervisee affect and uses that affective demonstration as a tool for further exploration.

Supervisors may keep these guidelines in mind when supervisees present with affective responses:

- Beware the urge to move into a counselor role. Take a moment to remind yourself who you are in relation to the supervisee and his or her clients.
- Beware the urge to diagnose or pathologize such affect.
- Consider the possibility that the affective demonstration serves an underlying purpose. You will not respond with suspicion or dismissiveness, but may keep this in mind if the supervisee appears unwilling or unable to fully explore the response.

*Activity: Make a list of your personal and professional characteristics that will help you be an "ideal" supervisor. Which characteristics need strengthening or repair prior to entering or continuing on as a supervisor? Now, make a list of the characteristics that your current or prior supervisors demonstrate that made them effective or ineffective as supervisors. Which of these characteristics would you like to demonstrate? Which would you like to minimize or avoid altogether?*

## EFFECTIVE VERSUS INEFFECTIVE SUPERVISION

The aforementioned ideal supervisor characteristics are necessary components of effective supervision but are not sufficient to create an effective, impactful supervision experience. Supervisors, in addition to having ideal characteristics, must also be skilled in supervisory behavior and techniques. While the field continues to investigate the constructs that make supervision effective, there are a multitude of known variables that create effective and ineffective practice. Some of these variables lend themselves to supervision that is not only ineffective but actually harmful to the supervisee and potentially even client care (Worthington, 1987). Worthington (1987) noted in his review of the literature on supervision that "a good theory of lousy supervisor behaviors is missing" (p. 203). However, Magnuson et al. (2000) provide us with the following model of ineffective supervision that serves as a caution to supervisors and supervisees alike.

## A MODEL OF "LOUSY" SUPERVISION

Magnuson et al. (2000) examined the supervision experiences of counselors who had 5 or more years of professional counseling experience in various work settings. These counselors were either practitioners or professors of counselor education. From their interviews with these counselors, the researchers found the following six "Overarching Principles of Lousy Supervision."

Principle One: Unbalanced. Some supervisors may have difficulty managing and infusing all key elements of supervision into the supervision process. They may overemphasize one supervision task or focus to the detriment of others. On the contrary, balanced supervisors are able to maintain both a detail orientation and, perhaps more importantly, an objective overview of the "big picture." The unbalanced supervisor, on the contrary, may get particularly over focused on certain details or concepts to the detriment of other important items or areas of need. It may be that a well-balanced supervisor is effective at maintaining "super" (objective) "vision" at all times; that is, the ability to balance affective, cognitive, and conceptual experiences while minding the core thematic issues of a session, rather than engaging fully and solely in one nongeneralizable domain.

Principle Two: Developmentally inappropriate. While it is safe to assume that most counselors will develop and change with experience (Worthington, 1987), there is a fundamental disconnect when the supervisor does not adjust to meet the evolving developmental needs of the supervisee. Consider what happens when a parent who provides a five-year-old child with a toy designed for infants: the child will likely reject the toy, get annoyed at the parent for providing it, and will inevitably look outside of the relationship to find a toy that will meet the developmentally appropriate need for intellectual stimulation, growth, and learning. The supervisee, as he or she advances, will need the supervisor to adjust accordingly. The developmentally appropriate supervisor will find and implement new tools, strategies, and techniques that fit the developmental stage of the supervisee. Most importantly, the supervisor will continually assess and evaluate the supervisee's developmental stage to ensure appropriate supervision (see Chapter 3 for further discussion of developmental theories of supervision).

Principle Three: Intolerant of differences. Supervisors who are viewed as intolerant of differences contribute to poor supervision experiences in a variety of ways. A supervisor's goal is often to help a supervisee develop into his or her best therapist self. However, a supervisor who is intolerant of differences is not going to tolerate a supervisee exercising different manners of conceptualization, intervention, and practice in general. This supervisor may be trying to create a clone of sorts or may not fully understand that supervision is not a duplication process. Instead, a supervisor who tolerates difference will allow the supervisee the flexibility and space to develop his or her own theory and methods of practice, and will tolerate therapeutic concepts that do not mirror his own.

Next, a well-formed, effective supervisory alliance has room for disagreement. The tolerant supervisor will allow differences of opinion, philosophy, and conceptualization. A tolerant supervisor will question, probe, and facilitate ongoing thought, while an intolerant supervisor may try to argue or command a supervisee out of his or her clinical opinion. The danger with intolerance, besides obvious ruptures to the supervisory alliance, is that a supervisee who is sent a message of intolerance is likely to shut down for protection. After all, the supervisor holds power (by definition), and most supervisees have learned not to risk offending a person with power (especially a person who is demonstrating intolerance). The supervisee may continue to think and act in ways that feel right for him or her, but will learn not to be forthright about this in supervision. Thus, the supervisor, through intolerance, has taught the supervisee to only share agreeable items in supervision. The supervisee is thus trained to reveal only certain parts of his or her practice, and the supervisor has now forfeited the ability to provide complete oversight of the supervisee's work.

This does not mean that a supervisor readily accepts all a supervisee suggests. Instead, a supervisor allows full discussion and uses skilled supervision techniques to help a supervisee fully consider all options and consequences. Through skillful supervision, a supervisor and supervisee can together protect the clients. This requires tolerance, patience, and acceptance of the supervisee's unique process.

Principle Four: Poor model of professional or personal attributes. Consider the discussion of standards of practice and codes of ethics earlier in this section. The majority of issues relevant to this principal have to do with violations of basic standards of practice. For instance, one supervisee in the study described supervision as a time when the supervisor was attempting to provide individual therapy. Another supervisee was aware of a supervisor forming a sexual relationship with a supervisee, and yet another participant revealed that the supervisor leaked confidential information. Understandably, the supervisory alliance was damaged following such an incident.

Principle Five: Untrained. This study indicates that supervisees are hindered in their growth and performance when working with supervisors who are untrained and lack professional maturity. Supervisees, when paired with unskilled supervisors, notice that the supervisor may be uncomfortable with their role, their responsibility, or perhaps the supervision process itself. While experienced supervisors may find themselves wishing they had more time to spend with their supervisees, these researchers found that an inexperienced supervisor may even end supervision early as the supervisee runs out of content to discuss.

Principle Six: Professionally apathetic. A supervisor who lacks passion or commitment would naturally be a source of frustration or discouragement to a committed and enthusiastic supervisee. Supervisees in this study frequently described their supervisors as "lazy." Further, some supervisors simply do not fully engage in the task at hand (e.g., viewing session tapes). A supervisor who is demonstrating a lack of commitment or an acceptance of "shortcuts" will inevitably find that his supervisees engage in that same apathetic attitude or demeanor. While they may begin supervision with plenty of enthusiasm and dedication, it is difficult to maintain such enthusiasm in the face of apathy. Consider the supervisee who is delighted to share with his supervisor information he gained in a workshop about trauma. The apathetic supervisor may inadvertently unwelcome or shut down the supervisee's excited sharings about what he learned. The supervisee may decide to try some of the new techniques without the supervisor's knowledge or awareness. This is not borne of malintent; rather, the supervisor sent a message that new information was not welcome and inadvertently (or blatantly) closed the conversation. Instead, the supervisee is left to figure out where the novel techniques shall be applied and, in the worst case scenario, may inappropriately apply techniques or concepts in a manner that ends up harmful to a client. Finally, consider the parallel process here. If a supervisor demonstrates apathy that becomes frustrating or discouraging to a supervisee, that supervisee is likely to experience those feelings beyond just the supervision relationship. In that clients may often appear apathetic, the supervisee may unwittingly engage in a parallel process where his frustrations toward his supervisor are unleashed on the client with similar aphetic presentation. In this scenario, the supervisee is not being provided the oversight or outlet to explore the parallel process nor the supervisory relationship, and a client may be damaged or dismissed from therapy as a result of the supervisee's response to a strained supervisory alliance.

*Activity:* *Which of these principles of lousy supervision have you experienced as a supervisee? How were you affected professionally? How did the principle affect the supervisory relationship and your feelings about your supervisor or the supervision process?*

The preceding six overarching principles are found within the following three general spheres of lousy supervision. In any general sphere, we might find several overarching principles at work.

General Sphere One: Organizational or administrative. In this sphere, the supervisor did not provide appropriate parameters and structure for supervision to occur. Supervisors have the responsibility of creating a safe container for the supervisory process. In this sphere, the supervisee experiences supervision as a process that lacks clear guidelines, standards, definition, and expectations. The supervisee may be uncertain of how to act, how to prepare, and how to engage in the process appropriately.

Further, the supervisor does not provide continuity in the supervision process. Supervision is a process where one session builds upon the prior sessions. Lousy supervision occurs when each session is treated as a separate entity that does not logically follow from prior sessions. Further, supervisors hold a great responsibility to follow up on supervision assignments, items of concern, and supervisee growth and development. The unprepared supervisor will likely neglect to uphold this responsibility, thus inviting the supervisee to also "forget" to follow through on items of clinical importance.

Supervisors who lack organization may fail to accurately assess a supervisee's needs or may miss the supervisee's statements of need. Further, the supervisor may overlook such needs in favor of other, less important items of relative nonconcern.

General Sphere Two: Technical or cognitive. Supervisees will likely have a difficult time working with supervisors who they do not have professional respect and confidence in. In this sphere, we pay attention to the supervisor's technical competence and skill level. Supervisors must be skilled practitioners to effectively supervise. While a supervisee may never directly witness a supervisor at work with clients, a supervisor's technical competence is evident when providing feedback and assisting in case conceptualization. By extension, when a supervisor is unskilled at supervision, the supervisee notices and feels the effects of the supervisor's floundering. It is safe to assume that most counselors are eager for intellectual discussions that stimulate their desire to understand, make sense of, and successfully intervene with clients. A supervisor who cannot skillfully assist in this process will inevitably lose the respect and confidence of any supervisee, especially as that supervisee becomes increasingly skilled and complex in his development.

Additionally, supervisors who utilize only one model of counseling (and perhaps supervision) may be viewed as incompetent or lousy. Since supervision is a process of helping supervisees explore their many options and develop their ideal therapist self, a supervisor who has a narrow breadth of practice is not going to benefit a supervisee who wishes to explore and practice expansively.

General Sphere 3: Relational or affective. This sphere addresses the importance of the supervisory relationship and the ability of the supervisor to create and maintain a safe supervisory environment. Supervisors create a safe environment by introducing and supporting the humanization of the supervision practice. Supervisors who understand and practice supervision in a human, authentic, and compassionate manner are more likely to keep a supervisee engaged, honest, and willing to share the worst elements of their practice that can use the most support and adjustment.

Lousy supervision occurs when supervisors engage in emotionally unsafe interactions with their supervisees. For instance, a supervisor who is viewed as overly critical or negative is likely to diminish the self-efficacy of the supervisee while damaging the supervisory alliance in the process. Further, the supervisee is likely to disengage or withhold weaknesses in the hopes of avoiding ego damage or further terror. In these cases, the supervisor inevitably fails to maintain adequate oversight as the supervisee has now disengaged and is not freely sharing information. A supervisor who withholds honest, clear, and constructive feedback may be just as ineffective. Supervisees in this study discussed their displeasure with supervisors who did not provide them with enough quality feedback. A supervisor who fails to provide impactful feedback is seen as relationally (and technically) ineffective. Further, counselors are often faced with the oft-difficult task of providing feedback to their clients. When a supervisor does not utilize supervision as a time to demonstrate effective feedback skills, the supervisor is losing a great chance to improve the supervisee's skills through demonstration and discussion. A supervisor who can effectively deliver feedback while maintaining a strong supervisory alliance is providing the supervisee with technical and relational skills that cannot be learned anywhere except in actual practice.

Supervisors who impose their personal agenda or are guided by external criteria (such as agency needs) may irreparably damage the trust and confidence of their supervisee. The supervisee will likely not feel important or valued in the process and may recognize that his or her clients are, by extension, not central to the supervision process either. This dynamic will inevitably create a divide between the supervisor and supervisee as the supervisee becomes more protective of himself and his clients, while the supervisor works more forcefully to get his or her agenda across to this ever-disengaging supervisee.

Consider the list of ideal supervisor qualities discussed earlier in this chapter. Many of those qualities are particularly important when considering the relational or affective sphere of lousy supervision. A supervisor who is not well able to tolerate affect, differences, and open, honest dialogue is going to struggle to provide effective supervision. Further, a supervisor who perceives supervision as a chore or requirement rather than a dynamic, beneficial process is likely stripping the relational or affective opportunities from the supervision process. In this instance, the supervisee loses a valuable chance to practice and get feedback about the interpersonal and relational skills that create optimally effective therapy and client care (e.g., Rogers, 1957). The supervisory alliance is discussed in much more explicit detail in Chapter 5. However, at this point, readers are encouraged to recognize that one instance or a brief period of one principle or incident of lousy supervision is not likely to destroy a well-formed supervisory alliance. Instead, skilled supervisors and strong supervisory alliances can withstand moments of "lousiness." Of greater concern are patterns of ineffective supervision and how beneficial and intact the personal and professional characteristics of the supervisors are.

*Activity: Think of your own experiences with "lousy" supervision. Conceptualize your experiences in terms of the aforementioned spheres. How would you describe your supervisor's skills in terms of those spheres? Which of those spheres will be the most problematic for you and why?*

## EFFECTIVE SUPERVISION

Effective supervision may be conceptualized in a number of ways. First, effective supervision serves the dual purpose of protecting client welfare and helping a supervisee develop and maintain clinical skill. Next, supervision may be considered effective if a supervisee is satisfied with the course of supervision, although supervisee satisfaction alone is not an adequate measure of supervision effectiveness. For instance, consider a supervisee who would rather not be supervised; a supervision session that ends after 10 minutes may be considered unsatisfactory and ineffective to most, but the avoidant supervisee will likely feel quite satisfied with another chance at successful avoidance. Worthen and McNeill (1996) posit that two factors indicate positive supervision experiences: a good supervisory alliance and focus on counseling skill development. While we will cover the supervisory relationship in much greater detail in Chapter 6, we will keep in mind that the supervisory working relationship remains the vehicle through which these additional features of effective supervision occur. Personal characteristics were discussed in detail earlier in this section and are crucially important as well. The remaining features of effective supervision are divided into domains based on common central themes.

### Environmental Factors of Effective Supervision

Effective supervisors role model the attentiveness and tuned-in demeanor that they would like to see their supervisees demonstrate with their clients. Effective supervisors take great care to construct an environment for supervision that is most conducive to good work and focus. When supervision occurs in the supervisor's office, a supervisor and supervisee should turn the ringers off of any phones, including cell phones. The computer is turned off (or at least the monitor), and a "do not disturb" indicator is on the door. The supervisor begins the session exactly on time after spending at least a few minutes of preparation ahead of time to review notes and transition into a supervisory mindset. If a supervisor rushes into supervision from another event, the supervisor may use the first moments of supervision to refocus and prepare. However, this should be done with the supervisee present rather than keeping a supervisee waiting. The supervisee and supervisor can refocus and get present to the workspace together. The supervisee might even use this uncommon occurrence as a trainable moment to discuss the difficulties of balancing multiple roles and demands. The supervisor's focus is on the supervisee's experience, so any self-disclosure is delivered as a means of facilitating discussion or normalizing the difficulties of multiple demands.

Supervisors will pay attention to the proxemics, the physical distance or space between the participants, just as counselors do. Supervisors will take great care to sit at eye level to the supervisee (beware the "supervisor-gets-the-throne, supervisee-gets-the-couch" dynamic). Supervisors may find that having rolling chairs for all members of the supervision session allows for greater movement and spontaneity. The effective supervisor has appropriate supervision equipment readily available; that is, the supervisor may have a computer or DVD player for viewing session videos (depending on how the supervisee records) or may have a dry erase board, sand tray, or other tools that can be spontaneously engaged for various supervisory techniques. The supervisor has the supervisee's file, the Diagnostic and Statistical Manual of Mental Disorders (American Psychiatric Association [DSM-IV-TR], 2000), and other relevant diagnostic tools, and both the supervisor and supervisee are prepared to actively take notes throughout the session.

Often times, supervisees seek supervision from someone outside their practice setting. In these cases, supervision often happens in the supervisor's office. Supervisors may not have an understanding of the supervisee's work environment or practice setting. Instead of maintaining a blind distance, supervisors may make initial or regular visits to the supervisee's practice site to gain a better understanding of their work setting and their client's experience.

Supervisors may wish to conduct a supervision session at the supervisee's practice setting within the first three supervision visits. The supervisee is asked to provide the supervisor with the same directions or instructions a client would typically be given to locate the practice site. The supervisor then arrives and is greeted in the same way a client is, that is, by a front desk receptionist, or perhaps waiting on a bench outside of one's office. The supervisor then enters the supervisee's office with the same fresh eyes a client has as he or she enters the space. Look around: What is hanging on the wall? What is the feel of the room? How is seating arranged? Is it conducive to good proxemics and a warm environment?

This writer recalls traveling to a supervisee's newly opened private practice for a supervision session. My intention was to arrive early; however, between evening rush hour traffic and a dire parking situation, I arrived barely in time for our session. When I arrived at the building, I found the building locked. My supervisee's name was not yet in the directory. Luckily, I had her suite number with me and could dial in. After gaining entrance, I selected one of three elevators and made my way up to her floor...slowly. My supervisee greeted me warmly as I stepped off the elevator, but I could not help but wonder how a client would feel being greeted by a counselor in the midst of dozens of other people who were on their way to and from the same locale. It certainly did not lend to the air of confidentiality and privacy one would hope for. As my supervisee and I entered her office, I was struck by the beautiful décor, warm lighting, and comfortable seating. I also noticed that sinking into the comfortable armchair meant that I was a foot below my supervisee's eye level. I also was ready for a nap after a long hike from my car to her office, and the chair's comfort was more conducive to sleep than to active therapy work. My supervisee spent our first five minutes together arranging a beverage and snack tray while I noticed the beautifully framed art on her wall, including several verses of scripture. This experience, alternating between hassle and comfort, provided me with invaluable information for our next few supervision sessions. While we turned our focus to client care, I found natural points of entrance through which I could provide feedback and invite discussion about the religious items present throughout the office, the proxemic difficulties, and client retention. When my supervisee continued to wonder aloud why her clients were not returning after an initial session, I wondered if the logistical difficulties may factor in. When my supervisee noted that her previously energetic clients were treating therapy more as "coffee talk" than "work" time, I noted that the beverage and snack trays, overstuffed chairs, and dim lighting may be contributing to excessive comfort. If discomfort leads to change, did she really want her clients dismissing all experiences of discomfort?

The effective supervisory environment reflects the same warm, distraction-reduced features that we expect to see in a counseling environment. Supervisors conducting "visiting supervision" in their supervisee's workspace can guide supervisees in creating a climate most conducive to effective treatment and can allow the supervision session to be the learning laboratory in which this occurs.

*Activity: Consider the space in which you will provide supervision. What factors need to be adjusted to allow for the most concentration and the fewest interruptions? Is there anything that may occur in the supervision environment that should not occur in a therapeutic environment? If so, consider your role as a role model for the supervisee. How might you adjust the environment so that you are effectively demonstrating the appropriate context for intimate, valuable exploratory work?*

## Developmental Factors of Effective Supervision

The developmental models of supervision are discussed in Chapter 3 of this text. However, certain factors are necessary and desired across all developmental stages. These factors include a supportive stance (Black, 1988), normalization of their professional and/or personal struggles, and a reframing of such struggles so that mistakes or tumult can be viewed more productively as a learning experience (Worthen & McNeill, 1996).

*Activity:* How well supported have you felt in the course of your career? When did you have the most support and from whom? The least? Has your sense of being supported grown over time or decreased? Have you had consistent professional support when you needed it? If not, what kept you from having the support you needed at crucial times?

Make a list of those who provide you with professional support at this point in your career. Consider those who provide you with personal counseling, professional oversight, consultation, supervision, emotional and psychological support in difficult times, etc...How have you built your support network? Is your support network sufficient in meeting your professional needs? What additional support do you need in order to be an effective supervisor? How will you secure that additional support?

## Technical Factors of Effective Supervision

While a supervisor's relational skills and personal characteristics matter, a supervisor's technical skills are also important. Undoubtedly, personal and relational characteristics impact the delivery of technical skill. However, effective supervision involves several technical components specific to supervision practice. One technical skill is the adherence to a supervision theory. In one study, researchers found that supervisees experienced some of their worst instances of supervision with supervisors who claimed an "eclectic" theoretical orientation. In these cases, the supervisors seemed to overlook the importance of being grounded in theory and did not appropriately ground their discussion of clinical intervention in an appropriate, theoretically driven context (Allen, Szollos, & Williams, 1986). Effective supervisors have determined a theoretical approach to supervision and use that theoretical approach to inform and guide their practice (Watkins, 1997).

Supervisees consider supervision more effective when the supervisor has a higher level of expertise and addresses personally meaningful "artistic" elements of therapy (Allen, Szollos, & Williams, 1986). Interestingly, participants did not equate opportunities to observe the supervisor work as relevant in a meaningful supervisory experience. Perhaps, the participants recognized that effective supervisors will support, develop, and value the supervisee's approaches above his or her own.

Finally, the research reveals that supervisees, in their best supervision experiences, experience their supervisor's feedback as straightforward and honest. They experience their supervisor as welcoming of mistakes (which were further viewed as learning experiences) and skillful at confronting "blind spots," resistances, and areas of weakness. Effective supervision experiences occur when supervisees are given the space and encouragement to actively explore areas of needed personal growth and the impact of life experiences (Allen, Szollos, & Williams, 1986).

# THREE

# Identifying Your Model of Supervision

## SUPERVISION: COMBINING SCIENCE AND PRACTICE

Clinical supervision is a professional endeavor with a scientifically informed base and several intended key outcomes. First, supervision aims to protect the welfare of the clients involved with the supervisee (Wampold & Holloway, 1997). Second, supervision helps further develop a supervisee's skills and competence (Bernard & Goodyear, 2004; Falender & Shafranske, 2004). Next, and perhaps a combination of the prior two, supervision *hopefully* improves the therapeutic outcomes for the client(s). It may be difficult for some practitioners and recipients of effective supervision to imagine that supervision is only *hopefully* impactful. Many supervisors can provide impressive anecdotal and experiential evidence that supports the theory that supervision effectively improves client care and clinician performance. However, this has been difficult to prove through research (Holloway & Neufeldt, 1995) because there have been difficulties operationalizing the definition of "clinical supervision." Clinical supervision has been defined by many authors in the helping professions, and these definitions are not always congruent nor concrete (Faugier, 1994). These difficulties make it challenging to conduct strong research of supervision practices to learn whether supervision is truly as advantageous as so many believe (Milne, Aylott, Fitzpatrick, & Ellis, 2008).

Despite these methodological shortcomings, many scholars in the supervision field as well as practicing supervisors assert that supervision is beneficial to both the supervisee and his or her clients and that a theory or model of supervision is necessary for effective supervision practice (Bradshaw, Butterworth, & Mairs, 2007; Haynes, Corey, & Moulten, 2003). There are several models to select from, and supervisors should carefully consider their options in terms of their work context, supervision setting, supervisee characteristics, and beliefs about how professional change and development occurs. Often times, supervision models are categorized based on similar underlying beliefs and principals. For instance, several models are based on the idea that supervision is a process of helping a supervisee develop and mature over time, from beginning to advanced practice. These models are all categorized as "developmental models" of supervision and are similar in their underlying beliefs, but the specific approaches and techniques between development models are different. This chapter provides information about three major categories of models: developmental models, counseling and psychotherapy-based models, and social role models. This information is accompanied by guidance about how to select one's model of supervision and several exercises that help supervisors carefully consider the multiple and unique needs of their supervisees and practice setting.

*Activity: Consider the setting(s) in which you will be providing supervision and the people whom you will be supervising. Make a list of the top 10 professional needs of the supervisees in that setting. Rank order that list by importance: first, according to your opinion of important needs, next according to the supervisees' opinions (you may have to use your best guess here, or ask a supervisee or potential supervisee to help you with this, if possible), and, finally, rank order the priorities based on what you believe would be the agency or employer's order of importance (again, it is useful to have the agency or agency representative complete this, if possible).*

*You may use this exercise in an initial consultation meeting with an agency manager or representative when setting up supervision relationships. This will help ensure that all parties have an understanding of each other's priorities and may attempt to come to a mutually agreeable consensus before engaging in supervision.*

*Consider this list as you explore theories and models of supervision. One theory or model may be better suited to the priorities you will be addressing, even if it is not your "favorite" theory initially.*

## THE IMPORTANCE OF USING A SUPERVISION MODEL

In that, clinical supervision is a distinct intervention (Bernard & Goodyear, 2004) and is not merely a replication of the therapeutic process (Watkins, 1995); supervisors use supervision-specific theory or model of clinical supervision practice that guides their work. While a *theory* is not the same thing as a *model* by definition, these terms are often used interchangeably in the supervision literature (Watkins, 1997) so will also be used interchangeably here. A model of supervision is the "systematic manner in which supervision is applied" (Leddick, 1994, p. 1) and helps the supervisor conceptualize and make sense of experiences and dynamics. Supervision models provide "a theoretical description of what supervision is and how the supervisee's learning and development occur" (Haynes et al., 2003, p. 109). A supervisor's theory or model influences his behaviors, roles, approaches, and attitudes (Goodyear, Abadie, & Efros, 1984) and shapes the form and function of a supervision experience.

Models are useful to supervisors in that they provide a framework in which to gain conceptual clarity and a sense of direction. According to Holloway (1995), models ideally assist supervisors in understanding and interpreting complex phenomena. Indeed, models certainly can help supervisors make sense of the vast amount of information that could be attended to, as the options at any given moment are plentiful. Haynes et al. (2003) state that "effective supervisors have a clearly articulated model of supervision: they know where they are going with the supervisee and what they need to do to get there" (p. 109). Further, identifying and engaging with a practice model may help a newer supervisor transition from a counselor mindset to that of a supervisor. This shift in roles may be complex and more difficult than it originally seems, and having a practice model for one's role as a supervisor may help develop and maintain clarity and professional identification (Borders, 1992). Effective supervisors act with clarity and intention, and an identified supervision model helps both the supervisor and supervisee develop and maintain focus in this highly complex, multidimensional experience.

Supervision models are considered adequate, according to Haynes et al. (2003), when they contain six main components. First, a supervision model should describe how learning and development occurs. Next, the model should explain the role of individual and cultural differences in the supervision process. The model should additionally include elements that structure the goals of supervision, the role of the supervisor, and intervention strategies. Finally, the model should describe the role of evaluation in supervision (Haynes et al., 2003).

## EVIDENCE-BASED PRACTICE

The literature is ripe with concern about the many models of supervision (Milne, 2009). While the multitude of models may offer a useful framework, scholars question the effectiveness and appropriateness of the existing models (Maggs, 1994; Milne, 2009). Derek Milne, a noted scholar in the clinical supervision field, comments that "many models of clinical supervision are impressively strong on imagination, but worryingly weak when subjected to careful evaluation" (2009, p. 47). A model with a sound theoretical base should be able to be pulled apart, examined, tested, and utilized to predict outcome (Milne, 2009). Most supervision models simply cannot perform to such a level. However, it is widely agreed upon that supervisors who practice without a model are simply less effective than those who utilize a model in their supervision practice (Haynes et al., 2003; Holloway, 1995). So, supervisors are wise to select and adhere to a model of supervision despite a lack of evidence-based information that indicates whether any supervision models are more effective than others. It may be that supervision models parallel the phenomena that occurs with counseling theories in general. That is, no actual theory on its own is the most crucial contributor to successful intervention, as there are multiple other factors that contribute to the effectiveness of the therapeutic experience (e.g., Hubble, Duncan, & Miller, 1999; Sexton, Whiston, Bluer, & Walz, 1997). Supervision likely operates in a similar fashion to therapy in that clients will often "profit about equally (but in different ways) from the different therapies" (Gelso & Carter, 1985, p. 234). At the very least, adhering to a theory provides positive role modeling for the supervisee who is expected to adhere to a therapeutic model or theory as well.

While many supervisors may not be interested in the scientifically unsound leanings of most theories of supervision, they are typically quite interested in knowing whether their chosen theory is going to help them successfully accomplish the goals of supervision. That is, will the selected theory be effective in protecting clients, helping the supervisee develop, and positively impacting client outcome? As discussed earlier, it is not yet known whether one supervision theory is more effective than another. So, a model is selected even with recognition that there is little confirmation or grounding in scientific rigor. Instead, supervisors recognize the complexities of developing a strong evidence base for supervision practice and select a model of supervision that best suits their skill set, personality, professional beliefs, supervisee needs, and the context in which supervision will occur.

In this chapter, supervisors will learn the major categories of supervision models and will be briefly introduced to some of the key models within those categories. This chapter does not provide comprehensive enough information to be considered proficient in any given model: Optimal competence requires additional learning, training, and supervision of one's practice. This chapter intends to help supervisors narrow their focus and interest down to one or two specific models that they can then learn more about. At the end of this chapter, there is a list of additional resources that provide a more intimate knowledge and understanding of these models in practice. Supervisors should carefully consider their personality, beliefs about training and development, and practice context, and then consider how well those features synchronize with each of the following models.

## SELECTING A MODEL

The following models are all based on theories and beliefs about *how* supervision is conducted, *what* makes supervision effective, and *who* and *how* the supervisor is in relation to the supervisee. When considering which supervision model(s) to adopt, remember that additional learning is typically needed to fully appreciate what the model is and what it is not. While gathering knowledge through additional reading is useful, it is also crucial to gain experiential knowledge of the model. Gaining experiential knowledge means that the model is being actively applied in a manner that is faithful to its unique features and attributes. Additionally, supervisors who are using a model will likely benefit from engaging in supervision-of-supervision with a more seasoned supervisor who is well versed in using that model. Supervisors have an ethical obligation to explain to their supervisees which model of supervision is being used (ACES, 1993) and should be able to explain the basic premises of the model to a supervisee so that the supervisee understands the supervisor's conceptual approach. So, it is necessary to select a model that matches ones beliefs about how counselors grow and develop, how supervisors should think about their role and influence with supervisees, and what the necessary tasks and foci of clinical supervision should be. While reading the following sections that describe the major developmental models of supervision, remember that this book provides an introduction to the models and not a comprehensive description and examination of each. After you find one or two models that are most appealing and align with your supervisory context, you will follow the reference list to find additional reading so that you can build an appropriate amount of familiarity with the model prior to practical application.

*Activity: As you learn about the following theories, consider this: What supervision theories have your own supervisors used? Were they explicit ahead of time about which model or theory they would use? If your supervisor did not appear to be using a theory or model, how do you think the absence of theory impacted the supervision process? What do you think would have been different if your supervisor had used a specific model of supervision?*

### DEVELOPMENTAL MODELS

The developmental models of supervision are perhaps the most widely accepted and embraced supervision models (Milne, 2009; Worthington, 1987; Watkins, 1995; Stoltenberg & McNeill, 1997). Developmental models of supervision share the same basic idea that counselors develop in stages from professional infancy toward professional maturity. Further, counselors and supervisors both improve as they gain experience (Worthington, 1987), although experience alone is not sufficient to gain improvement. The developmental models posit a stage theory of counselor development where (a) each stage is distinctly different from prior stages and (b) supervisor interventions and behaviors align with the supervisee's hypothesized stage of professional development (Worthington, 1987). Change is a constant, and supervision relationships will change and evolve as the supervisee develops.

In order to align supervisory interventions with supervisee development, the supervisor conceptualizes the supervisee's stage of counselor development in accordance with the specific model of development that supervisor subscribes to. These models will be discussed in further detail later in this chapter, but the underlying intention is consistent across models; that is, supervision is intended to enhance counselor growth and development from the current stage into the next level of counseling competence (Worthington, 1987; Stoltenberg & McNeill, 2010).

Developmental models center on the concept of change over time (Stoltenberg & McNeill, 1997). Supervision will change and adjust so that it appropriately aligns with the counselor's experience, developmental level, and evolving needs. The supervisor makes decisions about intervention strategies and techniques based upon his or her conceptualization of the supervisee's performance, knowledge, and experience (Worthington, 1987). Once the counselor advances to the next, distinct stage of professional development, the supervisor adjusts the supervision experience to align with the needs and abilities of the increasingly developed supervisee (Worthington, 1987; Stoltenberg & McNeill, 2010).

This chapter discusses developmental models of supervision; that is, models that have been developed specifically for the supervision process. Supervisors using a developmental model of supervision should not conceptualize supervisees in the same way they would a client, even though these models seem to parallel developmental therapy models. Instead, supervisors should avoid bringing the psychotherapy-based developmental models into the supervision process by maintaining clarity about their role as supervisor, not therapist (Loganbill, Hardy, & Delworth, 1982; Stoltenberg & McNeill, 1997).

*Activity: Before you examine these models in more detail, consider how you conceptualize counselor development. What are the key stages of counselor development? How do you imagine counselors' progress from one stage of development to the next? Is a developmental model appropriate for the counselors and context in which you will supervise?*

*How do you conceptualize your own growth as a counselor? What sorts of interventions, techniques, and experiences were the most formative for you in your training and professional experience thus far? Did those experiences happen in or outside of supervision sessions? How did those experiences get brought into supervision? Did supervision further the impact of these learning experiences? Had these experiences not occurred, would you be as professionally advanced as you are today?*

Some developmental models of supervision are stage based and suggest that the supervisee develops in stages from early or beginning to advanced. Others suggest that counselors develop by cycling and recycling through stages with ever-increasing depth and understanding (Hess, 1986; Loganbill, et al., 1982). Finally, other models examine development in terms of the resolution of crisis or conflict at certain stages. While these models all share similar underlying beliefs, we will now examine one widely accepted developmental model of supervision, the Integrated Developmental Model (IDM). The IDM is one of the most oft-researched models of supervision (Stoltenberg, 2005) and continually evolves in response to evaluative feedback and ongoing critical examination from the primary creator of the model and researchers in the field.

## The Integrated Developmental Model

The Integrated Developmental Model (Stoltenberg & McNeill, 2010; Stoltenberg, McNeill, & Delworth, 1998) is built upon the premise that a supervisee may function at different levels in different domains of practice, and will need supervision appropriate for his or her functioning in each area (Stoltenberg & McNeill, 1997). For instance, a supervisee might be quite skilled and well practiced at individual counseling, yet may be rather unskilled when faced with the complexities of couples counseling. This model provides supervisors with a framework in which they can conceptualize the supervisee's functioning in each of these practice domains and can tailor interventions to meet the supervisee's varying needs.

This model additionally consists of three overarching structures to monitor supervisee development through three levels across various practice domains (Stoltenberg & Delworth, 1987; Stoltenberg & McNeill, 1997). First, we will examine the three overarching structures Self- and other awareness, Motivation, and Autonomy. Next, the developmental levels are explained. Finally, the practice domains are detailed to provide supervisors with a complete framework in which to conceptualize their supervisee's development.

## The Overarching Structures

Self- and other awareness (cognitive-affective): This structure allows the supervisor to assess the supervisee's self-pre-occupation and awareness of their client's experiences in terms of both cognitive and affective components. Supervisees are likely to have greater focus on themselves than their clients in the beginning phases of their work (Stoltenberg & McNeill, 1997; 2010). They are motivated and eager learners and will lean on their supervisors and others with expertise and will look for solid answers to avoid the uncertainty and insecurity of this initial period. They will spend expend plenty of energy keeping track of their own skills and abilities and are quite concerned with their "performance" and competence. Supervisees in the initial training phase, Level I, often pay exclusive attention to their internal processes at the expense of authentic connection and empathy. However, as the supervisee transitions to the next development stage, Level II, he develops a greater capacity for empathy and cognitive understanding of the client's viewpoint.

Motivation: At this same time, the supervisee may experience a drop in motivation as frustration sets in; that is, early techniques are proving less useful as the relationship becomes increasingly two-person and complex. Motivation may be greater when the supervisee feels confidence in the work and may decrease when the supervisee feels confused and ambivalent (Stoltenberg & McNeill, 1997).

Autonomy: Supervisors continuously consider the supervisee's level of autonomy and assess whether that level is appropriately aligned to the supervisee's skill and development level. Autonomy levels will fluctuate over time with supervisees demonstrating independence, dependence, or counterdependence.

## Levels of Development

Supervisors consider a supervisee's developmental level in relation to various practice domains. Supervisees are assessed as Levels 1, 2, or 3, with a final designation of 3i for the most advanced practitioner. Supervisors concern themselves with accurate assessment of the supervisee's development so that they can deliver activities and interventions that align with the supervisee's developmental needs. If a supervisor intervenes with a supervisee who is more advanced than the supervisor recognized, the supervisee will not feel adequately challenged and supported. If the supervisee is less developed than the supervisor assessed, the supervisor may provide challenges that hinder the supervisee's development or can cause confusion, a drop in confidence, and a strain in the supervisory alliance.

Level 1: The Level 1 supervisee has likely had some limited exposure or personal experience with counseling and helping practices but is likely somewhat uncomfortable in the counseling role. These supervisees are usually quite motivated to learn and improve, as they usually do not like feeling inexperienced or ineffective (Stoltenberg & McNeill, 1997). Level 1 supervisees look to their supervisors, instructors, mentors, and senior peers and colleagues for guidance and instruction. They typically appear fairly dependent and eager to learn. Many Level 1 supervisees are avid consumers of movies, books, and training opportunities as they seek to emulate others' work. The dependency demonstrated by Level 1 supervisees is appropriate as the supervisee is not yet skilled enough for fully independent work; in this stage, a supervisor is providing strong oversight, training, skill shaping, and positive feedback (Stoltenberg & McNeill, 2010).

Recall that, in this stage, the supervisee likely has a strong self-focus, high motivation, and low autonomy. This is all appropriate at this phase. As the supervisee begins to master initial counseling skills and early conceptual understanding, the supervisee begins to build some confidence and is ready to move toward a bit more independence. The supervisor, during this transition time, will watch carefully to ensure the supervisee does not attempt to progress too far too quickly; that is, sometimes supervisees strive for more independence than is warranted. Additionally, since motivation may decrease during this time, the supervisor will monitor for ongoing education and skill development to ensure the supervisee does not neglect necessary ongoing training and development. While Level 1 typically refers to supervisees still early in predegree training programs, it is possible (depending on the supervisee's training and education) that a supervisee may appear to be Level 1 when beginning work in the counseling field as a postdegree professional. More likely, early professionals could be in later Levels 2 or 3 in some practice domains, but may still be Level 1 in domains that were not focused on in their training program.

Level 2: The Level 2 supervisee has likely mastered most initial counseling skills and has experienced some effectiveness working with clients (Stoltenberg & McNeill, 1997). This supervisee is likely examining the elements of his practice in terms of variable levels of effectiveness with different clients. The supervisee may experience some feelings of angst or helplessness as he discovers his own skill limitations or the limitations of the counseling process itself. At this point, the reality of the experience is likely setting in. The counselor learns that he will not be able to "fix" anyone and learns that he may not have the skills yet to help as effectively as he might otherwise. At this point, the supervisee's confidence and motivation may drop. The supervisee struggles with autonomy versus independence and may feel uncertain about how independently he should be practicing. Some supervisees may question whether they should be practicing at all, or whether their degrees of ineffectiveness at this stage indicate a poor fit to the profession (Stoltenberg & McNeill, 1997).

The Level 2 supervisee has shifted focus from self-awareness to other awareness, so she will inevitably experience such common phenomenon such as countertransference, enmeshment, overidentification, and alliance strains. Since the focus has shifted to the client's experience, the supervisee may not have the necessary objectivity to appropriately conceptualize and contend with such phenomena. Further, the supervisee may not understand his role or influence in such processes. The supervisor's main tasks in this phase are to support the supervisee in getting conceptual and interventive clarity in these experiences while avoiding direct advice-giving or answer-providing. Since the supervisee is getting into riskier practice, the supervisor will maintain appropriate oversight but will encourage the supervisee to conceptualize and create interventions with an increasing degree of autonomy and initiative. At times, the supervisor may need to provide directive intervention for the sake of client welfare; supervisees should be reminded of the supervisor's role in these instances and should remember to provide appropriate follow-up to ensure the supervisee does not behaviorally resist the supervisor's directives.

Stoltenberg and Delworth (1987) termed this stage "trial and tribulation," and supervisors should keep this in mind as they supervise Level 2 supervisees. In this stage of turbulence and experimentation, supervisors may begin to view the supervisee as competent enough to receive less supervision. However, in this level, supervisors should acknowledge the increased risk and responsibility to protect client welfare. Supervisors should actually increase oversight and accurate feedback through video or audio reviews or direct observation (Stoltenberg & McNeill, 1997). Self-report is not sufficient, as an increase in relational complexity and supervisee experimentation make the supervisee perhaps less reliable as an accurate reporter. Since the supervisee will inevitably have little or no objectivity in some instances, supervisors who rely upon self-report alone will miss some crucial opportunities for supervisee development and client protection. The supervisee, at this level, should not be fully directing the content of supervision sessions. The supervisor must maintain appropriate oversight of all cases, especially the cases the supervisee may wish to avoid discussing.

Level 3: The Level 2 supervisee has endured the trials and tribulations of Level 2 and is ready for increasingly stable, consistent practice at a more complex and competent level. Motivation increases once again and the supervisee is eager and excited about his work. The supervisee feels stable and competent, but has a realistic view of his weaknesses and limitations. The supervisee feels like a "real" counselor at this point and is comfortable making decisions and taking interventive initiative with a fair degree of autonomy. Level 3 supervisees have a broad range of skills and intervention choices, and these counselors are able to absorb and integrate feedback from multiple sources (i.e., client, supervisor, self-reflection). A Level 3 supervisee may work at Level 1 or 2 in some domains, especially new areas of practice, so the focus of supervision is to address areas of lesser development so that the supervisee can reach Level 3 development in all areas. The supervisor working with a Level 3 supervisee needs to provide support and appropriate amounts of confrontation and exploration so that the supervisee continues to feel challenged to develop and practice optimally. While most counselors are Level 3, some reach a stage of masterful integration.

Level 3i: The Level 3 Integrated supervisee has the flexibility and consistently effective skill base to move from one practice domain to another with competence and ease (Stoltenberg & Delworth, 1987). These counselors have mastered all practice domains to a masterful level and are interested in exploring each domain with additional depth and analytic sophistication. Stoltenberg and McNeill (2010) acknowledge that very few therapists ever reach full mastery of clinical practice across all domains and explain that "In development, staying the same is regression" (p. 135).

*Activity:* *What are your levels of self- or other awareness, motivation, and autonomy at this time? What would be effective in helping you increase self- or other awareness? Motivation? Autonomy?*

## The Practice Domains

According to the IDM (Stoltenberg & McNeill, 2010), counselors have eight domains of professional functioning in which they will progressively gain competence. These domains are as follows:

Intervention skills competence: This domain refers to the counselor's professional efficacy; that is, the counselor's confidence and ability to implement therapeutic interventions.

Assessment techniques: This domain involves the counselor's ability to conduct and utilize psychological assessments and measurements.

Interpersonal assessment: This domain refers to the counselor's ability to use one's self when conceptualizing the interpersonal dynamics.

Client conceptualization: This domain includes diagnosis, both formally and less formally. While there is a necessity to be able to accurately and ethically provide diagnosis through formal diagnostic channels, counselors also conceptualize clients in terms of contextual life circumstances and background.

Individual differences: This domain involves the counselor recognizing the presence and impact of individual features such as gender, worldview, personality features, cultural characteristics, and other qualities unique to that client.

Theoretical orientation: This domain involves the formal constructs of psychotherapy theory and approach, and the counselor's ability to understand and engage in the complexities of such approaches.

Treatment plans and goals: This domain refers to the process by which a counselor organizes his work with clients in terms of goal-setting, intervention planning, and treatment progression.

Professional ethics: This domain focuses on how the counselor's professional ethics and standards influence and are influenced by personal ethics and standards.

*Activity: Review this list of eight practice domains. Indicate beside each domain your current level of development. Which domains do you still need to improve at this point? How will you make such improvements so that your supervisees' levels of development do not exceed yours?*

*Intervention skills competence*

*Assessment techniques*

*Interpersonal assessment*

*Client conceptualization*

*Individual differences*

*Theoretical orientation*

*Treatment plans and goals*

*Professional ethics*

## COUNSELING AND PSYCHOTHERAPY-BASED MODELS

Theory plays an important role in the counseling profession, and clinical supervisors are important facilitators who help counselors further shape and develop their theoretical orientation. While counselors in training typically become familiar with at least one model of counseling through their initial training, the emphasis during early counselor training is usually on skill-building and technical aspects of counseling activities (Goodyear & Bradley, 1983). However, as counselors become increasingly skilled and developed, they typically need a more complex means of structuring their conceptual view of clients and treatment (Goodyear & Bradley, 1983). Counseling theories give counselors a way to structure and conceptualize the many variables involved with any client and therapeutic relationship (Watkins, 1997). Regardless of the theory selected, a counselor's theory (or theories) of practice allow the counselor to organize information so that therapeutic interactions and interventions are made in a thoughtful, well-informed fashion. Typically, counselors learn about a myriad of counseling theories, and then narrow their options down to one or select few theories that they have a particular interest in practicing. At times, the work setting or range of clientele influence or dictate the theoretical orientation the counselor will use, and the counselor has the opportunity to develop proficiency using one or a few core theories.

While all supervisors have the responsibility to help their supervisees develop and further hone their theoretical stance, some supervisors elect to do so through a practice of psychotherapy-based supervision. Many clinical supervisors (who presumably are experienced counselors) have proficiency with at least one or several theoretical approaches and select a supervision model based on a specific approach that they like and are familiar with. Psychotherapy-based supervision models are models whose theoretical underpinnings parallel those of psychotherapy or counseling theories by the same name. While the supervision approach differs from how the theory is used in therapy, many of the counseling theory's key constructs are utilized in the supervision process (Watkins, 1997).

There is little evidence to point to the effectiveness of selecting a particular psychotherapy-based theory of supervision (Goodyear & Bradley, 1983;

Milne, 2009), but Milne (2009) notes that there are advantages to extending one's preferred therapy model into the supervision process. One advantage is familiarity and intimate knowledge of a theory or approach. Since supervisors typically enter supervision practice after many years of counseling experience, many have likely developed a strong working knowledge of at least one or two theories of practice. Certainly, supervisors who have practiced with a certain model for years will be able to provide guidance and training with that model to their supervisees. On the converse, when extending a counseling model into supervision, the boundaries between supervision and counseling can become blurred and confusing. For instance, there are different power dynamics in the supervision relationship than there are in the counseling relationship. Supervisors hold a significant amount of direct power in a supervisor relationship and hold necessary evaluative power over their supervisees (Holloway, 1995; Milne & Westerman, 2001). The inherent and necessary power dynamics present in supervision may negate the effectiveness of the therapy-based approach in that the tasks of supervision differ so greatly from those in a typical therapeutic experience. Milne (2009) explains that therapeutic techniques have little place in supervision because supervision is an educational and professional experience, and "treatment for the supervisee's personal functioning or growth" is inappropriate in this context (p. 40). So, supervisors need to remain clearly in their role as supervisor, which can be difficult when espousing a counseling-based supervision model.

Early psychotherapy-based models include approaches such as psychoanalytic (Dewald, 1997) and a person-centered approach (Patterson, 1974). In recent decades, additional approaches such as Adlerian (Tobin & McCuyrdy, 2006) narrative, solution-focused, and systemic models (McDaniel, Weber, & McKeever, 1983; Rigazio-DiGilio, Daniels, & Ivey, 1997) have gained increasing attention. These models of supervision are typically developed from the core principles and practices inherent to the specific therapy model they align with. The therapy model is then adjusted to include or exclude tasks so that the model best fits the purpose of supervision, but the core beliefs and major techniques remain constant.

## COGNITIVE-BEHAVIOR THERAPY SUPERVISION

As the helping professions focus ever-increasingly on evidence-based practices, many supervisors are being called upon to provide supervision utilizing a theory-specific model of supervision that aligns with the supervisee's specific, evidence-based theory of counseling. One well-accepted counseling model-based approach to supervision is cognitive-behavior therapy supervision (Rosenbaum & Ronen, 1998). As the focus on manualized evidence-based treatment increases, cognitive-behavioral theory (CBT) approaches are increasingly implemented in community mental health/agency settings. Oftentimes, manualized treatment protocols include specific supervision requirements and instructions. Since the manualized approaches typically show effectiveness when practiced in a specific manner, supervisors are charged with ensuring that the supervisee maintains fidelity to treatment. Fidelity to treatment refers to the counselor's alignment with specific treatment protocol and instructions. While supervisors typically have the responsibility to protect client welfare and facilitate supervisee development, they also may find themselves taking on additional training and assessment duties when a manualized treatment protocol influences the supervision process. It is important to note that there is no strong empirical support for cognitive-behavioral supervision practice on its own (Milne, Pilkington, Gracie, & James, 2003; Townend, 2008), but a manualized supervision protocol lends itself to empirical research much more readily than other forms of supervision do.

Cognitive-behavior therapy (CBT) supervision approaches have been in practice for many decades and there are several models of CBT supervision to select from. When one considers the wide range of cognitive-behavior therapy approaches that exist, one can imagine how variable the selection of CBT supervision models are as well. Cognitive-behavioral approaches may be challenging to define, as there are variances in how much "cognitive" and how much "behavioral" one incorporates into practice (Goodyear & Bradley, 1983). Some reduce cognitive factors in favor of more pure behaviorism (e.g., Wolpe, 1973) and others highlight cognitive approaches as more significant components of their model (e.g., Kindsvatter, Granello, & Duba, 2008).

Cognitive-behavioral supervision is "educational, interpersonal, and skill-based" (Ladany & Bradley, 2010, p. 175). Cognitive-behavioral supervisors readily acknowledge the importance of the supervisory relationship (Townend, 2008) and engage in a collaborative supervision process that involves agreement on a supervision agenda and ongoing monitoring of progress and development (Bernard & Goodyear, 2004). Bradley and Gould (2001) provide a description of cognitive-behavioral supervision as an approach whose foundational premise is that a supervisee's behavior and emotional experience is influenced or controlled by their cognitions. Further, consequences serve to reinforce and maintain behaviors. So, the goal of supervision is to increase and maintain beneficial, skillful counseling behaviors and reduce or eliminate inappropriate, unhelpful behaviors (Ladany & Bradley, 2010).

One early model of CBT supervision introduced by Schmidt (1979) proposes a series of phases for the supervision session in which the supervisee initiates discussion of a challenging issue, and then the supervisor and supervisee formulate some hypotheses about the meaning of the issue. After that, the supervisee shares his or her emotion responses to the issue and those responses are discussed, followed by further conversation about therapeutic interventions and approaches. At the conclusion, the supervisee summarizes the discussion (Schmidt, 1979). This process is intended to reduce the supervisee's experience of negative affective experiences, while the supervisee learns to propose and test hypotheses about client's behaviors. The model also includes a training component where supervisees improve their ability to implement specific behavioral techniques. The premise of the model is that supervisees need to have the cognitive ability to function in a fairly anxiety-free manner, while developing and testing hypotheses and utilizing the appropriate techniques to help clients change (Schmidt, 1979). More recent models present variations on these goals, yet maintain similar core beliefs and assumptions. Rosenbaum and Ronen (1998) present a model with similar intent and suggest that the ultimate goal of CBT-based supervision is to empower supervisees who will, in turn, empower their clients to become optimally resourceful and skilled.

*Activity: Consider what you know about CBT-based supervision. When might this be a good fit for your practice or your supervisees? What appeals to you about this model? Are there any components that do not align well with your ideas or beliefs?*

## SOCIAL ROLE MODELS

Social role models focus primarily on the roles of the supervisor in the supervision process (Holloway, 1995). A clinical supervisor holds several roles within the supervision context (e.g., trainer, consultant). The supervisor, when engaging in a particular role, fulfills the expectations and anticipated behaviors that are congruent with that role (Holloway, 1995). Because the supervisor's role at any point is accompanied by consistent and fairly predictable patterns of behavior, the supervisee can experience a sense of security and predictability in the supervision process (Holloway, 1995; Pfeffer & Salancik, 1975). This chapter provides two examples of social role models: the Discrimination Model (Bernard, 1997) and the Systems Approach to Supervision (Holloway, 1994).

## THE DISCRIMINATION MODEL

The Discrimination Model (Bernard, 1979; 1997) is a widely accepted and utilized model that is appreciated for its flexible yet structured format. This model helps beginning and more experienced supervisors approach supervision in an organized, clearly intentioned manner. The model presents supervisors with a three by three matrix (three focus areas and three supervisor roles) of options from which to choose. The *focus areas* include intervention skills, conceptualization skills, and personalization skills (Bernard, 1997).

The *supervisor roles* include teacher, counselor, and consultant. It is important to recognize that the supervisor does not espouse the role in a literal sense; that is, a supervisor will not actually become a counselor, consultant or teacher to the supervisee. Instead, the supervisor draws from the skill base related to that role and incorporates those types of skills into the supervision activity (Borders & Brown, 2005).

This model is a social role model in that the focus of the model is largely centered on the role the supervisor takes when intervening and interacting with the supervisee. The teacher role is used when the supervisor is providing instruction, feedback, and modeling skills for the supervisee. This role is best utilized when it seems as if the supervisee will not be able to integrate or understand a less structured approach (Luke & Bernard, 2006). The counselor role is when the supervisor elicits reflection and introspection from the supervisee so that the supervisee is sharing his or her internal experience and reality. This role should not be misinterpreted: that is, the "counselor" role indicates that the supervisor is utilizing a counselor role but is not providing therapy to the supervisee (recall from Chapter 2 that providing therapy to a supervisee is a dangerous and ineffective supervision practice, at best). Finally, the consultant role is when a supervisor operates as an available resource for the supervisee who facilitates some direction but leaves the supervisee largely responsible for their own professional ideas, conceptualizations, and psychological and emotional experiences of their own work (Bernard, 1979; 1997).

The supervisor also selects from three focus areas. One foci is *intervention skills*, which refers to the supervisee's observable actions during a session. Next, *conceptualization skills* refers to how the supervisee thinks about and organizes the many aspects of the counseling experience (e.g., identifying major themes, making sense of interpersonal dynamics). Finally, personalization skills refer to how the supervisee's personality and personal style factor into the therapeutic process (Bernard & Goodyear, 2009).

So, the supervisor, at any given moment in supervision, will select one focus area and will evaluate the supervisee's ability in that particular focus area. The supervisor, after making that determination, selects the role best suited for that ability level. A teaching role would be inappropriate when a supervisee is exploring an issue in which he or she has a strong fund of knowledge already and is readily accessing that knowledge; instead, a consultant role may be more useful in that instance. It is important to remember that the roles and foci may shift several times within a session, and this model allows for that shifting so that the supervisee's needs can be met in any given moment of a supervision session (Bernard & Goodyear, 2009).

*Activity*: *Consider what you have learned about the Discrimination Model. When might this be a good fit for your practice or your supervisees? What appeals to you about this model? Are there any components that do not align well with your ideas or beliefs?*

## THE SYSTEMS APPROACH TO SUPERVISION

Holloway (1995) introduced the Systems Approach to Supervision to help supervisors conceptualize the supervision experience. The supervision relationship between the supervisor and supervisee is the core dimension that supports the weight of an additional six dimensions. In addition to the *supervisory alliance*, the following interrelated dimensions together describe the supervision experience in its entirety: *supervision tasks, supervision functions*, and the supervision context. The contextual factors include *the supervisor, the supervisee, the clients*, and *the agency* or organization in which the therapeutic experience occurs (Holloway, 1995).

Tasks are the pieces of work expected of the professional counselor, so *supervision tasks* are the pieces of work that the counseling field expects a supervisee to demonstrate competence in (Holloway, 1995). The SAS model contains five tasks of supervision (which can otherwise be conceptualized as areas of counselor competence): (1) counseling skill, (2) case conceptualization, (3) professional role, (4) emotional awareness, and (5) self-evaluation. *Supervision functions* are the actions or activities that are endemic to a supervisor's role. These functions are as follows: (a) monitoring and evaluating, (b) instructing and advising, (c) modeling, (d) consulting, and (e) supporting and sharing. According to Holloway (1995), a supervision task combined with a supervision function equals the supervision *process*.

At any given time in a supervision experience, the supervisor determines the task and function combination and approaches supervision through that framework. Picture a five by five matrix, with supervision tasks along one axis and supervision functions along the other. Supervisors select one task in combination with one function, and they use that combination to inform their intervention. For example, a supervisee is struggling to understand why he felt emotionally reactive with a client during a session. The supervisor determines that the intervention (a discussion) should focus on the task of *emotional awareness* as the supervisor would like to help the supervisee gain clarity about the emotional experience of that client, both in session and during supervision as he recollects the situation. The supervisor decides that a supporting and sharing function is most appropriate for this particular situation and believes that function will best help the supervisee make sense of his experience. So, the supervision process, at this point, is comprised of the task (emotional awareness) and the function (sharing and supporting). As a supervision session unfolds, the supervisor will continue to combine tasks and functions, all the while paying attention to the supervision relationship, which must remain strong to allow these interventions to reach full efficacy.

*Activity: Consider what you have learned about the Systems Approach to Supervision. When might this be a good fit for your practice or your supervisees? What appeals to you about this model? Are there any components that do not align well with your ideas or beliefs?*

# FOUR

# Preparing for the Initial Session

C linical supervisors enter supervision in a variety of ways: some are assigned the task as part of their job description, some enthusiastically volunteer to supervise interns or trainees in their work setting, and others eagerly enter the practice as private practitioners. Regardless of how one comes into the role, the clinical supervisor holds a great deal of responsibility for ensuring that the supervision experience is a positive and effective one that meets its multiple goals and demands.

Foremost, supervisors are responsible for role modeling professional standards and creating a safe, structured environment for effective supervision to occur (Whitman & Jacobs, 1998). To meet these responsibilities, supervisors engage in a thorough preparation process before beginning work with a supervisee. This chapter guides supervisors through the many steps of presession preparation, beginning with a discussion about making the decision to supervise. Next, the Pre-Supervision Interview is introduced as a tool to help supervisors and supervisees make thoughtful, intentional entry into a supervision relationship. Following that is a detailed review of professional documentation that must be readied before the initial supervision session, including the professional disclosure statement and the supervision contract.

## TO SUPERVISE OR NOT TO SUPERVISE?

Prospective supervisors have a difficult decision before them. Although supervision is a rewarding and central task of great importance to the field, it can also be considered a high-risk/low-reward activity. Supervisors take on a great deal of responsibility and liability for therapeutic interactions and interventions that are performed by another, less developed professional. Supervisors hold the responsibility for their own caseload in addition to every client with whom their supervisees come in contact. Although the American Association of State Counseling Boards Approved Super Model (AASCB, 2007) recommends that supervisors provide supervision to no more than five supervisees, many supervisors find themselves involved with a much larger number. The responsibility and liability is exponentially greater and more perilous with each additional supervisee.

Before entering into a supervision relationship, potential supervisors should answer the following questions. (You may not have answers to these questions immediately. Some questions may require you to gather additional information depending on your unique situation.)

1.  **What is my motivation for providing counselor supervision?**
    Be clear about what drives you to provide supervision. In that this task is one that may be, at times, high risk and low reward, the motivation ought to be one that is internally driven, borne of enthusiasm for shaping the next generation of professionals, and holds the potential to increase job satisfaction or professional fulfillment.

2.  **Do I truly have the time and availability to engage in supervision?**
    As you consider the amount of time you should allot to supervision, remember that a responsible supervisor is available and able to provide additional oversight and guidance in difficult times (Kadushin & Harkness, 2002). A supervisee who seems "easy" will still have difficulties at times, and a supervisor holds the duty to be available for that supervisee. The following questions can help guide you in your decision making:

    a.  If a supervisee calls me at any given point on any given day, will I be able to return the call within 2–3 hours?

    b.  If my job or leisure time involves a lot of travel, will I be willing and able to have a backup supervisor available; or will I be personally available despite being out of town or out of the country?

    c.  If I need to be available to help my supervisee(s) through a crisis or difficult time, would I still be able to provide the most optimal services to my own clients?

    d.  Do I have the emotional space and time to take care of my own psychological needs, which may increase as I experience my supervisee's difficulties and stressors? (Be cautious not to underestimate the power of vicarious trauma. No one is immune!)

    e.  Do I have adequate time to complete the necessary training, continuing education, and documentation needed to provide supervision? (Do you know at this time where you will fit that into your schedule?)

    If you answered "no" to any of these questions, you will likely need to pause at this stage and consider how you will resolve some of the time management and workload dilemmas that may prevent you from providing appropriate and responsible oversight. These issues need to be resolved before taking on the responsibility of a new supervisee and will not "naturally" resolves themselves later.

3. How many supervisees should I supervise?

    This question holds different meanings based on several contextual variables. First, consider the supervisee's educational and licensure status. If a supervisee is an intern in a training program, consider the plethora of responsibilities and commitments that are involved when working with students. There are numerous training demands that are compounded if you are also in a position to provide managerial supervision for the trainee as well. There are a number of training program demands set forth by the college or university and their accrediting bodies. The Council for the Accreditation of Counseling and Related Educational Programs (CACREP, 2008) requires that supervisees receive 1 hour of supervision per week and 1.5 hours of group supervision (staff meetings do not count; this must be actual group supervision of a clinical nature). In addition, most programs require site visits and formal evaluations. Some programs require supervisors to attend trainings or meetings, and others ask site supervisors to oversee work sample or portfolio projects. It is necessary to learn from the university training program what the requirements are before agreeing to supervise one or multiple students.

    If the supervisee is working toward state licensure, reflect back to Chapter 2 and what you learned about your state's licensure requirements. How many supervisees does the state regulatory board allow a supervisor to work with? Many states have limits to the number of prelicensed supervisees one can supervise. What are the numbers of hours each of the supervisees will require per week or month? Will your supervisees have the resources (time, money, and willingness) to be available for you to provide appropriate and thorough oversight? Finally, consider whether the supervisee's schedule will match well with your availability. Do your schedules align well enough that you will be able to find common meeting opportunities on a regular basis?

    Next, consider the supervisee's job in terms of the intensity and clientele. The supervisee's work setting often influences the amount of supervisory support needed. A supervisee with a small private practice may need a lot less emergency-type support than a supervisee working full time in community mental health with high-intensity mentally ill and/or suicidal clients. When supervisees have higher-acuity client populations, you can expect that you will need to be more readily accessible for assisting the supervisee through professionally and emotionally difficult times. Supervisees who work with higher-need populations will likely need to access you for additional support or guidance when crises or ethical and legal dilemmas arise.

Finally, consider your state's prelicensure reporting requirements. How much additional time outside of supervision sessions will you be spending on completing and submitting reports? Be certain you are familiar with current reporting requirements (as they may have changed since you went through licensure) and consider the worst case scenario: If you have a supervisee who is not an appropriate candidate for licensure, how much documentation will you need to complete? Consider whether you have time to fully engage in that level of responsibility.

Prospective supervisors should also consider the possibility that a supervisee may need additional, increasingly intensive oversight at some point in his or her experience with you. If the supervisee experiences difficulties with a particular client or has overall performance impediments, will you have time to watch video, listen to audio, or provide direct live supervision? If, at some point you question your supervisee's competence and their ability to be safe with clients, you hold the responsibility to provide increased oversight for the protection of the client. It may be hard to imagine that your counselor supervisee may at some point become incompetent or dangerous, but beware prejudicial conceptualizations. For instance, even your most competent supervisee may experience a life-altering event that affects his mental health. There is simply no way of predicting which supervisees will need additional oversight and to what degree. So, imagine every supervisee having a crisis at once. If that were to happen, how many supervisees can you effectively manage while keeping your professional sanity and not impeding the quality of care you provide to your own clients?

4. Have I resolved any remaining grudges/resentments/ruptures/bitterness that I may have toward my own former supervisors?

   The quality of the supervisory relationship is a key determinant in how impactful and effective the clinical supervision experience is (Holloway & Johnston, 1985; Stoltenberg, McNeill, & Delworth, 1998). Further, successful supervision involves the appropriate and productive conflict resolution that naturally occurs in the supervisory dyad (Nelson & Friedlander, 2001). If conflict in your own supervision experience was not effectively resolved and residual negativity remains, you may inadvertently work through such unresolved conflict in your role as supervisor. Potential supervisors should work through their own unresolved conflict or negativity toward supervisors or the supervision process before engaging in the process as a supervisor.

## THE PRE-SUPERVISION INTERVIEW

The Pre-Session Interview is a dual-purpose tool that supervisors may use either to screen potential supervisees or, when screening is not an option, to initiate a positive supervisory working alliance. Many supervisors, especially those in a community mental health or other agency setting, may have little or no voice in selecting a supervisee. They may be assigned to work with supervisees whom they have never met or whom they have concerns about supervising. Others have the ability to screen and interview potential supervisees to mutually determine whether they are a good match for one another. Because the supervisory alliance and structure are so central to the supervision process (Holloway, 1995), presupervision interviews can assist a supervisor in creating a well-structured, mutually agreeable beginning with a supervisee who has been "assigned" to them.

Whether the presupervision interviews are used as a screening and selection tool or as an initial supervisory activity depends on the manner in which the supervisee and supervisor are matched. If the match has been predetermined and cannot be "undone," the interview should be presented as a presupervision meeting where the supervisor and supervisee can learn about one another and exchange initial thoughts about their expectations and hopes for the supervision process. If the duo have already met and have worked together for a period of time in a different capacity, the supervisor will use this meeting as a time to discuss the shifting relationship and any resultant feelings or concerns that may impact the new relationship. If the duo has not met and is "assigned" to one another, the supervisor can share his enthusiasm about the supervision process and may open a conversation about the "choiceless" matching process to ensure no resultant negativity of that process is carried forward. The supervisor will not defend the selection process but will instead use this meeting as a time to discuss any feelings that result from the process if needed. Supervisors can validate the difficulties in being paired without the power of choice, but assure the supervisee that once supervision begins, the power to structure that experience is largely determined by the supervisor and supervisee together.

When a supervisor decides to willingly engage in supervision with someone over whom he has little administrative power, that supervisor is entering into a risky and highly libelous relationship (see Chapter 12 for further discussion). One common example of this is the private practice supervisor who is supervising a counselor employed by an agency or in private practice. Because of the supervisor's increased risk in these situations, the screening and selection process is critically important to the supervisor, supervisee, and clients' best interests. In an effort to effectively select low-risk supervision situations, "judicious supervisors typically engage in supervisory contracts only after careful deliberation" (Magnuson, Norem, & Wilcoxon, 2002, p. 54). Effective and protective supervision practice hinges on making wise choices about whom to supervise. In this case, the Pre-Supervision Interview is actually a screening process and should be presented as such. This is a time for the supervisor and supervisee to learn more about one another and expectations of the process, so that they may mutually determine whether they are an appropriate professional match.

When a potential supervisee approaches a potential supervisor, there are a number of factors the supervisor should pay attention to when making the decision to enter a working relationship. The following questions may be asked of potential supervisees to help make this important decision.

*Activity: As you read the Pre-Supervision Interview Questions below, rank the questions in order of importance based on the setting in which supervision will be provided. Be certain to add any additional questions that seem important to you and include them in the ranking.*

Pre-Supervision Interview Questions:

- What license/credential is the supervisee working toward? Determine whether you are qualified to supervise toward such credentials. If not, be sure to let the supervisee clearly know that you are not qualified to provide such supervision, and the supervisee should seek supervision elsewhere. Beware of the seduction of a supervisee who asks you to supervise them in general and plans to get specific credential-related training from an additional supervisor. There are a number of potential pitfalls in this arrangement, and the risk may be much greater than the benefit.
- Where did the supervisee get his or her training and education? Are you familiar with the training or graduate program and feel comfortable that the supervisee has received well-rounded, foundational information? If the program is accredited, you may be able to assume a certain level of clinical training and prior supervision. If not, are you certain that this supervisee is ready to work autonomously? Also, be cautious of placing too much importance on the degree itself. Many programs have to allow students to graduate even when their performance has been less than optimal, even though they would prefer not to. The licensure process serves the necessary function of preventing credentialing counselors who may be unsafe. Supervisors are the intermediary between licensing boards and the counselor and are often well positioned to evaluate readiness for licensure. So, you should feel fairly confident in the supervisee's education and training background before accepting liability and responsibility for that supervisee's performance.

■ What is the supervisee's philosophy of change/theoretical approach to counseling?

In that supervision is not a cloning process, it is not necessary that your theoretical orientation(s) and beliefs match the supervisees. However, the supervisor needs to have familiarity and competence in working with each of the theoretical orientations the supervisee would like to practice. If a potential supervisee claims an "eclectic" or "integrative" approach, learn what specific approaches are drawn from. An integrative approach involves the fusion of strong components of two or more theoretical perspectives, whereas "eclectic" is fairly haphazard in nature and indicates that the counselor has technical expertise but no primary guiding theory (Levitt & Bray, 2010). The potential supervisee needs to understand and be open to additional training and practice in several areas of orientation so as to develop true, masterful implementation of his primary theory/theories of choice.

■ What are the supervisee's perceived strengths?

A supervisee's description of his or her strengths can often be quite illuminating. A potential supervisee who has been in the field for 1 year states that her specialty is "intense trauma recovery work," which might be hinting at a practice that is out of her scope (and without the understanding of such scope of practice issues). A supervisee who appears personable, competent, and genuine may state that he has not developed any strengths yet; this may be a hint at self-efficacy or confidence issues. As the potential supervisor, you may ask as many clarifying questions as you like to try to determine whether the candidate has a realistic sense of his development, his role, and appropriate boundaries. During a presupervision interview, one potential supervisee indicated to this writer that her greatest strength is that she "loves her clients until their illness disappears, because love is the ultimate healing." It is no surprise, then, that this potential supervisee went on to explain that she was having great difficulties with her agency administrators who believed that her therapeutic effectiveness was hindered by inappropriate boundaries and a tendency to pathologize mild client concerns.

■ Has the supervisee ever had a complaint lodged against him or her with a state licensing board or other entity? What was the situation and what was the outcome?

Many licensing boards make complaint information public or semi-public, so that the consumers are protected from counselors known to create harm or violate legal and ethical standards. As a supervisor, it is often worth taking some time to discuss past troubles with the supervisee and to check in with the state regulatory board for confirmation of any information the supervisee has shared. Be cautious of your assumption that a supervisee looks too "innocent" to have had a complaint filed against him. In many cases, complaints and transgressions are born of great intentions. Every counselor is vulnerable to grievance (arguably some more than others). As a potential supervisor, you are interested in knowing specifics about these situations. What happened, was anybody harmed, and what was the outcome? It is reasonable to expect a potential supervisee to share situations that involved unfounded complaints as well. Although this may cause embarrassment to the supervisee, many counselors are interested in making sure their supervisor knows of such situations as they are often interested in trying to avoid such an ordeal in the future. If a supervisee leaves such information out and you learn of an incident through another party, you can reasonably expect that it will be difficult to trust this supervisee's self-report when something goes wrong or he/she is in distress (at a time when honesty and cooperativeness is imperative).

■ What feedback has the supervisee encountered that he/she has disagreed with?
The information gathered from this question is not necessarily going to help you make a decision about whether or not to accept a supervisee. Instead, it may give you some insight about how this supervisee accepts and integrates feedback, how well the supervisee asserts himself or herself, and the quality of prior supervisory relationships.

■ Is the supervisee willing to give you permission to speak with former supervisors?
Sometimes it is helpful to speak with a supervisee's former supervisor, especially if the supervisee indicates that the supervisor had concerns about his or her practice or if you are having a difficult time understanding why the supervisee stopped working with the supervisor. Likewise, supervisees may request to speak with a supervisor's other current or former supervisees. This is an appropriate practice that allows each party to get a sense of personal and professional amity and helps each to determine whether they indeed have mutual interests (Magnuson, Norem, & Wilcoxon, 2000). Supervisors should not, however, base their opinion solely on others' reports and should recognize that the supervisee will respond differently in a new setting with a new supervisor (Borders & Brown, 2005). Further, supervisors should keep in mind that the helping professions are a business of change, and it is quite possible that a supervisee has changed some of the behaviors or dispositions that were concerning to earlier supervisors. Although prior supervisor reports may be useful as you conceptualize your supervisee's needs and development, your own current assessment is likely more valuable.

Supervisors may wish to direct potential supervisees to the article by Magnuson, Norem, and Wilcoxon (2002). This article instructs counselors-in-training and prelicensed counselors about how to engage in a thorough and intentional search for an effective supervisor and supervision situation. Supervisees are given an overview of how to initiate supervision, what to look for in a supervisor, and how to engage in the supervision process. Supervisor–supervisee fit is addressed, and supervisees are encouraged to ask their supervisor to conceptualize a hypothetical case, so that the supervisee can get a sense of the supervisor's work style, approach to practice, and general orientation and beliefs about counseling. In addition, supervisees need to know about the cost of supervision and scheduling arrangements before beginning supervision.

## SUPERVISION FEES

Supervisees will undoubtedly be interested to know the cost of supervision. Supervisors should determine their fee schedule before the Pre-Screening Interview, so that they may share this information with the supervisee. Cost may be an influencing variable in determining goodness-of-fit, so supervisors need to be explicit about the cost of services. Supervision should not be seen as a "for profit" activity in the same vein as other private practice endeavors. Instead, counselor supervision is a service that helps protect clients, sustains the profession, and allows the profession to remain self-governing as more senior members help the junior members to meet performance standards. Supervisors should keep a number of variables in mind when determining fees. First, what do you need to earn to cover your overhead fees, including supervision-specific insurance and uncompensated paperwork or documentation time? Second, what fee range is typical in your area of practice? (Speak with others who provide clinical supervision, or check with your state licensing board). Next, what fee arrangement will be sustainable to your supervisee? The supervision relationship extends over time, and often supervisees stay with the same supervisor until licensure and beyond. What is affordable to a supervisee in your area and can be reasonably sustained? It is within reason to ask your supervisee to consider his or her budget. Does his or her salary support the ongoing cost of supervision? Encourage supervisees to determine when they will begin making student loan repayments and to be realistic about salaries if they have not yet secured a job. A sustainable fee schedule that is consistent and steady for years is more desirable than an arrangement that will ultimately fail, leaving a strain or break in the supervisory relationship. Supervisors have flexibility with their fee schedule and may exercise such flexibility when working with a supervisee to find a sustainable rate. However, the supervisor should be cautious not to generously set a fee that is too low and will result in resentment if the supervisee becomes problematic in the future. The arrangement should be acceptable and sustainable to both parties.

Supervisors should not charge additional fees for ethical and responsible oversight. That is, supervisees should not pay for video reviews, emergency consultation, and evaluation or assessment documentation. The financial strain serves as a disincentive to supervisees and indicates that such services are "extras" and are not a necessary part of the supervision process. Supervisors may charge a fee for additional supervision time that is not urgent; however, supervisors may help initial supervisees figure out what "urgent" means before imposing such a fee. This fee may be useful for supervisees who have a difficult time working autonomously. Instead, supervisors can use exercises such as the one discussed in Chapter 11 to help a supervisee move toward more confident self-supervision and support-gathering.

Finally, there must be an agreement about when payment for services occurs. Supervisees may pay every session or monthly but should not be allowed to accrue a balance of more than 1 month's worth of services. This can lead to anxiety and tension between both parties, especially when evaluation time arrives. Supervisors may not refuse their reporting responsibilities because a supervisee is not current on his payments, nor can such a situation impact the objectivity of a supervisor. The supervisor needs to present an arrangement that will not, at any time, impact his or her objectivity when working with the supervisee.

*Activity: If you will be providing supervision for a fee (rather than as part of your work setting job functions), consider how much you will charge for supervision. Contact three supervisors in your area who share similar levels of education, supervision training, and credentials. Find out how much they are paid for supervision (remember, what they charge may not be what they are paid, as many supervisors allow supervisees to pay a reduced fee). Consider what amount you need to charge to cover your expenses, including increased liability insurance and unreimbursed time. Although it may feel wonderful to provide reduced cost service in an effort to help the next generation of counselors, it is also important that you make enough profit to sustain your positive feelings about engaging in this endeavor.*

## SCHEDULING

At this point, you have already determined whether your schedule can accommodate the responsibilities of a supervisory relationship. The next challenge is to determine whether the potential supervisee's scheduling needs match your availability. In some cases, supervisees must receive supervision outside of their regular work hours. Some supervisees are only available in the evenings, others experience a change in availability regularly depending on school or work schedules, and yet others simply have no idea of their availability as they are not yet employed or have not yet built their practice. Regardless, supervisors should enter the Pre-Supervision Interview with a clear idea of their availability and flexibility, and limitations therein. Supervisors should take great care to prevent a situation that impedes the continuity of supervision service. For instance, if both the supervisee and supervisor experience schedule changes at the same time, they may find themselves in a situation where they do not have a mutually open meeting time. They should speak upfront about the conditions that may cause such a situation and should agree on a backup plan if this were to occur. Some backup plans may include agreeing to temporarily meet on a weekend or nonwork "day off," referring the supervisee to another supervisor once a schedule conflict appears inevitable (at least a month's notice would be optimal in this case), or determining ahead of time that the supervisee should work with a supervisor with greater flexibility.

Once supervisor and supervisee determine they are an appropriate match for one another and agree on payment and scheduling arrangements, the supervisor tailors his or her preparatory process to specifically address the needs of that particular supervisee. The supervisor prepares the supervision contract, makes necessary arrangements with regulatory or credentialing bodies, and connects with the supervisee's work setting (when applicable).

## SETTING THE STAGE FOR SUPERVISION: THE SUPERVISION CONTRACT, INFORMED CONSENT, AND PROFESSIONAL DISCLOSURE STATEMENT

### The Supervision Contract

The supervision contract is a written agreement between the supervisor, supervisee, and any involved agency of employment (such as the supervisee's employer) and is initiated by the supervisor at the beginning of the supervisory relationship (Osborn & Davis, 1996; Sherry, 1991). This contract is not a legal document and is usually not expressed in legal language. Instead, it is a formal but understandable written document that describes the terms of professional agreement between all parties regarding the tasks, roles, functions, and limitations of the supervision process. Supervisors and supervisees enter into a contract when they begin working together, although often times the contract is merely implied and not discussed in great detail or formally documented (Proctor, 2006). However, leaving the working agreement vague and undefined leaves room for misunderstandings, assumptions, and unfulfilled expectations, which can strain the supervisory relationship unnecessarily. The supervisor, supervisee, and supervisory alliance all benefit from explicit clarity about how supervision will operate logistically, relationally, and in accordance with optimal practice standards (Liddle, 1988; Osborn & Davis, 1996).

Written contracts serve many purposes, and Osborn and Davis (1996) describe five reasons for a formal supervision contract. First, supervision contracts clarify the methods, goals, and expectations of each party in the supervision arrangement. Second, a contract honors the collaborative spirit between supervisor and supervisee by allowing parties to share their expectations and wishes, which they discuss and document. Third, a contract aligns with the principles of ethical practice in a number of ways. The supervisor can include items on the contract that instruct the supervisee to follow appropriate ethical and legal practices (e.g., gaining informed consent, making mandated reports) and can ensure the supervisee clearly understands parameters of confidentiality. Supervisors can also include information about multiple relationships and the handling of such, both in the supervisory relationship and with clients. Fourth, a contract details the services that are to be provided by both the supervisor and the supervisee. Each party knows clearly their responsibilities and duties to one another and for the protection of client welfare. Fifth, a contract professionalizes the supervision practice and parallels the contractual practices present in both therapy and consultation services (Osborn & Davis, 1996). Further, contracts help minimize covert agendas and can help reduce the likelihood of supervisory abuses of power (Falvey, 2002; Tanenbaum & Berman, 1990).

Contracts should be treated as fluid in that they may be modified as the supervisee's practice and needs change, and a mechanism for such modification should be in place (Storm, York, Vincent, McDowell, & Lewis, 1997). Supervisors may routinely review supervision contracts as a supervisee's practice changes or perhaps on a schedule of every 6 or 12 months to ensure the contract is still meaningful and current. Supervisors may alternatively elect to review the contract with the supervisee during every formal evaluation or reporting time.

A thorough and specific initial contract ensures clarity and a mutually agreed-upon set of expectations, which is essential to an effective supervisory experience (Inskipp & Proctor, 1993). Contracts should be detailed, thorough, and thoughtfully designed. Although a supervisor may prepare the framework for the contract before meeting the supervisee, many features of the contract are based on mutual agreement between the supervisor and the supervisee. The contract is finalized in alliance with the supervisee; it is not a document that is created independently then handed to the supervisee for a signature.

Clear, effective supervision contracts should include the following items (based on the work of Borders & Brown, 2005; Cobia & Boes, 2000; Proctor, 2006; Magnuson, Wilcoxon, & Norem, 1999; Osborn & Davis, 1996; Ronnestad & Skovholt, 1993; Teitelbaum, 1990):

1. *The purpose and intent of the supervision arrangement*: Explain the purpose of the supervision arrangement. In some cases, a supervisee

is engaging in supervision during a time-limited training period such as during internship or while on a mandated work improvement plan. Other times, supervision is for the purpose of additional prelicensure oversight or simply professional growth and development. Be clear and as specific as possible, while remembering that this purpose may change at some point (e.g., a prelicensure supervision arrangement may become a postlicensure arrangement once the supervisee is licensed and yet still values the supervision process).

2. *The supervisor and supervisee's goals and expectations of the supervision process*: The contract should include a statement that explains the purpose of supervision (e.g., monitoring client welfare, supervisee development, meeting professional practice standards).

3. *The duties and responsibilities of the supervisor and supervisee*: The duties and responsibilities of each party should be stated clearly and with unambiguous language, so each member of the supervisory dyad knows what to expect from the other. Supervisors should also clearly indicate issues that are outside their scope of responsibility, when appropriate.

4. *Scope of practice/competence*: Supervisors should explicitly detail their scope of professional competence and qualifications. Supervisors and supervisees should also make explicit any information regarding supervision toward a specific credential and will ensure the supervisor is appropriately qualified to supervise toward the credential or licensure sought by the supervisee.

5. *Logistical information such as*:
   Meeting days/times/session length
   Frequency of supervision sessions
   Absenteeism/tardiness procedures
   Fee for supervision services
   Payment methods/practice
   Modes of supervision (individual, triadic, and group)

6. *Supervision monitoring and professional development methods*: Supervisors will detail the types of activities in which the supervisee will participate and should consult with the supervisee about the feasibility of such activities. Activities may include video or audio recording of sessions, live observation, theory-specific assignments, transcription, chart reviews, and such. Supervisors will include a statement about session recordings, indicating that the supervisee is responsible for gaining consent from clients to record sessions for use in supervision. The supervisor should also discuss the protection of session recordings, especially when in transport.

7. *Preparation expectations*: Include information about what the supervisee will do to prepare for supervision sessions. For instance,

a supervisee may be required to bring his supervision portfolio (see Chapter 5 for further detail) to each session, along with one video recording and a current list of all clients. It is not necessary to be quite that specific in the initial contract, but at times, a supervisor may find the need to further clarify expectations and might adjust the contract accordingly.

8. *Evaluation and reporting practices and schedule*: Supervisors should ensure they know the specific evaluation and reporting requirements for prelicense and student supervisees, so they can fully comply in a timely manner. This should all be documented in the contract, including a specific breakdown of responsibilities when applicable. For instance, if a prelicense supervisee needs a term report submitted, detail who is responsible for tracking the due date and bringing the report into session for review. Be certain you are familiar with any evaluation tools that will be used, so that you can accurately complete the instruments. The contract should also include the contact information of the contact person who serves as the liaison between the supervisee's agency or work setting (or training program) and the supervisor in case difficulties arise. The contract should make clear that the liaison will be contacted if problems arise and that there will be no secrecy or confidentiality in cases of performance difficulties or threats to client welfare.

9. *Informed consent*: When a counselor is receiving supervision, the counselor has the responsibility to inform the client of the nature of the supervision experience (Falvey, 2002). Supervisees inform their clients that they are receiving supervision, detail from whom they are receiving supervision, and should be clear about what that means to client confidentiality (Borders & Brown, 2005). Because supervisors are responsible for the client's welfare, supervisors are privy to confidential information about the client. Client confidentiality extends into supervision, but clients need to know clearly that their information will be shared. Clients should also be informed about who is involved in the supervision process, and if the supervisee is involved in group or triadic supervision, the client should be made clearly aware of that. In addition, the client should be provided with information about how to directly contact the supervisor if the need arises (Falvey, 2002). This information may be provided in an informed consent document or in the supervisee's professional disclosure statement as instructed by state rules and laws and national standards. Further, a supervisor may at times need to be in direct contact with a client, such as when a client contacts the supervisor with a grievance or in the case of a compromised supervisee. The contract may detail how a supervisor can access clients if needed and can include a statement that the supervisee agrees to provide client contact information at the supervisor's request.

**10.** *Names, signatures, dates, and contact information*: The supervision contract should be signed by all parties, and the date of agreement should be included. When the contract is revised, the revision date should be supplied. All parties should also include contact information and emergency contact information, and this information should be updated anytime a change has occurred.

*Activity: Create your supervision contract. Appendix D contains a sample contract (Osborn & Davis, 1996) you may follow or you may create your own. After you create your contract, have a supervisor or colleague review it and provide you with feedback. Make sure it is flexible enough to allow for collaborative co-creation with your supervisee.*

## Supervision and Informed Consent

In the counseling process, informed consent refers to a client's right to be made fully aware of all aspects of the counseling process and treatment, so that he/she can decide whether to willingly participate in the treatment (McCarthy et al., 1995). It is an ethical and legal matter that is a core concern of any counseling practice, and the concept has been extended into the practice of clinical supervision. Informed consent in supervision refers to a supervisee's rights to know the parameters of supervision including methods, mutual and individual responsibilities, evaluation and feedback procedures, and supervision requirements (Sherry, 1991; McCarthy et al., 1995). Supervisors who thoroughly cover all the aforementioned features of a clinical supervision contract with their supervisee, plus provide the supervisee with a supervision professional disclosure statement, will have effectively provided the information necessary for a supervisee to make a well-informed decision to engage in the supervision process.

## The Supervisor Professional Disclosure Statement

Just as the professional disclosure statement in counseling intends to inform and protect clients, the supervision professional disclosure statement informs and protects the supervisor and the supervisee (Lee & Everett, 2004).

The supervisor professional disclosure statement discloses several key aspects relating to the supervisor's practice. These disclosure statements differ from the supervision contract in that they are a static document that will not often change and are not individualized to fit specific situations. Instead, it is a document that details the professional service that the supervisee will be receiving and provides the supervisee with the necessary information to fully understand the supervisor's scope and methods of practice (Cobia & Boes, 2000).

Applicants seeking the Approved Clinical Supervisor (ACS) credential (Center for Credentialing and Education [CCE], 2009) are required to submit a supervisor professional disclosure statement as a requisite for the credential. In addition, individual states may also require that supervisors provide disclosure statements to their supervisees at the start of a supervision experience.

The ACS credential requires that supervisory professional disclosure statements include the following elements (Center for Credentialing and Education [CCE], 2009):

1.  Name, business address, and telephone number
2.  A listing of degrees, credentials, and licenses
3.  General areas of competence in mental health practice for which the applicant can provide supervision
4.  A statement documenting applicant's training in supervision and experience in providing supervision
5.  A general statement addressing the applicant's model of or approach to supervision, including role of the supervisor, objectives and goals of supervision, and modalities (e.g., video review, live observation)
6.  A description of the evaluation procedures the applicant uses in the supervisory relationship
7.  A statement defining the limits and scope of confidentiality and privileged communication within the supervisory relationship
8.  When applicable, an indicator that the applicant is under supervision and that the supervisee may be discussed with the applicant's supervisor
9.  A fee schedule, when applicable
10. Emergency contact information for the supervisor
11. A statement indicating that the applicant follows the relevant credentialing body's Code of Ethics and the ACS Code of Ethics (Center for Credentialing and Education [CCE], 2009)

In addition, supervisors may include statements that describe how multiple role situations will be managed, a process for addressing supervisee grievances or concerns, and how the supervisor typically manages fee and payment issues (e.g., supervisee pays by cash or check at the time of service).

*Activity:* Create your supervision professional disclosure statement. You may use the statement from Appendix E as an example or create your own. Provide a copy to a colleague or supervisor and ask for evaluative feedback. Incorporate that feedback into your final product and disseminate your statement to all current (and future) supervisees.

# SUPERVISION IN ACTION

# FIVE

# The Initial Session

*T*he initial supervision session serves the same purpose as an initial counseling session: to collect and share necessary information and to establish the working relationship (Gladding, 2009). Although the tasks, goals, and functions of this working relationship are quite different from a counseling experience, it is quite typical for a supervisee and supervisor to approach the new experience with the same nervousness, hopefulness, and curiosity a counselor and client may feel on first meeting.

The initial supervision sessions will feel anxiety producing and awkward to the unprepared supervisor and supervisee. However, those who have followed the steps outlined in Chapter 4 have already met with their supervisee for a Pre-Supervision Interview and have prepared well for the business of supervision. Supervisors, during the Pre-Supervision Interview, shared their philosophy and model of supervision and informed the supervisee about what he or she can expect of the supervision process.

Now that supervision is "officially" beginning, that same information will be covered once again in a more personalized, meaningful way. The supervisee will discuss professional goals and the supervisor will consider how to assist the supervisee in meeting such goals. The supervisor and supervisee will create a format for their sessions that is influenced by the supervisee's professional goals and the supervisor's model of supervision. The supervisor will start making intentional decisions about where his or her emphasis will be while further assessing the supervisee's strengths and weaknesses. The supervisee will leave the initial session with a clear sense of what he or she needs to do to prepare for future supervision sessions. The preceding information will be documented in the supervision contract that the supervisor and supervisee review and sign, and any areas of concern or question are clarified at this time.

This chapter discusses each of these tasks in greater detail, and supervisors are provided with a First Session Checklist that can be followed to ensure all initial tasks are covered. This checklist should be adjusted to fit the unique needs of each supervision relationship and setting. Supervisors should plan a 90-minute initial session, so that a sufficient amount of attention can be paid to the necessary initial points of discussion and the supervisee and supervisor get comfortable in one another's presence. An hour-long initial session may feel rushed and incomplete. In that the supervisory relationship is vital to a successful supervision experience (Borders & Brown, 2005), it is wise to spend plenty of time at the beginning acclimating the supervisee to the supervision process while getting to know one another in a more relaxed, "pre-business" alliance building time. The chapter concludes with a discussion of collaborative goal setting, so that the supervisor and supervisee can launch their work together with thoughtful and deliberate intention.

## THE SUPERVISION ENVIRONMENT

When supervisors think back to their early days as novice counselor preparing for their first sessions, they can usually recall that their concerns were mostly centered on the few things they felt they could actually influence: the therapeutic space, how they greeted the client, and what kinds of questions they could ask to most certainly avoid 50 minutes of awkward silence. Over time, they grew less concerned about these elementary ideas as their practices and skill sets grew increasingly complex. Although their initial concerns seem elementary in hindsight, the basic building blocks of one's practice remain important even as they shrink from the forefront.

Supervisors also must contend with seemingly elementary features that may not feel terribly important but actually impact the supervisory climate a great deal. Supervisors must model appropriate distraction-reduction techniques and take great care to ensure supervision is a time of work and focus rather than casual or interruptible conversation. The supervisor is fully attentive and engaged as a supervisor. Although the supervisor may have multiple roles in the supervisee's life, the supervisor takes great care to minimize the influence or impact of those other roles on the supervision experience. When a supervisee is welcomed into supervision for the initial session, that supervisee is likely to feel uncomfortable and may be uncertain about what to expect. Conversely, the supervisee may have enough experience with supervision that he knows what to expect, but those expectations may not align with his new experience with his supervisor. So, as supervisors welcome a new supervisee into the work space, they make sure to acquaint the supervisee with the practice space the same way a therapist would with a new client. Supervisors provide supervisees with a brief tour and ensure he knows how to access the restrooms and is aware of any logistical issues before they become a problem (e.g., parking rules, fragrance-free workplace rules).

The supervisee is then invited to consider the office a mutual workspace where he should be comfortable and able to focus on the matters at hand with a minimum amount of distraction. The supervisors "unplug" various forms of technology (e.g., desk phone, computer screen, cell phone), and the supervisee is asked to do the same. The supervisor and supervisee decide together whether the supervisee will make use of a laptop computer or other device during supervision. In many cases, the use of computers during supervision is unnecessary and may serve as a barrier to impactful interpersonal dynamics. However, in some instances, it makes sense for a computer or other device to be used throughout the session. Supervisors should allow the use of technological devices when they enhance the supervision process (like for video review or specific activities) but should ask supervisees to refrain from the use of technology when it impedes the supervisory process or the supervisory alliance in any way.

*Activity: What will you need to adjust in your environment to model a constructive, distraction-free work setting? How will you ensure your practice space is most conducive to optimal concentration, thinking, and learning? What specifically needs to change in your practice environment to make the space more suitable for supervision?*

## BEGINNING THE SESSION

As supervisors remember their first sessions as a counselor in training, they inevitably probably remember their eagerness to say the "right" thing. They probably learned in their training program that the first moments of a session may set the tone for the remainder of the session or the relationship as a whole (Guindon, 2011). Supervisors now extend those ideas into the supervisory experience. They consider carefully how to begin supervision sessions and recognize that the tone and attitude with which begin the first sessions will influence and shape the supervisory alliance.

*Activity: Recall from Chapter 2 the characteristics of effective supervisors. How will you present yourself in a manner congruent to that ideal? How will you initiate your sessions, so that your supervisee understands the tone, the direction, and the process of your time together?*

Once the supervisee has been welcomed into the mutual workspace, the supervisor shares the initial meeting outline or checklist so that the supervisee knows what to expect. The supervisor explains to the supervisee that this meeting will be unique but that it is crucially important to create a work experience that will be optimally beneficial to everyone involved. The supervisor explains that supervision is a place for collaboration and sharing, not simply further training and instruction. The supervisee is invited to ask for clarification or elaboration about anything that seems unclear. The supervisor is certain to focus on building a supportive and empathic alliance, but remains professional and focused on engaging in the first-session tasks.

The supervisor might even explain to the supervisee that the first supervision session process is similar to what counselors often experience with clients: both parties are eager to "get to the good stuff," yet the crucial introductory phases cannot be hurried as they are quite critical to an effective, long-lasting working relationship.

## THE FIRST SESSION CHECKLIST

The following items should be discussed in detail during the first supervision session. In Chapter 4, the professional disclosure statement and supervision contract were covered in explicit detail. At this point, the supervisor has developed those documents and arrives at the initial supervision session ready to share and discuss them at length. However, supervisors should be cautious that the discussion does not take the form of a "document review" but instead is a dynamic conversation where the supervisor and supervisee thoughtfully consider the contents of those documents and how those features will impact the collaborative experience. Many of the items on this checklist are based on the Initial Supervision Session Checklist by Prest, Schindler-Zimmerman, and Sporakowskis (1992), which was initially intended for marriage and family therapy supervisors but is appropriate and useful for all counselor supervisors.

- Supervisor Professional Disclosure: As discussed in Chapter 4, supervisors should provide supervisees with a written supervisor professional disclosure before the first session. During the first supervision session, invite the supervisee to ask questions about the disclosure if there is a need for clarification. Because the disclosure is a generic document that includes nonnegotiable items, it serves a unidirectional informational purpose only. Discuss items that need clarification but move efficiently along as the majority of the initial session time will need to be spent mutually creating the supervision contract.
- The Supervision Contract: The supervision contract was discussed in great detail in Chapter 4.

Recall the encouragement to create a dynamic contract framework that can be solidified in the first supervision session. Now is the time to engage in collaborative discussion with the supervisee about all items on the contract. Encourage the supervisee to consider each item in terms of work style, personality, work setting, clientele, professional experience, and life circumstances. Explain that the contract is a professional agreement that will be revisited and modified as needed and is simply a way of ensuring that everyone begins the experience with mutually agreeable understandings.

If there are any points of disagreement that cannot be worked out through discussion, you as the supervisor will decide how to proceed. For instance, is the disagreement a logistical one, such as figuring out the best day and time to meet, and can be worked out with some reasonable effort? Or, is the disagreement about an item that may put you or your supervisee into a professional, ethical, or legal bind at some point? For instance, if the supervisee refuses to video or audio tape and will only work with a self-report method, then you may rethink your decision to supervise this counselor in that you will not be able to provide appropriate oversight (especially in times of concern for client welfare). All items of the supervision contract should be agreed on and mutually acceptable by both parties before signing, and both parties should have copies of the contract for their reference.

■ The Supervision Portfolio: Supervisors may encourage supervisees to keep a "supervision portfolio;" that is, a binder or folder that holds supervision-related documents and is brought to each supervision session. This portfolio is an organizational tool that assists the supervisee in keeping supervision-relevant documents portable and accessible during and between supervision sessions. In addition, the portfolio allows for continuity of discussion from session to session, as the supervisee can examine historical data from prior supervision meetings. This portfolio should be protected in the same way other confidential materials are protected, as it will contain sensitive client information. The portfolio should include sections to help the supervisee maintain organization and accessibility. Although a portfolio should be individually designed and tailored to meet the supervisee's specific needs, the following format may be used as a guiding example of how to organize supervision-relevant documents.

Section 1: Client-Specific Documents

A list of current clients
Case conceptualization forms
Treatment plans
Resource and referral lists

Section 2: Supervision Documents

The Supervisor's Professional Supervisory Disclosure Statement
The Supervision Contract
Goals list
Professional documents
Internship/Licensure/Continuing education items
Copies of insurance coverage information
Job description
Professional Disclosure Statement

Section 3: Codes of Ethics

Copies of all relevant ethical codes
An ethical decision-making diagram or similar document

Section 4: Supervision Notes

This section is where the supervisee keeps notes that he takes during supervision sessions. If there is a formal supervision document that must be used per agency or treatment-specific protocol, this is where the supervisee can store such information. At times, it is useful to have the supervisee review his supervision notes to look for patterns of feedback, struggle, or discussion. The supervisee can also be instructed to review prior supervision notes and decisions and compare those decisions with what actually happened in client sessions, then examine the mechanisms that lead to a divergence from the agreed-upon plan.

Section 5. Training and Education

This section includes formal homework assignments and readings that the supervisee will complete. If the supervisor assigns the supervisee to comb the literature for information about a topic, then read and report back, the supervisee may decide to include an article or reflection in this section for future reference.

This section is not intended to serve as a growing library of references; instead, it should include materials being actively used in supervision and self-reflection, and those materials should be moved to more permanent storage once the supervisee feels she has absorbed the necessary information.

- The Supervisor's Supervision Chart/Supervisee Information Form: The Supervisor's Supervision Chart (SC) and the contents of that chart will be discussed in greater detail in Chapter 13. During or before the initial session, however, the supervisor should collect some key information from the supervisee and document this information on a Supervisee Information Form. It is often helpful to send the supervisee this form ahead of time and ask them to complete it ahead of time and bring it to the presession interview or first session. Supervisors should tailor their supervisee information form to fit their setting and the unique situations of each of their supervisees. The following list contains some general information that should be collected of all supervisees, then provides some items specific to training-level supervisees and pre-license supervisees, agency counselors, and private practitioners.

General information to collect from all supervisees is as follows:

Contact information: Name, address, phone numbers (cell, home, office), email address

Emergency contact information (personal contact—close friend, housemate, family member): Name, phone number(s), email address, relationship to the supervisee

Emergency contact information (professional contact—employer, business partner, office mate): Name, phone number(s), email address, relationship to the supervisee

Are there any medical or health-related conditions that may impact your ability to provide client care at times or may create a medical emergency? (Note: if you are an employer of the supervisee, you may decide not to ask this question. Consult with your human resources specialist for guidance.)

Educational history: List your degrees (type, specialty, year earned) and any postdegree trainings that were significant to you.

Licensure and certification status: List all licenses earned and specialty certifications. List the license type, issuing organization/state, license number, and whether license is current.

Pending/future credentials: List any degrees, licenses, or other credentials that you are currently working toward. Describe the credential, issuing organization, or body, and describe your progress toward that credential. Indicate whether you expect your supervisor to oversee your work toward that credential.

Supervision history: Where/from whom have you received counselor supervision? List all supervisors and what degree or credential they were providing supervision for, if any. Have you been supervised using any of the following modalities: live supervision, two-way mirror, bug-in-the-ear, audio review, video review, reflecting group, or others?

Theoretical orientation(s): List your theoretical orientations and any additional practice models/modalities. If there are any additional theoretical orientations that you have been trained in but do not practice, indicate that as well.

Training/work history: Attach a resume or list your work settings, job duties, and client populations. Add notes to your resume to more fully describe your experiences and practice in the counseling-related training and work settings.

History providing assessments/diagnosis: Describe your training providing assessment and diagnosis. What assessment tools are you proficient at? When was your most recent training in diagnosis? What kind of assessment/diagnosis do you utilize in your current work and how is it used?

History working with the following populations/modalities: Newer counselors, list approximate number of client contact hours; more experienced counselors, approximately how many hours per week for how many months or years?
> Individuals
> Couples
> Families
> Children
> Group (psychoeductional)
> Group (process/therapy)
> Severely mentally ill
> Suicidal/homicidal
> Clients with active addictions
> Describe the populations you have worked with specifically in terms of age, gender, cultural variables, diagnosis, etc.
> Are there any populations you are hoping to work with to expand your breadth of experience?
> Are there any populations you are concerned about working with or would rather not work with?
> What do you consider your professional strengths and weaknesses?
> Which personal characteristics contribute toward your therapeutic effectiveness and which characteristics may hinder effectiveness?
> Do you currently have an established relationship with a therapist who you can access when/if in need?

Information to collect from Agency Supervisees

> Agency contact information: Phone, physical location, mailing address
> Administrative supervisor contact information: Name, position, phone, email address, typical work days/hours
> Is your agency aware that you are seeking outside supervision? What is your agency's policy on such supervision arrangements? (This is discussed in greater detail later in this chapter)
> Position responsibilities: Attach a copy of your job description or contract

Private practitioners

> Practice location: Physical address, mailing address, phone number
> Business name:
> How long have you been in business?
> What marketing strategies do you use?

Do you communicate with clients through electronic means (like email or Skype)? If so, describe the protective measures to protect confidentiality and reduce risk.
Where do you complete and store your documentation?
Who else has access to your locked space and client files?
If you are unable to practice due to an emergency, who is assigned to contact your clients and how will that person access client contact information?

Postlicensure Supervisees

What has prompted you to seek supervision at this time?
Have you ever been investigated or reprimanded by any state licensing board or professional organization? Describe the situation and the outcome.
Continuing education requirements: What are your continuing education requirements to maintain your credentials?
Do you maintain membership in local, state, or national field-related organizations? Which ones?
Do you engage in field-related leadership activities at a local, state, or national level? Please describe your involvement.

- "Use of Self" Features: Prest, Schindler-Zimmerman, and Sporakowski (1992) recommend discussing professionally relevant personal features during the initial supervision session. These features may include the supervisee's family structure, key relationships, living situation, and significant current and past life events that shape and influence the supervisee's work. For instance, imagine a supervisee who is in the middle of a divorce after 12 years of marriage. The supervisee's spouse quite suddenly left the home after announcing that he had been involved in an extramarital relationship with a same sex partner. Naturally, these significant and current life events can impact the supervisee's work with a number of clients, and a well-informed supervisor can help the supervisee make certain that her objectivity and optimal client care are not impeded by the difficult personal circumstances she is working her way through.
- The Counselor's Counselor: Supervisors should learn in the first session whether the supervisee is currently working with a mental health counselor. If so, the supervisor should learn how accessible that counselor is if the supervisee were in crisis or in need of emotional support. It is appropriate to ask how often one sees the counselor and whether they plan to continue on with that counselor. If the supervisee does not currently have a counselor, a supervisor can recommend that the supervisee begin a search for a counselor,

then develop a relationship with a counselor that they think will be helpful to them if and when the need arises. Supervisors should encourage counselors to be actively engaged in their own counseling, so that they have a venue in which to attend to important psychological experiences that naturally arise from doing helping work of such an intimate nature. Further, the supervisor needs some assurance that when he recommends to a supervisee that a particular topic or phenomena needs to be discussed in personal counseling, and the supervisee will have a counselor at the ready to discuss the topic of concern. If the counselor does not already have a relationship with a counselor, he or she may have to begin the search for one when a crisis or traumatic situation arises. Instead, supervisors should ensure that the supervisee has a counselor readily available for when he or she is needed.

- The Supervisee's Workplace: Prest, Schindler-Zimmerman, and Sporakowski (1992) recommend discussing the supervisee's work setting in explicit detail to gain an understanding of the workplace logistics, dynamics, administrative structure, and organizational structure. Further, it is often useful to have a thorough understanding of the referral systems, reporting requirements, documentation demands, and availability of collegial, administrative, and managerial support available to the supervisee. A flowchart or diagram may come in handy as the supervisor tries to make sense of the supervisee's work context. If the supervisor works in the supervisee's agency, it is still useful to do some review of the supervisee's understanding of the organizational structure and hierarchy. This information will likely be quite useful later on in the supervision experience.

- The Supervision Goals Form: Although many supervisors include the supervision goals on the initial supervision contract, it may be useful to have a specific form designed to specify and track supervision goals. This form may parallel the treatment planning process, and supervisors may elect to use a format identical to the treatment planning format used by the supervisee for clients. The supervisor can role model effective treatment planning and progress tracking techniques while ensuring that the supervision experience is one of ongoing progress and development for the supervisee. The goal setting discussion should not be hurried; in fact, it often makes sense to conclude an initial session after some discussion of goal setting, with a promise to return to the topic at the start of the second session. The supervisor can assign supervision homework to the supervisee and instruct him to return with a carefully considered list of three to five potential goals for supervision. The goal setting process is a critical one, as the mutual agreement of goals and tasks is foundational to an effective working relationship (Bordin, 1979).

*Activity:* Prepare a model supervision portfolio for your supervisees to see. Make it simple, but organize it in a way that allows your supervisee a clear understanding of what you expect or suggest of them. Allow your supervisee flexibility to deviate a bit from your sample; you might be surprised at how useful and innovative their "product" may be.

*Activity:* Prepare Supervision Charts for each of your supervisees. Create a supplies list ahead of time, and list the materials you need. Create charts for your current supervisees and be sure to have extra material on hand to create the skeletons of additional charts for future supervisees. If you do not have supervisees yet, create a prototype that you can follow in the future.

## COLLABORATIVE GOAL SETTING

Formalizing the goal setting process is as crucial in supervision as it is in counseling. According to Milne (2009, p. 112), "good objective-setting can contribute hugely to the success of supervision." Goal setting is a collaborative process that is heavily reliant on self-reflection and evaluative feedback. Some supervisees are easily able to articulate realistic, appropriate goals, and others have more difficulty. The supervisor might lead the supervisee in a goal setting process that consists of several questions such as the following:

> What have you received feedback about that you would like to improve? (Consider feedback you have received from supervisor(s), colleagues, and especially clients.)
> What has caused you/will cause you the most anxiety about your clinical work?
> As you consider the many skills needed to do this work, what areas or practice skills do you think are weaker than others?
> What personal characteristics, habits, or defense mechanisms are impacting/do you think will impact the effectiveness of your work?
> What types of skills would your clients benefit from you improving upon?
> What phenomenon have emerged that are the most concerning to you as you consider your more complex sessions/cases?
> What has caused relational strains with your clients and/or colleagues recently?

The supervisor's task is to assist the supervisee in identifying and finding goals that are authentic and relevant. If the supervisee arrives with prior evaluative feedback, the goals may naturally emerge from such feedback. If the supervisee seems to have difficulty finding goals, the supervisor might make some generic suggestions and agree to revise the goals after having the chance to observe the supervisee's work. Border and Brown (2005) state that goals must be realistic, developmentally appropriate, and attainable in the supervisee's work setting. Supervisors may consider the goal setting process an opportunity to assist supervisees in conceptualizing their own performance with greater clarity while practicing goal setting skills.

Milne (2009) provides the acronym SMARTER to help supervisors and supervisees remember the key criteria needed to create good objectives.

S: Specific
M: Measurable
A: Achievable
R: Realistic
T: Time-phased (scheduled)
E: Evaluated
R: Recorded (written down)

So, the supervisee initiates a goal (the way a client produces a "presenting concern") and then the supervisor helps the supervisee shape the raw development goal into a SMARTER format (analogous to helping a client fit the initial concern into a treatment plan format). Supervisors are not limited only to goals brought forth by the supervisee; supervisors may also suggest goals, and the goals form can be adjusted at any time. This writer suggests, however, that goals not be discarded too readily in favor of more "current" goals. Instead, thoughtfully review progress toward a goal before discarding it in favor of other goals. Decide together whether the goal has been met, is "in progress" and can be addressed again at a later time, or should still be an area of necessary focus. Borders (1992) suggests three to five goals a semester for counseling students, and the same suggestion may be considered for prelicensure and postlicensure supervisees. However, supervisors may consider the sophistication and complexity by which their supervisee approaches conceptualization and problem solving. Highly advanced supervisees who engage in complex analysis with a skill for bringing to light overarching themes that impact multiple clients may need only one or two goals to frame their process. Multiple goals may add too much complexity and reduce the ability to fully investigate each area of growth and inquiry, so perhaps one or two goals is sufficient for the well-experienced supervisee.

A truly collaborative goal-setting effort involves the full investment of both the supervisee and supervisor. Since goal-setting relies heavily on self-evaluation and en examination of critical feedback, it is natural that defensiveness may arise. Some supervisees may become avoidant, others may feel a desire to set goals that are easily achievable, and yet others may set goals that are too far advanced in an effort to skip the painful early stages of development. Supervisors should proceed with caution when they disagree with the goals a supervisee initiates, or when the goals appear developmentally inappropriate. At times, supervisees may introduce goals that seem quite ideal on the surface but are actually well mastered already by the supervisee. The supervisee who expresses a desire to focus on "better listening" should explain what the intention of that goal is, so that the supervisor can understand why this already skilled listener needs to improve. The supervisor may suggest variations on the goal proposed by the supervisee, and the collaborative discussion continues until the supervisory dyad has reached a mutual understanding and agreement on the goals of supervision. Once goals are agreed on, they are documented for ongoing reference.

Borders and Brown (2005) state that a goal document should be a separate entity, not included amongst other documents that are more procedural in nature (such as the supervision contract). This writer suggests that the supervisor create a document for goal setting that is congruent with his model of supervision and the supervisee's practice approach. For instance, if a supervisee practices from a strictly cognitive-behavioral approach, a supervisor may use a treatment planning style model of goal setting to provide professional role modeling. Regardless of the format in which the goals are documented, the supervisor and supervisee should each maintain copies of the goals form someplace easily accessible. The supervisee may keep the goals form in the front window of her supervision portfolio, so that the goals are constantly noticeable, and the supervisor may keep the goal sheet as the first page of the SC or may also place it directly on the front of the chart. Allow goals to emerge naturally during the course of supervision, and celebrate the attainment of new developmental milestones as development objectives are completed.

*Activity: To practice and enhance your goal setting abilities as a supervisor, engage in a process of self-reflection about your goals as a clinical supervisor. Use the questions in the "Collaborative Goal Setting" section of this chapter, then follow the SMARTER method to specify three goals that are intended to enhance your competence as a supervisor. Make certain that you document these goals in the same manner in which you will be documenting your supervisee's goals. Store your goals document in a place where they can be easily accessed for ongoing review. If you have a supervisor who supervises your supervision practice, bring the goals to that supervisor and make this a collaborative process.*

*How will you keep these goals in mind as you engage in your supervision practice?*

*Next, list as many sources of feedback you can think of; that is, who can help you evaluate progress toward these goals? (Consider your supervisees, colleagues, supervisor, manager, and mentor.) How will you ensure that your perception of progress matches another relevant and credible source's impression? What will you do if there is incongruence in these perceptions?*

# SIX

# The Supervisory Alliance: Building the Relationship

## THE SUPERVISORY ALLIANCE

The supervisory relationship, also referred to as the supervisory alliance, is the core mechanism of supervisee development regardless of supervision model or practice method (Holloway, 1987; Ronnestad & Skovholt, 1993). The quality and features of the relationship between the supervisor and supervisee matters at all stages of a supervisee's development, whether the supervisee is a new counselor or is quite experienced (Fisher, 1989; Ronnestad & Skovholt, 1993) and is essential in achieving positive supervision outcomes (Worthen & McNeill, 1996). The supervisory working alliance figures prominently in the learning process of supervision (Efstation, Patton, & Kardash, 1990) and impacts the positivity of the supervisee's therapeutic working alliances (Patton & Kivlighan, 1997).

In this chapter, we will examine the supervisory alliance from many angles. First, we will examine many important components of the supervisory working alliance. Next, we will examine dual roles and managing multiple roles within the supervision context.

The supervision relationship, while admittedly crucial to effective supervision, is "difficult to describe and nearly impossible to prescribe" (Borders & Brown, 2005, p. 67). Thus, readers will view this chapter as the foundation for self-reflection and consideration but understand that there is no magic formula for an impactful and positive supervision relationship. Instead, readers will consider the characteristics and skills that have helped them build and sustain effective professional relationships with colleagues and clients. That self-awareness, in combination with information gathered from this chapter, will prepare the supervisor to create and sustain impactful and positive supervision alliances.

## IMPORTANT COMPONENTS OF THE SUPERVISORY ALLIANCE

The supervisory relationship has been long considered the core condition in which all other dynamic elements of supervision occur (Holloway, 1995;

Ronnestad & Skovholt, 1993). Borders and Brown (2005, p. 67) posit that the clinical supervisor's capacity for developing and maintaining "a positive working relationship is as important—or more important—than technical supervisory skills." Many noted researchers in the clinical supervision field pay exquisite attention to the facilitative and crucial role of the supervisory alliance in both effective supervision outcomes (Lambert & Ogles, 1997) and, by extension, positive therapeutic outcomes (Bordin, 1983).

*Activity: Consider your own experiences with supervision and the importance of the relationship between you and your supervisor(s). How would you describe the quality of your working relationship? How did the supervision relationship impact the experiences you had in supervision and as a result of supervision? How did the supervisory relationship impact your work with clients?*

### Three Core Conditions of a Working Alliance

The critical role of the therapeutic alliance has been acknowledged in the literature for decades, and one early researcher introduced a relationship-based model of supervision based on his knowledge of therapeutic working alliance. In his early work on the therapeutic working alliance, Bordin (1979) identified three essential features. First, the client and counselor must have mutual agreement upon the goals of treatment. Next, there must be agreement about the therapeutic tasks; that is, a clear and mutually acceptable plan of action to achieve the goals. Finally, there is an emotional bond that develops when two people share a common experience. The underlying assumption is that there must be some liking, caring, and trust that develops to sustain a relationship and work together to accomplish the tasks at hand (Bordin, 1983). The model of supervision by Bordin is based on the preceding three elements of the working alliance but recognizes that those three elements alone are not sufficient for an effective supervisory experience. Instead, the alliance is considered the context in which change happens in supervision, and with a stronger supervisory alliance comes a greater ability to effect change (Bordin, 1983; Rose Burke, Goodyear, & Guzzard, 1998).

The work of Bordin is carried forward by Holloway (1995), whose Systems Approach to Supervision highlights the supervisory relationship as the central component of the supervision experience. In addition, the Systems Approach highlights the significant role of clear expectations between the supervisor and the supervisee.

### The Supervisory Contract/Expectations

Supervisors and supervisees each bring a set of expectations to the supervisory relationship (Holloway, 1995). These expectations may be largely influenced by past professional and personal experiences and will undoubtedly inspire the development of the supervisory relationship. Supervisors and supervisees certainly have expectations of one another's behaviors and interpersonal abilities, and have expectations about the tasks and usefulness of supervision. Supervisors who engaged in the Pre-Supervision Interview likely initiated a discussion about expectations, and certainly supervisors explored mutual expectations during the initial supervision session. Although those prior discussions may have brought some information forward, there is great value in engaging in an ongoing conversation about expectations. Expectations will likely transform and evolve as the supervisory relationship develops and changes over time. The supervisor will inevitably expect different behaviors, cognitions, and levels of therapeutic sophistication over time, and the supervisee may expect supervisor behaviors to adjust as needs change. Negotiating and discussing changing expectations is essential to an increasingly effective and secure working relationship.

*Activity: What are your expectations of the supervisory relationship? How have past supervision experiences influenced those expectations? What do you expect of your supervisee(s)? What do you expect of yourself as a supervisor? How will you make these expectations transparent?*

## Power and Involvement

*Power* and *involvement* are crucial constructs in understanding the supervisory relationship (Holloway, 1995). The supervision relationship is hierarchical in that the supervisor's role involves evaluation and gate keeping to the profession. So, the supervisor maintains formal and *legitimate* power or the power that comes with a particular role. Many supervisors are concerned about the notion of having power over someone in such an impactful manner, especially considering the empowering stance many supervisors are used to taking in their therapeutic work with clients. However, supervisors should remember that "the supervisor's power is typically what the supervisee is paying for" (Grant, 1995). That is, supervisees willingly engage in a process of supervision with the knowledge that another professional will have oversight of their work for the purposes of client welfare and skill development. In addition, supervisees understand the supervisor's gate keeping functions and recognize that supervisors must have the power to prohibit practice when necessary for client welfare. Imagine supervision where the supervisor does not have the power to protect clients, influence the supervisee's development, or keep poorly practicing counselors from the profession. The power to protect and influence supervisee development is a necessary component of the supervision process, and supervisors must get comfortable with the power that is inherent and crucial to their role.

Sometimes supervisors attempt to minimize their power and evaluative responsibilities, which may seem helpful to the supervisory alliance in the moment but is likely quite damaging overall (Borders & Brown, 2005). In fact, a minimization of power may be perceived as a betrayal when power differences become necessarily present. Borders and Brown (2005) suggest that acting as if the evaluative power does not exist, or is not of significant importance, is dishonest as both parties are clear that evaluation is a necessary part of the process and will, at some point, happen. Although evaluation becomes less formal as the supervisee gains experience and credentials, the supervisor still maintains some power of evaluation. Imagine a longtime therapist who relapses into alcohol abuse after many years of sobriety. That therapist's supervisor holds the power to determine whether that therapist is safe to practice, at that time, with clients. If the therapist does not reach that decision on his own, the supervisor may have to exert his power to ease that therapist temporarily out of practice for the sake of client welfare.

On the converse, supervisors should not exert inappropriate amounts of power or use their positions of power to coerce or intimidate a supervisee. Supervisors should never use the supervision relationship as a venue for meeting one's need for power or control over another. This would result in the relationship becoming personal in nature rather than professional. Further, supervisors need to be cautious not to utilize their position of power as a means to further their own agenda. Supervisors must maintain clarity that supervisory power is useful in protecting clients and the profession and is useful in motivating supervisee development. Supervisory power is inappropriately abused when supervisors attempt to clone themselves through their supervisees, use their supervisees to further a personal or political agenda (especially prevalent in agency settings), or use the supervisory relationship to satisfy personal needs (e.g., the need for power, ego fulfillment, sex). Imagine a supervisor who asks a supervisee to disclose personal information about a life circumstance. The supervisee may not feel comfortable disclosing but may feel pressured by the supervisor because of the supervisor's position of power. The supervisor may be well intentioned; that is, he may hold a legitimate concern that the supervisee's personal circumstance is causing a negative impact on particular clients. However, the supervisor should be cautious about what information he presses for and in what context, so that the supervisee is not unduly pressured (Allen, Szollos, & Williams, 1986; Worthen & McNeill, 1996).

Supervisees hold power as well. Supervisors and supervisees engage in a reciprocal influence where they each hold some power to influence one another. This influence occurs during interpersonal transactions, a dance of sorts. During this dance, each participant engages more personally relevant material to predict one another's behaviors and responses, which effectively reduces personal uncertainty. The supervisor and supervisee find themselves increasingly involved in the supervision process. In this case, *involvement* refers to the level of participation and attachment one contributes to the supervisory process (Holloway, 1995). The supervisor and supervisee will each determine their level of attachment to one another and the process, and the nature of the supervisory alliance may become more professionally intimate as involvement builds.

Supervisors should engage in an ongoing examination of power and involvement dynamics as impactful components of the supervisory alliance (Holloway, 1995). Further, an intimate and clear understanding of power, involvement, and privilege in the supervisory alliance is a precursor to multicultural competence and effective supervision practice.

*Activity: How have power dynamics impacted your supervision experiences? Describe the dynamics in detail: How was power exhibited during supervision interactions? Was the power appropriately used and exhibited, or was power present in a way that was stressful to the supervision relationship?*

*How did your supervisor facilitate your empowerment or cause disempowerment? Do you believe that you became more empowered as supervision progressed? If so, how did that empowerment happen? Describe memorable incidents in detail.*

*How did power shift during conversation or interactions? How did each party respond to shifts in power (e.g., with flexibility or rigidity? with a welcome demeanor or perception of threat?) Were there ever times that you resented your supervisor's power? Were there ever times you believe your supervisor resented his or her own power? What was the impact of that on your supervision relationship?*

*You, as a supervisor, will be in a position of power. How do you feel about holding the power that comes with the supervisor's role? Do you expect you will hold power in appropriate balance, or are you concerned you may minimize or exploit the power inherent to the position? What are your concerns as you consider the power dynamics in a supervision relationship?*

## Multiculturalism

In the past decade, the counseling field has focused increasingly on the belief that all counseling is multicultural counseling (Pederson, 1991), and all interactions are multicultural (Bernard & Goodyear, 2009). The same can be stated about supervision; that is, anytime there are two people working together, especially given the inherent power imbalance of the supervisory relationship, a multicultural experience is taking place. The supervision experience is an ideal venue for supervisees to explore and make meaning of cultural variables as they relate to the therapeutic experience (Tummala-Narra, 2004).

Supervisors are responsible for integrating an acknowledgement and understanding of race, culture, gender, and social justice issues both within the supervisory dyad and in the larger systemic context (Tummala-Narra, 2004; Constantine & Sue, 2007).

Supervisees, as mental health professionals, are increasingly expected to achieve and maintain an impactful level of multicultural competence in their work with clients. Competence, in this domain, refers to a supervisee's ability to both identify cultural factors affecting the client and be able to integrate the impact of these variables when conceptualizing client treatment (Ladany, Hofheinz, Inman, & Constantine, 1997). To achieve such competence, supervisees need to be invited and continually welcomed to identify, discuss, and conceptualize the impact of multicultural variables on their significant professional relationships. Supervisors need to gain comfort and skill in facilitating cultural self-awareness and other-awareness in their supervisee. To do so, the supervisor needs to be a culturally competent counselor and supervisor as well.

In recent years, counseling training programs are placing increasing importance on multiculturalism and social justice. This means that many supervisees have more multicultural expertise and knowledge than their supervisors who were trained less formally and thoroughly in such domains (Constantine & Sue, 2007). Supervisors, to ensure they have equal or, ideally, greater skill and knowledge than their supervisee, should engage in both study and additional supervision or consultation to ensure their competence is strengthening.

Supervisors should maintain constant awareness that cultural variables may impact the supervisory relationship in a number of ways, directly and indirectly. A supervisor who is oblivious to a supervisee's experiences of racial-cultural issues as they impact the therapeutic process is missing an important component of the supervisee's conceptual framework. A supervisor who is insensitive or inadvertently demonstrates racism or cultural inappropriateness is placing a strain on the supervisory alliance and, in some cases, doing psychological or developmental harm to the supervisee. In addition, supervisors may overemphasize cultural explanations for client or supervisee difficulties, or may overlook crucial cultural variables that impact the therapeutic and supervisory dyads (Killian, 2001; Priest, 1994). Instead, supervisors should remain open and aware of multicultural variables as they present in the supervisee, supervisor, and the supervisory dyad. Further, multiculturally competent supervisors will invite and initiate discussions about culture and contextual factors and will pay sincere, genuine attention to such matters (Inman, 2006).

Although supervisors are responsible for creating the environment where multicultural exploration and discussion can safely occur, supervisors often believe that they are more attentive to multicultural issues than what their supervisees report (Duan & Roehlke, 2001). Supervisors should remember that supervisees will likely need to revisit common themes and issues of multiculturalism repeatedly as they develop and become more advanced in their practice (Borders & Brown, 2005). Discussion alone is not sufficient in addressing multicultural issues and their impact on client care. In fact, studies have revealed that when supervisors are not culturally competent or have anxiety about discussing racial and cultural issues, discussions may be harmful to the supervisory relationship and the supervisee (Constantine & Sue, 2007).

To help develop culturally competent supervisees, supervisors need to be certain that they have adequately addressed and continue to address their own cultural self-awareness and competence. Supervisors should examine and explore the impact of their own biases and assumptions. Further, supervisors should elicit feedback from colleagues, their own supervisor, and others about the integration of cultural competence in their work, so that undetected biases and assumptions may be acknowledged and addressed (Borders & Brown, 2005; Tummala-Narra, 2004).

Although many supervisors will quickly acknowledge the importance of addressing such variables, it is difficult to know how to engage in competent multicultural supervision. Supervisors should keep the following in mind when considering competent multicultural supervision practices:

1. Research demonstrates that many supervisees wish their supervisor had addressed multicultural issues more often and more explicitly (Constantine, 1997).
2. The supervisor should pay attention to multiculturalism in several relational configurations: the supervisor–supervisee dyad; the supervisee–client relationship, and the supervisor–client relationship.
3. Supervisors hold the ultimate responsibility for moving their supervisees to culturally competent practice. Thus, the supervisor has the responsibility to continue to develop and move toward optimal competence in therapeutic and supervision practice. Supervisors should engage in exploration and self-knowledge activities, in which they can then have their supervisee engage when appropriate.
4. Racism is not always deliberate and can exist unconsciously (Constantine & Sue, 2007). So, supervisors should accept that racism will likely be present in supervision and should welcome the experience, so that it can be worked through and appropriately addressed and resolved.
5. Colorblindness, or the minimization or denial of racism and race, will likely have negative consequences on the supervisory alliance, counselor development, and ultimately, client care (Sue, 2004).
6. Supervisors should initiate the conversations and raise racial and cultural issues to build a respectful, constructive supervisory relationship (Goodyear & Guzzardo, 2000). Supervisors will be proactive in starting this exploration rather than reactive in waiting for the topic to "naturally" emerge.

7. A strong working alliance allows for conversations and exploration of multicultural issues to occur; further, the occurrence of these conversations, when effectively managed, further strengthens the supervisory alliance (Sue, 2004; Constantine & Sue, 2007).

Supervisors who are practicing in a multiculturally competent manner may disclose aspects of their culture beyond the visible racial and ethnic features. In this case, as with other cases of self-disclosure, the supervisor will attempt to meet supervisee developmental and training needs foremost and will dismiss temptation to disclose when it is not going to serve a useful purpose to the supervisee or the supervisory alliance.

*Activity:* Examine the Association for Multicultural Counseling and Development (AMCD) Multicultural Counseling Competencies document (Appendix C). Rate yourself on each component of the competency list. Use the following scale:

> *1 = I have not yet addressed this competence*
> *2 = I am in the process of addressing this competence*
> *3 = I believe I am competent in this domain and am willing to further explore when the need arises*

As you score yourself, recognize that some items may cause you greater concern than others. Keep track of those areas of greatest concern as they will become your highest priorities as you continue to increase your multicultural counseling competence.

Examine your scores and look for patterns. Do most of your lower scores fall into knowledge, beliefs, or skills?

Based on what you notice about your scores, formulate a development plan to address your priority growth areas. List at least three competencies that need to be addressed and your plan for addressing them. For instance, if you need to become actively involved with minority individuals to broaden your perspectives (Section II.c.2), you may decide to engage in a community event that allows you to network and increase social contacts in a culturally diverse setting.

## Attachment

Many mental health professionals are familiar with the impact and implications of attachment theory in the context of the therapeutic milieu (Ainsworth & Bowlby, 1991). Attachment theory, by extension, provides an interesting and useful way for supervisors and supervisees to develop clearer understanding of interpersonal characteristics that impact the supervisory relationship (Neswald-McCalip, 2001). Further, this theory allows supervisors a way to conceptualize supervisees' attachment and apparent involvement in the supervision experience.

Attachment theory posits that humans have a need for accessibility and closeness in an emotionally significant relationship that provides security and protection (Bowlby, 1988). Humans have behavioral systems that are existent before birth and fulfill the need for safety, security, and a safe anchor from which to explore the world. Further, environmental stimuli, especially from other people, will either activate or terminate the behavior system (Neswald-McCalip, 2001). As supervisees and supervisors form a relationship, it is likely that elements of *attachment behaviors* (internally motivated behaviors that serve to fulfill an important survival need) will present themselves in the supervisory context. These behaviors, over time, can become *attachment patterns* (Bowlby, 1988). These patterns are precisely what supervisors will examine when conceptualizing the supervisory alliance in terms of attachment theory.

Supervisors will consider the three main attachment patterns when conceptualizing the working alliance: the secure attachment pattern, the anxious-resistant pattern, and the anxious-avoidant pattern (Bowlby, 1988). These patterns describe the quality of the *secure supervisory base*; that is, the supervisor's position of availability and safety by which the supervisee can explore interpersonal and professional features of the therapeutic and supervision relationships.

The supervisee with a *secure pattern* of attachment typically has a positive attitude toward exploration, challenge, assistance, and a confidence that help will be available when needed. This individual views his or her supervisor and support system as readily accessible when needed (Neswald-McCalip, 2001).

An *anxious-resistant pattern* is demonstrated by an individual's experience of the supervisor as inconsistent and unreliable. Further, the supervisee is uncertain whether the supervisor will be available when help is needed, and, if physically available, may not be psychologically present or attentive to the supervisee's support and technical needs. These supervisees may be nervous and anxious when challenged or provided with evaluative feedback and may be viewed as needy and lacking autonomy.

An *anxious-avoidant supervisee* will view the supervisor as inaccessible and absent and is fairly certain that no help will be available when needed. This supervisee expects to be overlooked and ignored and may attempt self-sufficiency as a result (Bowlby, 1988; Neswald-McCalip, 2001). This supervisee may appear to resent or reject the supervisor's availability or help and may go to great lengths to avoid supervision when available.

Supervisors will aim to form secure attachment patterns with their supervisees. With a secure attachment base, the supervisee will feel safe and supported, especially in times of crises or angst (Neswald-McCalip, 2001). A secure supervision base provides protection to the supervisee in several ways. First, the secure base lets the supervisee know that he or she is not working in a professional vacuum and is supported in his or her work. Next, the supervisee knows that he or she has an available and invested resource who is there for them when needed. Finally, the supervisee understands that his or her work is monitored and appropriate oversight is being steadily provided (Pistole & Watkins, 1995).

*Activity: Describe your own patterns of attachment as a supervisee. In your current or most recent supervision relationship, did you notice signs of secure, anxious-resistant, or anxious-avoidant? What were these signs? How did the attachment pattern impact your growth, learning, security, and job or placement satisfaction? How did your attachment impact your work with clients?*

*As a supervisor, do you believe you might have difficulty working with a supervisee with any of these attachment patterns? What might cause the difficulty? What will you do to manage the relationship?*

## Supervisor Self-Disclosure

Supervisors are likely quite familiar with the term self-disclosure as it relates to the therapeutic process. In therapeutic settings, self-disclosure is defined and is done with great care and forethought to maximize therapeutic value and appropriateness. In supervision, self-disclosure may be quite powerful when used at the right time in the right way (Ladany & Walker, 2003). There are five categories of supervisor self-disclosure statements, as follows:

1. Personal material: self-disclosures about the supervisor's personal life (such as personal stressors, family issues, or other items not directly related to the professional role or tasks).
2. Therapy experiences: self-disclosures about the supervisor's work and experiences as a therapist.
3. Professional experiences: self-disclosures about professional experiences beyond working with clients (such as administrative or managerial functions, employee dynamics).
4. Reactions to the supervisee's clients: self-disclosures relating to one's reactions and responses to a client that the supervisee is working with (e.g., the supervisor feels annoyed at a client when watching a video of the session and shares this feeling with the supervisee).
5. Supervision experiences: self-disclosure about the experience of being a supervisor engaged in the supervision process.

Supervisors also consider the following dimensions when considering self-disclosure: nonintimate-intimate (how personal the disclosure is to the supervisor), discordant-congruent self-disclosures (how much the supervisor's disclosure relates to the supervisee's training needs and concerns), and service of the supervisor versus service of the trainee (whether the disclosure meets the supervisor's needs or prioritizes the supervisee's training needs). Self-disclosures that focus on the supervisee's training needs are considered more meaningful than supervisor-centric disclosures (Ladany & Walker, 2003). Similarly, disclosures that are congruent with the supervisee's concerns and are more personally intimate are considered more impactful. Further, supervisor self-disclosure may influence supervisee self-disclosure and can help build trust and attachment when used appropriately. Supervisors who use disclosure skillfully may find it a useful tool in providing training through role modeling or didactic mentoring (Ladany, et al., 1999).

Supervisor self-disclosure, like disclosure in therapeutic settings, comes with some risk. Supervisors who use the aforementioned categories and dimensions will inevitably engage in a thoughtful decision-making process that is actually very fast once one is familiar with this process. When used appropriately and thoughtfully, supervisor self-disclosure can have a positive impact on the supervision experience and relationship (Ladany & Walker, 2003). When disclosure is not used appropriately, the impact on the supervisory alliance can be quite disruptive.

*Activity: Describe some memorable incidents of disclosure in supervision. What was the nature of the disclosure (which category does it fit into)? What was the supervisor's intent? Was the disclosure effective in strengthening the supervisory alliance or facilitating growth in the supervisee, or did it have a detrimental effect? How?*

Although many instances of supervisory self-disclosure are going to be positively impactful or perhaps unimpactful enough that they go largely unnoticed, some cases of disclosure will be harmful to the supervisory alliance. The following are some examples of supervisory self-disclosure patterns that highlight the risk involved with supervisor self-disclose gone awry (Ladany & Walker, 2003):

1. "The Uncontrollable Narcissist": This supervisor self-discloses excessively, thus reducing the availability of time and attention for client or supervisee concerns. In this case, the supervisor is bringing material in that is discordant with the supervisee's training needs and is in the service of the supervisor, not the supervisee.

2. "Whatever You Can Do I Can Do Better": In this case, the supervisor uses disclosure to elevate his or herself to a superior status and meet his own need to feel important and valuable. The supervisee will likely either act in awe of the supervisor or may refute the disclosure. Either way, the energy is spent addressing the supervisor's needs at the expense of addressing supervisee concerns or training needs.

3. "The Indomitable Altruist": A supervisor may disclose, from time to time, an anecdote about their own experience as a therapist working with a client. In moderation, this can be quite useful and may enhance the supervisee's conceptualization skills. On the contrary, the supervisor may carry this intervention too far and may share for less appropriate reasons. For instance, the supervisor might disclose to prove that he or she knows the "correct" way to provide treatment. In these cases, the supervisee is not given the chance to think critically and self-reflect, but is instead redirected to focus on the supervisor's work and skill.

4. "When I was Your Age": In this scenario, the supervisor uses disclosure to normalize or validate the supervisee's anxiety-producing events (such as making an error out of inexperience, or expressing a feeling of inadequacy). Although this may be useful when brief and truly empathic in nature, it can go awry when the disclosure ends up creating additional fear or feelings of inadequacy in the supervisee. A supervisor might do this by highlighting the supervisee's inexperience or highlighting the skill differences between the supervisor and supervisee.

5. "The Hyde or Jekyll Supervisor": In this case, the supervisor might use disclosure maliciously, like to highlight the supervisee's poor performance in therapy and supervision. One example is a supervisor saying to a supervisee "We all had to go through supervision, the sooner you accept the fact that I'll be watching your work, the better."

6. "The Unabashed Bigot": This pattern of disclosures refers to the supervisor using oppressive prejudicial statements, such as generalized comments about one gender or one culture. The range of comments or questions may be quite broad and the common effect is one of strain to the supervisory alliance and discomfort, at the very least, to the supervisee (Ladany & Walker, 2003).

*Activity: Which of these disclosure patterns might you engage in, perhaps quite accidentally? What might trigger such an event? How would you extricate yourself from it and make amends with your supervisee if a relationship strain resulted from the interactions?*

## Trust

Participants in any helping relationship know the critical value of trust between a service provider and a recipient. However, many people have also learned to exercise caution when dealing with people in authority, especially during initial encounters (Shulman, 2006). Supervisees may feel some hesitance to open up to their supervisors as they experience the typical sensations of performance anxiety, fear of repercussion or ridicule, and desire to be viewed in a positive light by someone with greater expertise and evaluative power. Supervisors, similarly, understand the liability they accept when working with a supervisee and may feel some hesitance and trepidation as they learn about their new supervisee's skills and abilities. Although trust in a relationship inarguably requires reciprocal effort, the supervisor ultimately holds the responsibility to create an emotionally safe working environment in which the supervisee can make mistakes, report errors, and feel a growing sense of power and effectiveness.

Trustworthiness has been described as one's openness, sincerity, and a lack of motivation for personal gain (Heppner & Handley, 1981). A supervisor who presents with these qualities is likely to be viewed initially as trustworthy by the supervisee; however, these qualities are not sufficient to sustain trust in the supervisory relationship. A supervisee must be able to trust that the supervisor is an emotionally and psychologically safe person with whom to reveal sensitive and confidential issues (Edwards et al., 2005). Further, the supervisee has to experience the supervisor as someone who will treat them with respect, positive regard, and value, even in the face of dreadful errors or embarrassing clumsiness.

As discussed earlier, supervisors sometimes are hesitant to acknowledge to themselves or their supervisee that they possess evaluative power that influences the work. However, supervisors should be transparent, honest, and clear about evaluation and reporting practices to avoid feelings of betrayal later on. If a supervisor is making reports, formal or informal, to third parties, the supervisor may consider making such reports in a transparent and open fashion, so that there are no surprises or miscommunications that would inevitably strain the supervisory relationship. For instance, let us imagine that a supervisor in private practice is contacted by the supervisee's managerial supervisor. This manager asks for information about whether the supervisee is discussing particular issues in supervision and wants to learn specifically what the supervisee is doing to address certain problem areas. The clinical supervisor, rather than engaging in a spontaneous discussion, should invite the managerial supervisor into a triadic meeting or conference call with all parties present. This helps decrease the likelihood of triangulation, mixed messages, and covert communication that would reduce the supervisor's trustworthiness.

*Activity: Consider your prior experience as a supervisee. What did your supervisor(s) do to gain your trust and openness? What kinds of things made it difficult to trust your supervisor(s)? Was the difficulty related supervisor-specific (perhaps the result of your supervisor's words, actions, or role) or was the difficulty specific to you (such as your feelings about supervision, your personality, or a particular circumstance)? Was there ever a strain in the relationship as a result of a breech in trust?*

*As a supervisee, what kinds of indicators did you look for that let you know it was time to trust or not trust your supervisor? How will your own supervisees know that you are trustworthy?*

## Supervisor Style

Supervisor style is the supervisor's manner of actually doing supervision; that is, the supervisor's way of approaching, responding to, and intervening with supervisees (Friedlander & Ward, 1984). Understandably, the supervisor's style must, to some degree, match the supervisee's needs. When considering supervisor style and the impact of style on the supervisory alliance, we focus on interpersonal, relationship-centered features. There are three categories of style to consider:

1. Attractive (demonstrates the collegial aspects of supervision through warmth, friendliness, supportiveness, openness, flexibility)
2. Interpersonally sensitive (demonstrates a relationship-oriented approach and may show investment, commitment, perceptiveness)
3. Task-oriented (demonstrates a content-focus and may demonstrate goal-oriented behaviors, is thorough, practical, and structured) (Friedlander & Ward, 1984)

Supervisors determine their primary style, so that their approach aligns with the supervisee's developmental needs (Ladany, Marotta, & Muse-Burke, 2001). Supervisees who are newer counselors likely need a more structured, task-oriented approach with a more actively guided direction (Holloway & Wampold, 1986; Stoltenberg, McNeill, & Crethar, 1994), whereas the more advanced supervisees benefit from more mutual collaboration and exploration in an increasingly consultative stance (Miars et al., 1983; Ladany, Marotta, & Muse-Burke, 2001). Although many supervisors will use components of all three styles at once, it may be useful to consider these styles in relation to the supervisee's needs: which style does the supervisee typically respond most favorably to? Which style would best help the supervisee remain open, engaged, and invested in the process? Which style would most effectively provide the supervisee the appropriate amount of challenge necessary for development and deeper conceptual understanding?

*Activity: Using the categories described above, how would you describe the style of your prior supervisors? Did their style match your needs? If not, which style would have been a better fit for you? How did your supervisor's style, matched or mismatched with your needs, impact the supervisory relationship?*

## ROLE CLARITY: MANAGING MULTIPLE RELATIONSHIPS

The term *multiple relationships* refers to a supervisor having a relationship or role with the supervisee in addition to the supervisory relationship. The relationship may have preceded the supervisory alliance or may have formed after supervision began. The additional relationship or relationships may be professional, personal, sexual, or business related (Westfield, 2009). Multiple relationship issues are nearly unavoidable, especially when the supervisor is a university supervisor or is the supervisee's managerial supervisor as well (Borders & Brown, 2005; Disney & Stephens, 1994; Gottlieb, 1993). However, multiple roles may significantly and negatively impact the development and maintenance of an effective, positive supervisory alliance for several reasons. First, supervisors hold a position of power and advantage over their supervisees (Harrar, Vandecreek, & Knapp, 1990). Next, supervisors are in a position of trust and, in that position, are expected to proceed in the best interest of the supervisee and, by extension, the supervisee's clients (Harrar, Vandecreek, & Knapp, 1990; Gottlieb, 1993). When the inherent power or trust is violated, even by a seemingly willing supervisee, the supervisor has failed in his or her duty to maintain objective professional judgment and act in the best interest of the supervisee and clients (Disney & Stephens, 1994; Harrar, Vandecreek, & Knapp, 1990). The ethical issues inherent to multiple roles are discussed in much greater detail in Chapter 8. At this point, it would be remiss to overlook the potentially detrimental effects of multiple relationships on the supervisory alliance.

Effective and positive supervisory alliances are built on clear expectations, appropriate respect for inherent power differences, role clarity, trust, and many other factors discussed earlier. One can easily conclude that a sexual relationship between a supervisor and supervisee would violate most or all of those factors. Regardless, sexual relationships between supervisees and supervisors occur with surprising frequency (Glaser & Thorpe, 1986; Neufeldt, 1999). Sexual boundary violations are considered the most egregious of multiple relationships (Falvey, 2001) and are perhaps the most obviously impactful to the participants. However, many other multiple relationships can occur that may strain the foundational fibers of a strong supervisory alliance.

When considering the impact of a multiple relationship on the supervisory alliance, a supervisor should consider two factors: first, the supervisor should not be involved in a relationship with the supervisee that will cause impairment in objectivity or judgment. Second, the supervisor should not engage in any relationship that is exploitative or has the potential for exploitation of the supervisee (Borders & Brown, 2005; Harrar, Vandecreek, & Knapp, 1990). Finally, the supervisor should recognize that any multiple relationship may influence the power structure, role clarity, and trust in the supervisory dyad. With this realization, supervisors should carefully consider how to manage any relationship that exists with the supervisee beyond the supervisory one. The supervisory relationship is considered central, and all other relationships need to be managed in a way that honors the needs and demands of the central supervisory relationship.

## MANAGERIAL VERSUS CLINICAL SUPERVISION

Many supervisors experience the inherent dilemma that comes with holding multiple roles in one setting. Perhaps the most common of these dilemmas is when the *clinical* supervisor is also the *managerial* supervisor. By definition, a managerial or administrative supervisor is someone who oversees or manages staff (such as clinicians, students, and support staff) in a bureaucratic organization (Holloway, 1995). That supervisor's responsibilities are primarily to the organization and the functional aspects therein. On the contrary, a clinical supervisor is someone whose responsibilities are first to the client, next to the development and ongoing formation of the counselor (Kaiser, 1997). Despite the inherent disparities, these two activities often seem to exist within the same job description (Holloway, 1995; Powell, 2004). These supervisors who are both managerial and clinical supervisors are in a dual relationship with their supervisee/employee. In these cases, agency or administrative needs may take precedence above clinical focus and supervisee development, and the supervisor's two roles may be in direct opposition. For instance, clinical supervisors often make great efforts to ensure the supervisee feels safe and comfortable to discuss times of professional incompetence and needed development. However, many supervisees may find it difficult to divulge professional weakness to their direct manager who has great control or influence over their ability to be promoted, given a raise or bonus, approved for vacation time, and the like.

In addition, the supervisee may be keenly aware of the divergent responsibilities and may view this split as a betrayal of sorts. Inevitably, there will be situations where the supervisor will have to decide whether to act on the best interest (or necessary interest) of the agency at the expense of the best interest of the supervisee. If the supervisee needs the supervisor to be compassionate and empathic about a heavy caseload, but the supervisor is the person who assigned the caseload, the supervisee may not feel safe and welcome to engage in such a conversation or seek support. Further, if that supervisee indicates an inability to handle the assigned job, the clinical supervisor may have to utilize such information at some point, such as during a time of layoffs. This dynamic likely impedes the necessary trust and involvement levels necessary for a maximally effective clinical supervision alliance. Imagine additionally a situation where the clinical supervisor of a crowded residential treatment facility is keenly aware that a supervisee is experiencing burn out, compassion fatigue, and is considering leaving the counseling profession altogether. The supervisor understands that the supervisee is ineffective and on the verge of being harmful and needs at least a few days off to rebalance. The clinical supervisor, in the best interest of the clinician and his clients, may agree that the absence is a necessary beginning to professional respite. However, the same supervisor, wearing a manager's cap, may be fully aware that the agency will not be able to function if employees are on vacation and subs need to be hired. Further, that same manager recognizes that there is an upcoming audit and this clinician needs to be caught up on paperwork in time. A vacation would prohibit that from happening. Now consider the impact this multiple role has on the supervisory alliance and the supervisor's ability to make objective, beneficial decisions. The dilemma is clear, and this multiple role, although common, should be carefully monitored and minimized whenever possible (Bond & Holland, 1998; Maki & Bernard, 2003).

This multiple role issue is so significant that the Association for Marriage and Family Therapy has specified in its "Responsibilities and Guidelines for AMMFT Approved Supervisors and Supervisor Candidates" that administrative supervision (in this case, supervision that does not focus on the quality of therapy being provided to the client) is not an acceptable component of clinical supervision (American Association for Marriage and Family Therapy, 1993). Further, the supervision guidelines put forth by the Supervision Interest Network (Association for Counselor Education and Supervision [ACES]/Supervision Interest Network) do not mandate a separation of administrative and clinical roles, but instead state that:

> Supervisors who have multiple roles (e.g., teacher, clinical supervisor, administrative supervisor) with supervisees should minimize potential conflicts. When possible, roles should be divided amongst several supervisors. When this is not possible, careful explanation should be conveyed to the supervisee as to the expectations and responsibilities associated with each supervisory role. (Section 2.09)

The literature indicates that administrative tasks may predominate supervision sessions, potentially at the expense of supervisee development and growth (English, Oberle, & Byrne, 1979; Herbert, 1997). However, studies have shown that the supervisory alliance is most supported by clear and clinically focused supervision from supervisors with one clearly defined role. Supervisees have reported dissatisfaction with such practices and indicate in several studies a preference for a clinical focus during supervision as opposed to an administrative one (Crimando, 2004; English, Oberle, & Byrne, 1979; Herbert & Trusty, 2006). One study of rehabilitation counselors found that counselors who indicated their supervisor "always" took an administrative role (engaging in administrative tasks) were most dissatisfied with their "clinical" supervision experiences. This same study indicates that counselors who were much more satisfied with supervision when their supervisors "often, rarely, or never" engaged in administration roles and focused instead on clinical tasks (Herbert & Trusty, 2006).

*Activity: Consider your experience as a supervisee receiving supervision from someone who had managerial or administrative oversight of your work. How did this dual role impact the supervisory working relationship? If the impact was minimal or nonexistent, what kinds of measures did your supervisor or the organization take to ensure the impact of these dual roles was minimized? If there was a negative impact on the relationship, what do you believe could have been done to decrease this effect?*

*Describe the multiple roles you will be engaged in as a supervisor. List specifically what your roles will be (e.g., clinical supervisor, managerial supervisor, group supervisor) and which supervisees will experience you with multiple roles. How will you minimize the impacts of these dual roles, so that the supervisory relationship does not suffer as a result of your multiple responsibilities?*

### Minimizing the Impact

In many instances, the impact of a multiple relationship will not be harmful to any parties. However, supervisors should always follow the guidelines set forth by the ACES in the Ethical Guidelines for Counseling Supervisors statement (ACES, 1993; see Appendix B). The guideline states that "supervisors who have multiple roles (e.g., teacher, clinical supervisor, administrative supervisor)...should minimize potential conflicts. When possible, the roles should be divided among several supervisors. When this is not possible, careful explanation should be conveyed to the supervisee as to the expectations and responsibilities associated with each supervisory role" (ACES, 1993).

Clinical supervisors who are in administrative and clinical positions may consider working with their agency to implement a structural change that reduces conflict and increases the effectiveness of supervision practices. When a supervisee can fully trust the allegiance and motives of the supervisor, that supervisee is likely going to allow the supervisor a much clearer glimpse into the work and greater influence through evaluative and cooperative feedback. More effective supervision relationships allow for greater oversight, more impactful supervisee development, greater protection for the clients, and a reduction in employee burnout (Edwards et al., 2006; Edwards et al., 2005; Ladany, Lehrman-Waterman, Molinaro, & Wolgast, 1999; Milne, Leck, & Choudhri, 2009).

# SEVEN

# The Supervision Alliance: Strains, Stressors, and Solutions

*R*esearchers have examined effective and ineffective supervision characteristics and events for many decades (e.g., Gray, Ladany, Walker, & Ancis, 2001; Hutt, Scott, & King, 1983; Miller & Oetting, 1966). In this chapter, the primary focus is on how ineffective and counterproductive supervision events impact the supervisory working alliance and, by extension, the supervision experience. The supervision relationship, like any personal or professional relationship, is vulnerable to conflict and discord at times. This chapter discusses the appearance of conflict in supervision and how to effectively conceptualize and manage such conflict. This chapter concludes with detailed descriptions of supervisee games and defensive strategies that invariably impact the supervision relationship and a supervisor's ability to make supervision maximally effective.

## COUNTERPRODUCTIVE SUPERVISION EVENTS

Supervisors should be keenly aware of many types of incidents and dynamics that are counterproductive to effective supervision. While ineffective supervision is of great concern, so is actual harm to a supervisee. Ellis (2001) distinguishes between "bad" supervision and "harmful" supervision. Bad supervision is supervision that is ineffective but does not traumatize or harm the supervisee, while "harmful" supervision does create harm or trauma for the supervisee (Ellis, 2001). This distinction is helpful when conceptualizing counterproductive supervision events in that some events are merely "bad," so the supervisory dyad can possibly repair and move forward with little or no lasting negative impact. On the converse, a "harmful" supervisory event or pattern is probably going to cause a lasting negative impact for the supervisee which, even more concerning, can also cause damage to vulnerable clients. So, supervisors seek to provide "good" (productive and positively impactful) supervision while minimizing "bad" supervision. Harmful supervision should be avoided entirely, though even well-intentioned supervisors may cause harm. One recent study reveals that 36% of supervisees report being harmed by a supervisor, and the intensity of that harm is quite alarming. Fifty-nine percent of respondents in the same study report receiving inadequate supervision from their current or a past supervisor (Ellis et al., 2001).

In this section, supervisors will learn many ways that supervision may be counterproductive (ineffective or harmful). The following examination is not all-inclusive, and supervisees will experience varying events with different interpretations based on context, personality, relationship variables, and such. The core concern here is the impact that these events have on the supervisory alliance. When supervisees experience supervision as unhelpful or harmful, the supervisor's ability to provide appropriate oversight, objectivity, and optimal development is reduced. The supervisor's objective is to prevent counterproductive events when possible, and effectively manage and resolve these events when they do inevitably occur. These events are typically a threat to the supervisory relationship (Ramos-Sanchez et al., 2002), but when effectively managed can provide the supervisory dyad a chance to gain a stronger and more invested bond.

Researchers have identified multiple events that are experienced by supervisees as counterproductive or harmful (e.g., Ellis et al., 2008; Gray et al., 2001). In this section, counterproductive events are placed into three categories: *ethical nonadherence, supervisor skill,* and *supervisor personalization.* Many concerns quite naturally overlap categories, but the more important focus here is on truly understanding the counterproductive events and considering how to prevent or manage them.

The first category, ethical nonadherence, particularly addresses supervisor behaviors that do not align with supervisor ethical guidelines. Research reveals that supervisors who do not adhere to ethical practices typically have weaker supervisory alliances and less satisfied supervisees. Ladany, Lehrman-Waterman, Molinaro, and Wolgast (1999) used a list of 12 supervisor ethical guidelines developed by the Association for Counselor Education and Supervision, as well as three additional guidelines added by the researchers to describe supervisor nonadherence to ethics (supervisor ethics are further discussed in Chapter 8). The items of ethical nonadherence discussed in this chapter are adapted specifically from Ladany and his colleagues' research.

While ethically lax supervision may be quite obviously detrimental to the supervisory relationship, additional harm or, at the least, ineffectiveness, occurs when supervisors lack effective *supervision technical skills.* It is now understood that clinical supervisors need appropriate training in supervision-specific skills, yet research has revealed that many supervisors are not adequately trained nor have had the benefit of highly effective supervision themselves (Bernard & Goodyear, 2009). Supervisors, like any humans, are prone to errors, instances of poor judgment, and well-meaning interventions that go awry. Most of these incidents will not create lasting harm or negative impact, especially if the working alliance is foundationally strong enough to withstand the strain. However, mishandled incidents or patterns of such incidents certainly can cause harm to the supervisee and, by extension, the client (Ramos-Sanchez et al., 2002).

The final category, supervisor personalization skills, refers to the intersection of the supervisor's style and presentation with the supervisor's personality characteristics and interpersonal skills; in short, how the supervisor's personal being influences his professional being. The manner in which a supervisor approaches supervision, his supervisees, and people in general can have a profound impact on the supervisory alliance, as can the supervisor's personality and emotional capacity. The supervisor's abilities to manage the intensity and intimacy of the supervision dynamic will greatly influence whether the supervisee can fully invest and allow vulnerability in the supervision process.

## COUNTERPRODUCTIVE EVENTS INVOLVING ETHICAL NONADHERENCE

Ethical breeches in supervision negatively impact the supervisory working alliance in several ways. First, a supervisor is providing inappropriate role modeling when engaging in an ethical breech. Second, breeches can take up time and energy in supervision that would better be invested in other supervisory tasks. Finally, breeches may convey a message of disrespect and lack of caring to the supervisee which, in turn, reduces the quality of the emotional bond (Ladany et al., 1999).

### Evaluation and Feedback

Evaluation and feedback are imperative and critical functions of the supervision process. However, the Ladany et al. (1999) study reveals that the most common ethical violation pertains to the evaluation process. Supervisees indicate that their supervisors did not provide them with appropriate evaluation of their counseling work. This can happen in several ways. First, a supervisor may not witness enough of the supervisee's work to adequately evaluate the job performance. Second, the supervisor may not provide the supervisee with feedback that truly matches the quality of the work. Third, the supervisor may not give ongoing feedback and surprises the supervisee with negative feedback when the formal evaluation reporting time arrives. Fourth, the feedback may be too sparse or infrequent to help shape or influence supervisee development. Finally, the quality of the feedback may be poor or inappropriate enough to hold little, if any, meaning or value to the supervisee receiving it. Failure to provide a supervisee with consistent, valuable feedback inevitably impedes the supervisee's development and opportunity to grow as a result of the supervisory experience (Ladany et al., 1999).

## Multiple Perspectives

Supervisors, as part of good supervision practice, remain open to supporting and discussing perspectives other than their own. This applies to theoretical orientation, ideas about treatment approaches, multicultural issues, and other pertinent supervision topics. However, some supervisors have difficulty providing support to supervisees who do not align with the supervisor's own theoretical beliefs. Research reveals that this misalignment can result in conflict and dissatisfaction with the supervision experience, thus damaging the supervisory alliance and weakening or eliminating the positive impact of supervision (Ladany, Lehrman-Waterman, Molinaro, & Wolgast, 1999; Moskowitz & Rupert, 1983). Supervisors who maintain a rigid, inflexible adherence to their preferred orientations inevitably strain the supervisory alliance and disallow their supervisees the appropriate space to practice and individualize treatment under objective oversight. Instead, supervisors should invite the supervisee to practice his or her own selection of theoretical orientation(s), provided that supervisee has an appropriate breadth of knowledge and understanding of the theory, has a solid concept of how that theory makes sense given the clients' presenting concerns, and can discuss the therapeutic rationale of utilizing such a theory in their practice context. Supervisors, at times, will have to exercise some authority if a supervisee runs the risk of harming a client, but supervisors should not prohibit a supervisee from appropriate practice on the basis of one's own loyalty and belief in a particular perspective.

## Confidentiality

Confidentiality in supervision is a very different concept than confidentiality in client relationships (see Chapter 8 for additional information). Supervisees are not guaranteed confidentiality the way clients are in a therapeutic relationship. In fact, supervision relationships often involve reporting and communication between the supervisor and outside parties (such as regulatory boards, university training programs, agency administrative supervisors). Supervisees, while not guaranteed confidentiality, should know from the beginning about the limits of confidentiality and privacy in the supervisory relationship to avoid unnecessary feelings of betrayal or mistrust between the supervisee and supervisor. A supervisor who betrays a supervisee's trust or confidence is creating an environment where the supervisee will remain guarded and self-protective. This does not mean that a supervisor must keep the supervisee's secrets; instead, the supervisor should make sure the supervisee is clearly aware of the limitations of confidentiality in the supervision context. The supervisor should make certain that the supervisee understands that he or she is granted some degree of privacy, but that confidentiality in supervision does not exist in the same manner as it does in a counseling relationship.

This matter is complicated given the intimate and disclosing nature of the supervisory relationship. Supervisors work hard to ensure their supervisee feels emotionally safe to disclose personal matters that impact client work. However, supervisors are also aware that these matters can, ultimately, impact client care negatively. Supervisors are ethically bound to protect client welfare foremost, but doing so can lead to a violation of trust, especially if the supervisor has implied a greater amount of confidentiality than actually exists. Supervisors may consider including a statement about confidentiality in the initial supervision contract and may revisit the issue often to make sure the supervisee understands the limitations and is clear about the situations and circumstances in which the supervisor will share supervision details with others.

A supervisor has to use his or her best judgment when deciding what information needs to be revealed from supervision sessions. If a supervisor determines that client welfare is at stake, the supervisor will necessarily have to communicate concerns and relevant information to the appropriate parties. The supervisor should proceed with caution and, for the preservation of the alliance, should be certain that the process is made transparent to the supervisee when possible. For instance, imagine a supervisee mistakenly believes that supervision is a confidential enterprise. During the course of supervision, the supervisee reveals that she maintains some cultural biases that she identifies as "deeply rooted" from her family of origin. She is insightful about the origins and ongoing presence of her biases and is willing to consider how these biases impact her current work, as she is experiencing great shame about this. Despite this willingness to engage in appropriate exploration, the supervisor notices that the supervisee mistreats certain clients with whom she carries a bias. Her language and actions clearly demonstrate the bias, and the supervisor believes the supervisee is violating ethical codes and is doing harm. The supervisor has to decide whether to report this to the state regulatory board, as the board is interested to know whether the supervisor has any concerns about the supervisee getting licensed. Further, the supervisor needs to decide whether this should be disclosed to the supervisee's managerial supervisor, as that person may need to adjust the caseload accordingly until the supervisee demonstrates significant improvement.

Undoubtedly, the supervisee will experience some pain of betrayal when the supervisor has to reveal some of the information about the supervisee's bias and resultant behavior. The supervisor may couch the evaluation with professional terms referencing multicultural competence and fair treatment of clients, but the supervisee will likely focus on the personal nature of the sharing she has done in supervision sessions and will be concerned about having such personally revealing discussions made "public." The supervisor's objective is to protect client welfare while trying to preserve the strength of the supervisory alliance.

## Session Conditions

Supervisees will likely feel disrespected or inadequately served when a supervisor does not uphold his commitment to the supervision process or does not maintain appropriate supervision conditions. Supervisors who cancel supervision, constantly reschedule, or shorten supervision time are demonstrating unprofessional behaviors and are diminishing the perception of supervision as an important professional endeavor. Supervisors should demonstrate the same behaviors that they expect their counselors to demonstrate in counseling sessions: respect for the therapeutic space and climate, minimization of interruptions, honoring the allotted time, and responsibly create a professional work environment.

## Orientation to Professional Roles

Supervisors are not to assume a supervisee knows how to be a supervisee; instead, supervisors assume a training role with supervisees and teach them how to make the most of appropriate, effective supervision. The research conducted by Ladany, Lehrman-Waterman, Molinaro, and Wolgast (1999) indicates that many supervisors fail to clearly explain the supervisee's roles and responsibilities. Supervisees need to understand their role as a supervisee and what is expected of them in that role, but they do not necessarily arrive at supervision with this knowledge (even if they have had years of experience being supervised). If the roles are not clear, supervisees may experience increased anxiety, dissatisfaction with work or supervision, and a poor supervisory alliance (Ladany & Friedlander, 1995; Ladany et al., 1999). Supervisors need to be certain that the expectations they present to the supervisee are congruent with evaluation criteria. Supervisees need to be clear about what they are expected to do, how they are expected to perform, and what their responsibilities are as a supervisee (e.g., preparing notes for session, bringing relevant video recordings). Supervisees may be provided such clarity through the supervision contract, where the supervisor spells out clearly what is expected of the supervisee. Should the supervisee demonstrate a need for clarification, the supervisor can always return to that initial document as the foundation for later discussions about roles and responsibilities.

## Modeling Ethical Behavior

Supervisors who do not role model ethical behaviors will likely find that the supervisee has a difficult time trusting or believing in that supervisor's professionalism. Supervisors should demonstrate ethical behaviors to supervisees and should expect the same of the supervisee. Supervisors who participate in unethical practices are likely compromising their credibility as a professional counselor and supervisor and are certainly not creating a climate of trust and emotional safety.

## Competence and Expertise

While most supervisees would probably prefer not to become a clone of their supervisor, supervisees often strive to become as clinically skilled and knowledgeable as senior members of their profession. Supervisees who view their supervisor as having weak or ineffective clinical skills are not likely to hold great trust in that supervisor's ability to appropriately guide and develop them over time. Sometimes, supervisees perceive their supervisor as lacking the appropriate expertise or knowledge in dealing with certain clients or diagnoses. In these cases, the supervisee's trust in the supervisor weakens and the supervisee may feel uncertain that his work is being appropriately evaluated and directed. When supervisors find areas of needed growth, they have a responsibility to consult with other professionals such as colleagues, a supervisor, or a counselor educator. A supervisor may use this process as an opportunity to role model appropriate assistance-seeking behavior and to normalize that no one is completely knowledgeable in all domains of practice. However, some supervisors do not seek additional help, perhaps because of a busy schedule or lack of a collegial support system. In this case, the supervisor is role modeling for the supervisee that one should not consult and should feign competence instead, which is, at the least, ethically irresponsible (Ladany et al., 1999).

## Disclosure to Clients and Informed Consent

A number of supervisees are not provided with instruction about how to identify their training or prelicensure status to clients. In many cases, mental health professionals are required to share a professional disclosure statement in which one's status as a trainee or prelicensed counselor is made clear. However, research reveals that, in some cases, trainees were actually informed by supervisors to misrepresent their status (Ladany et al., 1999). Beginning counselors may feel shy or hesitant to reveal that they are under supervision for fear that being in supervision indicates incompetence. However, supervisors can coach supervisees in how to speak about their supervision to clients. For example, a supervisor might remind a supervisee that supervision is available for the duration of one's career as a mental health professional and is indicative only of responsible practice. The supervisor can role-play with the supervisee to demonstrate how to speak to a client about supervision and one's own status as a trainee or prelicensed supervisee. The supervisor might demonstrate statements such as "I am committed to improving my performance as a counselor, so will receive supervision as mandated until I am licensed and then voluntarily after that. I believe this benefits my growth as a professional and, ultimately, makes me a better counselor for you and my other clients." Supervisees need to clearly understand that they have a responsibility to obtain informed consent from clients prior to treatment, and part of that consent process involves the counselor being clear and accurate about their training, background, and status (ACA, 2005). Supervisors also have a responsibility to show the supervisee how this is done and to ensure that the supervisee is engaging in this practice ethically and transparently. A supervisor asking a supervisee to engage in deception is obviously unethical (Ladany et al., 1999), and a supervisor failing to monitor the informed consent process is engaging in, at the very least, neglectful supervision.

## Crisis Availability

Supervisors are responsible for the direct client care services provided by their supervisees. Many supervisees, in times of crisis, need a consultative ear or some additional guidance from their supervisor. In some cases, the crisis may involve life and death situations. However, some supervisees find that, in these times, they cannot access their supervisor to get the urgent assistance that is needed (Ladany et al., 1999). Even supervisors who are usually readily available might have instances of inaccessibility, especially in cases when the supervisor is also a counselor or professor and is necessarily inaccessible at times. Supervisors have a responsibility to instruct supervisees about how to handle emergencies and who to contact should the supervisor not be available. It is a wise practice for the supervisor to review alternatives ahead of time and to review the crisis protocol with supervisees well in advance of a crisis occurring. While supervisees may have some general knowledge about how to handle various crises, the experience may feel different for the supervisee when the crisis actually happens. The supervisee may experience enough stress or anxiety to forget the knowledge or skill he already possesses, or he may astutely recognize that his emotions are interfering with his ability to make a nonreactive, objective decision in the client's best interest. Supervisors should keep in mind that they hold a great deal of liability for the supervisee, and what the supervisee chooses in a time of crisis has implications for the client and the supervisor. If things go awry, the supervisor's actions or inactions may be examined in times of grievance. An absent supervisor is a neglectful supervisor unless the supervisor has worked out a feasible and reasonable backup plan with the supervisee ahead of time.

## Multicultural Competence

As discussed in earlier chapters, supervisors have a responsibility for multicultural competence in both themselves and their supervisees. When supervisors are culturally unresponsive (overlooking, minimizing, or dismissing cultural issues), the supervisory alliance and, ultimately, client outcomes are negatively impacted (Burkard et al., 2006; Ramos-Sanchez et al., 2002). Cultural unresponsiveness can occur in a variety of ways. First, supervisors may wish to be responsive but may not have the training or self-awareness to identify or notice cultural issues as they arise. Similarly, supervisors may notice issues but not know how and when to skillfully address them. Next, supervisors may attend to some cultural issues and not others. In some cases, supervisors may actively seek to dismiss or shut down cultural issues or concerns when they arise. Supervisors who use transparency and have higher self-awareness around cultural and racial issues tend to have stronger supervisory alliances and stronger ratings of supervisee satisfaction (Gatmon et al., 2001; Ladany, Hofheinz, Inman, & Constantine, 1997). So, supervisors who are overlooking, ignoring, or dismissing cultural issues are likely straining the working relationship and failing to help their supervisees fully develop multiculturally competent practices.

Research has found that many supervisees report ineffective or inappropriate supervision practices relating to cultural issues (Ladany et al., 1999). For instance, some supervisors make culturally inappropriate, stereotypical, or racist remarks about clients. Supervisors may also reach conclusions about supervisees that are distorted or inaccurate because of a lack of knowledge or inaccurate perceptions and views of a client's cultural context.

Supervisor level of development around racial identity impacts the supervision relationship and interactions therein. Racial identity refers to the "sociopolitical construct that underscores the dynamic interplay between individuals belonging to dominant and nondominant cultures" (Bhat & Davis, 2007, p. 81). Supervisors may engage in four types of racial identity interactions with supervisees. Racial identity interactions indicate how often and thoroughly racial issues are likely to be discussed, and how well positioned the supervisor is to be facilitating and guiding the discussion. The four types of interactions are progressive, regressive, parallel high, and parallel low (Cook, 1994). Progressive interactions indicate that the supervisor has high racial identity development and the supervisee is lower, so the supervisor is well positioned to help the supervisee develop. Regressive interactions occur when the supervisee has higher development than the supervisor, so the supervisor is not well positioned to help the supervisee develop. In these cases, there is likely to be an alliance strain as the supervisee wishes for more conversation and exploration regarding cultural issues and factors (Bhat & Davis, 2007). Parallel high interactions indicate both members of the supervisory alliance have high levels of racial identity development, so cultural factors are more likely to be discussed than in parallel low relationships where both members have low levels of development and will probably overlook racial issues.

Supervisors are advised to approach multicultural competence in several ways. First, supervisors must examine their own knowledge, attitudes, perceptions, feelings, faulty cognitions, stereotypes, and biases (Bhat & Davis, 2007; Peterson, 1991; Priest, 1994). Supervisors will likely engage in more culturally competent supervision if they have a higher level of racial identity development, cultural self-awareness, and willingness to integrate cultural issues into supervision. Next, supervisors should receive supervision and consultation when possible, and as needed to further develop their ability to contend with areas where they do not have objectivity or awareness.

Further, since many supervisors did not receive adequate training in cultural competence, supervisors should seek additional training to fill in knowledge or development gaps that have emerged (Ladany et al., 1999; Nelson & Holloway, 1990).

Finally, supervisors should engage in active conversations with their supervisees about the presence or absence of culturally focused conversation in their supervisory dyad. If a supervisor recognizes that the conversations have not been occurring, or have been ineffective or harmful, the supervisor may initiate a conversation with the supervisee about his or her observations on that matter. For instance, a supervisor may say, "I've been thinking a lot about culture lately, and recognized that you and I haven't spoken about it much in here. You and I probably have some similarities and differences, and there is certainly a lot of variance amongst your clients. I'd like to start integrating cultural factors and issues into our discussions more than we have traditionally done in here. Do you have any concerns or hesitation about doing this together?"

## Multiple Relationships and Roles

The issue of multiple roles is one that has been addressed several times thus far in this book and is addressed commonly in the research literature. While multiple roles are nearly unavoidable in many cases, supervisors have a responsibility to minimize the impact of such roles and avoid engaging in multiple roles when possible (Borders & Brown, 2005). The reason supervisors should minimize the multiplicity of their relationships with supervisees is to reduce the risk of impaired objectivity and decrease the potential for supervisee exploitation (Disney & Stephens, 1994). Supervisors who do not take appropriate measures to reduce the risks, or who engage in exploitation of any sort, are engaging in ethically unsound supervision practice, which can impact the supervisees and have lasting implications for their careers, their experiences as a supervisee, and their clients.

Supervisors who actively seek multiple roles with supervisees may be doing so to meet personal or professional needs and are probably not paying attention to the power dynamics which impact and are impacted by multiple roles (Holloway et al., 1989). Similarly, supervisors who seek friendship or social interactions with supervisees should consider the discomfort this may cause the supervisee. In some cases, the supervisor's actions may be directly affecting the supervisee, like when the supervisor initiates a romantic or sexual relationship or business partnership that the supervisee feels powerless to refuse. Further, a supervisor who is engaging in multiple relationships with the supervisees may find themselves without objectivity during evaluation time. Likewise, a supervisor may have appropriate objectivity but may no longer have credibility at evaluation time as the supervisee wonders whether his or her actions impacted or will impact the veracity of the evaluation.

More commonly, supervisors are also managerial supervisors and hold conflicting responsibilities when providing supervision (as discussed previously in Chapter 6). Supervisors, in these cases, should recognize that it is appropriate for supervisees to feel concerned about the impact of these multiple roles. While supervisors should make the extent and impact of each of these roles explicit from the beginning of the supervisory relationship, they must recognize that conversations about the impact of the multiple roles should be ongoing and welcome. Multiple roles have an impact on the supervisory relationship and should seek consultation or supervision-of-supervision when possible to help maintain objectivity and transparency. Supervisors should be most concerned about covertness and secrecy with respect to multiple roles. In the interest of appropriate consent and honoring power dynamics, multiple roles should be made transparent and should be openly and ongoingly discussed between supervisor and supervisee.

In some cases, the supervisee may wish to seek supervision outside of the agency setting so that the discomfort of the conflicting responsibilities does not negatively impact his or her development. Supervisors who hold dual roles as managerial and clinical supervisors should carefully consider how they can help make this situation collaborative and most beneficial to all parties. If a supervisee is working with a supervisor external to the agency, the internal "assigned" clinical supervisor may consider working with the external supervisor to create a supervision contract that carefully delineates responsibility and oversight to ensure the supervisee's developmental and clinical needs are well taken care of.

*Activity:* Consider incidents of supervisor ethical nonadherence that you have experienced or witnessed. How did these incidents impact the supervision relationship? How did these incidents impact the supervision experience?

*Consider your own role as supervisor in your particular work setting. Which of these areas of ethical nonadherence are of greatest concern to you? What do you imagine could happen and how would it occur? Imagine an incident from beginning to conclusion. When, in this story, might you be able to do something to prevent or minimize the impact of the ethical breech? How will you address the breech with your supervisee?*

## COUNTERPRODUCTIVE EVENTS INVOLVING SUPERVISOR TECHNICAL SKILL

Supervision is an intricate and influential component of the therapeutic relationship, so supervision must be done well (Nelson & Friedlander, 2001). Supervisor skill deficit is frequently the culprit of ineffective supervision. Many supervisors readily acknowledge a lack of supervision-specific training, and this lack of training can certainly create the conditions for ineffective or "bad" supervision (Ellis, 2001). Supervisor skill deficits are not likely to cause trauma or emotional harm to the supervisee, but the supervisee may instead experience supervision as unhelpful, a waste of resources (time and money), unproductive, and frustrating. Supervisors need technical skills to maximize the effectiveness of supervision as well as strong interpersonal skills to maximize the strength of the supervisory alliance.

In this section, we review a number of ways that supervisors create ineffective supervision through skill deficits, thus negatively impact the supervisory alliance and losing the opportunity to fully enhance and develop their supervisee's skills. In later chapters, we focus more explicitly on building and enhancing supervisory skills and interventions. At this point, however, it is important to review counterproductive supervision events to consider the impact such events have on the supervisory alliance. Further, supervisors should consider the following list as a preassessment of sorts. That is, how do you rate your skill in each of the following domains, and where do you need to make the most improvement? While you may be quite skilled as a helping professional, how skilled are you in each of the following areas as a supervisor?

## Ability to Deal With Power Issues

Supervisors need to have awareness of their position of power, as well as how they use and experience that power. Skilled supervisors honor their position of power, recognize the implications of such power, and do not attempt to diminish it by pretending it does not exist. To do otherwise would inevitably weaken the supervisory alliance. Further, diminishing one's position of power means voluntarily reducing the influence the supervisor has to help the supervisee grow and develop through constructive feedback and evaluation. Skillful supervisors provide immediate, evaluative feedback that helps a supervisee develop and provide more effective services to clients. Supervisors who cannot accept the inherent power that comes with their position can create insecurity and role confusion in the supervisee. Supervisors who are overly eager for power may "pull rank" and present authoritatively when they would be better off responding from a place of responsive connection (Nelson & Friedlander, 2001). Supervisees who resent the supervisor's authority may maintain the supervisory relationship (especially when there are no alternatives) but will minimize vulnerability and control negative feelings by psychologically and emotionally distancing themselves from the process (Greer, 2002; Hutt et al., 1983).

## Intervention Effectiveness

Supervisors who are not well skilled at supervision may strain the supervisory alliance by asking meaningless or ineffective questions, engaging in off-topic activities, or an inability to match supervisor intervention with supervisee development level or conceptual ability. Further, supervisees understand that supervision is intended to increase their competence and help them move toward greater effectiveness. However, if the supervisee views the supervisor as ineffective, the supervisee will lose confidence that the supervisory relationship and experience can move forward in a helpful direction. Supervisees in this situation may attempt to get the challenge and developmental needs met elsewhere (such as through consultation or other means). If this becomes the norm, the supervisor will find himself less and less "useful" as the supervisee disengages further and further from the supervision experience. In this instance, the supervisor has lost the ability to provide appropriate oversight, and the relationship has likely disintegrated beyond repair.

### Supervisor Avoidance

*Experiential avoidance* occurs when a supervisor (or supervisee) is unwilling to stay connected to personal experiences (e.g., emotions, memories, cognitions, physiological sensations) and makes effort to reduce the frequency or change the context of such events. This allows unpleasant events to be dismissed or ignored (Hayes, Wilson, Gifford, Follette, & Strosahl, 1996). Supervisors may experience this phenomenon to some degree when feeling uncertain about how to respond to or guide a supervisee, or when experiencing excessive discomfort or reactivity. The supervisee, in turn, learns that certain topics or interactions should be handled through avoidance or are simply not acceptable to approach with this supervisor. Further, this approach reinforces the concept that unsatisfying interpersonal relationships or uncomfortable topics should be handled through avoidance rather than transparent and open communication. This norms the supervisory relationship as one of inhibition, avoidance, and eventually, mistrust.

## COUNTERPRODUCTIVE EVENTS INVOLVING SUPERVISOR PERSONALIZATION SKILLS

### Apathy

A supervisor's attitude about the field, the work setting, the supervision relationship, and the therapeutic relationships may all impact the supervisory alliance (Magnuson et al., 2000). A supervisor who demonstrates apathy, or a lack of enthusiasm or investment, is a mismatch for the supervisee who is eager, excited, and highly invested in the work. Apathy toward the profession, workplace, or clients may all be signs of professional burnout (Edwards et al., 2005), but must be managed so they do not manifest within the supervision context.

## Supportiveness

Supervisors who are not supportive of their supervisee's work, development, and exploration will likely harm the supervisory alliance. In that "supportiveness" may hold different meanings for different people; supervisors should engage in ongoing conversation with their supervisee about how support may be operationally defined in their relationship. The supervisor clearly understands that supervisees will have different types of support needs from session to session, or even within a session. For instance, a supervisee may feel somewhat stagnant in her work and wants to be challenged to approach some clients differently. She may view the supervisor who challenges her as supportive because the immediate need has been fulfilled. In the same session, the supervisee may be discussing a complex situation where she is experiencing countertransference that has not yet been fully examined. Since the supervisee already feels challenged by the situation, she may expect that "support" from the supervisor involves pulling back and allowing the supervisee to explore with a minimum amount of supervisor interference. Since supervisory alliance ruptures may occur when one member of the partnership does not behave in ways that meet the expectation of the other (Quarto, 2002), it makes sense to continually explore how to maximize supportiveness in this working relationship.

## Control and Flexibility

Supervisors who maintain flexibility and can adjust to varying levels of control in the relationship are likely to maintain a stronger supervisory alliance (Quarto, 2002). While supervisors maintain power by virtue of their position, they do not need to hold on to control over the supervisee or their actions. Instead, the supervisor may willingly accept the supervisee's growing empowerment and control as an indicator of developing professional maturity or growing confidence and efficacy (Holloway, 1994; Wiley & Ray, 1986). A rupture in the alliance can occur if a supervisor perceives a supervisee's increasing control as a challenge to the supervisor's authority (Quarto, 2002) or a personality deficit that must somehow be "corrected" through disempowering measures (Gray et al., 2001). Supervisors who are flexible to meet their supervisees' needs will create and maintain stronger supervisory alliances than supervisors who are inflexible and rigid in their approach (e.g., Hutt et al., 1983).

## Interpersonal Approach

The supervision relationship is inevitably impacted by how the supervisor approaches the supervisee verbally, attitudinally, and affectively. Supervisees are not likely to allow authentic vulnerability when their supervisor is demonstrating abrasiveness, hostility, a demeaning attitude, emotional reactivity, and other similarly negative expressions (e.g., Greer, 2002). Supervisees who are treated in a manner that leaves them feeling unsafe or upset may succumb to the supervisor's authority and withdraw their investment in the supervisory experience (Gray et al., 2001).

The aforementioned list of counterproductive events is not all-inclusive. In fact, there are numerous examples in the literature of additional ways in which a supervisor can weaken or permanently damage the supervisory relationship (e.g., Gray et al., 2001; Magnuson et al., 2000). The common factor among many of these items is that they may create conflict in the supervisory relationship and, oftentimes, that conflict can be skillfully managed and repaired.

*Activity: Which of these counterproductive events do you believe you will be the most prone to while providing supervision? What conditions may lead to this type of event? What do you need to strengthen personally and professionally to prevent such events from occurring?*

## CONFLICT IN SUPERVISION

Supervision is an intimate professional process. Supervisees are expected to maintain an openness to evaluative feedback while taking professional risks, engaging in self-reflection, and monitoring internal processes all the while (Nelson, Barnes, Evans, & Triggiano, 2008). It is no surprise then that the supervisory alliance is especially susceptible to tension, strife, and outright conflict (Ladany, Friedlander, & Nelson, 2005).

Conflict in supervision can be conceptualized on several continuums based on *intensity, transparency*, and *residence*. Intensity refers to the strength and impact of the conflict. Minor disagreements that are momentary and have little or no lasting effect are low impact, while high impact conflict is disruptive enough to the supervisory relationship or session that it must be resolved for supervision to continue. In some cases, the relationship is far enough beyond repair that the supervisory dyad should disband entirely.

Transparency describes the overt versus covert nature of the conflict. Covert conflict is not intended to be noticed or discussed, as it remains hidden and unspoken of. This conflict is usually known by only one participant or may be so nontransparent that even the person experiencing the conflict is not yet aware of its presence. On the converse, some conflict is quite transparent and its presence is readily known to both members of the supervisory dyad.

Residence refers to the location of the conflict, both in terms of its origin and where, relationally, it is currently located. Often times, conflict can transfer from internal to interrelation or vice versa, or from one dyad to another through a parallel process (discussed in Chapter 8).

For example, a supervisee experiences an internal conflict as she struggles with a client during a particularly difficult session. The supervisee struggles to find appropriate interventive words and strategies and finds she feels inept and upset. That internal conflict may go unexplored as the supervisee moves busily along to the next client, and finally the supervisee enters the supervision session where she has time to sit and notice her internal unrest. The supervisee attributes the unrest to the challenge being issued by her supervisor, rather than recalling that the unrest emerged during an earlier session. The conflict now resides interpersonally between the supervisor and the supervisee, as the supervisee is annoyed with the supervisor for issuing a challenge. The supervisor astutely notices that the supervisee is responding to the challenge in a manner that is not typical and asks the supervisee to explore together the difference between today's challenge and prior instances. The supervisee discovers, through some guided self-reflection, that she actually was experiencing some internal conflict from earlier and relocates her energy to focus on the original residence of the conflict, thus resolving the interpersonal conflict that appeared in supervision.

A supervisor who senses some unrest or conflict in the supervision relationship may first consider these three factors when decided when and how to intervene. For instance, when the supervisor believes that the supervisee is annoyed with her, the supervisor may first work to bring transparency to the situation by asking the supervisee if there is something uncomfortable happening that should be discussed. While discomfort is an expected and appropriate experience in supervision, the use of words like "discomfort" or "unrest" may be more inviting than more emotionally charged words such as "angry" or "conflict." This is an effort to bring some transparency into the relationship so that both parties are privy to the same information. At the same time, the supervisor will consider the possibility that she is actually the one experiencing some internal unrest, or the uneasiness may be relational and too newly emerging to be identified. The skilled supervisor is also willing to discard an incorrect hypothesis and will move on quickly rather than perseverate on an erroneous or premature conclusion.

Once the conflict is identified, the supervisor will consider the intensity of the conflict and will let the intensity guide the amount of energy that is focused on exploring and resolving the conflict. Conflicts that are seemingly unimpactful to the supervisee and the supervisory relationship should be resolved quickly so that energy can be spent on more impactful tasks. Conflicts that are greater in intensity likely warrant plenty of exploration and healing effort. This may be difficult for supervisors to commit to for a variety of reasons. First, some supervisors are less comfortable with conflict and will have a desire to avoid attending to the conflict. Next, some supervisors feel unskilled in working through conflict successfully, especially with a supervisee, and are hesitant for fear of creating more conflict. Finally, attending to and resolving conflict takes time. Supervisors and supervisees alike often feel pressed for time as there is much to discuss and accomplish during supervision sessions. It is difficult to remember that exploring and resolving the interpersonal conflict will likely have a positive impact on client care, since so much conflict actually emerges between the supervisee and client and simply exhibits itself in the supervisory relationship (known as the parallel process). Resolving the strains in the supervisory relationship allows supervisees to learn how to resolve strains in the therapeutic relationships and can help build their comfort with facing and managing conflict as it emerges (Gray et al., 2001).

Perhaps, the most complex and delicate function is determining whether the residence of the conflict is in the supervisory relationship, the therapeutic relationship, or is intrapersonal and exists solely within one person but is disruptive to the working alliance. The supervisor will proceed with caution here and will maintain a stance of objective curiosity, remembering that conflict in supervision, like conflict in therapy, is challenging to effectively manage (Nelson et al., 2008). Often times, the supervisee will figure out through self-exploration where the conflict emerged. Together, the supervisor and supervisee can examine and marvel at how the conflict travelled from one relationship or person to the next and can determine how and when the conflict should be resolved. The supervisor and supervisee can mutually determine what they would like the outcome to be and can together decide how to reach that goal.

Research has clearly indicated that supervisors who ignore, neglect, or mishandle conflict are contributing to counterproductive or harmful supervision and, by extension, counterproductive client care (Gray et al., 2001; Nelson & Friedlander, 2001). Supervisees who are not invited and encouraged to bring conflict to a transparent, resolvable ground will experience supervision as a negative, anxious experience where one should maintain a self-protective stance and avoid professional and personal vulnerability (Hutt et al., 1983). Supervisors should recognize that it is the supervisor's responsibility to address conflict skillfully with a nonjudgmental, nonpunitive stance. Supervisees should not be expected to bring conflict forth. While they may be readily able to address and contend with conflict, intra- and interpersonally, outside of supervision, and perhaps even with their clients, supervisors should recognize that the vulnerable and evaluative nature of supervision can make the presence of conflict more threatening and foreign to even a seasoned professional.

*Activity: Consider an experience you have had of conflict in supervision. Who were you in conflict with? Was the conflict transparent? How impactful was this conflict on the supervisory relationship?*

## Working With Conflict in Supervision

Effective conflict management is one critical element of a strong supervisory relationship (Nelson et al., 2008; Ramos-Sanchez et al., 2002). Many counselors do not receive training specific to conflict management and resolution and likely develop and hone their skills through experience and challenge. However, research has revealed that the most important feature in working successfully with conflict is the supervisor's attitude of *openness to conflict* (Nelson et al., 2008). Supervisors who are open to conflict consider conflict in the supervisory alliance to be necessary and helpful. Further, they welcome conflict into the supervision session because they envision supervision as an ideal time and place for the supervisee to learn to effectively manage conflict and contend with interpersonal challenges. These supervisors respect the power differences inherent to any supervisory relationship and honor the anxiety and guardedness that accompanies such an imbalance. Further, these supervisors demonstrate transparency, vulnerability, and genuineness while they welcome ongoing discussion of the supervisory relationship. These supervisors create safety for the supervisee by being appropriately open and utilizing appropriate disclosure of one's experiences in the moment, one's limitations, and their own vulnerabilities (Nelson et al., 2008).

Supervisors who effectively manage conflict utilize three types of strategies (Nelson et al., 2008). These three types are *reflective processes* (within the supervisor), *interpersonal strategies* (between the supervisor and supervisee), and *technical interventions* (conflict management techniques).

Reflective processes are the internal processes where supervisors carefully consider and pay attention to the contextual factors that pertain to the supervision relationship. They might consider the supervisee's developmental stage, features that contribute to or help sustain the conflict, additional life factors, and supervisee strengths. Supervisors also use a process that researchers (Nelson et al., 2008) call *self-coaching*, or talking oneself through conflict mentally prior to engagement with the supervisee. Finally, skilled supervisors also make active use of consultation or supervision when conflict arises. They are humble and recognize their own shortcomings or lack of objective at times and consult with trusted professionals to better understand, process, and strategize conflict management and resolution (Nelson et al., 2008).

Interpersonal strategies are used when the supervisor is working through the conflict with the supervisee directly. Skilled supervisors seek to empower their supervisee and will take care not to shame or punish the supervisee. Instead, the supervisor approaches the conflict in a reasonable, matter-of-fact, collaborative manner that allows the supervisee to feel supported in working through the conflict. Additionally, skilled supervisors will listen to the supervisee's experience of the conflict, will disclose his or her own feelings about the conflict (or their part in the conflict), and will use the information generated by the conflict as helpful in better understanding the supervisee's approach and therapeutic dynamics (Nelson et al., 2008).

Technical interventions are the specific approaches that supervisors can use to skillfully manage and resolve conflict. For instance, many effective supervisors provide early and frequent feedback to their supervisees. Some use humor or highlight the supervisee's strengths specifically. Some use specific problem-solving approaches or models to help the supervisee resolve conflicts, and in some cases supervisors recommended that the supervisee further discuss the conflict with their own personal therapist (Nelson et al., 2008).

*Activity: How do you typically avoid conflict in your personal and professional life? Do your approaches typically lead to a satisfactory outcome? Do your approaches allow the relationship to strengthen, or do you find that damage remains? What can you do to improve your own conflict management skills? How will you make these improvements? What will the impact on our supervisee(s) be if you do not make these improvements?*

*Now engage in a process of hypothetical self-coaching. How do you plan to approach conflict (as a supervisor) when it emerges? Which of your strengths and skills will you remember to utilize? What types of things will you do and say, and what will you AVOID doing and saying? Who will you consult with when situations arise? Is this person (or persons) someone who works as a supervisor and is skilled at resolving conflict?*

A supervisor's primary focus when dealing with conflict in supervision should be on the *process* of conflict management much more than the *content* of the conflict itself. Process, as discussed in earlier chapters, refers to the series of interpersonal and intrapersonal dynamics, whereas content refers more to the concrete story and accounting of events. In many cases, conflict arises when supervisor and supervisee do not agree on a therapeutic conceptualization or decision. Maintaining a focus on content will likely further exacerbate a disagreement. Instead, the supervisor will focus on the process of managing and resolving the conflict. In many cases, the supervisor and supervisee will simply continue to disagree, and this is often perfectly acceptable. The supervisor will prepare the supervisee for the fact that the disagreement may continue; however, the conflict will be resolved. Supervisors will show supervisees that it is acceptable and common for two people to share a relationship that includes differences in professional (and personal) opinion. In fact, counselors will often experience the stress of having different opinions and choices than their clients do. Supervisors can use conflict in supervision as an opportunity to demonstrate how to agree to disagree while maintaining a respectful, healthy interpersonal relationship.

In some cases, the supervisor will need to accept the disagreement but may need to use supervisory authority to request certain actions occur, even when the supervisee disagrees. For instance, if a supervisee would rather not make a call to report child abuse, but the reporting criteria has been met and the supervisor is certain a report needs to be made to satisfy legal requirements, then the supervisor may need to insist that the report happen. In this case, the supervisor maintains his role as conflict-manager and uses the entire experience as a time to role model. The supervisor may present the supervisee with the dilemma as a way to continue the collaborative spirit. As an example, the supervisor may say, "I'm feeling really conflicted here. I know you would rather not make this report, on the one hand. On the other hand, I know that I have a responsibility to ensure you are upholding the law. In my opinion, the requirements for a report have been met and the call has to be made. However, I'm concerned that this will create more upset between us. This doesn't feel good, does it?"

Oftentimes, maintaining a focus on content or the subject of actual disagreement will lock the supervisor and supervisee into a power struggle of sorts. Instead, the skilled supervisor will look for ways to empower the supervisee and hand over decision making and resolution control to the supervisee. The supervisor will help navigate the process and will assist the supervisee through immediate feedback (e.g., "I like this direction, we're coming up with ideas! Terrific.") or supportive suggestions (e.g., "Let's keep considering the options before evaluating this one") whenever possible, keeping a spirit of supportive collaboration all the while. The supervisor's intent during times of conflict is to help develop the supervisee's skill around conflict management, to ensure the welfare of the clients, and to maintain a positive working relationship with the supervisee. Supervisors will remember that they hold the responsibility to make certain that the effective management of conflict is a productive, although not always enjoyable, supervision experience. Avoidance, neglect, and power struggling will turn the experience into a counterproductive supervision event, which will prove ineffective or even harmful in the long run.

## DEFENSIVE STRATEGIES AND STRATEGIC GAMES

Supervision is a process that requires personal and professional vulnerability and an ability to integrate challenging and sometimes distressing feedback. Supervisees frequently attempt to engage in behaviors that will yield as much approval as they can gain from their supervisor and will minimize disapproval or disappointment (Kadushin & Harkness, 2002). This is considered a typical part of the supervision dynamic and is common in relationships where one's work is the subject of evaluation and professional scrutiny. Supervisees will often respond to feelings of anxiety, stress, and fear with stress-reduction strategies that are referred to as "games" (Kadushin, 1968).

The concept of "games" originated from Eric Berne's (1964) conceptu-alization of two-person interactions and the dynamics therein. Berne (1964) proposed that dyads engage in transactions that are goal-directed and have ulterior motivations. Kadushin (1968) extended this concept into supervision dynamics and posited that supervision games are *recurring* interactions that contain a reward ("payoff") for one of the involved members of the supervi-sory dyad (Kadushin, 1968). Supervisors remain alert to these games, as the games typically prevent the necessary tasks of supervision from being carried out. Further, sometimes a game's predictable reward benefits the supervisor rather than (or in addition to) the supervisee, which makes it difficult for a supervisor to disengage. So, supervisors become familiar with the follow-ing games so that they can minimize the impact of such games when they appear. Note that supervisors will not notice all games immediately since games are recurring. One incident of any of the following does not necessar-ily indicate a game. However, a game is probably occurring when there is a repeating pattern of behaviors during which the supervisor feels blocked from effectively performing supervision

The following four categories contain games that are grouped because they have common tactical approaches. The following games are all described in Kadushin's (1968) article, "Games People Play in Supervision" and are described below.

### Manipulating Demand Levels

This category of games refers to the games that help reduce the level of demand or challenge the supervisee experiences (Kadushin, 1968). One of these games is called "Be Nice to Me Because I Am Nice to You." This is when the supervisee uses flattery and compliments that may seem innocent at first, but actually induce a sense of disablement in the supervisor, who inevitably feels mean or unjust when attempting to hold the supervisee to appropriate levels of demand and expectation. This game is especially seductive to the supervisor because the supervisor, ultimately, seeks to help the supervisee and want some reassurance that he or she is useful and effective in his role as supervisor. The supervisee's flattery provides such reassurance. However, the supervisory dyad is the focus of this game and supervisors may find it quite difficult to shift focus onto client care once locked into the rewarding game of being "nice."

Another game, "Two Against the Agency," might be especially entic-ing to supervisors who are both managerial and clinical supervisors. This game involves a supervisee who is rather good at the work of therapy but is annoyed by agency protocol and procedural requirements. This supervisee highlights client needs and wonders if he could have a reduction in docu-mentation demands so as to better utilize his clinical talent. The supervisor may initially find this game seductive, as the supervisor likely empathizes and agrees with the supervisee's argument. The supervisor may, in fact, reduce demands or reduce the negative consequences to the supervisee of not meeting such requirements, and the supervisory dyad is now aligned against the agency's policies and procedures (Kadushin, 1968).

## Redefining the Relationship

This category is similar to the previous one in that supervisees continue to seek a reduction in demand. In these cases, supervisees attempt to reduce demand by redefining the supervision relationship and creating ambiguity (Kadushin, 1968). One such game is "Treat Me, Don't Beat Me." In this game, the supervisee would prefer to not have his work addressed, so he presents personal issues and elicits help from the supervisor to resolve these issues. Supervisors are typically experienced counselors who find that slipping into the counselor role is comfortable and gratifying, perhaps even flattering. The supervisor then feels intimately connected with the supervisee's vulnerability and will reduce the level of demand in supervision to match the new, redefined relationship.

The supervision relationship may also be redefined as a friendship or social relationship, as happens in the "Evaluation Is Not for Friends" game. In this game, the supervisee introduces numerous social components into the relationship in an attempt to redefine the relationship as a friendship, which makes it difficult for the supervisor to hold evaluative authority in the relationship (Kadushin, 1968). Another version of this game is "Maximum Feasible Participation." In this game, the roles move from supervisor or supervisee to peer colleagues with equal and democratic participation. This might seem reasonable at first, but actually enables the supervisee to control the agenda and reduce the supervisor's ability to provide appropriately demanding levels of expectation and challenge (Kadushin & Harkness, 2002).

## Reducing Power Disparity

This category of games functions to lessen a supervisee's anxiety by diminishing the power difference between the supervisor and supervisee (Kadushin, 1968). The supervisee may undermine the supervisor's power on two levels; first, the supervisor's inherent power that comes with the position and, second, the supervisor's advanced skills and expertise (Kadushin & Harkness, 2002).

A supervisor's expertise may be called into challenge during the "If you Knew Dostoyevsky like I know Dostoyevsky" game. In this game, the supervisee makes reference to material that the supervisor may not be knowledgeable about (such as a literary work or scholarly piece). The supervisor and supervisee experience a role reversal as the supervisee proceeds to educate the unlearned supervisor. The supervisor then feels badly for not having more knowledge than the supervisee, and the supervisee feels comfortable at having more knowledge and undermining the supervisor's expert status for at least a short while.

Another game with similar dynamics is the "So What Do *you* Know About It?" game. This game involves the supervisee highlighting areas of wisdom or life experience that the supervisor does not share (e.g., marital status, parenting, working directly with clients) (Kadushin & Harkness, 2002). This game allows the supervisee to diminish the supervisor's feelings of knowledge and control, thus decreasing the supervisor's threat and authority as a power figure.

## Controlling the Situation

This category of games involves the supervisee eliciting control of the supervision session through tactics intended to weaken the supervisor's control, thus weakening the threat of examining performance weaknesses or shortcomings (Kadushin & Harness, 2002). The "I Have a Little List" game is quite effective at keeping the supervisee in control of the agenda. In this game, the supervisee arrives at supervision with a list of topics to be explored or discussed. The supervisee expects that each questions or item will elicit some mini-lecture or unilateral discussion from the supervisor, in which time the supervisee can sit and listen (or not listen) to the response. The supervisee, upon sensing the supervisor is winding down, can then repeat the cycle with the next question or item, engaging in this pattern until session time is up. The supervisor engages in the game for many reasons: at first, the questions seem reasonable and perhaps the supervisee really needs the knowledge. Next, the supervisor feels excited to share about a topic of particular interest or knowledge to him. Finally, the supervisor feels useful and helpful to the supervisee and may even feel more competent at the practice of supervision. The supervisee has effectively maintained control of the session and has avoided evaluative feedback and critical analysis of her work.

The supervisee may also play the "Heading Them Off at the Pass" game, an especially useful game for supervisees who are certain that evaluative critique is forthcoming (Kadushin & Harkness, 2002). In this game, the supervisee takes a proactive approach by acknowledging errors openly. The self-derogatory nature of this interaction induces the supervisor to provide reassurance, perhaps to even attempt to bolster the supervisee's suffering ego. Any further discussions of the supervisee's inadequacy are replaced by sympathy and perhaps even praise (Kadushin & Harkness, 2002).

The "Pleading Fragility" game is similar and involves the supervisee presenting a fragile and tenuous state of emotional health. A supervisor presenting too much challenge could conceivably cause great harm to the supervisee, so the supervisor avoids any topics or feedback that may send the supervisee into psychological destruction.

"Little Old Me" is a game often played by newer supervisees who have genuine inadequacies and highlight these inadequacies to the supervisor. The supervisor is then invited to shoulder increasing amounts of responsibility as the supervisee repeatedly asks what the supervisor would do or say next (Kadushin & Harkness, 2002). The more capable supervisor provides a plethora of assistance to the supervisee who is now controlling the content of the session and the supervisor's workload.

Following "Little Old Me" comes "I Did As You Told Me." This game occurs after the supervisor has told the supervisee how to proceed or has provided suggestions that the supervisee then implemented in some fashion (Kadushin, 1968). The supervisee becomes distressed when he carries out the supervisor's orders and the interventions were unsuccessful. The supervisor is left feeling defensive, and the supervisee successfully evades evaluative feedback—after all, the supervisor cannot provide critical feedback about his own directives!

The "It's All So Confusing" game involves the supervisee consulting with other authority figures in an attempt to reduce the authority and power of the primary supervisor (Kadushin & Harkness, 2002). The supervisee then claims confusion when multiple authority figures provide different feedback. The supervisor's expertise is diminished in relation to these other, possibly entirely unskilled authority figures, and the supervisee questions the supervisor's credibility and evaluative feedback.

Supervisees, according to Kadushin (1968), can also utilize distancing techniques to decrease a supervisor's control. "What you Don't Know Won't Hurt Me" is a game of selection. That is, the supervisee selects what to share with the supervisor to control the amount of critical and evaluative feedback that may be given. The supervisee will select content that is not representative of the work, is distorted, or presents a favorable picture of one's work. The report might contain minutiae that is of no relevance to the clinical performance or conceptualization, but effectively allows the supervisee control of the supervision discussion. This also allows the supervisee to keep a rigid boundary around his work with the client so that session content may be kept secret and covert (Kadushin & Harkness, 2002). This phenomena may be especially harmful in that there is an illusion of oversight, but, in actuality, the supervisor has little or no idea about what is going on in the therapeutic relationship.

### Neutralizing the Game

A game is effective when there is a predictable payoff (Kadushin, 1968); a supervisor who becomes aware of a game is well positioned to remove the payoff so that he can guide the dyad toward more effective supervision experience. Kadushin (1968) proposes that the simplest way to deal with a game is to refuse to play. Admittedly, this is difficult because supervisors also receive some payoff from many of the games. So, the supervisor has to be willing to give up the rewards that accompany the game. Discarding a game may come at a cost to the supervisor. The supervisor may have to engage in activities that are uncomfortable for him, such as providing critical feedback or acknowledging weaknesses (Kadushin & Harkness, 2002).

Another solution is to openly confront the game (Kadushin & Harkness, 2002). In this instance, the supervisor brings transparency to the interaction in an attempt to help the supervisee discard the tactics through exposure and exploration. Supervisors are to be cautious when using this confrontational approach. Supervisees use a game to reduce a perceived threat or anxiety; if the supervisor is not skillful in confronting the game, the supervisee's anxiety and threat levels may increase, thus further precipitating the need for games. While supervisors are not advised to collude in keeping the game covert, they do need to be cautious and thoughtful to protect the supervisee's ego in the process (Kadushin & Harkness, 2002). Supervisors should remember that the game was likely initiated with intent to preserve one's self-image (Milne, Leck, & Choudhri, 2009) and that need should be honored through the neutralizing process. Supervisors can remember that games serve a useful function in helping humans learn to socialize and relate to others (Middleman & Rhodes, 1985; Kadushin & Harkness, 2002), so games in supervision should be viewed as helpful and informative events that provide supervisors a chance to further shape and develop the supervisee.

*Activity: Which of these defensive strategies have you used as a supervisee? What prompted you to use them? How often did you engage the strategy? What was the predictable payoff? What would have been different had you not used the strategy? What would the positive and negative consequences of not using the strategy have been?*

*Which strategy or "game" are you the most fearful of encountering in one of your supervisees? Why? What will you do if and when it appears? What do you think the impact of your action will be?*

*What can you do to reduce the need for defensive strategies in supervision? You will not be able to prevent them altogether, but consider carefully how you might be able to help alleviate the supervisee's need for such strategies.*

# EIGHT

# Beyond Self-Report: Supervision Modalities and Methods

$S$elf-report in supervision is the process of a supervisee providing a narrative account of what transpired in the counseling sessions and is subject to distortion, bias, and inaccuracy (Noelle, 2002). While it is commonly practiced, its low reliability and validity (Noelle, 2002; Romans, Boswell, Carlozzi, & Ferguson, 1995) make it a risky and, at times, irresponsible practice at best.

When a supervisor relies on self-report alone to understand the dynamics, events, and conversations from a counseling session, he is relying upon a distortion-prone method (Klitzke & Lombardo, 1991) that cannot possibly represent the client's experience in session with full accuracy. Instead, the supervisee presents information that reflects his own experience in session, and the clients' experiences and perspectives are represented only through the supervisee's unique lens and filter. Further, one of the core intentions and benefits of clinical supervision is the benefit if "super vision." That is, a supervisor is meant to have objectivity and distance to notice phenomena that the supervisee may not notice or may not be willing to acknowledge (Goodyear & Nelson, 1997). The self-report method does not typically allow a supervisor a glimpse into those "missing pieces" that are typically much more obvious when one observes a session directly.

When a supervisee is doing his best to accurately and fully represent the happenings of a session, he is limited by his humanness; that is, all humans are equipped with a unique worldview, biases, personal experiences, and cultural context that inevitably impact one's understanding and subsequent account of any event. This humanness, combined with the intimate and interrelated nature of the therapeutic experience, prevents supervisees from ever being able to report the happenings of a session with complete, impartial objectivity. Further, the human condition impacts counselors in that supervisees often experience some performance anxiety or a concern about impression management that pulls one toward inaccurate or partial reporting (Goodyear & Nelson, 1997). Supervisees may feel compelled to misreport or withhold data out of fear, especially given the supervisor's role as evaluator and gatekeeper. Supervisees are often concerned that they will receive negative evaluation or consequence or will appear incompetent to their supervisor (Noelle, 2002). Ladany and colleagues (1996) studied nondisclosure in supervisees and found that 97% of supervisees withheld information at some point and 44% knowingly did not reveal clinical errors. A clinical supervisor holds liability for a supervisee's work, so the potential of not knowing that an error occurred is a reasonable cause for concern in any supervisor.

Despite these shortcomings, self-report remains a frequently used method of supervision in school psychology training programs and clinical psychology programs (Romans et al., 1995). Self-report has some appeal in that it is easily accessible and low cost as no technological equipment is necessary. Additionally, some supervisors find great interest in observing the dynamics that transpire in the supervision session as self-reports are provided. For instance, supervisors may be quite fascinated by supervisor or supervisee dynamics that occur and seem to mirror the dynamics present in the counselor and client relationship. This mirroring, or parallel process, is informative and can be used to inform the supervisee about dynamics and interpersonal features of relationships with other clients as well. Further, self-report can provide plenty of useful material for a supervisor to work with in session in terms of helping the supervisee work through his own reactions and responses to a client or the session dynamics (as interpreted through his individual lens). In fact, the material provided through self-report methods may be plentiful and rich enough to keep supervisors and supervisees busy through entire sessions. However, supervisors should maintain clear awareness that the information provided is merely an account of the supervisee's experience and aftermath of that experience, and does not represent the client and the session dynamics with complete, unbiased accuracy.

Clinical supervisors relying solely on self-report may find that the risk involved with such a method is not worth the limited benefits. In this instance, supervisors will find a number of options available to them to enhance their access to actual session data, either during the session itself through concurrent supervision or after the session through ex-post facto methods of supervision.

This chapter examines concurrent methods of supervision, including live observation and multiple methods of live supervision, and then examines ex-post facto supervision options. The chapter then examines some activities involving the use of video and audio recordings in supervision, and then concludes with an analysis of eSupervision, or supervision that relies on technology to connect the supervisor and supervisee.

## CONCURRENT AND EX-POST FACTO SUPERVISION METHODS

Supervision interventions can be categorized into two time-related groupings: concurrent supervision and ex-post facto supervision. *Ex-post facto*, or retroactive, supervision occurs after the therapeutic encounter (Hernandez-Wolfe, 2010). Concurrent supervision is supervision that occurs at the time of the therapeutic encounter and includes such methods as live observation and live supervision.

Due to the dynamic effectiveness of concurrent supervision techniques, counselor education programs are encouraged to have in-house clinics where students and faculty supervisors can be actively co-involved in the therapeutic experience (Romans et al., 1995). The following descriptions of concurrent supervision methods begin with *live observation*, where the supervisor is minimally involved, followed with *live supervision*, which involves increasing levels of supervisor involvement and, often times, the use of technology.

## CONCURRENT METHODS OF SUPERVISION

### Live Observation

Live observation is a unidirectional process where the supervisor observes the supervisee in therapeutic action. Live observation does not involve any interaction between the supervisee and supervisor during the course of the session (Bernard & Goodyear, 2009). Live supervision, on the contrary, involves the active involvement of the supervisor during counseling sessions and will be discussed later in this chapter.

Live observation involves the supervisor actually witnessing the therapeutic encounter in real-time and is frequently utilized in counselor education and psychology training programs (Bernard & Goodyear, 2009). Supervisors may be watching sessions from behind a one-way mirror or through a closed circuit television monitor, which allows them to view the session as it happens. Supervisors may elect to take notes including their observations from the session, and these notes may be later shared with the supervisee.

According to Bernard and Goodyear (2009), live supervision is highly favorable for a number of reasons. A supervisor who is able to directly monitor a session is immediately available to respond to crisis situations. This may be particularly useful in the case of supervisees working with suicidal clients or clients with particularly concerning mental health or medical issues. Next, a supervisor is able to provide timely and immediate feedback to a supervisee, either through written notes or a supervision session directly following the session. Supervisees who receive feedback on the day of the session often appreciate the immediacy of such feedback. Immediate feedback allows them to integrate objective information from the supervisor with their own subjective experience of the session while the experience is still fresh in the supervisee's memory. The supervisee now has this information to aid him in the conceptualization and planning tasks that should transpire prior to the next session. Finally, live observation affords supervisors the opportunity to include other supervisees in the viewing of the session, in which case the supervisor has the chance to provide instructional and observational feedback as the session occurs, though Bernard and Goodyear (2009) caution that this technique could be detrimental to the supervisory alliance when not used appropriately. If the supervisor discusses feedback in front of the collegial observers that is too frank or revealing, it can diminish the group's trust in the supervisor and the process. The supervisor has to remember to provide all feedback to the supervisee directly, as the supervisee will inevitably lose trust in the supervisor if not given feedback directly (Bernard & Goodyear, 2009).

When colleagues are invited into a peer observation climate, the supervisor has the responsibility to ensure that the behind-the-mirror discussion is kept to a minimum so that observers are not overly distracted by conversation (Powell, 2004). Further, the colleagues may engage in unsupportive discourse that can create mistrust, anxiety, or undue stress on any of the participants. Supervisors are charged with protecting the best interest of the supervisee who is in session (Powell, 2004) and should be an appropriate role-model of supportive, professional behind-the-mirror behavior.

Supervisors who are overseeing a group of collegial observers may want to provide the observers with the following instructions prior to the session beginning:

1. Remain quiet and keep talking to a minimum to avoid interrupting the session or the observation experience.
2. Use a tool to help conceptualize what is happening in the session being observed. Tools may include a family genogram, a cultural genogram, a sociogram, a case presentation outline, or some other organizing activity.
3. Avoid the temptation to continually consider what you would do or say. While you should consider how you might approach the session, you should balance that with examination of the process and dynamics of the therapy session in front of you.
4. Give feedback according to the supervisor's instructions.

The supervisor should decide ahead of time what the feedback process will be so that the supervisee is not inundated by feedback from multiple sources. For instance, feedback may be integrated into group supervision or may be provided through brief consultative formats initiated by the supervisee so that he may pace the feedback. The supervisee should be made aware of what the feedback process will be like so that he does not experience an overabundance of evaluative anxiety prior to or during the session.

## Live Supervision

Live supervision is similar to live observation in that the supervisor witnesses the session as it occurs. However, in live supervision, the supervisor provides feedback, guidance, or direction by intervening in the process as it unfolds (Costa, 1994; West, Bubenzer, & Gold, 1991). As with live observation, this method enables supervisors to be readily available to assist in the case of emergency or crisis situations, so client welfare is better protected than in the absence of the supervisor (Bernard & Goodyear, 2009; West et al., 1991). Further, supervisors can help influence the course of the session through immediate feedback. This feedback may be offered through several techniques: cotherapy (in vivo supervision), supervisor entry, phoning in, bug in the ear, bug-in-the-eye, taking a break, or exiting the room for a consult (Liddle & Schwartz, 1983).

*In vivo* supervision resembles direct observation in that the supervisor observes the session as it is happening. However, there are two key differences: first, the supervisor is present in the therapy room and second, the supervisor consults with the supervisee during the session. This consultation happens in front of the client so that the client or clients are able to experience all information that is discussed about their case (Bernard & Goodyear, 2009). When utilizing this technique, the supervisor must be cautious to provide feedback that will not undermine the supervisee's efforts and will contribute to the therapeutic climate. The supervisor, just through his presence in the room, becomes part of the therapeutic experience and will role model the professionalism and involvement that accompanies that position. The supervisor also must remain cognizant of his level of involvement in the session; that is, if he is over involved, he runs the risk of the client or clients preferring to work with him and disengaging from their work with the less experienced supervisee.

A slightly more removed method is the "knock and consult" method (sometimes known as "calling out"), where the supervisor views the session from behind a one-way mirror. Then, the supervisor knocks on the session room door and calls the supervisee outside of the therapy room for a consultation (Scherl & Haley, 2000; Smith, Mead, & Kinsella, 1998). This method resolved some early frustrations that supervisors had with merely providing live observation. With this method, a supervisor does not need to sit idly by while a supervisee flounders or teachable moments expire. Instead, the supervisor can consult with the supervisee while there is still time to take corrective action for the betterment of the client's experience (Scherl & Haley, 2000). Bernard and Goodyear (2009) warn that supervisors should be cautious about taking too much time out of session because the session may lose momentum by the time the supervisee returns, rendering the corrected intervention ineffective. One important consideration to make, however, is the client's experience while the counselor is out of the room. One study found that the client felt abandoned or criticized (Cotton, 1987 in Smith, Mead, & Kinsella, 1998). The private conversation between the supervisor and supervisee may lead the client to speculate and may cause some distress to clients who are not privy to the content of the conversation. The supervisee might diminish this concern by briefly reporting to the supervisee what was discussed, when appropriate, or the supervisor might decide to use the following method to increase transparency.

The "knock and enter" method is when the supervisor again knocks on the therapy room door, only in this case the supervisor enters the session and provides feedback to the supervisee in front of the client. This method poses similar disadvantages as the knock and consult method in that client session time is taken up by consultation and the supervisee may have less credibility in his client's view because of the "need" for supervision. Additionally, the supervisor, in this method, could potentially change the dynamic of the therapeutic alliance by inadvertently undermining the supervisee's efforts, so the feedback given needs to be well considered and honoring of the supervisee's therapeutic intention. The knock on the door techniques were replaced, in time, with the phoning-it-in method.

The "phoning-it-in" method involves the supervisee answering a ringing or beeping phone or, more typically, a phone with a flashing light feature that minimizes distraction. The supervisee listens for the supervisor's feedback, then hangs up the phone and proceeds to make the corrections instructed by the supervisor. As one might imagine, a phone may be distracting during the session so should be used minimally. Phoned-in directives should be brief, with no more than two instructions per phone-in (Borders & Brown, 2005).

A less intrusive method of speaking to the supervisee while in session is the "bug-in-the-ear" method. This involves the supervisee wearing an earphone receiving device that gets messages from a microphone in the observation area (Klitzke & Lombardo, 1991). During the session, the supervisor is able to speak to the supervisee so the supervisee receives real-time feedback. The advantages of this method parallel the aforementioned advantages of any life supervision method. The disadvantages are also similar to other live methods; that is, the bug-in-the-ear device can be distracting to the supervisee, especially if the supervisor's feedback is excessive or vague.

A similar method is the "bug-in-the-eye" system, which is a teleprompter device of sorts (Klitzke & Lombardo, 1991). This system involves the supervisee being positioned so that he can see a monitor in the therapy room. That monitor is typically up behind the client's head so that it is not distracting to the client and is easily viewed by the supervisee. The supervisor types words into the teleprompting device while watching the session from an observation area, then word prompts appear on the monitor to instruct or advise the supervisee. The supervisee, using this technique, can examine the feedback with the luxury of more time than the bug-in-the-ear method allows. The supervisee may find this method less obtrusive and might not cause the same anxiety that bug-in-the-ear prompts might cause.

Once the supervision method is determined, the supervisee is prepared for the experience through the presession phase. During this phase, the supervisor and supervisee converse about the goals, plans, and strategies for the session. Next, the in-session phase occurs. This is the phase when the counselor is in session and the supervisor provides feedback through one of the aforementioned methods. The postsession phase involves a debriefing between the supervisor and supervisee (Liddle & Schwartz, 1983; West, Bubenzer, & Gold, 1991).

Regardless of how the immediate feedback is delivered, the intent of live supervision is to be useful and facilitative rather than interruptive and distracting. With that intent in mind, the supervisor should consider the following four questions, recommended by Liddle and Schwartz (1983) when deciding when to intervene:

1. What are the consequences if I do not intervene at this time?
2. If I wait a bit longer, will the supervisee possibly make the intervention himself/herself?
3. Is the supervisee actually able to implement the guidance at this time?
4. If I intervene, am I causing undue dependence for the supervisee? (Liddle & Schwartz, 1983).

Further, once the intervention has been implemented, an additional three questions should be asked to evaluate the effectiveness of the supervisor's intervention:

1. Did the supervisee implement the directive?
2. If not, how come? (Was this due to supervisee skillset, confidence, trust in the supervisor's interventive decision, etc...?)
3. If the supervisee did follow through, how effective and impactful was the intervention?

Supervisors and supervisees must lay a strong foundation for live supervision before entering into such an arrangement. Supervisors are encouraged to follow these guidelines when engaging in such a practice (based on Elizur, 1990; Lee & Everett, 2004; Montalvo, 1973):

- Include the agreed-upon method of live supervision as part of the supervisory contract (after fully addressing any of the supervisee's concerns or reservations).
- Engage in some practice rounds prior to using the techniques in actual sessions.
- Agree that the supervisor will allow the supervisee room to explore so that the experience does not become a robotic "do as I command" operation in which the supervisee is a clone carrying out the supervisor's therapeutic wishes.

■ Recognize that the process is likely to be more directive at the beginning and that autonomy will increase as supervisee skills develop.

■ The supervisor and supervisee discuss and agree upon the rules of operation. For instance, how the supervisor will issue directives, what kind of language will be the most clear and useful, and how and when the supervisee decides to ignore or dismiss the supervisor's instructions or feedback.

■ Supervisors will keep in mind the welfare of the client and of the supervisee, and will honor that welfare by providing feedback with sensitivity to the participants' feelings and psychological experience of the feedback.

■ Supervisors recognize that live supervision can be viewed as a threat and will help the supervisee keep anxiety to a manageable level to best facilitate learning and good client care.

When deciding to engage in live supervision, supervisors have a number of items to consider. First, consider the therapeutic context. In many instances, supervisors may believe that they do not have time to provide person to person supervision as well as live supervision. However, supervisors might consider occasional live supervision, perhaps with clients who are in crisis or with whom the supervisee feels ineffective. While live supervision is common in training contexts, agency supervisors may find that live supervision helps their post-Masters counselors stay actively aware of their own skill development and performance, especially when and if stagnation sets in. Live supervision may also be an effective tool in preventing legal concerns. That is, if a supervisee is concerned about a specific situation and feels held hostage by a client's threats of litigation, the supervisee may be able to more effectively work with the client when the supervisor is helping to make the therapeutic decisions. The supervisee feels the release of the threat, thus restoring the therapeutic balance of power by sharing some interventive responsibility with the supervisor.

Next, the supervisor needs to consider the logistics and equipment needs to provide live supervision. Some methods cost nothing and require no equipment (e.g., the planned consultation, the knock on the door techniques) but others require some equipment expense and appropriate space configurations (e.g., bug in the eye, closed circuit video monitoring).

Finally, the supervisor should be thoughtful about his or her intention in providing live supervision. This intention should be made explicitly clear to the supervisee. Live supervision is intended to help develop a supervisee's skill base and provide more effective oversight through direct observation and intervention (Bernard & Goodyear, 2009; Bubenzer, West, & Gold, 1991). Implementing live supervision with a supervisee as a result of performance concerns may be a risky endeavor, especially in terms of the supervisory alliance. A supervisee who believes he or she has additional oversight as a result of supervisor performance concerns may feel mistrustful, paranoid, or excessively anxious. Some supervisees may feel that the supervisor is attempting to "catch" the supervisee engaged in poor practice or "messing up." The supervisee may feel that the supervisor is providing extra critical scrutiny which could impede the supervisee's performance, directly opposing the intended consequence of providing live supervision. To prevent this scenario, supervisors may wish to introduce live supervision to the supervisee at the beginning of the supervision relationship. Even in cases where the supervisor can only provide limited live supervision, it might be useful to engage in live supervision at least intermittently so that it is normed as part of supervision practice. Then, if a supervisor develops increasing concern about the supervisee or client welfare, the supervisee already has familiarity and practice with live supervision and is less likely to incur the amount of stress one might experience otherwise.

Live supervision may have a detrimental effect on performance and development, so supervisors may consider the following when using live supervision methods. Supervisee anxiety is of particular concern in live supervision. While supervision often generates some anxiety because of its evaluative, impactful nature, live supervision includes an added level of exposure and involvement that may contribute to even more anxiety for the supervisee (Costa, 1994). While a moderate level of arousal is reportedly beneficial in that it keeps a supervisee readily engaged to learn and acquire new skills (Breunlin, Karrer, McGuire, & Cimmarusti, 1988), an excessive amount of anxiety may be paralyzing or drastically inhibiting to a supervisee and may negatively impact his performance. Supervisee anxiety should be discussed and addressed directly (Costa, 1994). Further, supervisees will likely sense and reflect the anxiety or ambivalence the supervisor feels about using live supervision. So, if the supervisor has any misgivings or doubts, those should be resolved so that the supervisee is not dissuaded from willing and eager engagement. Supervisors may elect to engage the supervisee in some practice rounds of live supervision using a colleague as the "client." This way, each party gets familiar with what the technique involves and can provide feedback in advance about how to most optimally engage in the technique. The "client" can also provide some useful feedback about how the technique was employed and may be able to make suggestions about logistical arrangements and such. For instance, a colleague might notice that the view from the client's chair looks directly into the one-way mirror and is distracting and unnerving. At the same time, the supervisor behind the mirror notices that he has trouble seeing the supervisee's facial expressions. So, the practice round allows for simple reconfigurations to occur so that the experience can be optimally beneficial and comfortable for all.

Supervisors should also consider that supervisees are moving toward increasing autonomy in their practice and will parallel that dynamic in supervision. In early phases of live supervision, supervisees will likely appreciate more directive, specific intervention (West, Bubenzer, Pinsoneault, & Holeman, 1993). In this stage, supervisors should be cautious not to provide excessive amounts of feedback or direction, lest the supervisee become dependent on the supervisor to guide the session. Instead, supervisors should refer to the four questions posed above to determine when and if to provide live feedback. In later stages of development, supervisees may desire more autonomy and would prefer supervisors stay less involved in the session (West et al., 1993). Again, the supervisor will determine whether feedback is timely and useful and may prefer to wait a bit longer than in sessions past to allow the supervisee space and time to proceed autonomously. At this point, supervision may shift from live supervision to a live observation format where the supervisor eventually remains totally uninvolved in the session. This is not recommended for counselors who are still in training programs, but is usually more appropriate for supervisees who are competent and skilled in most domains. As with any supervision experience, feedback should be documented. Information about documenting live supervision sessions can be found in Chapter 13.

## EX-POST FACTO SUPERVISION

Ex-post facto ("after the action") supervision occurs after a counseling session has already happened. This may be hours, days, a week, or, in more drastic situations, as far as several weeks after the actual session. The problems with the self-report method of supervision have already been discussed at the start of this chapter, but this section begins with a further examination of the verbal report method of ex-post facto supervision. Following that, this section covers additional forms and techniques of supervision, including no-technology, low-technology, and high-technology methods.

### The Verbal Report or Case Consultation Approach

In some instances, supervisors have not yet brought their practices to standard and are still relying on verbal report alone. This method, sometimes called the "case consultation method" relies on verbal report as the foundational premise of the work to be done. The supervisor relies solely on the supervisee's recollection as the singular representative of the therapeutic experience (West et al., 1993). This means that the verbal report of the sessions is provided through the supervisee's individual lens, complete with inherent biases, emotional influence, and blind spots. However, if the supervisor is engaging in this method of supervision, he or she should consider this method more than merely "talking about clients" (McCollum & Wetchler, 1995). Supervisors using this method are prohibited from being able to accurately examine the dynamics and intricacy of any therapeutic interaction for the reasons already discussed. However, McCollum and Wetchler (1995) present four supervision areas that may be adequately addressed by this method:

1. Understanding the architecture or structure of the therapy process in general
2. Assisting supervisees to build theoretical models of change
3. Assisting supervisees to understand the clients' broader context and contextual factors that affect the therapeutic process
4. Assisting supervisees to understand their own broader, more general context

These areas seem more applicable to the case consultation model of supervision. However, supervisors may find themselves concerned that these areas do not necessarily include direct, case-specific client oversight. McCollum and Wetchler (1995) further recommend that supervisors review cases with their supervisees to help them organize a full case conceptualization around each client. They recommend that supervisors ensure that cases are discussed longitudinally and that client progress is reviewed from one supervision session to the next. The following questions are proposed by McCollum and Wetchler (1995) to help in this process:

- How does the current intervention plan align with the broader treatment goal?
- What steps should be taken to help the client move from how they are doing today to resolving their ultimate treatment goal?
- How does today's work with the client relate to prior work from one or many sessions ago?
- If your interventions are effective today, how will you work with this client in the future?
- If you are changing the direction of treatment, how will you explain that to your client?

In addition to helping a supervisee organize a case conceptualization, supervisors work collaboratively to facilitate deeper thought and theoretical clarity.

Supervisors, according to Bronson (2010), may ask questions such as "What theory are you using to better understand the client's presenting concerns?" and "How does that theory relate to the interventions you are using?"

The supervisor's role is to assist supervisees in making connections between seemingly unrelated features of a particular case or set of cases (e.g., Prieto & Scheel, 2002). Supervisors may use *case reports* or *case note documentation* to help meet these objectives.

Case reports are written conceptualizations of several key features of the counselor's experience with a client. These reports are written by the counselor following a session and are then presented to the supervisor, usually verbally, for further discussion. Case reports may include client data (demographic or identifying data), the client's initial concerns, counseling goals, treatment plans, assessment and evaluation data, and information about the client's progress in treatment (Bronson, 2010). Supervisors may present a written form to the supervisee to complete, or supervisees may develop their own narrative. The intent is to engage the supervisee in a process of fully considering the many variables pertinent to the client's treatment so that the supervisee has a better idea of how to proceed. Ideally, supervisees should approach this activity from a particular theoretical stance. That is, their theoretical orientation will help supervisees determine the most important and relevant features of a case and helps the supervisee conceptualize the relationship between client concerns, treatment options, and outcomes. (Sample case conceptualization forms are provided in Appendix E.)

One particular model of case reporting is the STIPS format of case documentation introduced by Prieto and Scheel (2002). This model involves the supervisee documenting case information through five sequential sections as follows:

*Signs and Symptoms:* This section aligns with a mental status examination (MSE) format where seemingly relevant observable behaviors (e.g., appearance, speech) are noted. Supervisees document the client's level of functioning and makes note of any changes in functioning since prior sessions. Supervisees also include relevant diagnostic information and symptoms that may be diagnostically relevant.

*Topics of Discussion:* In this section, supervisees include information about major points of discussion from the session. Significant changes relating to these issues are also noted here.

*Interventions:* Supervisees will document specific counseling interventions in this section. They should note how those interventions relate to the treatment goals. Homework assignments and other treatment-related features should also be included in this section.

*Progress and Plan:* This section is where the supervisee summarizes the progress the client has made toward reaching treatment goals since the time of the last session. The supervisee also documents their plans for the next session and notes the specific interventions they plan to use as well as the intended outcomes.

*Special Issues:* In this section, supervisees document any critical issues or new issues that have arisen. Issues may include suicidality, threats to harm, mandatory reporting concerns, or medication management. This section has been termed the "red flag" section and is for issues of clinical significance. It is not an area where the supervisee should document notes to his or herself for later reference (Prieto & Scheel, 2002).

Supervisees complete this case document then present it in supervision. This document allows supervisors to quickly locate the most critical information and can help supervisees find relevant case information by clearing away irrelevant distracters and minimally related material. The creators of this format assert that this format helps supervisees avoid neglecting critical issues because they essentially get trained to examine each important domain of client functioning. Further, supervisees learn to differentiate between what they meant to do in a session versus what actually happened during the session (Prieto & Scheel, 2002).

These STIPS notes may typically be a half to full page in length. If a supervisee continually writes notes that are much longer than that, they may be having trouble deciphering the relevant material from the irrelevant. The supervisor can assist the supervisee through ongoing discussion about clinical relevance. For instance, if the supervisee indicates in the "topics of discussion" section that "The client discussed the weather," the supervisor might ask the supervisee how that discussion relates to the treatment. If the supervisee indicates that the weather conversation was small talk as the session opened, the supervisor may help the supervisee understand that the relevance is too minimal to note. However, if the supervisee indicates that the client has suicidal ideation when she sees storm clouds welling, that information is then considered relevant. The supervisor then helps the supervisee connect the relevance of that conversation to the larger clinical picture.

The verbal report method of supervision, as described at the start of this chapter, is a problematic enough supervision method that it can be considered ethically remiss to rely on this method alone. Various forms of technology have become so inexpensive and easy to use that supervision simply must include some supervisor access to "raw material" of the therapy encounter (McCollum & Wetchler, 1995).

## Audio or Video Review

Audio and video reviews are among the most common activities of clinical supervision for good reason (Romans et al., 1995). There are typically many life events and happenings between the time of most therapy sessions and the time of supervision. Accessing the actual session content through audio or video recording provides the supervisor and supervisee access to the raw material of the actual session, reducing the negative impact of "tainted" recollection and helping the supervisor gain a better understanding of what happened in the session. Further, supervisees may experience a session quite differently upon later review. It is not unusual for a supervisee to "hear" something a client said only when reviewing the session later; supervisees will make statements such as "Why didn't I hear that then?" or "Wow, I didn't even catch that when I was in the room with him!" Further, the physical and temporal distance between the session and later review allows the supervisee a chance to approach the same counseling scenario from a different, more objective perspective than when actually in the same room and locked in the process with the client or clients.

Additionally, the use of video recordings in supervision is beneficial in that video recordings allow the storage of raw data for historical reference (techniques using historical data are discussed further in Chapter 9). Video recordings also allow a supervisee the chance to observe the supervisor experience the counseling session and client as well. The video recording allows the supervisee and supervisor to review the same sections of a session multiple times to pull different information from the session as needed. Most importantly, the data found on video recordings assist the supervisor in closing the gap between the supervisee's biased, naturally flawed recollection of the session and the actual proceedings of the event (Huhra, Yamokoski-Maynhart, & Prieto, 2008).

Many training programs mandate the use of audio or, more typically, video recordings so many supervisees have already had some experience with this practice. However, some supervisees express resistance or hesitance when a supervisor requests the use of audio or video recordings. Supervisees will typically argue that such recordings may be intrusive or will cause harm to their clients. While it is true that, in some select cases, video recording may cause distress to a client, that distress is usually only a small amount of anticipatory anxiety that is quite short lived (Huhra et al., 2008). The supervisor is wise to focus first on the supervisee's hesitance about the recording process, as often times the anxiety and resistance lies mostly within the supervisee, whose attitude about video recordings inevitably influences the client's attitude about the process.

In one study, practicum students were informed that they would have their sessions videotaped and reviewed. These students showed increased physiological signs of perceived threat as indicated by increased heart rate and higher skin temperature (Roulx, 1969). While the technology was different over 40 years ago when that study was conducted, the perceived threat response parallels what many supervisees demonstrate today. Supervisees might find it helpful to remember that audio and video recording therapy session is not a new activity in the counseling field. In fact, it has been a part of therapeutic practice for over sixty years, and supervisees may recall classic films and early television shows that feature a therapist turning on a recording device at the start of a session, with an unflinching client hardly noticing.

*Activity: Consider the reactions or responses you are having right now as you read about the use of video recordings. What are you experiencing? Be specific about your feelings. Are your feelings positive, negative, ambivalent? How do you believe your feelings will influence your supervisee's feelings or beliefs about the use of audio or video recording methods?*

*Make a list of the reasons you would prefer to use or not to use video or audio recordings in your supervision session. Now, make a list of the barriers to usage. Next to each barrier, indicate how you might be able to remove that barrier. Who has the power to help you deconstruct the barriers? Who can help you in your effort to advocate for more ethical counseling practices and better client protection?*

Supervisors may use video or audio review in supervision in a variety of ways. For instance, supervisors may ask a supervisee to bring in a video that is already cued to a segment of a session that the supervisee did not feel good about. Sharing this segment allows the supervisor to help the supervisee explore the session in explicit detail to get a better understanding of where the supervisee needs more development (Baird, 2008). Similarly, the supervisee may be instructed to bring in a session cued to a segment that they feel positive about. The supervisor and supervisee can explore what went right in that segment and can utilize that understanding to further build and capitalize on the supervisee's strengths (Baird, 2008).

Supervisors, when deciding how to use recordings in supervision, should ask themselves the following:

- What is my supervisory intention at this time? (What am I hoping to help the supervisee do?)
- Which part of a session will best help me accomplish that? (The beginning, middle, conclusion, or a random segment?)
- Should we be selecting the recording of a particular client, or will any session suffice?
- How much of the session should we view? (This should be somewhat spontaneous, as supervisors will notice that sometimes they need to view more or less time than initially planned, but it often helps supervisees to know how much of the video will be viewed)
- What should we be doing before, during, and after the video review?
- Should video review be spontaneous or planned? (Consider whether the supervisee is ready for spontaneous viewing or if that will cause excessive stress)

While supervisors will make sure that video and audio review expectations are made clear in the initial supervisory contract, the specifics about how this will happen can change as the needs change and as the supervisory alliance builds. For instance, a supervisor may be concerned that a supervisee has developed seemingly tender feelings for a client. The supervisee's presentation of this client appears different than the way she speaks of other clients. The supervisor is formulating a hypothesis that the supervisee has romantic feelings for the client that are interfering with her therapeutic objectivity. However, the supervisee is hesitant to discuss that and denies feeling any differently toward this client and expresses that the client is making no progress in treatment. The supervisor wonders if perhaps the supervisee is less effective with the client because of her tender feelings for him and wonders if the supervisee is eager to keep the client in therapy longer than necessary. So, the supervisor answers the aforementioned questions (supervisor responses in italics) which, altogether, form his intervention plan.

1. What is my supervisory intention at this time? (What am I hoping to help the supervisee do?) *I would like to do three things: First, I want to better understand the client's depression level from an objective stance; second, I want to establish an objective baseline for the depression level so that we can measure whether he is actually making progress in treatment; and third, I would like to see how my supervisee's countertransference is impacting the treatment and/or the therapeutic alliance.*

2. Which part of a session will best help me accomplish that? (The beginning, middle, or conclusion, or a random segment?) *I think any part of the session would be useful, so perhaps I will have the supervisee decide what she would like to share.*

3. Should we be selecting the recording of a particular client, or will any session suffice? *My concerns are about this client's treatment, so I would like to start with video of this client. It might be useful to look at video of another client with depression as well so that we can notice differences and similarities in how the supervisee approaches each of them. She also might feel less "on the spot" if I ask her to bring in segments of two or three of her clients who exhibit depression.*

4. How much of the session should we view? (This should be somewhat spontaneous, as supervisors will notice that sometimes they need to view more or less time than initially planned, but it often helps supervisees to know how much of the video will be viewed.) *I think I will ask her to prepare 5-minute segments and will tell her that we may watch a few minutes more if we find it useful.*

5. What should we be doing before, during, and after the video review? *Before the review, I will ask her to share what her motivation was in cueing the video to those particular segments. During the review, we will just watch and take internal note of what we are seeing. After, I will ask her what she noticed and will ask her if she sees anything differently now than she did before watching the video with me.*

6. Should video review be spontaneous or planned? (Consider whether the supervisee is ready for spontaneous viewing or if that will cause excessive stress.) *Considering her hesitance to speak about this client, I think this should be planned. I think she gets nervous talking about her clients and her nerves make her tongue-tied; with some prep time, she will still be nervous but will have more time to consider how she would like to talk about her clients.*

The supervisor has now created a thoughtful and intentional intervention plan, a process that took merely moments. The more the supervisor uses this sequence of questions, the more efficient and comfortable he will become at devising intervention plans where the intervention matches the supervisory intent. This process parallels treatment planning with clients; one typically knows the objective or goal, then thoughtfully considers how to best reach that goal. The supervisor may consider being quite transparent with the supervisee about the plan. For example, the supervisor may say, "I'm thinking about how I can best assist you in figuring out what's going on with the clients who have depression. When I watch the segments you select from the two videos, I'll take a look at how the client's are presenting, how the interactions are, and whether I notice things that are facilitating or blocking progress. We'll even get to compare the differences and similarities in your approaches between clients. What do you suppose we'll notice?" The supervisor can then engage in a preliminary discussion with the supervisee about what she anticipates they will notice, and these guesses become some hypotheses that the supervisor and supervisee make note of. For example, the supervisee may say "I think I am a lot gentler with these clients than most, perhaps even more so with (client A) because I think he's in more pain. I also think you'll see that I'm doing all I can with them. They just have the winter blues and probably won't feel better until the spring." The supervisor then instructs the supervisee to find segments of the video that might help illustrate these dynamics, and expresses excitement at the chance to discuss more about these hypotheses together while reviewing the video in the next supervision session.

## TECHNOLOGY-ASSISTED REMOTE SUPERVISION

In recent years, the mental health professions have been adapting to advances in Telehealth practices. Telehealth is the use of electronic and telecommunications technology to provide and support long-distance clinical health care, patient education, and public health administration (Wood, Hargrove, & Miller, 2005). *Etherapy* is internet-based therapy and may include online mental health screening (Ybarra & Eaton, 2005), email exchanges, live chat through a chat room, or videoconferencing (Abbott, Klein, & Ciechomski, 2008). Similarly, remote clinical supervision, *eSupervision*, is supervision that is conducted through the same technology-assisted methods so that the supervisor and supervisee do not need to be in the same physical location (Baird, 2008). ESupervision may also be referred to as *cybersupervision* (Watson, 2003) or *technology-assisted distance supervision* (TADS) (McAdams & Wyatt, 2010). Remote supervision helps close some of the accessibility gaps that counselors have experienced in years past. Primarily, the field has been concerned with the experience of rural counselors and supervisees in training who may not have had access to supervision, or their access was limited to costly long distance calls. Now, with the growing popularity of computer-based and distance learning, counseling trainees may be engaging in clinical training several thousand miles away from their training program. Technology allows counseling student trainees and professional-level counselors to maintain connections with well-qualified supervisors in an innovative manner.

However, innovation is often accompanied by risk and growing pains. To help counselors mitigate the risks involved with technology-based service delivery, the mental health professions have introduced guidelines and rules that pertain to technology-based counseling. The ACA Code of Ethics, section A.12 is entitled "Technology Applications" and includes necessary guidelines regarding informed consent, Web site management, state laws and statues, and access concerns (ACA, 2005) and the National Board for Certified Counselors (NBCC) (2005) also introduced ethical guidelines for technology-assisted practice.

Telehealth practices are not entirely new to supervision. Early technology such as the telephone has been a supervision tool for years, but long distance costs used to make frequent use somewhat prohibitive. Now, supervisors and supervisees tend to have greater accessibility to one another through the use of cellular phones and unlimited, inclusive long-distance plans. Supervisors are accessible when they are on the move, and supervisees have greater flexibility to reach their supervisors in a more timely manner when emergencies or urgent needs arise. Additionally, some supervisors conduct supervision sessions by phone. While many find this undesirable, it can be a valuable tool when the supervisor and supervisee are many miles apart, or for the unique occasion when a supervisor or supervisee is temporarily unable to meet in person (e.g., because of maternity leave, conference attendance, caring for a sick family member, etc…) or has no internet access. Phone supervision has drawbacks in that the supervisor and supervisee lose their ability to observe nonverbal cues and behaviors, plus typically have to rely on verbal report to guide the session. The dyad additionally loses the ability to engage in spontaneous role play or utilize other techniques that can only be done in person. Recently, the advent of internet-based supervision resources and videoconferencing tools have helped ameliorate some of these challenges.

Recent advances in technology allow supervisors and supervisees to meet remotely through internet-based videoconferencing programs during eSupervision (Dudding & Justice, 2004). ESupervision presents the same challenges as phone supervision (such as the loss of nonverbal communication) with additional, more complex security challenges. When considering the use of technology, the supervisor and supervisee must consider whether they both can maintain pure confidentiality without any risk to client privacy. Confidentiality largely depends on *transmission protocol*, or how data are transmitted between locales. Further, supervisors and supervisees must have access to technical support to ensure that supervision can happen as scheduled in a fully secure manner. In addition to data security, supervisors often consider other factors when deciding upon eSupervision methods. These factors include ease of use, cost, portability, program compatibility between users, and whether the benefits of the method outweigh the risks (Dudding & Justice, 2004; McAdams & Wyatt, 2010).

ESupervision involves videoconferencing, or a meeting in which the parties can speak to and see one another. There are three categories of videoconferencing: desktop conferencing, group conferencing, or broadcast quality conferencing (Dudding & Justice, 2004). Desktop-level conferencing involves a computer, camera, speaker, microphone, and desktop collaboration software. There are dozens of options of desktop collaboration software that are appropriate for eSupervision use, and a simple internet search of "desktop collaboration software" will yield plenty of information about the range of available choices. Some graduate programs have had great success with the use of Adobe Connect™ and other videoconference programs. Group-level conferencing involves a videoconferencing unit with a self-focusing camera, microphone, and monitor (Dudding & Justice, 2004). This is likely more elaborate than what is needed for simple eSupervision and is typically more appropriate for training programs or group supervision formats where multiple users will meet regularly. A broadcast-level system is a professional level system that far exceeds the needs of an eSupervision experience.

Supervisors need to ensure that their equipment is compatible with the supervisee's equipment. Compatibility typically depends on transmission protocol, with formats such as ISDN (integrated services digital network) or TCP/IP (transfer control protocol/internet protocol) (Dudding & Justice, 2004). Further, bandwidth requirements must be compatible. Supervisors who are not well knowledgeable with all of these components should access a technical support person who clearly understands the unique needs of the supervision experience. The supervisee is responsible for ensuring confidentiality, which can be daunting when one relies upon another's expertise with such matters.

Counselors and supervisors using electronic communication rely on encryption to protect confidentiality of the information being shared. Encryption refers to the disguising of information as it is transmitted so that the information is not recognizable to anyone other than the intended receiver. Though encryption is recommended, encryption-protected systems are not totally safe as they are vulnerable to intrusion and violation (McAdams & Wyatt, 2010).

If the supervisor and supervisee feel satisfied that their electronic systems are protecting confidential information to the highest degree possible and are convinced that the benefits outweigh the risks, they may then engage in eSupervision practice. Counselors (supervisees) who are engaged in such supervision have a responsibility to update their informed consent practice to reflect this supervision method. In addition to the typical informed consent information regarding supervision, counselors must inform their clients of the following:

- That they are engaged in an electronic method of supervision.
- That eSupervision involves risk and that no security measure can entirely ensure confidentiality.
- That ethical guidelines exist regarding the use of technology in the counseling profession and those guidelines will be adhered to (ACA, 2005; NBCC, 2005).

While many counselors and supervisors may be familiar with videoconferencing in its more direct forms, such as through Skype™ or WebEx™, supervisors may wish to include video review of client sessions as part of their eSupervision practice. Some programs allow the supervisor to watch video in tandem with the supervisee, while maintaining video conferencing connections. So, the supervisor and supervisee can utilize video playback exercises (discussed in more detail in Chapter 9), and the supervisor can have access to raw session material just as he would with in-person supervision. Often times, videoconferencing programs cannot support great amounts of raw data. Instead, supervisees often have to use a digital delivery program that compresses large amounts of data (large files like videos) so that it can be directly uploaded into the conference program or sent to the supervisor. Programs such as YouSendIt™ or SendSpace™ allow videos to be sent securely and in a compressed format.

Finally, supervisors have some additional logistical considerations to clarify at the onset of remote supervision. First, payment arrangements need to be decided upon and specific. Electronic payment options are readily available and supervisees can typically arrange for automatic bill payment through their bank, or supervisees may simply mail the supervisor a check. However, they should decide the method and timing of such payment as part of the initial supervisory contract. Second, supervisors and supervisees may consider a "back-up plan" in case they learn that their eSupervision methods are not reliable. In one case, a supervisor found that she and her supervisee could not engage in eSupervision during times of high internet use in either of their service areas. They each had to work with their local internet providers to increase the sophistication of their service, which added additional, ongoing cost to their monthly internet service bills. While they were engaged in the troubleshooting effort, they had phone supervision while simultaneously playing the same video on their own computers. This created some minor annoyances, but served the purpose of providing continual oversight and support of the supervisee's work. Lastly, supervisors should remember that technology-based supervision is intended to improve access and enhance the supervision experience and should only be provided when the benefits clearly outweigh the risks (McAdams & Wyatt, 2010).

*Activity: If you work or will be working with prelicensed supervisees, visit your state licensing board's Web site to learn what the rules and acceptable practices are regarding phone or eSupervision practices. Additionally, investigate the rules regarding electronic counseling practices. Consider the following: Would you agree to supervisee a counselor who is engaging in etherapy practice? How will you be aware of how your supervisees use technology in their practice? How will you ensure your supervisees are following appropriate technology practices in their work?*

*Review the following with each supervisee:*

*Ethical guidelines around the use of technology (even the phone is technology!)*

*Their practices regarding the use of technology with clients (Do they use email to communicate with clients? How secure is that email? Are they informing their clients of the risks of such communication and are they obtaining consent?)*

*Their practice of getting written permission to audio or video tape a session*

*Their participation in web-based communities and how this may impact client care (If they use programs like MySpace and Facebook, have they taken appropriate measures to protect their privacy? Would they ever "friend" a client electronically?)*

*Their practice Web site and electronic communications. (Does the Web site follow the guidelines in the ACA Code of Ethics about Web site management? If information is submitted via the Web site, is that information secure? Are the limits to security clearly stated? How much access does the webmaster have to the data that is submitted?)*

# NINE

# The Supervision Process: Technical Tools and Tips

*S*upervisors and supervisees alike typically wish for a beneficial, valuable, and productive clinical supervision experience. Further, some wish for an experience that does more than merely provide additional oversight and some skill development; some wish for supervision that allows intellectual stimulation, renewed and reinvigorated interest in one's practice, and provides a bevy of learning experiences from which to grow and develop. Although this type of supervision requires dedication, hard work, and willingness for both the supervisor and the supervisee to accept the challenge, many report that phenomenal supervision is well worth the effort.

A phenomenon is defined as a "fact, occurrence, or circumstance observed or observable" (Dictionary.com Unabridged, n.d.). This chapter examines many observable occurrences and circumstances that are often present and are typically influential at some point in the supervision experience. Supervisors are wise to understand these many phenomena, so that they may identify them, incorporate them into their conceptualizations, and respond accordingly.

A phenomenon is further defined as "something that is impressive or extraordinary" (Dictionary.com Unabridged, n.d.). Although supervision may involve plenty of administrative and clinical minutiae, many supervisors find that the conceptual and interventive activities are quite fun and stimulating. Supervisors may find great delight in working to make otherwise "ordinary" supervision "extraordinary" through their attention to the phenomena and techniques described in this chapter. Many of the processes of supervision hold the same qualities as those of counseling; active engagement in attending to such dynamics and processes relies on the supervisor's most effective counseling skills, plus allows the supervisor the enjoyment of engaging in counseling-like processes without inadvertently slipping into the counseling role with a supervisee.

Further, supervisors may find professional fulfillment and interest in using varying techniques and interventions as this prevents supervision from becoming too routine, predictable, and uninteresting. In this way, supervisors can help prevent their own burnout and disengagement while they assist their supervisees in doing the same.

This chapter examines several phenomena and dynamics that are present in the supervision session and provides some tools and techniques for working through these occurrences with the supervisee in a facilitative, beneficial way. After an examination of many phenomena and features that are present in clinical supervision such as the separation-individuation process, self-efficacy, transference-countertransference and supertransference, the parallel process, and emotion in supervision. This chapter additionally provides specific strategies, guidelines, and techniques to improve the effectiveness of clinical supervision. The chapter concludes with specific tools and techniques to use when balancing administrative and managerial functions with clinical supervision.

## SUPERVISION PHENOMENA AND PROCESSES: MAKING SENSE OF IT ALL

Supervision is an intervention by definition (Bernard & Goodyear, 2009), and supervisors must be deliberate and intentional about how they intervene. Supervisors, like counselors, use their theoretical orientation or practice model to inform how they conceptualize a situation, then select interventions that are appropriate given that conceptualization. However, conceptualization in supervision is complex given the many layers of interpersonal relationship and intrapsychic features involved. Supervisors have to make sense of what happens in the counselor–client relationship, the supervisee–supervisor relationship, and the supervisor–client relationship. In addition, there are a number of contextual variables to contend with, superimposed on many layers of internal and cultural variables that are specific to each participant in the process. The following phenomena and processes will help supervisors to conceptualize and make sense of these many dynamics as they occur. Supervisors with conceptual clarity will be more adept at knowing how, when, and why to intervene.

## THE SEPARATION-INDIVIDUATION PROCESS

Counselor supervision is a process of, amongst other things, helping a counselor move toward independent, autonomous functioning as a competent service provider. Certainly, there are bumps and barriers on the road to autonomy, and the supervisory dyad will often experience the effects of the autonomy–dependency conflict throughout the supervision experience. Watkins (1992) describes four domains of autonomy versus dependency issues as they relate to counselor supervision: functional, attitudinal, emotional, and conflictual (Watkins, 1992).

## Functional Dependence/Independence

Functional independence refers to a supervisee's competence in performing counseling tasks with little or no help from the supervisor. These counseling tasks may include case conceptualization, treatment planning, interventive processes, assessing progress, making appropriate referrals, and terminating counseling. Functional dependence, conversely, is the opposite and refers to the supervisee who needs a great deal of supervisor involvement to carry out these counseling tasks and functions. The functionally dependent supervisee needs assistance from the supervisor before carrying out tasks and will oftentimes seek specific and directive guidance before taking any therapeutic action. This supervisee has low self-efficacy and believes that he needs the supervisor to instruct and inform his therapeutic functions (Watkins, 1992).

## Attitudinal Dependence/Independence

Attitudinal independence refers to the supervisee's attitude, opinions, beliefs, and values regarding the counseling process, which are unique and separate from the supervisor's attitudes, opinions, beliefs, and values. The attitudinally independent supervisee owns beliefs about how change occurs, which theoretical stance to espouse, and what kinds of tasks and functions belong in the counseling process. This counselor is not a "clone" of the supervisee nor has taken on the precise beliefs and attitudes of a professor, theoretical icon, or greatly admired colleague. However, the attitudinally dependent supervisee may be more likely to fit that bill. That is, the attitudinally dependent supervisee adopts the views of his supervisor or other key figures and has not yet fully developed his counselor "self" (Watkins, 1992).

## Emotional Dependence/Independence

Emotionally independent supervisees do not need excessive amounts of support, approval, and intimacy from their supervisor; instead, emotional sustenance is accessible internally (Watkins, 1992). On the contrary, the emotionally dependent supervisee needs plenty of assurance and support to feel secure and certain as a professional. This supervisee is likely to seek reassurance and confirmation regarding most therapeutic and professional decisions, and without such reassurance feels ungrounded and insecure.

## Conflictual Dependence/Independence

Conflictual independence refers to the supervisee's freedom from great levels of conflict-related emotions such as guilt, anger, anxiety, hostility, and resentment. This supervisee can experience supervision in a constructive manner, even in the presence of occasional conflict or discord. Opposite to that is the conflictually dependent supervisee. This supervisee engages in power struggles, territorialism, efforts to dominate or conquer the supervisor, and other similar struggles. This supervisee may undermine the supervisor, reject the supervisor's suggestions, or engage in excessive games that render the supervisor somewhat helpless. This supervisee may engage in an "advance and attack" manner with the supervisor or "retreat and withdraw" (Watkins, 1992). These methods are either aggressive or, in many instances, passive–aggressive or resistant, all dynamics which strain the supervisory relationship and paralyze the supervisory process.

These dynamics are particularly relevant in the supervision relationship in that the supervisor and supervisee can, at times, lose clarity about their respective professional roles. Dependency/autonomy struggles mimic the dynamics that parents and their children engage in, and the supervisor–supervisee dynamic may feel like a parent–child struggle as the supervisee works toward professional independence and identity (Ringel, 2001). A supervisor who believes that the supervision relationship is providing a pull in that direction may revisit this information to determine where the autonomy–independence struggles are centered. By addressing the struggles in terms of supervisee movement toward autonomy, both members of the dyad can regain and maintain clarity about their professional roles and the tasks at hand.

When a supervisor notices hints of a parent–child or similar type dynamic, the supervisor uses the four domains to conceptualize their supervisee in terms of self-efficacy and autonomous functioning. If a supervisee is more dependent in one area of functioning than others, it may be useful to examine the rationale for that dependency. Supervisors can then focus more energy and attention on that particular domain to help the supervisee gain more autonomy and proficiency in that area. For instance, if a supervisee is relatively autonomous in most domains, yet seems particularly emotionally dependent, the supervisor may wish to further examine that. It might be that the supervisee is particularly strong in his abilities to carry out the necessary tasks of counseling, yet may be frustrated or concerned that his clients are not demonstrating the improvement he hopes for. He may need a lot of reassurance from the supervisor that he is, in fact, an effective counselor and belongs in the profession. In this case, the supervisor may work with the supervisee to develop skills to elicit feedback from his supervisees. The supervisee may speak with the supervisor about the need for reassurance and will clarify the problem: In this case, the supervisee feels uncertain about the effectiveness of his work and his goodness-of-fit to the profession. Rather than offering endless amounts of reassurance, the supervisor may demonstrate or role–play for the counselor how to initiate conversations with the clients to determine whether therapy is effective for them. The supervisor instructs the supervisee that the clients are not meant to provide emotional reassurance and comfort, so shows the supervisee how to elicit feedback of professional relevance instead. The supervisor then may help the supervisee to draw conclusions about the more personal aspects of the issue; that is, he will have to determine whether he is competent and appropriate to be in the field and will have to find some security about that from within. The supervisor, in this case, may also wish to help the supervisee to institute formal evaluative or assessment tools in which the client rate the counselor's performance. For instance, the counselor may use the Session Rating Scale by Duncan and colleagues (2003) to provide real-time feedback from the client to the counselor. Regardless of how the counselor gathers feedback, the primary goal here is to shift the counselor away from seeking emotional reassurance from the supervisor and toward autonomous, emotionally steady functioning. A counselor is ready to practice autonomously when he develops a sense that he can deal with prospective situations with skill and competence, that is, when he has developed appropriate levels of *self-efficacy* and true competence across all functional domains.

*Activity: Consider your own experience as a supervisee currently (or, if more applicable, your most recent experience as a supervisee). Rate your levels of independence and autonomy in reference to the four domains: functional, attitudinal, emotional, and conflictual, using this 1–5 scale: 1 = completely dependent; 2 = fairly dependent; 3 = dependent at times; 4 = fairly independent; and 5 = completely autonomous.*

> *Functional:*
> *Attitudinal:*
> *Emotional:*
> *Conflictual:*

*Now, consider how you will gain or gained independence in the aforementioned domains. What kinds of support and experiences helps (helped) you to gain more autonomy? What specific interventions did your supervisor use to help you gain autonomy? Did supervision help you become more independent or less so? How? Describe in detail the events and occurrences that impacted autonomy.*

*Now, consider the dependent supervisee. Discuss how you will assist a supervisee who is dependent in one of the above domains gain independence. Be specific about your interventions and what impact you believe they will have.*

## SELF-EFFICACY

Counselor's self-efficacy is a counselor's belief about his competence and ability to perform counseling behaviors and to manage clinical circumstances and situations (Larson & Daniels, 1998). This is different from *self-esteem*, which refers to the positivity of one's global evaluation of him- or herself, or general fondness for oneself (Heine, Lehman, Markus, & Kitayama, 1999). Self-efficacy is a term derived from *self-efficacy theory*, which suggests that to successfully conduct a behavior, one must have knowledge, skills, and the belief that he has the ability to actually perform the behavior to create a positive outcome (Bandura, 1982). Further, this belief in one's ability to do something is acquired in four ways: (1) enactive mastery (e.g., achieving small successes), (2) vicarious learning (e.g., learning by witnessing others), (3) verbal persuasion (e.g., encouragement and verbal reinforcement from others), and (4) a reduction in emotional arousal (e.g., anxiety) (Bandura & Adams, 1977; Melchert, Hays, Wiljanen, & Kolocek, 1996).

Counselor self-efficacy is particularly relevant in several ways. First, one's belief about his ability to perform a set of tasks inherent to a particular role impacts one's ability to fully adopt that role. That is, if a counselor believes he can counsel effectively, he is likely going to more readily identify as a counselor and willingly engage in counseling tasks (Heppner, O'Brien, Hinkelman, & Flores, 1996). Second, a counselor who believes himself to be capable may be more able to instill such confidence in his clients, thus gaining credibility and client trust more readily. With credibility and client trust, the counselor may be more able to positively impact change, which may further strengthen one's self-efficacy. Finally, research reveals that counselor's self-efficacy positively correlates with satisfaction and negatively correlates with anxiety (Larson & Daniels, 1998). This is particularly interesting to supervisors who have a vested interest in their supervisees maintaining satisfaction in their roles. A satisfied counselor is able to engage in counseling and supervision in a manner that dissatisfied counselors often struggle with, especially when those counselors are experiencing burnout or resentment. Further, counselors with less anxiety are likely to be more autonomous in their overall functioning and can accommodate feedback and challenge that will help them to further improve their skills and performance. Given the relationship between self-efficacy and performance, anxiety, autonomy, role identification, and satisfaction, supervisors are especially interested in helping their supervisees strengthen this construct.

Supervisors may use a formal scale to assess counselor's self-efficacy. This is something that can be administered at several points in time to assess whether a counselor's efficacy has increased and, if so, in what areas. Supervisors can then target their supervisory interventions to match the areas where counselors do not feel as competent or able. One such scale is "The Counselor Self-Efficacy Scale" which has 20 items that relate to individual and group counseling skills and practices (Melchert et al., 1996). Although the items of this scale cover only a small range of specific counseling skills, it provides a useful tool to help discriminate between needed areas of improvement and is suitable for professional-level use. The scale includes items that focus specifically on a supervisee's self-efficacy regarding ethical issues, major psychiatric conditions, facilitating exploration, emotional reactions, and behavior change skills.

Self-efficacy measurements are useful in that they help supervisors to discern areas of needed improvement to make supervision interventions as focused and useful as possible. At times, supervisors and supervisees are tempted to focus on skill sets or practice areas that are already well-intact. Although this may be more enjoyable and is certainly more comfortable, supervision time is better spent addressing areas of needed development. Supervisors may address this quite directly with supervisees by asking questions such as "What do you feel most competent at?" or "Which skills do you feel the least competent at performing?" Although self-report is a useful starting point, supervisors will constantly compare their assessment of supervisee performance with the supervisee's self-assessment. Supervisors look for incongruence here: that is, does a supervisee feel especially inept at a skill that is actually quite well-developed? If this is the case, the supervisor may wish to explore this in depth with the supervisee. What does the supervisor (as the more seasoned clinician) notice or know that the supervisee does not see? For instance, a supervisee may report that she believes her ability to appropriately diagnose mood disorders is limited. She may be frustrated that she relies heavily on manuals, books, and supervision to help her in a differential diagnosis process. She says "I don't understand why it doesn't come more naturally to me. I still get so confused!" This provides the supervisor with the opportunity to help the supervisee to weigh her performance against developmentally appropriate performance standards. Although counselors are expected to know how to make appropriate and accurate diagnoses, this counselor has had a limited range of experience and has not had enough practice at doing such a task. The supervisor may acknowledge the supervisee's feelings of ineptness and provide the supervisee with some added perspective on how these skills take time and practice to develop. Further, the supervisor may note that mood disorders can be quite complicated to diagnose in certain cases, and many counselors find some difficulty with the task. The supervisee is then left with a feeling of normalcy and a reduction in her sense of inadequacy, which frees up her emotional energy to instead focus instead on developing her diagnostic skill without the added weight of anxiety or frustration.

Sometimes, supervisors will notice incongruence in the opposite direction. That is, supervisees may believe themselves to be particularly skilled in a domain that the supervisor assesses to be weak. This situation is bit more complicated, as the supervisor will not have the luxury of reducing distressed feelings; instead, the supervisor is going to introduce some feedback that will likely induce some distress. For example, a supervisee is discussing a situation in which he provides a client with his personal phone number and email address, so that the client can be in contact whenever the need arises. The supervisor questions whether the supervisee is concerned about the client having these pieces of personal information, to which the counselor replies, "Oh no, I told her not to use them unless she really needs it and I trust her. She won't abuse the privilege. We're really close and she won't risk straining our relationship." The supervisor further inquires about therapeutic intent, to which the supervisee replies, "Given her current emotional state, I just wanted to be sure I'm there for her in case anything comes up." The supervisor notes that the boundaries with this client appear different than with other clients, as the supervisee is usually protective of personal information, to which the supervisee responds, "Yeah, I like to individualize treatment to fit the client's needs. It's one of my strengths." The supervisor recognizes that she and the supervisee are at a point of incongruence: The supervisee conceptualizes her performance as helpful, client-centered, and professionally appropriate. The supervisor is concerned about professional boundaries, countertransference, and appropriate clinical judgment.

The supervisor now has to balance providing feedback to facilitate consideration about these issues, whilst keeping in mind the importance of the supervisee maintaining self-efficacy about the positive performance areas. The supervisee might say the following: "I think you quite accurately assessed this client's increasing emotional distress and were concerned about your availability during her difficult times. You also pride yourself on individualizing treatment to fit the unique needs of each client, and that type of thoughtfulness and concern is so very important, as you clearly know. I'd like for us to discuss some alternative interventions that might have better honored the client's resilience and independence, while honoring your personal and professional boundaries. Let's start by examining the therapeutic intent. What were you hoping to accomplish here? Let's clarify that, and then we'll consider a handful of other interventions that might be effective without compromising professional boundaries." Notice that the intervention began with an authentic summary of the supervisee's strengths: sensitivity to the client's emotional state and concern about his availability for his clients. This summary does not provide praise nor is it formulaic. Instead, it is a genuine acknowledgement of the supervisee's strong skills in this matter followed by an acknowledgement of the constructs on which the supervisee holds his efficacy (individualizing treatment).

Following that is a summary of the supervisor's concerns that are presented in an instructive manner: that is, the supervisor is not presenting concerns to which the supervisee must respond directly. The supervisor is presenting concerns as she guides the supervisee toward the subsequent discussion of alternatives. This helps the supervisee dive immediately into finding alternatives and leaning upon other areas of knowledge and competence, rather than having to defend or explain his actions. He may elect to discuss his rationale in further detail, but doing so after some initial problem-solving tends to diffuse the emotion surrounding such feedback a bit, thus lowering defensiveness, anxiety, or confusion about having "done something wrong." Oftentimes, supervisees can figure out the errors they have made by examining alternatives. In this case, the supervisee might examine the alternatives (e.g., "Well, I could have given her the crisis number instead, or talked to her about what she could do if a crisis occurs. She does have close family she can lean on") and might draw his own conclusions about the problems in his performance (e.g., "I'm a sucker for someone who cries! I don't know why, I just seem to want to bend over backwards when people are sad and hurting. It pulls at my heartstrings, I guess, and I'm worried I can't do enough for them."). The supervisor may then inquire about self-efficacy (e.g., "Do you believe your intervention skills are effective enough to help someone who is incredibly sad?") and now has a direction from which to continue working with that supervisee.

Although the literature is quite ripe with articles and scales that address the importance of counselor self-efficacy, supervisor's self-efficacy is less investigated. However, research reveals that supervisors, as they gain experience and training as a supervisor, experience an increase in self-efficacy as well (Stevens, Goodyear, & Robertson, 1997). This process is similar to that experienced by counselors; although experience may help one to feel more comfortable in the professional role, training, knowledge, and an increased belief in one's abilities may contribute to an overall increase in performance and competence. Further, an increase in self-efficacy is often correlated with a decrease in anxiety, which is another important construct in the supervision process (Larson & Daniels, 1998).

*Activity: Compare the amount of self-efficacy you have as a counselor with the amount of self-efficacy you have as a supervisor. Are the amounts similar? What happens to your competence and confidence when you are contending with a situation in which you have low self-efficacy? What measures do you take to ensure competent performance even when you are uncertain about your ability? How can you, as a supervisor, increase your self-efficacy?*

## ANXIETY

Anxiety is a particularly common experience in clinical supervision. Supervision is evaluative by nature and involves a more experienced colleague critically examining one's work; further, the work itself involves using one's personal characteristics, personality, and style along with professional skills to improve the emotional and psychological well-being of another human. This situation quite naturally lends itself to appropriate levels of nervousness and performance concerns. Supervisees typically want to do good work for the client's benefit and also to yield favorable evaluation and respect from the supervisor. Anxiety, to some degree, may benefit a supervisee's performance; excessive anxiety, however, is likely to inhibit one's ability to learn and perform well (Powell, 2004).

Self-efficacy and anxiety are intertwined through an inverse relationship (Bandura & Adams, 1977; Larson & Daniels, 1998). The more belief a counselor has in his ability to do the tasks of counseling, the less anxious he will be. Indeed, supervisees who believe they can handle most situations have developed professional autonomy as discussed earlier in this chapter. They are not afraid to consult or get supervisory assistance as they recognize that seeking assistance and consultative support is an indicator of professional competence. Anxiety in supervision is particularly relevant in that excessive anxiety may prevent a supervisee from appropriately reflecting on his own performance and may additionally prevent a supervisee from engaging in full discourse with a supervisor about his performance. In particular, supervisees may be hesitant to provide supervisors with material or information that reflects a poor performance. In an effort to maximize *self-presentation*, supervisees may withhold raw session material or information about one's experience of a session to preserve the supervisor's opinion of his work (or, in some cases, to preserve one's job or place in the profession). The greater the anxiety, the more likely one is to experience changes in the way he shows himself to others, albeit intentionally or unintentionally (Holloway, 1994).

*Activity:* Describe in specific details how anxiety impacted your work and development as a counselor. Describe how anxiety was managed and addressed in your supervision sessions. Did your supervisor have any notable anxiety? If so, how did that impact your work and your relationship? How was it addressed? How do you typically demonstrate and experience anxiety? How will anxiety impact your work as a clinical supervisor?

## SELF-PRESENTATION

Self-presentation refers to the manner in which the supervisor and supervisee present themselves to one another (Holloway, 1995). Self-presentation includes automatic behaviors that are ingrained and habitual as well as deliberately regulated behaviors (Holloway, 1995). This is typical human behavior; that is, in relationships that people find important, and it is common to act in a manner that will yield favor and positivity from others (Ward, Friedlander, Schoen, & Klein, 1985). This natural human dynamic places both supervisors and supervisees at a disadvantage in many ways. Ideally, clinical supervision is a safe place in which to examine one's weakest and most incompetent actions; however, human nature prefers that supervision is a place to applaud one's effective and brilliant performance. Supervision is where a supervisee typically wants assistance in finding his areas of poor performance and lack of objectivity so that he can make improvements; however, that same supervisee often calculates the risk of sharing such information. Although the risk to one's self-efficacy, ego, and confidence are noteworthy, supervisees are often aware that one also may be risking his job or career through certain revelations. This is especially significant when a supervisee is getting clinical supervision from someone who is also his managerial supervisor. The supervisee, in this case, has carefully weighed his options and has perhaps made the determination that he should not share anything that may factor negatively in performance reviews, layoff decisions, and other such consequential outcomes.

To further complicate matters, people need to hold a positive view of themselves (Heine et al., 1999). Further, a positive view of oneself is considered central to optimal mental health, at least in North American culture (Heine et al., 1999). Individuals' views of themselves tend to be "systematically biased toward an overly positive view of the self" (Heine et al., 1999, p.779). This is particularly relevant to the supervision process in a number of ways. First, supervisees and supervisors alike are humans, so are prone to this bias. Each may see their performance as stronger or more impactful than it actually was. Second, supervisors and supervisees alike will use strategies to maintain their positive self-views. They will engage in actions that enhance positive evaluation and feedback and reduce negative impressions. Finally, supervisors and supervisees will be selective about information that they disclose versus information they withhold, again as a defensive strategy or impression formation tactic. This next section discusses these phenomena in detail.

Consider the circumstance when a supervisee views his performance as more effective than it actually was (or, more likely, more impactful than the client experienced). The supervisee believes his performance to be strong and says, "It was a great session! We got along really well, there's a strong therapeutic alliance, and I feel really good about it." The supervisee is then perplexed when the client calls the clinic and requests another counselor. The supervisee wonders what went wrong. The supervisee is unable to see through his historical lens that although the session felt good and initial rapport was developed, the client's definition of an effective session simply differs from what the supervisee thought was good work. On closer inspection, the supervisee may notice that the session lacked challenge and appears more reminiscent of a talk amongst friends at a coffee shop. The supervisee may notice that the counselor appeared to be polite and engaged but become increasingly restless as the session progressed. The supervisee may have these recognitions later with the assistance of additional feedback (from the supervisor or, more rarely, from the client). However, the initial accuracy of the supervisee's performance is impaired by the distorted belief that the session was more effective than what the client or supervisor concludes.

Next, supervisors and supervisees alike will employ the use of various strategies to maintain their positive self-views. They purposefully or inadvertently aim to enhance positive evaluation and feedback and reduce negative impressions. One such strategy is to take responsibility for client successes while accepting responsibility for "failure" only in the absence of other plausible explanations (Ward et al., 1985). This can be a rather subtle strategy in supervision and may not be easily detected. For instance, a supervisee may express concern that her client appears to be stagnant in treatment and may be uninvested in making a change to her maladaptive behaviors. The supervisee goes on to explain that she assigns homework to the client, which the client fails to complete. The counseling supervisee expresses, "I wish she would show a bit more interest in changing, but she simply has no motivation to do these homework assignments. I can't help her change in just 50 minutes a week. She has to commit a bit more. I think she just likes to have problems!" The supervisor, in this case, might shift the locus of responsibility back to the supervisee by examining the supervisee's performance while resisting the urge to further examine the client's reported deficit. Instead, the supervisor says, "Well, let's take a look at these homework assignments and how they relate to the treatment plan. They may not be indicative of poor motivation, it might be that we're just on the wrong track here." The supervisor has gently shifted the focus off of the client's performance, toward the supervisee's performance.

At times, this strategy is more aggressive and obvious. Consider a supervisee who is questioned about the progress of a particular client. The supervisee exclaims, "Well, she's not doing well because she doesn't show up. She says she'll be there but she calls at the last minute with an excuse. I can't terminate her from therapy, I mean I have to believe her excuses are legitimate, but I get so tired of this game! I'm doing all I can here but she's so borderline, it makes it hard for me to do anything to help her." This type of proclamation is likely to make many supervisors cringe: After all, supervisors can empathize with the supervisees' perceived helplessness and distress about the inconsistent attendance, and at the same time, it is difficult for most supervisors to hear diagnosis-related terminology spoken out of emotion. However, the supervisor will recognize that the counselor is feeling a sense of inefficacy and helplessness, so is presenting that by attributing the negative condition to the client. The supervisor may shift the responsibility back to the supervisee by saying the following, "You are really frustrated because you want two things: a relationship with this client, and an effective way to help her reach her treatment goals. Let's examine each of those in further detail to figure out what you can do here to help those things happen." The supervisor must also attend to the diagnostic terminology the supervisee mentioned. If the terminology does not relate to a current diagnosis, the supervisor may say, "I heard you mention the word 'borderline' and I'm wondering if I've missed something along the way?. Has the client been diagnosed with Borderline Personality Disorder, or are you recognizing signs that need to be examined right now?" If the supervisee contends that signs and symptoms of a disorder are present, the supervisor must attend to that information as a diagnosis certainly informs the treatment planning process. However, the supervisor will bear in mind that a supervisee may lean more readily toward a diagnosis when she believes her performance is impaired; again, because of the strategy of preserving one's positive presentation, the supervisee may inadvertently heighten her concern of problematic "symptoms" in the client to offset the potential impression of therapist ineffectiveness.

*Activity: Consider your experiences as a counselor. What tools did you use to manage clients' impressions of you? Were the tools effective? What were the consequences of using such strategies (positive and negative)? Now, consider your experience as a supervisee. What kinds of tools did you use to manage the impression your supervisor had of you? Again, what were the positive and negative consequences of your self-presentation techniques?*

## NONDISCLOSURE

Another impression formation tactic is selectiveness about the amount and types of information is disclosed in supervision. Both supervisors and supervisees engage in various forms of nondisclosure. Nondisclosure may be quite intentional and deliberate or may be somewhat unintentional or subconscious. Either way, it allows only partial amounts of information to be worked with in supervision, which inevitably inhibits the effectiveness of the supervision process (Ladany et al., 1996). Consequently, the supervision process is not best able to meet its objectives: client care and supervisee development and training. Although supervisors increase their ability to oversee a session by accessing raw data (video, audio, and live supervision), supervisors are not privy to the internal experiences of a supervisee unless the supervisee decides to disclose those experiences to the supervisor (Ladany et al., 1996).

Ladany et al. (1996) conducted a study in which they investigated supervisee nondisclosure. They posited that supervisees avoided disclosure in supervision in three ways:

1. Passive nondisclosure: Supervisees simply do not mention material that the supervisor does not bring up.
2. Active nondisclosure: Supervisees inform the supervisor that they do not wish to discuss something after the supervisor makes mention of it.
3. Diversion tactics: The supervisee engages in another discussion or topic as a means to avoid the subject the supervisor has raised.

The study investigates nondisclosure along many dimensions, and the findings are quite profound. The study reveals that 97.2% of supervisees withhold information (Ladany et al., 1996). Further, the types of withheld information are particularly concerning and include negative reactions to the supervisor, clinical errors, evaluation concerns, and client observations (amongst others). The researchers are particularly concerned that supervisees do not reveal negative reactions to their supervisors. When a supervisee has a negative reaction to their supervisor, that supervisee has the opportunity to examine and work through conflict and disagreement. These skills are especially important in the mental health professions because so much of client work involves issues of conflict and conflict resolution. Further, as discussed in Chapter 7 of this book, successful conflict resolution is one key factor in effective supervision alliances (Nelson et al., 2008). If a supervisee does not reveal stressors and strains as they occur, the supervisor does not have the chance to model effective management of such strains.

Further, the researchers acknowledge that impression management is likely a key factor in supervisee nondisclosure of clinical errors (Ladany et al., 1996). Given the evaluative and often involuntary nature of supervision, it makes sense that supervisees will withhold information about clinical mistakes (Bernard & Goodyear, 2009; Ladany et al., 1996). However, supervisors hold the liability and responsibility for their supervisee's work, so concern about this type of nondisclosure is particularly well-warranted.

It is particularly noteworthy that the majority of nondisclosures were performed in a passive manner, as opposed to active or diversionary (Ladany et al., 1996). Supervisors did not ask questions that elicited the information, or supervisees simply did not offer the information forth. Supervisors, regardless of how intentional and wide reaching their supervision inquiries are, may simply not know the right questions to ask to elicit needed information. Further, if they do ask the "right" questions, supervisees will selectively offer forth information that may not address what the supervisee actually needs to know. So, supervisors should focus heavily on building the trust, transparency, and mutual respect necessary to assist supervisees in the disclosure process. Ideally, supervision is a process where members may be open, honest, and transparent with one another. However, supervisees and supervisors alike contend with issues of nondisclosure, which inevitably inhibits open, clear, and accurate communication pathways between all parties.

Supervisors, like supervisees, engage in nondisclosure strategies. Research reveals that the most frequently (74%) reported reason for supervisor nondisclosure is a supervisor's negative reaction to the supervisee's counseling performance (Ladany & Melincoff, 1999). This nondisclosure often occurs because the supervisor believes that the supervisee is not developmentally ready for such feedback yet or may not have the well-formed cognitive schemas enough to make good use of the information. The researchers note, however, that this may have yielded an unexpectedly negative consequence to the client; that is, the supervisee may have needed that feedback provided in a direct manner so as to best promote optimal client care (Ladany & Melincoff, 1999). The second most common reason for supervisor nondisclosure was that the issues were personal in nature (67%; Ladany & Melincoff, 1999). This nondisclosure may be effective boundary setting and is appropriate in most cases. However, supervisors in certain settings, such as agencies, may be especially cautious about what types of personal information is withheld; that is, if the supervisee is likely to learn about profound personal information from other sources, that supervisee may experience feelings of betrayal or confusion about not hearing this information from the supervisor directly. Consider the case of a supervisor whose son committed suicide. The supervisor took some time off and then returned to work without sharing the specific reason for her absence with her supervisees. However, her supervisees had learned of the loss from another coworker. The supervisees did not bring up the loss in supervision as they wanted to respect the supervisor's boundaries, but these supervisees were also concerned about the supervisor's ability to provide adequate supervision at that time. The supervisees cared for the supervisor and wanted to be sure not to provide any additional stress, so they carefully avoided all topics in supervision that might have added to the supervisor's burden. However, the supervisees grew increasingly frustrated, as they wished for help with certain cases and did not feel their supervisor was competent to provide such help at that time. Further, the supervisees felt hurt that the supervisor had not entrusted them with information about such a profound life event. The unspoken concerns remained unspoken, much to the detriment of the supervisory relationships. In this case, some disclosure might have been useful to preserve the supervision relationship and to restore the supervisee's faith in the supervisor's competence.

In addition, 56% of supervisors in the study by Ladany & Melincoff (1999) reveal that they do not disclose negative reactions to the supervisee's performance in supervision. That is, how the supervisee behaves in the supervision session. Supervisors may be best served to discuss these dynamics as they occur; at the very least, to model the use of immediacy and open communication to the supervisee. At best, the observation may lead to behavioral change that helps the supervisee to make supervision a more effective and impactful experience.

*Activity: Consider your experience as a supervisee. Describe in detail three items or events that you did not share with your supervisor. Be detailed in your consideration of the event. Did you nondisclose intentionally or unintentionally? What was your rationale for the nondisclosure? What could your supervisor have done to help elicit the disclosure? Do you think, in hindsight, the nondisclosures were a good idea? Why or why not?*

*What will you do to help your supervisee disclose more fully and honestly? Be specific about how you will approach your supervisee in terms of communication style, supervisory approach, and your own transparent and honest style.*

## LYING

Although nondisclosure may, at times, be considered lying by omission, lies of commission (or delivering misinformation) also occur in supervision. Lying in supervision is an impression formation strategy and is similar to the process that occurs between clients and counselors; however, in supervision, counselors may have ever more motivation to lie, as they are not granted the same unconditional acceptance and nonjudgmental favor that is present in counselor–client relationships. Lying in supervision may be conceptualized as a transaction of sorts between the supervisor and supervisee, rather than as the result of an internal process specific to the supervisee (Hantoot, 2000). Supervisees will often lie to affect the transactions that occur within the context of the supervision experience; that is, supervisees lie to avoid losing the approval of their supervisor, to enhance praise or commendation, or to avert painful consequences and evaluation. Supervisees may tell a supervisor that they have enacted protective measures that they actually failed to enact (e.g., performing a suicide assessment, making a mandatory call to protective services) or they may state that they attempted interventions based on supervisor's suggestion when they, in fact, decided not to do so. Supervisees may exaggerate certain aspects of case material or client presentation or may attribute responsibility to a client when it actually belongs to a supervisee (e.g., saying a client cancelled a session when the supervisee actually did). Although lying certainly can have grave implications concerning client care, the supervisory relationship will also endure significant strain with the presence of dishonesty. In that trust is a core condition of a positive supervisory alliance, supervisors are wise to attend to contextual factors that influence honesty and disclosure in supervision.

There are several steps a supervisor may take to try to enhance honesty in the supervision process. First, supervisors should begin to discuss honesty and trust right from the initial presupervision interview. Supervisors should normalize the difficult nature of the supervision process and the temptation most supervisees experience to hide, withhold, or distort information. Supervisors may ask their supervisees how they together can create a climate most conducive to honesty and truthfulness. Supervisees are often quite insightful about what conditions need to be present for vulnerability to occur and that is a worthwhile discussion. The supervisor then discusses with the supervisee how those conditions may be honored in the supervision process, and no false promises are to be made. For instance, if a supervisee says "I can't say whatever's on my mind if I know you can just turn around and report that to the human resources department." In reality, a supervisor cannot promise confidentiality to a supervisee in that regard. So, the supervisor may respond with, "It's true, you might at some point reveal something that needs to be shared with human resources. Let's talk about what those things are and imagine how you and I would deal with that sort of situation together." Further, a supervisor may help a supervisee to examine the consequences of nondisclosure before the fact. The supervisor might say, "I know you are concerned that I may have to report things you share with me here to our human resources department. Let's imagine one of those scenarios and let's imagine what happens if I don't make a report. What happens to our client? What are the consequences to you, internally and externally?"

Next, supervisors will keep an alert eye out for signs of nondisclosure or dishonesty throughout the course of supervision. Note times when the supervisee is most vulnerable (such as when strong emotions are elicited in response to a client event or interaction). In addition, note instances when the supervisee appears defensive or guarded. Although supervisors may use direct inquiry to initiate conversation, sometimes an indirect approach is the least threatening. Imagine a supervisee who is withholding information about a client who has relapsed on his drug of choice. The supervisee recognizes that the client is likely in need of a higher level of care as individual sessions are not sufficient to manage his now active use. However, the client has no resources for additional care, and the wait lists for subsidized service is lengthy. Further, the counselor believes that if the client was dismissed from treatment per the "no active use" policy, his use would worsen and might be life threatening. The counselor has decided to continue to see the client even though she knows that he is in need of a different form of treatment and that she is working in direct opposition to agency policy. A supervisor who asks the counselor directly about how the work with this client is progressing may get a response such as, "It's okay. He is really going through a lot right now, so we're still working on stress management and coping skills." After all, the supervisee cannot reveal the relapse, as that would inevitably mean the client's dismissal from treatment, and she cannot reveal the actual treatment goal that is to help him discontinue drug use or get into a higher level of care. No matter what the supervisee asks, the supervisee is likely to lie to protect her actual treatment plan. However, the supervisor may take an indirect approach to inquiring about the client by examining the supervisee's affective state instead of her words. For example, the supervisor may say, "I notice that you seem quite tense as we talk about him. What about his situation causes you more tension than you have with other clients?" The supervisee's response will probably be minimal in content, such as "I don't know, I guess I feel really bad for him." The supervisor can then followup that affective lead with, "Feeling sorry for a client usually coincides with some shaky or broken boundaries. I wouldn't be surprised if you felt some temptation to loosen some boundaries with this client. My hope is that we can work together to get that figured out as it happens." That observation alone sends a message to the supervisee: the temptation is common and normal, and the supervisor is invested in working through that with the supervisee. The supervisee may have no idea what is actually going on, but sensing the added tension can reasonably assume that something is awry. The supervisor issues an invitation to provide assistance in figuring the dilemma out. If the supervisee has enough trust and confidence in the supervisor, he may decide to discuss the situation.

Finally, supervisors will monitor closely his or her reaction and responses to supervisees when they reveal difficult information. Supervisors will remember the fear and anxiety that often accompanies a revelation of error and will treat the supervisee's feelings with appropriate sensitivity. Supervisees learn quickly whether it is safe to reveal errors to their supervisor or not by monitoring the supervisor's reactions early in the relationship. If a supervisor reacts to an error, however small, with condemnation or scorn, the supervisee will work hard at making certain not to elicit a similar or worse reaction in the future. Supervisors may wish to first recognize the difficulty in sharing such information before attending to the content of the information itself. For instance, if a supervisee reveals in supervision that she failed to perform a thorough suicide assessment with a client, the supervisor should turn all attention to the affective experience of the supervisee before addressing the content of the message. The supervisor may first say, "Wow, I'll bet you have been pretty worried about this. Further, you came in here and told me about it. That couldn't have been easy for you. How are you?" The supervisee then has a chance to express her feelings and gain support from the supervisor, plus is able to maintain control of the content of the supervision session for a few moments, rather than having to brace for the inevitable repercussions. Further, supervisees will often turn the attention to client care and will preempt any examination of consequences and repercussions. In this case, the supervisee responds "I've been worried sick about the client and was really scared about telling you about this. I feel so incompetent! And what if she kills herself? I keep thinking it will be all my fault and I should have done more!" The supervisor then informs that supervisee that the focus will first be on client care, then on supervisee skill. The supervisor says, "I know you're worried that you messed up, and that I will see you as negligent. That's not my concern right now. Our first concern is to figure out how we can make sure your client is alright. Then, we'll figure out how things could have gone differently, so that you can be more skilled at this next time. What are some ideas you have right now about what should be done to make sure this client is alright?" The supervisee recognizes that the supervisor and she are in a collaborative process of client care and that no performance attack is imminent.

Further, the supervisee understands that she will later have a chance to examine her performance for the betterment of future behaviors and is not viewed as "all bad" by the supervisor who is still willing to elicit her professional opinion.

## TRANSFERENCE—COUNTERTRANSFERENCE

*Transference* refers to the unconscious experience in which a client displaces thoughts, feelings, and behaviors onto the counselor, although these thoughts, feelings, and behaviors originally stemmed from a relation with another significant figure in his or her life (Miles & Morse, 1995).

*Countertransference* refers to the counselor's feelings toward a client based on issues internal to the counselor or in reaction to the client's presentation or behaviors (Ladany, Friedlander, & Nelson, 2005). Supervisors have long been interested in their supervisees' countertransferential experiences and the management of those experiences in the supervision setting (Fawley-O'Dea & Sarnat, 2001; Teitelbaum, 1990). Supervisors are particularly concerned with the behavioral manifestations of countertransference and how countertransference informs and influences the therapeutic relationship and treatment processes.

Further, supervisors are concerned with how countertransference extends into the supervision experience. In particular, supervisors are especially concerned with helping supervisees to utilize and manage countertransference, so that they may provide optimal client care. Supervisors are often faced with countertransference issues in a number of ways. First, supervisees often present the countertransference itself and ask the supervisor what to do with it. Sometimes supervisees are distressed by the very presence of countertransference; after all, most counselors are trained to be objective, so any potential block to that objectiveness may be perceived as a threat to one's competence. Supervisors, in this instance, should normalize the presence of countertransference and remind supervisees that countertransference is to be embraced as a welcome messenger. Next, supervisors help supervisees decode the message: Is there a message about something the supervisee needs to examine internally? Perhaps, the supervisee is learning something about the client, or how the client interfaces with others. Regardless, the supervisor and supervisee welcome countertransference into the supervision experience.

Next, supervisors often experience countertransference that they do not directly address in supervision. Sometimes they purposefully withhold it; other times they are simply unaware of it. The supervisor, in these cases, notices the behavioral signals of such countertransference and decides how to intervene. Sometimes a simple and immediate observation of a behavioral change is sufficient. For instance, a supervisor may say to the supervisee, "I notice that as you are speaking of this client, you have clenched your hands into fists and your voice has gotten louder. What are you feeling as you discuss him?" Other times, the supervisor may elect to share her own responses or reactions as a way to normalize and facilitate a discussion. For instance, a supervisor may say, "As I hear you talk about this client, I find my heart pounding and my palms getting sweaty. I feel anxious just hearing about him. I wonder what your experience must be like since you are even more involved with him than I am?" Finally, supervisors may notice that supervisees appear to have countertransference that they may prefer to minimize or deny the existence of. These cases may be especially difficult, and supervisors may find that supervisees disengage upon even hearing the word "countertransference." Supervisors must still address the countertransference, although will be strategic and cautious in how they do so. In these cases, the supervisee may need to work with their personal therapist, especially when the supervisee is unwilling to engage in discussion of the countertransferential response in supervision.

Ladany, Friedlander, and Nelson (2005) provide an approach to help supervisees work though countertransference. They acknowledge that it is particularly difficult to figure out what specifically needs to be addressed in relation to the countertransference, so suggest that the supervisory alliance should be well intact before attempting to gain clarity about the countertransferential issue. Further, supervisors should remember to maintain absolute clarity about their role in this process; that is, they are supervisors, charged with using their super (objective) vision to help supervisee gain clarity, which can then affect the therapeutic relationship. The supervisor is not the therapist and should resist any urge or temptation to enter this role. Supervisors can ensure ongoing clarity on the part of both parties by repeating their role aloud during the process. For instance, a supervisor may state, "We're examining this from a professional stance, although the material is undoubtedly personal." The supervisor may also say, "That's something you will bring to your personal therapist; our job here is to figure out how it impacts the therapy experience with (client's name)."

The approach of Ladany, Friedlander, and Nelson (2005) is as follows: first, the supervisor and supervisee examine what may be happening in the therapy experience that is outside of the supervisee's awareness. This is when the supervisee may discover the source or "trigger" of the countertransferential reaction. Next, the supervisor helps the supervisee examine his current feelings toward the client compared to how he has felt toward the client previously. The supervisor and supervisee discuss the behaviors that elicited the countertransference and attempt to make sense or meaning of this. Following that discussion, the supervisor and supervisee interpret the parallel process, if that process exists and exploration of it makes sense, and then the supervisory dyad comes to resolution by planning how the supervisee will reenter the therapeutic experience after this exploration (Ladany, Friedlander, & Nelson, 2005).

## SUPERTRANSFERENCE

Teitelbaum (1990, p. 244) introduced *supertransference* as a term to describe a supervisor's "unresolved conflicts, blind spots, or inappropriate expectations." Supertransference refers to two phenomena. First, it refers to all responses the supervisor experiences in reaction to the supervisee, including the supervisee's personal style, way of speaking, personality features, feelings toward his clients, and overall way of being. Second, supertransference more specifically refers to a supervisor's "blind spots" or obstructions that are impactful enough to affect the supervisee's professional development, efficacy, or client care (Teitelbaum, 1990). Supervisors who feel inexplicably annoyed, angry, frustrated, anxious, and envious may be experiencing supervisor countertransference (Ladany et al., 2000).

There are several sources of such phenomena in supervision. According to Teitelbaum (1990), supervisors have personality characteristics that may interfere with objectivity or the supervision process. For example, supervisors may wish to be liked and approved of by their supervisee. Supervisors may also have inner conflicts that are elicited or ignited by the supervision experience (Teitelbaum, 1990). An example of this is a supervisor who wishes to be viewed as a skilled and talented supervisor, so expects for her supervisees to perform exceedingly well so as to reflect her superb work as a supervisor. This supervisor may view supervisee deficits or errors as a threat to her own competence (or how others will view her competence), so begins to feel resentment or hostility toward the supervisee who delivers such a threat. In addition, supervisors may have transferential reactions to the therapist that are inappropriate and subjective (Teitelbaum, 1990). For instance, the supervisor may simply dislike the theoretical approach the supervisee uses, so may feel some resistance or disengagement from that supervisee. More concerning is the situation where the supervisor perceives the supervisee as perhaps being more talented or skilled than he in this case, the supervisor is experiencing a narcissistic threat and will behave accordingly (Teitelbaum, 1990). Finally, a supervisor may experience a reaction to the counselor's countertransference. Imagine a supervisee who presents countertransference to his supervisor. The supervisor has a reaction to the supervisee's countertransference, thus inhibiting the objective exploration of the countertransference. The supervisee is left feeling confused and perhaps disappointed, as his situation has now grown more complex rather than increasingly clear, as he had originally hoped. At times, the supervisor will find himself engaging in a pattern of transference-countertransference that mimics the therapeutic relationship. This is likely a case of *parallel process* and is explored in the next section.

*Activity:* Have you ever had a supervisee or coworker who elicited strong and uncomfortable feelings for you? What if someone just like that becomes your supervisee? Describe how you would manage your supertransference and how you would build a positive supervisory alliance while feeling such discomfort. What specifically would you need to do and how would you do it?

## PARALLEL PROCESS

*Parallel process* refers to the supervisor and supervisee's interactions that often mirror the supervisee's interactions with clients (or a particular client) (Ekstein & Wallerstein, 1972). Supervisors and supervisees must attend to the parallel process as this phenomena is both informative (McNeill & Worthen, 1989) and transformative. The parallel process, referred to in early literature as the *reflective process*, is happening when certain aspects of the therapist and client relationship are also present in the supervisor–supervisee relationship (McNeill & Worthen, 1989). Early theorists posited that the parallel process is a response to the counselor identifying with the client at a subconscious level (Searles, 1955), and this identification causes the supervisee to "bring" the client into supervision through subconscious enactment. The supervision process then helps the supervisee gain awareness and resolution around the issue, and that awareness and resolution can then be brought back into the therapeutic experience. For example, a supervisee may recognize that she is hesitant to ask the supervisee questions that seem very personal in nature. She does not understand why she feels this hesitance and is disturbed by it. Similarly, the supervisor notices that, in supervision, he feels hesitant to ask the supervisee particular things about the client. In that this hesitance is unusual, he notices it and wonders about the meaning of this unusual occurrence.

As with any supervisory intervention, supervisors need to be deliberate about how to use the parallel process (McNeill & Worthen, 1989). Supervisors may believe a parallel process to be occurring but have to determine whether to disclose such a belief or merely hold it as an undisclosed hypothesis. Further, the supervisor and supervisee, on noticing a parallel process, need to determine how to make useful meaning of the process. Returning to the prior example, the supervisor has made note of his experience of hesitance in asking the supervisee about her client. The supervisor may decide to comment on this experience to the supervisee by saying, "I'm noticing that I feel hesitant to ask you more about this client. I want to, but something holds me back." The supervisee responds with, "I know what you mean! I have that happening in my sessions as well. I don't know why, but there are some things I just can't seem to bring myself to ask about." The supervisor asks the supervisee whether she feels any hesitance to answer particular questions, hypothesizing that perhaps a "don't ask" message is emanating from the client and has been carried into supervision by the supervisee.

The supervisee responds, "No, I'm not afraid of you asking me about anything, really, I just wish I had better answers for you. The right answers, I guess. I'm not sure I can tell you the right things." The supervisor asks the supervisee if perhaps the client holds a similar concern, about not saying the "right" things in counseling. The supervisee agrees to hold that hypothesis and returns to the next session with that in mind. The supervisee notices a time in session when she feels that familiar hesitance to proceed and notes that aloud to the client. The client responds with "I'm not sure what you want to hear from me" and the supervisee responds with, "I see. You're concerned that you won't say the right thing in here" and the client responds affirmatively. The client and counselor are now able to reform their relationship, so that the client feels more free to speak and the counselor feels more free to probe and inquire as needed.

To heighten the benefit of the parallel process as a useful supervision intervention, supervisors need to be intimately aware of their own cognitive and affective responses (Morrissey & Tribe, 2001). Further, supervisors need to get to know how their supervisee typically functions in those same realms: cognitive, affective, and behavioral. The supervisor can then more adeptly notice when any of these functions appear different than usual, as the different functioning is typically the indicator of a parallel process at work. Astute supervisors will notice when a supervisee's response to a client or presentation of a situation is different than what would typically be expected of that supervisee. Further, supervisors may notice that the supervisor–supervisee interactions sometimes seem outside the realm of what is typical and might be able to attribute that to a parallel process. For example, imagine a supervisor and supervisee who are typically quite positive and hopeful in their interactions. They engage in conversation that often includes an awareness of strength, resiliency, and hope. However, during one particular session, they are engaging in what seems like a typical discussion of a client case. The supervisee notices that she is starting to feel "depressed" and is not sure why. The supervisor notices that the conversation has been littered with negativity in a way that is not typical and wonders aloud what could be going on. The supervisee becomes aware that she is feeling in supervision the same way she feels at the conclusion of sessions with this client and expresses concern about that, and the supervisor and supervisee hypothesize about the meaning of this phenomenon. They draw the conclusion that perhaps the client is inwardly a lot more depressed than what he is expressing in session and that perhaps he also leaves therapy with a sense of gloom. The supervisee begins her next session with this client by inquiring about what happens directly following session and learns that the client goes to bed for the remainder of the day, paralyzed by sadness.

Researchers caution supervisors against overusing the parallel process as a supervisory intervention (Feltham & Dryden, 1994), especially when that allows the supervisor and supervisee to ignore dynamics that are actually exclusive to the supervisory relationship. The parallel process concept may be more suitable for supervisees who are more experienced and well practiced at exploring complex conceptual features of the therapeutic process (Morrissey & Tribe, 2001). Because the parallel process involves transference and countertransference, an examination of the phenomena will be useful only with supervisees who are self- and other-aware enough to explore such intrapsychic and interactional elements.

*Activity: Examine your own experiences as a supervisee. Did you and your supervisor ever engage in a process that aligned with something happening in one of your sessions? Describe the situation in detail. How did your experience with the client mirror the experience you were having with your supervisor? How did your supervision impact the client experience and vice-versa?*

## EMOTIONS

Supervisees are often confused about the role of emotion in counseling and, by extension, supervision. They may believe that they are effective counselors only if they can successfully inhibit emotion; on the converse, some use their emotional experience of a client as a primary source of information and conceptualization. Further, some believe that a show of emotion in supervision will yield them a negative evaluation by their supervisor, who may experience them as "unprofessional" or "neurotic." Yet others view supervision as an "emotional outlet" in which they can experience a cathartic release of tension and professional difficulties (Nordentoft, 2008). Although there are no specific rules that govern the appropriate quality or quantity of emotion in the supervision experience, supervisors are wise to consider how emotional experiences might be best used for the betterment of client care and supervisee performance.

Supervisees, like any other humans, inevitably have emotional experiences and reactions in the course of their relationships with others; whilst many are concerned or embarrassed about revealing these emotions to an authority figure (the supervisor), supervisors and supervisees should recognize that the very nature of supervision lends itself to emotional exploration and expression at certain junctions. Further, if supervisors or supervisees engage in active prohibition or inhibition of affective experience, they may consider it fairly logical that similar dynamics may appear in the counselor–client relationship as well.

Clinical supervisors may find great value in engaging their supervisees in a discussion about their views of the role of emotion in the therapeutic process. Supervisors can learn a great deal about their supervisee's views of change, development, client relations, and insight by simply asking, "Where do emotions fit in the therapeutic process?" Further, supervisors and supervisees should discuss the role of emotions in the supervision process as well.

Supervisees reveal dissatisfaction with supervisors who dismiss their feelings or affective experiences (Gray, Ladany, Walker, & Ancis, 2001). It seems like the most acceptable, and certainly, the most addressed emotion in the supervision literature is anxiety and its function in the supervision experience. Other emotions and their role in supervision are left largely unexplored.

Cooper & Ng (2010) acknowledge that a supervisee's emotional experiences related to clients and in the supervision process inevitably impact their learning and growth and, ultimately, client care. There are several layers of emotional experience to pay attention to: the client's emotional experiences the supervisee's emotional experiences and the supervisor's emotional experiences (Cooper & Ng, 2010). More specifically, the client's emotional experiences are represented in supervision directly through raw data (audio and video review), which give the supervisor observable entry into the client's affective experience and, indirectly, through supervisee report and filter, which likely contains various levels of distortion. Supervisee emotion may be related to their experience of the client, the therapy sessions, their supervisor, the supervision sessions, their job or employment situation, contextual stressors, or personal difficulties. Supervisor emotion, similarly, relates to the supervisor's experience of the therapeutic process, the supervision experience, contextual factors, and personal issues that typically remain largely undisclosed (Ladany & Melincoff, 1999). Given this multitude of emotional variables, supervisors need a plan of action to be able to make appropriate sense and meaning of emotion in the supervision context.

Supervisors are tasked with determining how emotion should be conceptualized and worked with in the supervision process. Supervision sessions are typically time limited and are intended to provide client oversight and supervisee growth; thus, supervisors have to ensure that supervision sessions do not carry so much emotion that they feel like therapy, and so little emotion that clients become sub-human "cases" to be "solved." Supervisors may ask themselves the following questions when a supervisee becomes emotional in supervision:

*What are the emotions being expressed here?* Get specific and name the feeling. This may be as simple as asking the supervisee, "What specifically are you feeling right now?" Oftentimes, merely getting specific or labeling the emotion helps to diffuse it. For example, a supervisee is speaking angrily about a client's tendency to argue and refute her feedback. The counselor states, "I'm angry!" when asked to clarify her emotion. She then laughs and says, "Well, I guess everyone's angry at this client. I've joined the club!" The supervisee regains objectivity and recognized her anger is typical given the context.

Further, the specific emotional experience is often countertransferential, so finding a specific word to describe the feeling may help the supervisee to gain insight into the client's experience. For instance, a supervisee expresses a combination of frustration and sadness with a client ("she's just so nasty to me! I wish she would stop being so sarcastic in session. It's hard to connect with her when she treats me like the enemy.") The supervisee states that she feels a mixture of melancholy and irritation as she thinks of the client and has some dread about seeing her. The supervisor wonders aloud to the supervisee whether the melancholy is the client's experience as well, and whether the irritation is an appropriate emotional response to large number of irritants the client must contend with daily. The supervisee thoughtfully considers this and experiences a sense of empathic awareness as she recognizes the quality and depth of the client's emotional turmoil.

*Is this emotional expression appropriate given the context?* For instance, if a supervisee's client dies, it is appropriate for a supervisee to cry. If a supervisee's client is 20 minutes late to session, those tears may seem contextually inappropriate. When an emotional expression seems contextually inappropriate, supervisors may further explore to learn what may be happening. First, the supervisee may be experiencing general transference where her emotional experience of one client represents a more general experience she is having of many clients (e.g., "They are all so disrespectful to me! I feel so used by them, they don't even have the courtesy to call me when they're late!"). Second, the supervisee may have a related transference issue that is magnifying her emotional experience with the supervisee (e.g., "This client's dog died on the same day my dog died. It's just so sad!") Third, the supervisee may have some difficulties managing her emotions and may need to continue her own therapy work to further develop her own emotion regulation or management skills or deal with the emotional impact of emotionally straining work. Finally, the supervisee may be experiencing issues beyond the relationship with clients, such as general burnout, vicarious trauma, or personal issues.

Once clarity is achieved, the supervisor asks himself, *How does this impact client care?* In some cases, supervisees who are able to connect to their emotion may be better able to experience empathy with their clients (Lambert & Barley, 2001). In other cases, supervisors identify countertransference that can be worked through before the counselor reengaging with the client. In more extreme circumstances, supervisors may recognize that the supervisee is dealing with personal or professional issues whose impact is significant enough that the supervisee should not be working directly with clients at this time.

Regardless, emotion is present in supervision whether it is demonstrated or not. Supervisors should recognize, normalize, and acknowledge the experience of emotion as a natural and critical component of the supervisory process. To discount emotion is to discount a significant component of the human experience. However, supervisors must maintain clarity about their role with the supervisee in contending with the emotional experience.

## SUPERVISION TECHNIQUES

### Reflective Practice

As supervisees move toward autonomy and independence, they need to develop the ability to critically and evaluative examine their work and the impact of their work. *Self-reflective thinking* or *reflectivity:* Self-reflective thinking is a process of ongoing examination of one's theories, beliefs, and assumptions that influence a counselor's conceptualization and interventive choices (Griffith & Frieden, 2000; Orchowski, Evangelista, & Probst, 2010). Reflectivity is critical in the counseling profession (Nelson & Neufeldt, 1998). Reflectivity builds a counselor's procedural knowledge and understanding of the counseling process and features therein, plus amplifies his ability to understand how affective and cognitive experiences inform and are informed by client–counselor interaction (Orchowski, Evangelista, & Probst, 2010; Safran & Muran, 2000). Supervisors assist supervisees in developing their reflective practice, so that they can effectively self-supervise. Although counselors should never work in a vacuum, the work by nature is fairly independent and requires a counselor to be skilled at making in-the-moment decisions based on solid therapeutic rationale. Ultimately, supervision has reached its epitome when the supervisee has internalized the process and can make decisions that optimize client care and fully engage one's most competent skills.

Although supervisors may often feel tempted to provide answers, teach supervisees didactically, and be directive, supervisees are more likely to become self-reflective practitioners if the supervisor engages them in a process by which they have to look inward and produce their own thoughts, evaluative feedback, and solutions.

Self-reflective practice, in supervision, means that the supervisor is assisting the supervisee in reviewing and considering his work from a self-evaluative lens. The supervisee considers the multitude of features that contributed to his choices and considers the impact of those choices on all parties.

This next section presents a multitude of techniques that are used in supervision and may facilitate reflectivity. Again, supervisors remember that what they are ultimately doing is helping the counselor become able to self-monitor and self-evaluate.

### Selecting Supervision Interventions and Techniques

Supervisors select their techniques based on what they believe will most effectively optimize client care while developing supervisee skills. Supervisors should consider thoughtfully which skill or competence they wish to develop and then utilize techniques that will best address those skills. Supervisors consider features such as experience, supervisee personality, learning style, work setting, and resources when deciding which interventions to use. Supervisors should not select interventions out of convenience, habit, or carelessness. The following sections include techniques and tools for use in supervision sessions and outside of supervision sessions. These lists are a menu of interventive options that supervisors can use as described or with creative twists that better suit the work setting. These techniques represent the actual "work" of supervision, and supervisors select interventions with the same thoughtfulness expected of their supervisees when selecting client interventions.

## In-Session Tools and Techniques

### The Socratic Method: Systematic Questioning

Systematic questioning is a commonly used part of the Socratic method and helps supervisors to facilitate supervisee reflection and insight through a collaborative exploration process. Systematic questioning involves careful forethought about the type of question, content of the question, and questioning process that the supervisor will use (Overholser, 1993). In counseling, this form of questioning is intended to help a client to find logical responses to a problem and draw conclusions about how to act in the future (Corsini, 2002). Similarly, Socratic questioning in supervision holds the same intention: to help supervisees engage in a reflective and critical thought process by which they can find solutions to dilemmas and plan future behaviors and interventions accordingly.

Although the mechanisms of the Socratic method is not made explicitly clear in the counseling literature (Carey & Mulan, 2004), this framework will help supervisors to engage in a process that aligns with the intentions of the Socratic method; that is, to engage the participant in critical thinking and discourse that allows for the most expansive breadth of options possible followed by logical, reasonable, and beneficial conclusions.

There are several types of question a supervisor may ask: memory, translation, interpretation, application, analysis, synthesis, and evaluation (Overholser, 1993). Memory questions involve the supervisee recalling historical information ("How did the client greet you when he came into your office?"). The content itself is not typically important but is elicited when it is leading toward something of greater impact. For instance, if followed up with "How did that greeting impact the tone of the session?," the content information takes on a more significant meaning. Supervisors should consider moving away from having supervisees try to recollect facts from their sessions; typically, the "facts" are simply not relevant enough to warrant supervision time. Instead, the focus is on the impact or meaning of the events. Memory questions should be used sparingly in supervision and only with specific intent.

Translation questions invite the supervisee to make new meaning of information and identify and resolve gaps in the supervisee's understanding of the information (Overholser, 1993). For instance, a supervisor may facilitate discussion with a supervisee about a dilemma by asking, "When you consider the code of ethics and this situation, what do you see as the relationship between the two?" The supervisee then recognizes the dilemma is an ethical one and can approach further discussion from that viewpoint.

Interpretation questions are questions that invite the supervisee to discover relationships between various features and components of the issue with the goal of using one's prior knowledge to resolve current dilemmas (Overholser, 1993). For instance, a supervisee informs the supervisor that she feels nervous about working with a particular client based on the initial phone call with that client. The supervisor asks, "Does your fear about working with this client remind you of any other situations you have recently experienced?" The supervisee then recalls that this particular client reminds her of another client who she also felt fearful about working with. The supervisee states, "Oh, that's right! I was really nervous about working with that client, too, but then realized that she wasn't as scary in person as I thought she would be." The supervisor might further inquire, "What lessons did you learn from that experience that might be applicable to this one?"

Application questions invite supervisees to use skills or information that they already possess to deal with and resolve a current issue (Overholser, 1993). Although the supervisee may already have the answers, they may not have considered using those answers in the current situation. So, the supervisor uses brief questions to facilitate problem solving, such as "What have you tried so far?" and "What are your other options here?" Further questions may include, "What else can you think of?" and "How are you going to implement that?"

Analysis questions involve the supervisor facilitating the supervisee in breaking down a problem into more manageable pieces. This type of question focuses on the thinking process of examining a problem and then drawing logical conclusions. These questions are appropriate for instances when a supervisee might have drawn an inappropriate or illogical conclusion. For instance, a supervisor asks a supervisee, "What evidence do you have that leads you to believe the client is unmotivated?," followed by, "What other things might be happening that would give this client the same presentation?"

Synthesis questions are questions that invite the supervisee to solve problems by using creative or divergent thinking (Overholser, 1993). This may feel like a brainstorming technique in that it is designed to help a supervisee find a wide range of answers and solutions. For instance, a supervisor may ask, "What are some other possibilities, besides continuing to use the cognitive techniques which the client is feeling adverse to?"

Finally, evaluation questions are questions that invite the supervisee to make a value judgment against a specific standard (Overholser, 1993). First, the standard is identified; a value judgment is made against that standard. For instance, the supervisee states, "I'm just not good at working with highly depressed clients. They just won't talk to me!" The supervisor asks the supervisee to describe the typical relationship between someone who is very depressed and a new person who enters their life. The supervisee recognizes, "Oh, I guess when you're really depressed it's hard to really feel excited about meeting anyone new." The supervisor then asks the supervisee to determine whether the therapeutic alliance is stronger or weaker than it might be with another counselor in similar circumstances. The supervisee says, "Well, I think anyone would have a hard time really bonding with this client. I guess I'm not so terribly unique."

Once the supervisor has determined which type of question to ask, the supervisee decides what to say. The key here is that the supervisor is the guide and will use questions only to facilitate further exploration and insight. The supervisor takes great care not to interrupt the process or prematurely halt the process; instead, the supervisor creates questions that will keep the supervisee thinking, reflecting, and then resolving.

### Beyond Systematic Questioning

Supervisors will find that they often do not have time to engage in such an in-depth process with the supervisee about all of his clients and may wish to employ questions that allow the supervisee to consider multiple clients at once. Supervisors may use *linking questions* or *generalization questions* to effectively engage the supervisee in critical thinking and reflection about more individuals than just the one who is the focus of current discussion. *Generalization questions* are questions that invite a supervisee to consider which other clients specifically may benefit from the solutions considered during the reflective process. If a supervisee decides that an art therapy approach may be useful for a client who prefers not to verbally discuss his problems, the supervisee is then encouraged to consider which other clients might benefit from a similar intervention. *Linking questions* involve the supervisor asking the supervisee about other clients who had similar issues. The supervisee is asked to consider how those clients resolved such issues and considers how those solutions may be used in this particular client's situation. In this case, the supervisee is being asked to draw upon information and competence he has already developed that can be applied in a new situation.

To elicit the most information possible, supervisors need to ask *open-ended questions*. *Open-ended questions* are questions that cannot be answered briefly or with dichotomous responses such as "yes" or "no." These questions are designed to provide the supervisee with something to think about and consider, rather than routinely or thoughtlessly answer. For instance, asking "Did that intervention do what you thought it would do?" may be answered with a simple "yes" or "no" and will not likely lead to further contemplation. On the converse, a supervisor can ask, "What else might you have done to achieve a more optimal outcome?" that encourages the supervisee to engage in a thoughtful, reflective process of considering alternatives.

### Interpersonal Process Recall

Interpersonal Process Recall (IPR) was originally developed by Norman Kagan and his colleagues based on their observations of a particular phenomenon they encountered in their work with counselors (Kagan & Kagan, 1997). They found that if people are video recorded then showed these recordings directly after the interaction, they are able to recall the thoughts and feelings they had during the initial interaction with great depth (Kagan & Kagan, 1997). IPR is a supervision approach that capitalizes on this phenomenon and helps supervisees to gain greater depth into their interactions and act on perceptions and realizations that they may not otherwise attend to (Cashwell, 1994; Kagan & Kagan, 1997). IPR is based on the concepts that people need one another yet fear one another as others have the ability to invoke physical and emotional pain (Kagan & Kagan, 1997). Further, humans are the greatest source of stimulation for each other (Kagan, 1980). As a result of these premises, Kagan and colleagues developed a model that allows supervisees to explore their work with a minimal amount of threat and "feigned naivete," or the tendency to acknowledge and label only a fraction of the information they perceive (Kagan and Kagan, 1997).

IPR is conducted through these steps (adapted from Cashwell, 1994; Kagan & Kagan, 1997):

1. *Tape review.* The supervisee reviews audio or video recordings before the supervision session and selects a segment of that recording that holds meaning to the supervisee.
2. *Introduce the activity.* Make certain the supervisee is clear about the intentions of the activity and the expectations of the activity. Speak in advance with the supervisee about the human tendency to attend to certain stimuli and tune other stimuli out. Inform the supervisee that she is to focus her reflection on the thoughts and feelings that were present in the session at the time of the recording.
3. *Play the recording.* Interrupt the recording at intervals to provide prompts (see below for examples) to the supervisee, which will help the supervisee in the reflection process. The supervisor may pause the playback, or the supervisee may do so. Both should have access to a "pause" button and either can initiate a pause at any time.
4. *Supervisor's role.* The supervisor's role during this process is to facilitate reflection. Supervisors should resist the urge to enter into a

didactic or teaching moment; instead, allow the supervisee to carry the weight of reflective discovery. The intention here is to help supervisees tune in to dimensions and information they might have not been attuned to during the session. The supervisee will benefit from noticing and discovering intrapersonal and interpersonal dynamics.

Facilitative prompts (or "leads") might include:

How do you feel about the session right now?
What was the intention in that moment?
What were you feeling about the client at that moment?
What do you wish you had noticed/done/said right then?
What were you hoping he would say/do?
What was she hoping to get from you at that point?
What feelings did you notice during that interaction?
Where in your body were you experiencing your reaction?
What would you like to say to the client right now?

Supervisors using IPR should maintain the stance that supervisees are the "best authority on their own dynamics and the best interpreter of their own experience" (Kagan & Kagan, 1997, p. 306) and should be treated as such. IPR is not a venue for a supervisee to demonstrate his knowledge or observations; rather, it is the venue to use optimal facilitation skills to help the supervisee bring his discoveries, observations, and learning to light.

### Recording Review Techniques

Although supervisees may initially feel hesitant about providing raw data to supervisors through video or audio recordings, supervisors may make the process more enticing for supervisees by highlighting the usefulness of having such data present. For instance, if a supervisee is attempting to describe a client, the supervisor may say, "Pop in a video, let me take a 10-second look to save you the trouble of describing him." Many supervisees, especially those who are newer at video review, appreciate the supervisor viewing the client rather than supervisee (of course, the supervisor cannot help but observe both). Further, incorporating audio and video review in small doses tends to help supervisees view the process as less threatening and more palatable, so that more in-depth, longer viewings are eventually more comfortable. Several techniques help to incorporate the use of audio and video recordings into the supervision session.

One simple technique is *introducing the client*. This is when the supervisee selects a 15-second clip of video that "introduces" the client to the supervisor (or group, in the case of group supervision). Even in cases when the video camera is able to record only the back of the client, it is often helpful to get a quick view of the client, the client's nonverbal presentation, affective presentation, and vocal tone. This introduction occurs the first time a counselor introduces a client into the supervision experience. Over time, many supervisees ask that the introduction extend to several minutes in length, so that the supervisor is able to get an understanding of the counselor–client interactions.

Another technique is *hypothesis testing*. Hypothesis testing may happen as an in-session activity or as a homework assignment and is somewhat spontaneous. Hypothesis testing is initiated when a supervisee wonders aloud about a particular clinical skill or feature. For instance, a supervisee is exploring why a particular client does not seem to opening up to her and says, "I wonder if I might be sending him messages that I really don't want to hear what he has to say?" The supervisor asks if that is internally accurate and the supervisee confirms that she is ambivalent, stating, "I am just afraid that if he tells me he really was sexually abused as a child, I'll have to know what to do or say about it and I'm not sure I do." Rather than speculating further, the supervisor invites the supervisee to play a random segment of the video for just 60 seconds to see whether the supervisee is sending a closed message. The supervisor may instruct the supervisee to examine verbal and nonverbal messages. In some cases, it is useful to play a video without sound and simply examine the nonverbal communication. The random review is not typically seen as threatening as the supervisee has initiated the self-reflection, and 60 seconds is a short amount of time to view video. In many instances, the supervisee will request to keep the video playing as she reflects and gathers further information to confirm or disconfirm the hypothesis. The supervisee then provides self-evaluative feedback (or the supervisor may offer a short prompt such as, "Well, what do you think?"). This method is fairly nonthreatening but does require access to multiple video recordings at once because of its spontaneous nature. This method is easiest when the supervisee is recording onto discs or memory sticks, as opposed to video tapes.

A similar technique is *checking for patterns*. The checking for patterns technique involves the supervisor or supervisee developing an initial hypothesis about supervisee behavior (or, in some cases, client behavior), then playing a video or audio recording at spaced intervals to check for patterns. For instance, a supervisee may state that she is not certain why she has difficulty challenging a couple of her clients. She says that she believes that the clients do not seem open to being challenged yet faithfully return to therapy. The supervisor suspects that perhaps the supervisee has slipped out of a professional role with these clients, and the relationships have become more friendly and casual, thus inhibiting the counselor's ability to effectively challenge the clients. The supervisor asks the supervisee to bring forward recordings of one or more of these clients and informs the supervisee that they together will examine tone, interactional style, nonverbal cues, or any features that make sense given the hypotheses. The supervisor then plays the recordings at random but spaced intervals for short amounts of time (such as 10–15 seconds) to see if any patterns of interactions are obvious. In this example, the supervisor notices that the supervisee is smiling in each of the clips and appears to be very casual and relaxed. The supervisee notices that her voice is light and friendly through the entirety of the sessions. The supervisee says, "Wow, I never really settle down to business, do I?" and recognizes that she is inadvertently sending a message that therapy is an enjoyable time for light discussion rather than a climate for challenge and change.

A variation of the aforementioned technique is to *compare and contrast* between recordings. When the supervisee identifies a concern about a client, the supervisor may ask the supervisee to provide video of that client (the "target" client) and any other client (this is the contrast" session and is preferably chosen at random). The supervisor plays two 30- to 60-second clips of the target client session at the 20- and 40-minute marks. Without discussion, the supervisor then plays video clips at the same marks of the contrast session. The supervisor then asks the supervisee to compare and contrast the differences in his presentation between the two clients. Although this may seem rather arbitrary, the supervisee will typically notice something in his presentation or interpersonal style that is contributing to the issue he is contemplating in supervision. Following the supervisee's insight and discovery, the supervisor may wish to revisit the target client video and play a small selection, perhaps 2 minutes, and will ask the supervisee how those 2 minutes may have gone differently had he used his newfound knowledge at that time.

### Representational Chair

Many supervision techniques require no technology at all. Supervisors may find a number of uses for a *representational chair* in the supervision experience. The representational chair is simply an extra chair (or chairs) that are present in the supervision space and represent the presence of the client(s) in the supervision room. A physical object such as a chair is large enough to remind the supervisor and supervisee of the primary focus of any and all supervision interactions: the betterment of client care. When a chair is present to symbolize the supervisee's place of importance in supervision, supervisees and supervisors alike may find themselves addressing the chair as they would the supervisee. This is typically inadvertent and many supervisees will not even notice they are doing it. For instance, a supervisor and supervisee may be discussing an interaction the supervisee had with his client. The supervisee begins to, unwittingly, gesture toward the chair while discussing the client's responses. The supervisor may then engage the chair spontaneously as a form of intervention. The supervisor can ask the supervisee to speak directly to the client (chair) to practice a response or interventive tactic. The supervisor may bring the chair further into the space between the supervisor and supervisee and ask, "Let's examine what he (the client) would say about our plans." The supervisor may ask the supervisee to have a seat in the client's chair and examine a situation from his perspective. This is especially useful with empathy building or when trying to facilitate a supervisee's view of multiple perspectives.

Although this may seem reminiscent of the Gestalt empty-chair technique, the use of the representational chair is not conducted with the same type of planning, practicing, and curative impact. Instead, techniques related to the representational chair are most often useful in that they are spontaneous, can be initiated by either the supervisor or supervisee, and hold little or no psychological threat. In fact, at times, the use of the representational chair may be the source of humor to lighten an otherwise intense supervision session. This writer recalls one supervision session in which a supervisee described having spent much of a recent session with a client, teaching her about appropriate communication skills. This writer joked to the supervisee while motioning to the chair, "I see what you mean. She's learned a lesson from that and hasn't said a word ever since." The supervisee chuckled and then said somberly, "Yep, I guess I probably did talk too much. I guess I treated her like she wasn't even there. My lesson in communication skills was actually just a terrible example of someone talking too much!"

### Genogram

Another no-technology supervision tool is the genogram. Supervisors may draw family or cultural genograms of their supervisee's clients as part of their supervision notes or may use a white board or shared paper to draw a genogram as the supervisee describes a case (note that the supervisee can also draw the genogram, although that tends to slow the supervision process). Further, supervisees may be instructed to bring a genogram into supervision, or may be asked to draw one as a supervision assignment. Supervisors should be specific about their rationale for utilizing a genogram. That is, a supervisor may say, "These relationships are starting to feel confusing to me. I wonder if a genogram would help us keep this all clear? I worry we might get mired in the story and not have clarity around the core issues if we don't get some immediate clarity." Genograms are especially critical when providing supervision of family therapy, as genograms help diagram and reveal the emotional processes and structures within a family system (Kerr & Bowen, 1988), as well as intergenerational patterns and trends. Genograms may also be useful when working with supervisees who have multiple pieces of seemingly relevant information about family members but are having difficulty understanding the connections and meaning of these pieces of information. Further, genograms are useful with supervisees who are having difficulty understanding the client within a broader context (Magnuson & Shaw, 2003).

One particularly informative use of the genogram is to have the supervisee construct a genogram of his own family. Although many supervisees may do this as part of their training program, if they have not constructed a genogram in the past couple of years, it is useful to have them do another one. Supervisors may specifically ask supervisees *not* to share the genogram in supervision; that is, supervisors ask the supervisee to construct a genogram, but that supervisee is told that he is not to show that genogram to the supervisor. Instead, the supervisee will use the genogram as a tool for self-discovery. His discoveries *as they impact his work with clients* are appropriate points of discussion for supervision; the genogram itself is not.

Supervisees may be instructed to look for the following as they construct their own genograms and client genograms (Magnuson & Shaw, 2003):

1. Tendencies toward underfunctioning and overfunctioning
2. Distancing and pursuing dynamics
3. Triangulation
4. Cultural variables and patterns
5. Views of human nature
6. Views about change/change process
7. Family roles

Further, genograms are useful tools in helping a supervisee understand and build an understanding of the client's cultural context. Supervisees can increase their cultural competence by constructing cultural genograms that allow a more thorough understanding of a client's cultural influences, belief systems, practices, and power dynamics (Shellenberger et al., 2007).

Sometimes supervisors will find that simply drawing a genogram in the supervisee's sight as they discuss a client's case is sufficient to prompt discovery. For instance, a supervisee was curious about a client who developed a drug addiction and was seemingly the only addict in her family system. As the supervisee described the family members, the supervisor drew a genogram. On closer inspection, the supervisee noticed that each of the family members had some sort of addiction-related behavior. Although the client was the only illegal drug user, other members of the family had food, sex, shopping, and a bingo addiction. The supervisee was able to return to the client with an adjusted concept of the client's "only addict in the family" designation and helped lead the client to a similar discovery.

### Homework

*Post-Counseling Session Reflection Prompts:* Supervisors may provide supervisees with a list of questions that they respond to directly after a therapy session. These questions are designed to explore cognitive, affective, behavioral features and decision-making, theory-based, and interpersonal components of the session. These questions may be designed by the supervisor and tailored specifically to the supervisee or may be gleaned from the literature (Holloway & Carroll, 1999; Neufeldt, 1999).

*Journaling:* Supervisees may be instructed to write reflective entries in a journal after therapy sessions. These may be paper journals or letters that the supervisee brings to supervision or perhaps posted to a private discussion board, chat room, or via email. Supervisors may respond to the musings electronically or may prefer to address the reflective writing during the subsequent supervision session.

# TEN

# Models of Supervision: Triadic and Group Supervision

While individual supervision is often the most practiced and preferred form of supervision (Enyedy, 2003; Ray & Altekruse, 2000), many counselors will at some point experience triadic or, more commonly, group supervision. At times, individual supervision is not available, accessible, or affordable. In these instances, triadic or group supervision may be an equally effective alternative (Ray & Altekruse, 2000).

However, triadic and group supervision are not to be considered merely alternatives for individual supervision. Instead, these modes of supervision have benefits that are simply not available in the dyadic (individual) format. Multiple participants add multiple perspectives, voices, and relationships, each of which hold the potential for great impact on the supervision experience and, ultimately, for the benefit of client care.

Triadic supervision is supervision provided simultaneously to two supervisees who meet with one supervisor (Altfeld & Bernard, 1997). Group supervision involves several counselors meeting together with one clinical supervisor and is a commonly practiced form of supervision (Enyedy, 2003). This chapter first examines the benefits and drawbacks of triadic supervision and introduces a model for triadic supervision. Next, this chapter examines the benefits and drawbacks of group supervision, which is followed by an examination of group supervision dynamics and activities. The chapter concludes with an examination of hindering events in group supervision.

## TRIADIC SUPERVISION

Triadic supervision is recognized as a viable and effective modality of supervision (Hein & Lawson, 2008). This form of supervision has been approved by CACREP for use with counseling trainees and is allowable as an alternative to individual supervision (CACREP, 2008).

## BENEFITS AND DRAWBACKS

In that many mental health agencies and counselors are experiencing the ongoing impact of poor economic conditions and understaffing, triadic supervision may prove an effective, time and money-saving activity. Triadic supervision allows supervisors to provide appropriate oversight and guidance to supervisees who typically would not be able to access individual supervision. Further, triadic offers more individualized attention than a group format typically allows. Agencies may consider triadic supervision a wise, economical option, especially if the alternative is no clinical supervision at all.

Triadic supervision may also be a time-saver for supervisors. Triadic supervision allows supervisors to provide oversight and development to two supervisees at once, an appealing prospect to many agency supervisors who feel the strain of heightened workloads. Additionally, the supervisees who work in the same setting may provide additional guidance and support for one another through collegial consultation between sessions. This is especially useful in an agency setting, where support and additional collegiality can greatly impact one's job satisfaction, likelihood of burnout, and quality of client care.

Additionally, triadic supervision is beneficial in that supervisees enjoy multiple perspectives, the chance to learn vicariously through the other supervisee, and may experience more comfort than during a larger group supervision process (Lawson, Hein, & Stuart, 2009). Triadic supervision is often synergistic; that is, the impact of the three counseling professionals coming together to work collaboratively can be greater than the impact of those individuals working alone or in pairs. The supervisor and supervisees collaborate to initiate ideas, feedback, problem clarity, and subsequent solutions (Oliver, Nelson, & Ybanez, 2010). Finally, research indicates that a sense of community is a core product of triadic supervision (Oliver et al., 2010). The sense of community is reflected in the supervisees' feelings of a true collaborative spirit where others have a deep, meaningful investment in the growth and development of all members and a true concern for each other's clients.

Some may express concern about the effectiveness of triadic supervision when compared to other modalities. One recent study compares supervisees in individual supervision with the experience of supervisees in triadic supervision. This study reveals that supervisees who participated in triadic supervision had a similar experience to supervisees in individual supervision in terms of the supervisory relationship, interpersonal dynamics, and level of satisfaction with supervision (Newgent, Davis, & Farley, 2005).

At times, however, triadic supervision poses some difficulties. Supervisees may experience some internal conflict as they try to make sense of conflicting or opposing feedback they receive from their colleague and their supervisor (Lawson, Hein, & Getz, 2009). Further, the presence of an additional supervisee may inhibit the supervisor from providing necessary critical feedback or fully engaging in the gate keeping functions that are a critical and inherent responsibility of any supervisor (Lawson et al., 2009). Additionally, triadic supervision is prone to the same relationship strains and challenges of any other form of supervision. The supervisor may have a difficult time getting supervisees to challenge one another. The supervisor may find that one supervisee overpowers the session or presents as "needier," thus prompting an imbalance of supervisory attention and focus, perhaps to the detriment of the collegial relationships.

## SUPERVISION STRUCTURE

To help prevent such dynamics, supervisors may find it useful to follow a specific and consistent format for supervision. Following a predictable structure allows the triad to manage time effectively and ensure that both supervisees have the chance to contribute and gain from the process. Supervisors may use a split-focus method where both supervisees share half the focal time in a session, or a single-focus method where one supervisee maintains the attention one session, the other supervisee the next (Lawson et al., 2009).

Lawson et al. (2009) introduce the following format for weekly, one-hour triadic supervision sessions:

- Supervisee One: Brief check-in to follow up on prior week's counseling sessions and to present immediate concerns which are immediately addressed by the triad
- Supervisee Two: Presents an approximately 15-minute video segment that he has preselected to reflect some work that he is concerned about and asks some guiding questions for Supervisee One and the Supervisor to consider
- Supervisee One and Supervisor: Address Supervisee Two's questions and concerns and provide additional feedback
- Supervisee One, Two, and Supervisor: Engage in discussion of any additional items of inquiry the video has aroused

The following week, this order is reversed so that each supervisee brings a video every other week. It is important to note that the researchers who present this model share feedback from some supervisees who engaged in this form of triadic supervision. Several supervisees indicated that they had less time and attention than they otherwise would using this format (Lawson et al., 2009). This was possibly a comparison between this format and individual supervision or perhaps other forms of triadic; when comparing the experience to group supervision, supervisees would likely report that they appreciate having more focal time and attention than they otherwise would.

This format is highly structured and may be most useful for beginning counselors and counselors who are at earlier stages of their development. More sophisticated counselors may appreciate a bit more flexibility in the structure of triadic supervision.

One flexible model of supervision may be useful for supervisees who are more autonomous, professionally mature, and have some ability to conceptualize cases fairly independently. This model involves the supervisor and supervisees beginning with setting a brief collaborative agenda for the session. The supervisor writes down a few keywords presented by each supervisee to represent each item (e.g., "suicidal ideation in males" or "Harry who shoplifts"). The agenda should have no more than three items from each supervisee, and the agreement is that the items lower on the list may not be reached in that session. It is also agreed that any items concerning client harm, threat of harm, mandatory reporting, or legal and ethical issues will always be the top priority. The supervisees then examine the supervisor's list to determine the rank order of the items. Often times, two items will be paired together if they share a common theme or element (such as "suicidal ideation in males" from Supervisee One and "depression with suicidality" from Supervisee Two).

The supervisee with the first agenda item briefly introduces the concern in the form of a brief case conceptualization. For example, this supervisee, Supervisee One, may say, "The client is a 32-year-old male with severe depression for three months. He is now beginning to have increasing thoughts of hopelessness and ideas about dying to escape the depression. There's no history of suicidality, but I'm concerned that I am not acting effectively enough and that he is getting worse. What else should I be doing here?" The supervisor may, at this point, ask Supervisee One to demonstrate a moment of video so that Supervisee Two and the supervisor can get a better feel for the client's presentation. While viewing video (if possible), the supervisor and Supervisee Two will formulate some thoughts and additional questions about what Supervisee One is presenting. Following the brief video, the supervisor and supervisees will discuss Supervisee One's initial inquiry: "What else should I be doing here?" The supervisor's role in this instance is purely facilitative; that is, the supervisor's goal is to help the supervisee find thoughtful resolution to her inquiry through a thorough yet efficient discussion. If the discussion appears to be tangential, the supervisor may help either supervisee stay focused on the relevant information through prompts. For instance, if Supervisee Two asks, "Has he just had a change in medication?" that question may be helpful to the process if tied back to the original inquiry. If the supervisees immediately begin discussing something else, the supervisor may prompt them to return to fully complete the exploration (Supervisor: "Let's revisit this idea of a medication change. What has changed and how might those changes have affected his mental health?"). If a supervisee poses a question that appears off-topic, the supervisor may say,

"(Supervisee), tie that question into the original one, 'What else should I be doing here?'"

This form of triadic supervision is intended to be active and dynamic. The supervisor may engage in spontaneous role plays with one or both of the supervisees. For instance, if a supervisee proposes an idea, the supervisor may say, "That's an idea. Let's role play that and see how it unfolds. (Supervisee One), you play your client, and (Supervisee Two), bring your idea to life. I'll just sit here and see how it plays out." As the supervisees role-play, the supervisor may help them work through worst case scenarios or alternatives by inserting suggestions from time to time (e.g., "And what if he says…what happens next?"). The supervisor can also engage the supervisees in a discussion about how it felt to be the client and/or the client's counselor. This helps develop empathy and a better awareness of the parallel process in action (discussed more in Chapter 9, parallel process).

The supervisor ultimately keeps track of the pace and timing of the session and helps supervisees transition from one agenda item to the next, recognizing that some items are so encompassing that they may address other items incidentally. Each discussion should be closed with the supervisor asking the supervisee whether she got what she intended to out of the discussion, then asking the other supervisee what they got out of the discussion that could be applied to their caseload as well. After a few sessions, the supervisees typically memorize the format and volunteer this information without prompting which helps the sessions move along efficiently. When five minutes remain, the supervisor should inform the supervisees that time is winding down and ensure no last minute issues have arisen. If so, those issues are to be dealt with; otherwise, the session concludes with each supervisee reflecting back to the triad about what lessons or ideas they will take out of triadic supervision and use in the coming week(s).

Another model of triadic supervision is the reflective model of triadic supervision (RMTS), which is based on the reflecting team concept most often practiced in the family therapy field (Stinchfield, Hill, & Kleist, 2007). The RMTS was specifically designed for student trainees but could be adapted to an agency or private setting. This model relies upon the reflective process, when supervisees will experience inner and outer dialogues. Outer dialogues happen when the supervisees are engaged in verbal discourse with one another to actively create meaning. Inner dialogues, as one might imagine, occur internally and refer to the ideas one forms internally while engaging in the outer dialogue (Stinchfield et al., 2007). During RMTS, supervisees attend to both the inner and outer dialogue during supervision. Supervision sessions are 1.5 hours per week and the supervisees have the opportunity to discuss any urgent clinical issues before the video review portion of supervision begins. In the process of showing video and afterward, the supervisee showing video engages in dialogue with the supervisor while the other supervisee observes the conversation. The supervisee who showed video then enters a reflective role where the internal dialogue may be attended to, and the observing supervisee then reflects back verbally thoughts from his or her inner dialogue (Stinchfield et al., 2007). Supervisors who plan to engage in this process can refer to the original work by the researchers for a more thorough description of the model in action and will find it useful to understand more specifically how the supervisees switch roles in the course of the supervision session (Stinchfield et al., 2007).

According to some preliminary research on RMTS, supervisees appear to appreciate the observing role when they can hear feedback and listen without the demands of verbal dialogue. They also seem to like the vicarious learning component of the process and appreciate generalizing ideas and lessons to their own client cases (Stinchfield et al., 2007). Conversely, some supervisees feel isolated or left out of the process when they are in the observer role (Stinchfield et al., 2007) so supervisors may consider forewarning supervisees of that phenomena and may have a discussion about how they will contend with that experience if it occurs.

## COMPOSING THE TRIAD

Triadic supervision may be a delicate balancing act for all parties. By design, there are several relationships to attend to: Supervisees One and Two, Supervisee One and Supervisor, and Supervisee Two and Supervisor. Each relationship must be equally nurtured and honored throughout the process. Incompatibility between the two supervisees can be detrimental to the experience for all (Lawson et al., 2009). The working relationship between the supervisees has proven to be a crucially important aspect of this modality (Lawson et al., 2009). Supervisors should consider the following elements of compatibility as they select their triadic participants:

1.  Developmental level: Supervisees at similar developmental levels are likely to be more compatible. Incompatibility in this domain could lead to frustration and feelings of inequity among the supervisees, especially if one feels as if she has to "pull the other up" or spend time explaining more elementary concepts.

2.  Supervision needs: Supervisees have different primary needs. For example, certain supervisees will require more attention and crisis management because of a high-acuity clientele, while others require more thoughtful, in-depth reflection because of their long-term approach to therapy. Supervisors should ensure that the supervisee's core needs are well matched for each other. They do not need to be exactly the same, but should align well enough that the pace, focus, and style of supervision is a suitable fit for the triad.

3.  Personality match: Supervisors should ensure to the best of their ability that the supervisees seem compatible in terms of personality

features (Hein & Lawson, 2008). Again, they do not need to be exactly alike; however, they should be compatible enough that personality differences do not interfere with the supervisory process. Supervisors will keep in mind that the trust and safety between the members is critical, as is the ability to relax with each another enough to engage in this process (Lawson et al., 2009).

4. Logistics: Supervisors need to ensure that the supervisees are available at the same time and can meet in the preferred location regularly. Further, some supervisees have schedules that change as they progress through their training program or as their work schedule demands. In these instances, it is necessary for the supervisor to exercise forethought in setting up triadic supervision to ensure that logistical arrangements will work for both supervisees now and in the future.

Triadic supervision has benefits and challenges but is proving to be a viable, impactful method of supervision that is cost-effective, time-saving, and can meet the needs of supervisors and supervisees alike.

*Activity: Consult with your state licensing board or supervisee's training program before you suggest triadic supervision.*

*Is there a time or place in your practice or agency where triadic supervision would make sense? What are the benefits and risks of this method of practice for you, the supervisor? What are the benefits and drawbacks for the supervisees?*

## GROUP SUPERVISION

Group supervision allows a combination of mental health professionals to gather with shared intentions: to improve client care, help facilitate skill and conceptual development in one another, and gain valuable insight and support from colleagues. This section discusses the goals, benefits, and drawbacks of group supervision. Next, leader qualities and the format of supervision are examined, followed by a discussion of group supervision dynamics and some conditions that may hinder the group supervision process. The chapter concludes with an assortment of activities that group supervisors may use in their group experiences.

## GOALS OF GROUP SUPERVISION

Edwards and Heshmati (2003) present four primary goals of group supervision. The first goal is to build a community where supervisees can learn while supporting and challenging each other. The second goal is to provide an organizational structure where the group supervisor can earn the supervisee's confidence in his or her leadership ability. Third, group supervision provides a forum where each group member may thoroughly describe his work and voice his needs to group members. The final goal is to create a group where multiple voices can be listened to and fully appreciated (Edwards & Heshmati, 2003). Group supervision, like other forms of supervision, is intended to attend to the clinical and clinically related administrative concerns of the counselor supervisees (Rowell, 2010). Group supervision is similar to individual supervision in that client welfare is the most important concern, followed by supervisee development and growth (Bernard & Goodyear, 2009).

## BENEFITS AND DRAWBACKS OF GROUP SUPERVISION

Group supervision allows supervisees to gain more accurate perceptions of their self and work through feedback from others, plus helps supervisees build empathy and intellectual community (Hayes, 1989). Additionally, supervisees can gain greater creative insight while enjoying a more collaborative, shared sense of authority than what individual supervision typically affords (Altfeld & Bernard, 1997). Further, Ray and Altekruse (2000) assert that group supervision promotes counselor effectiveness and development as well.

On the contrary, group supervision poses a challenge to supervisors in that group supervisors are not able to provide the type of case oversight that individual or triadic supervision allows. Instead, supervisees have the opportunity to present cases infrequently or without the amount of time they may wish to spend to thoroughly explore a situation (Altfeld & Bernard, 1997). Further, group supervision largely depends on the group climate and the skills of the group supervisor to create and maintain an environment conducive to sharing and collaboration (Boethius, Sundin, & Ogren, 2006).

## GROUP SUPERVISOR CHARACTERISTICS

Ideal group supervisors lead groups with a nonauthoritarian style and an accepting, confirming approach (Reichelt & Skjerve, 2001). The group supervisor works diligently to help all members of the group contribute, especially in instances when they share differences in opinions and views (Edwards & Heshmati, 2003). Ideally, the group leader will provide structure, encourage feedback, and help supervisees conceptualize events that occur during the course of the group (DeLucia-Waak & Kalodner, 2005). The leader also strives to keep each member engaged in the process to help each member learn and develop.

Group supervisors need to build and practice expert group leadership qualities for two reasons: first, for the betterment of the group supervision experience as a whole and, second, as a means of role modeling effective group leadership for those supervisees who facilitate counseling groups. Rubel and Kline (2008) reveal three core concepts regarding expert group leadership: experiential influence, leader resources, and leadership process. Experiential influence is the leader's cumulative breadth of experience with groups and the impact of those experiences on their group leadership. Leader resources refers to the prior knowledge base and attitudes the leader uses while leading groups, and leadership process refers to the leader's understanding of group process and how they make decisions while facilitating the group.

Experiential influence refers to the idea that a leader's experience with groups influences that leader's attitude, knowledge, relationships with group members, and conceptualization of group interactions (Rubel & Kline, 2008). Experiential influence may relate to increased confidence and increased knowledge. A leader may find he has more confidence because of his experience as he has learned to trust the group process and the members therein (Rubel & Kline, 2008). Additionally, someone with group experience may have increased knowledge of group dynamics and processes that extends beyond textbook learning into the practical, dynamic processes that one has to experience to fully appreciate.

*Activity: Consider "experiential influence" as you answer the following:*

*What have your experiences in groups been? (Consider therapy groups and supervision groups you have participated in either as a client, counselor, supervisee, or leader.)*

*What did you learn from those groups about how groups develop, collaborate, deal with conflict, and problem solve?*

*Which group dynamics or processes were surprising to you?*

*Did you experience trust in the group setting? What made that trust possible?*

*What did you appreciate about the group experience(s)? What could have made group a better experience for you?*

*Consider the concept "leader resources." What knowledge base and attitudes do you have about group supervision? Be specific. Include your positive and negative thoughts and feelings about group supervision, including any unresolved "grudges."*

*With what prior knowledge are you entering group supervision? What have you learned about how group supervision functions? Do these concepts match what you have learned and read (and are reading about here)?*

*Now consider the "leadership process."*

*Which leader characteristics influenced the group(s) you have been a part of and how? Be specific.*

*What characteristics and skills do you possess that will help you be an effective group supervision leader?*

*Write a brief "job description" for the group supervisor. Explain what you believe the group supervisor's roles and tasks are. Consider how you developed these ideas about what a group supervisor should/should not do? Are there any ideas about group supervisors that you carry that you would rather dismiss? If so, why?*

## GROUP COMPOSITION

Group supervision can feel safe, supportive, and invigorating in many instances, but supervisors should address several conditions while creating the optimal group supervision experience. One important factor is group size. As group size increases, the amount of time each supervisee gets to spend presenting cases decreases (Boethius et al., 2006). However, a group needs enough members to maximize the number of talented minds upon which to draw information and ideas. So, when a supervisor determines the group's composition, he should aim for five supervisees when possible (Boethius et al., 2006). Group supervisors should also take into consideration the accreditation or licensure requirements set forth by a supervisee's training program or state regulatory board. Counselor training programs accredited by CACREP follow CACREP's requirement that no more than ten supervisees are present in group supervision (CACREP, 2009). Additionally, state regulatory boards sometimes require that group supervision for prelicensed counselors is limited to a certain number of supervisees. Further, sometimes there are rules issued by the state licensing boards that specify how much group supervision a prelicensed supervisee can use toward supervision requirements.

*Activity: Check your state licensing board rules about group supervision. How many people can be in the group? Do all members of the group have to be clinical professionals of similar licensure status? How much group supervision may count toward licensure supervision requirements? (Is there a minimum or maximum?)*

## FORMATTING THE GROUP

Edwards and Heshmati (2003) offer a guide for beginning group supervisors which, although intended for family therapy group supervisors, is easily generalizable to most any group supervision experience.

The authors present the phases of a group supervision meeting intended to last for two hours (Edwards & Heshmati, 2003). These phases are as follows:

1. Checking in: The checking in process is approximately ten minutes and allows group members to reconnect and refocus on the tasks at hand. The authors suggest asking group members to

describe a clinical success they have experienced in the past week. (Additional check-in suggestions are provided later on in this chapter.)

2. Case presentation: The case presentation portion of group lasts about 15 minutes as one supervisee gives each group member a written description of a client. Supervisors present a formal written case presentation format that the supervisee fills out ahead of time and copies for each group supervision member. The supervisees each read and review the presentation, then ask clarifying questions as needed.

3. Questions for the audience: This 30-minute portion of the group is when the presenting supervisee's colleagues ask questions that help clarify, develop, and further deepen the supervisee's conceptualization and comprehension of the counseling work. The questions may elicit further thinking about contextual factors, ethical dilemmas, countertransferential responses, and other features that were not initially clear to the presenting supervisee (Edwards & Hasmati, 2003).

4. Video review: The video review process, also 30 minutes, relies upon the preparatory work of one of the initial supervisee's colleagues who is designated the "commentator." That is, a colleague is selected ahead of time to view the presenting supervisee's video and will decide upon the segment to show the group. The commentator explains to the group the rationale for selecting that portion of the video, then shows the video to the group.

5. Commentator reflections: The commentator then engages in a 10-minute process where he presents his feedback to the supervisee (this feedback was prepared as he previewed the video prior to supervision). First, positive features of the counselor's work are highlighted. Next, concerning aspects of the work are raised. Lastly, the commentator presents suggestions for future work. The presenter then responds to the commentator and they have a brief discussion about the feedback.

6. Audience reflections: This segment lasts about 25 minutes and involves the group members all presenting their views in a similar format: strengths, weaknesses, and future directions. Edwards and Hasmati (2003) warn supervisors to be especially active during this phase so that the feedback is useful and not overly aggressive or critical. The supervisor should help keep the supervisee from feeling attacked or inundated with excessive information.

7. Postsupervision supervisor reflections: The supervisor provides the supervisee with a written reflection on what transpired in supervision. The supervisor summarizes the initial question the supervisee posed to the group, the suggestions and feedback that were shared, and impressions of the supervisee's strengths and plans to move forward. The supervisor shares this letter with the supervisee as soon as possible after the group session.

The authors of this format (Edwards & Hasmati, 2003) invite readers to modify the format to meet their contextual needs. In some cases, this format may be too lengthy or involve more preparation than what an agency counselor and supervisor can manage regularly. So, agency supervisors may shorten the length of the group to 90 minutes, perhaps, or may reduce the preparation work by eliminating supervisee or the commentator's written components and asking for a verbal report instead. The purpose here is to create a well-structured, predictable group supervision format that is clearly clinical in nature and allows supervisees a chance to fulfill the many intentions of effective group supervision.

Another quite popular form of group supervision is Borders' (1991) Structured Peer Group Format (SPGF). The author indicates that the group meets weekly or biweekly for 1.5–3 hours and is typically a small group of three to six counselors and one trained supervisor. The sequence of activities for each group session are as follows:

- A counselor asks the group for feedback about a specific client or video segment. The feedback is specific to the counselor's performance.
- The other counselor supervisees are given duties or roles to engage in as they review the video. These include observing counselor or client nonverbal communication; observing a specific counseling skill or intervention; assuming the counselor, client, or other significant person's role; viewing the segment from a certain theoretical stance; or creating a metaphor for the client, counselor, or the counseling process as a whole.
- The video segment is presented.
- The colleagues provide feedback in accordance with the roles or duties described earlier. The initial question posed by the counselor should inform and guide this feedback.
- The group supervisor is the moderator and process observer and facilitates ongoing discussion and reflection.
- The group supervisor recaps the discussion with a summary statement and asks the presenting supervisee whether the initial inquiry was fully satisfied.

Borders' method can also be adapted for use in individual and triadic supervision and allows every supervisee to engage actively and thoughtfully in the supervision process. The flexibility and elasticity of this format make it desirable for use in a number of settings, with counselors of all developmental levels.

*Activity: Design your supervision group by responding to the following questions. If you are initiating a group or advocating for a group supervision experience, your responses to these questions can be written as a narrative group proposal.*

*How many participants will you have in your group? Be certain to address group number limitations that apply to prelicensed and in-training supervisees.*

*How will group membership be determined? What are the inclusion and exclusion factors that you will examine? (Consider developmental factors and logistical factors here.)*

*How will you determine the day/time of your group? (Remember, group day and time should be consistent.)*

*How frequently does the group meet? Weekly or every other week?*

*How long will the group last? (60/90/120 minutes?)*

*What is your intention in providing the group supervision experience?*

*The structure of the group: How will you format your group? How will you get group members reintroduced and refocused when they arrive? How will you ensure they have time to mentally "wrap up" before they leave? What is the process like?*

*What preparatory work is expected of each group member?*

*What will you do when a group member is absent?*

*What are your supervision group rules/guidelines? How will the group's safety be established and maintained?*

*How will you ensure your supervisees follow through on suggestions made by the group, especially in higher-risk situations or with legal and ethical dilemmas?*

*How will you, as supervisor, manage group conflict?*

*How will you, as supervisor, create professional safety?*

## BRINGING THE GROUP INTO ACTION

Counselors and supervisors alike readily acknowledge that without emotional and psychological safety, groups cannot function well (Rowell, 2010). Group supervisors hold a lot of power to get the group started in a positive, impactful manner (Rowell, 2010). To effectively do so, supervisors should carefully consider how they will introduce the group members to one another and introduce the group members to the group supervision process itself. Supervisors may be tempted to skip this step if group supervisees have already had experiences in group supervision or if the supervisor is stepping into an already-formed group. However, the supervisees need to be acclimated to the supervision process as it will now occur, not as they have experienced it in the past. The key differences are the leader and, possibly, the format. Supervisees should be invited to consider their past experiences in group supervision and groups in general. Encourage them to share elements of their experiences with the current group to influence the initial shaping of the group and to further understand one another's history with group counseling and/or supervision, for better or worse.

The following "First Group Session Checklist" can serve as an agenda for group supervisors to follow during the first group meeting. The supervisor should inform members ahead of time that the first group is largely administrative in nature and that they should not expect a lot of clinical process in the first meeting. This forewarning gives supervisees some comfort in knowing what to expect and helps avoid the disappointment that would occur if a member expects to process some clinical situations but does not have the chance to do so.

First session checklist: These are some items to cover in the first group meeting. It includes any additional items that are important to you in your specific work setting.

- Introduce members to each other through a nonthreatening introductory activity. If they already know each other, have them reintroduce in a novel way (see "group exercises" for ideas).
- Describe the intention of group supervision.
- Describe the format of group and explain how this format will help fulfill the intentions of the group.
- Explain the roles of the supervisor and supervisees.
- Discuss and explain safety-making in the group so participants know how safety is created and maintained.
- Provide direction about how to provide feedback.
- Lead a discussion about how conflict will be handled. Reassure supervisees that you will step in as actively as needed to maintain safety and, in time, they will do the same.
- Address any concerns or questions supervisees have.

Rowell (2010) cautions supervisors against treating the first session discussion of rules and procedures as mundane. Instead, supervisors shall fully engage and invest themselves into the necessary "setup" work as it is crucially important in influencing the future safety and effectiveness of the group experience. While many members are eager to engage in client-centered work, supervisors should remind supervisees that the relationship is central to an impactful and positive group experience. So, the foundational "business-type" items actually assist the supervisor in beginning to fulfill the three components of a positive supervisory working alliance described initially by Bordin (1979) and in Chapter 6 of this text: agreement on the goals, agreed-upon tasks and methods to reach those goals, and a bond between the involved parties. In this case, group members may not fully buy into the methods the supervisor is introducing, but they will have the chance to understand the rationale and have any questions answered before the engagement phase of the group process begins.

## ENGAGING THE MEMBERS

It is natural and expected for some group members to feel hesitant when they are new to the group supervision experience, have had bad experiences in groups, or feel anxious about the activities that will happen in group. These group members may not express that hesitation, or it may be quite obvious through verbal or nonverbal cues. Group supervisors should allow these members time to gain comfort with the group and the group process; however, these members should not be allowed total disengagement. Instead, all members are drawn to action from the initial group forward, beginning with the check-in activity.

The group check-in serves three key functions. First, the check-in reorients the members to the task at hand. Second, the check-in invites participation from members who may otherwise not contribute verbally. Third, the check-in allows the supervisees a chance to reconnect with one another and re-engage in their collegial relationship.

Group supervisors may conduct their check-in process in a number of ways. The group supervisor may elect to lead the check-in process in a different way every session, or he may introduce a check-in activity that will remain standard from session to session. The group supervisor may also decide to defer leadership to the group after the first week or two through the "Filling the Toolbox" activity.

"Filling the Toolbox" involves the group supervisor instructing the group members to come prepared each session with a group check-in activity. At the beginning of group, the supervisor asks which supervisee is prepared to do the check-in activity. Each member must facilitate one check-in before anyone gets a second chance (and the supervisor should keep a list to track this). If no one volunteers, the supervisor will select a member. If the member is unprepared, he or she will use their best spontaneity skills and will come up with a check-in on the spot or can elicit help from the rest of the group.

Supervisees are instructed that their check-in activity must meet the following criteria: it can be adapted for use in group counseling, it can be fully completed within 10 minutes, and it is different from check-ins that have been used in prior groups. These criteria allow supervisees to build their repertoire of available check-in tools that they can use when they are conducting counseling groups and help them share leadership responsibilities with the group supervisor. Further, it gives them practice at facilitating group check-ins while providing them with the chance to set the tone for the day's group. Finally, supervisees get to personalize the group experience by sharing a technique that reflects their professional or personal passion.

During the check-in process, group supervisees are instructed to remove all distractions and pay exquisite attention to the person checking in, the way they would pay attention to a client. This encourages reconnection and reminds supervisees that they are in group as counselors (not clients), so will utilize their professional counseling skills during the personal process of checking in. This brief role clarification statement seems rather insignificant, perhaps, but actually provides some role clarity that allows a supervisee to reorient themselves to their role in the group supervision experience.

The supervisees should be encouraged to use the group as a time to experiment, get creative, and have fun. If an activity flops, it is better to learn that in a safe setting than with clients. Further, members should be encouraged to make note of the activities that they really like so that they can use similar activities when they are facilitating group counseling. Since even "fun" activities typically elicit interesting material, supervisors should resist any urges to treat check-in time as supervision process time. Supervisees should be allowed to check in fully before any process work begins.

Following is a list of group supervision check-in activities that range from the commonly encountered "ABC" activity to the more creative "I Am..." activity.

- The ABC activity: Counselors are instructed to describe how they are feeling about their clinical work in terms of Affect, Behavior, and Cognition. Another variation is to instruct the counselors to describe how they are doing today in terms of their affect, behavior, and cognitions.
- The Hope Circle: Counselors are instructed to express a hope they have for one client in particular. The counselor can be as specific or general as he wishes. After all counselors have expressed their hope for the client, each member shares a hope they have for the supervision group today as it relates to that particular client. (The instructions should be given fully in advance so that supervisees can consider the activity on both levels: the client–counselor level and the counselor–supervision group level.) Not surprisingly, counselors will almost always select a client with whom they are struggling and planned to discuss in supervision anyhow.
- The "Excitement/Dread" activity: Counselors are invited to share one thing they are excited about in their work and one thing they experience dread about. The facilitator reminds the counselors that there will not be any judgment and that they should be truthful with their answers. Supervisees will often find commonalities in what they share and often enjoy the bonding that comes with that. It is also fairly typical for a supervisee to share that they dread seeing a particular client. There are often some feelings accompanying this revelation, and it is appropriate at the conclusion of the check-in for the supervisor to invite the supervisee, if he or she wishes, to share further about this client relationship as part of the supervision process.
- The "Talent Show" activity: There are two versions of this activity, personal and professional. The personal version involves supervisees

sharing or demonstrating a talent that is not work-related. They may demonstrate or verbally describe. This activity is especially useful early in group to help supervisees get to know each other more fully and is also helpful with supervisees who are demonstrating signs of burn out, as it typically energizes the group and allows some fun and laughter. The professional version is when supervisees briefly describe something they are especially skilled at clinically. This is useful when certain members of the group seem less confident in their work and are hesitant to provide feedback to others who they view as more competent.

- The "Resident Specialist" activity: The supervisees are instructed to select a topic or technique that they feel especially skilled at and are hereafter going to be the "resident specialist" regarding that topic. They should explain what the specialty is, how they acquire such knowledge or skill, and how they may contribute this knowledge and skill to the group in the future. While some more seasoned supervisees will naturally select their specialty niche, newer counselors will often have difficulty viewing themselves as "expert" in any area. The supervisor or facilitator reminds the group that this is a "specialist" role, not an "expert" one, so the specialist does not have to know everything about that specialty. Instead, the specialist can be counted on to help the counselor in need find the answers.

For example, a supervisee might say "I took a workshop on working with clients with complex grief. I'm not really an expert in it, but I have always been interested in helping people realize their grief is normal. So, I think I will be the grief specialist and you all can check with me if you want me to share some of the great books I've come across about grief and grief work."

- It is helpful for the facilitator to share first so that the supervisees understand the structure of their response.
- The "Empty Chair" activity: This activity involves each counselor "speaking" to a client who is represented by an empty chair or a doll that is passed around the supervision group. (Note: the doll often adds humor to the situation, which is useful in some groups; other groups will benefit from a more serious approach of an empty chair; either approach tends to yield the same results). The counselor is instructed to tell the client about something he or she did recently that caused a strong feeling in the counselor. The counselor should conclude with a statement that begins with the words "I want…"

For example, a supervisee might say, "You really frustrated me this week! You keep saying you're going to leave your partner but then you keep going back! Why do you keep doing that? We spent another entire session and you just keep saying the same things! I want you to just leave your partner already!"

- Oftentimes, the counselor and other supervisees will laugh at the conclusion of the "I want..." statement. Counselors often recognize their own agenda for the client and tend to experience their internal thoughts differently once stated aloud in front of the group. Counselors will often want to process or discuss whatever they just spoke of. It is often most helpful for everyone to get a chance to participate before additional process time is allowed. Depending on the typical format of the group, supervisors may want to build the group's agenda out of this activity or may simply assign supervisees to keep thinking about their experience during check-in as the group unfolds. Inevitably, the supervisees will weave their newfound insight into that session's discussion.
- Sentence Stems: Just as the prior activity concludes with a sentence stem ("I want..."), facilitators can use sentence stems to address a number of different dynamics. One simple check-in is to provide the supervisees with a sentence stem and ask them to complete the statement. The stem may be as simple as "Today I feel..." or may be more complex, such as "I often experience countertransference when...." The facilitator should provide a time allotment to each group member and may ask members to elaborate with simple prompts (e.g., "say more") so that members are prompted to think and explore further.
- The "I Am..." activity: Counselors are given a sheet of paper and markers or crayons and are instructed to spend two minutes drawing symbols or pictures of their ideal counselor self. Each member then has a moment or two to describe to the group his "ideal counselor self" to the group. (The instructions are purposefully vague to allow interpretation in any way one wishes.) Members may elect to share their pictures if they like. The overall intent is to help members remember who they are striving to become as professionals (or who they have become). This activity is especially useful with supervisees who have forgotten to focus on their own skill development as they feel pulled to focus exclusively on client concerns.

## PROBLEMS IN GROUP SUPERVISION

Group supervision may be a positively impactful experience for the supervisor, the supervisees, and the clients. However, multiple supervisees with multiple perspectives, personalities, and presentation styles inevitably lead to difficulties from time to time. Group supervisors should be keenly aware of some of the more typical difficulties encountered in group supervision so that they can address these issues as they arise or, in some cases, preventatively. Enyedy and colleagues (2003) present a number of "hindering phenomena" that occur in group supervision. These elements may block group process and progress so should be considered carefully by group supervisors.

First, between-member problems may occur (Enyedy, 2003). As the name implies, these are problems that occur between group members. Supervisors may notice that negative supervisee behaviors occur (in this case, general complaints about how other group members act or behave), or they may notice that members have personal reactions to negative behaviors.

Next, Enyedy and colleagues found the most prominent cluster of hindrances focus on problems with supervisors. Problems with supervisors may include negative supervisor behaviors, supervisor's lack of experience, and supervisor's lack of clinical focus.

Supervisee anxiety and other negative affect is the next category, and includes supervisee experiences of emotions deemed negative by the supervisee, including fear, isolation, anxiousness, and similar feelings. While these may be considered typical of any supervision experience, it might be worthwhile to help supervisees understand the normalcy of such responses (similar to helping a client recognize that counseling will not typically feel good when the hard work is taking place).

Finally, poor group time management can hinder the supervision group. The group supervisor in these instances may lack effective organization skills or may not have had appropriate logistical components in place (such as an appropriate number of group members or a format for the group that allows for maximum participation).

The researchers who reveal the aforementioned hindrances (Enyedyl, 2003) encourage group supervisors to set a group agenda and enforce time limits whilst containing threats to group cohesion (such as one group member dominating the group or members providing excessive critical feedback without appropriate amounts of support).

*Activity: What, in your opinion, makes group supervision a beneficial experience? Write down everything you can think of.*

*Consider your own experiences in group supervision. What made the group effective? Ineffective? Be as specific as you can about what contributed to the effectiveness of the group.*

*How will you use this information to create a most beneficial group experience? What would you like to replicate from prior group experiences? What would you like to be certain to avoid? How will you accomplish that?*

# ELEVEN

# Creativity in Supervision

Creativity is an essential and foundational feature of the counseling profession (Gladding & Henderson, 2000) yet is easily overlooked in clinical supervision. Creativity in supervision practice, admittedly, often involves time, forethought, and planning, yet may serve a vital facilitative function. Creative practices help supervisors and supervisees from becoming stagnant or overly routine in their practice. While some amount of routine and predictability is useful in creating structure and psychological safety, supervisors should help supervisees avoid routine, homogenous thinking, conceptualizing, and problem solving in their work. Supervisors know that they should employ alternative methods when their supervisees engage in supervision discussions that are so routine that either member of the dyad can predict the forthcoming words or solutions. Further, supervisors should infuse creativity when either member of the dyad feels bored, uninspired, "stuck" or stagnant, or is experiencing overly narrow or simplistic ways of approaching any given situation. Creativity in supervision may take many forms and involves various levels of complexity. Some creative approaches involve no materials, no technology, and little or no preparation. Other techniques involve some materials or technological equipment, and still others require more complex materials and/or technology. This chapter examines several creative techniques for use in supervision, including the use of metaphor, drama, literature, and various forms of media and technology. The chapter begins, however, with an examination of the SCAMPER model of creativity as it relates to supervision practice.

## THE SCAMPER MODEL OF CREATIVITY

The SCAMPER model, originally described by Eberle (1971), is a model of creativity intended to spark the imaginative spirit and promote change in relationships and systems (Gladding & Henderson, 2000). Recently, this model has been provided in the family therapy literature to assist family therapists in employing creativity in their therapeutic encounters (Gladding &

Henderson, 2000). However, this model will now be adapted and applied to the supervision process with the same intent: to approach problems and relationships with creativity for the betterment of client care and service.

The acronym SCAMPER stands for Substitute, Combine, Adapt or alter, Modify or magnify, Put to other uses, Eliminate or minimize, and Reverse or rearrange. *Substitution* involves bringing in words or mental images that adjust the supervisee's conceptualization or impression of a particular incident or client. For instance, the supervisee may describe a client as "trying to avoid therapy." The supervisor may substitute the word "painful experiences" for "therapy" so that the supervisee considers the client's apparent avoidance to be a sensible, self-protective measure rather than a deviant or otherwise concerning act.

*Combine* refers to bringing the interrelated parties together with a common focus so that the efforts are not fragmented or fractured. In the case of supervision, this means that the supervisor and supervisee are aligned in their goals with regards to supervision as a whole and in respect to any particular case. By extension, this also means that the supervisor is focused on helping the supervisee align his or her intentions with the desires and wishes of his client(s). In some cases, there may be a team of professionals involved in a particular case. When considering *combining* in the supervision context, this may mean that the supervisor is assisting the supervisee in coordinating the care efforts of multiple helpers, which often involves a creative and collaborative approach if it is to happen effectively.

*Adapt or alter* refers to the process of changing one's approach or style from a fixed, homeostatic stance to one of flexibility and adjustment. In the case of clinical supervision, the supervisor and supervisee become flexible and adaptable to examining things differently and allowing processes outside of the norm to occur. The supervisory dyad changes their practice to meet unique demands rather than working steadily to maintain homeostatic functioning at a potentially high cost to deepening understanding or problem-solving ability.

*Modify or magnify* refers to the amplified attention given to positive events and occurrences, and the modifications made to improve occurrences that are not as satisfactory given the intended outcome. This is significant in the supervision experience as supervisors often feel discouraged or frustrated when a supervisee appears to be struggling in particular domains of competence or skill. The supervisor may typify that supervisee as an "impulsive problem-solver" or "poor communicator" and may fail to see the exceptions to that conceptualization. Similarly, the supervisee engages in a similar process with his clients. The supervisor, instead, will role model a complete and complex understanding of the desirable behaviors in relation to the intended outcomes, and will magnify those behaviors when they occur. For example, a supervisor notices that a supervisee who is typically impulsive or thoughtless in session is explaining his intention in providing a client with some feedback. The supervisor recognizes that the supervisee acted with intention; therefore, the supervisee engaged in a thoughtful process of considering what he would say before saying it aloud. The supervisor highlights this by saying, "You really considered both your words and the intended effect your words would have. That seems to be a very thoughtful and intentional process, exactly what is expected at this level of professionalism." Further modification may be added in the near future through feedback such as, "Earlier, I commented on your commendable thought process, when you clearly considered the therapeutic intention of your intervention. I wonder how that same process might have improved the interaction you're now describing."

*Put to other uses* refers to putting personal or professional traits or characteristics to other use. For instance, the supervisee who typically "hijacks" a group supervision with a flurry of questions may be less interruptive and more facilitative if his curiosity and investment in the process is put to another use. That is, instead of leaving him to questions that are seemingly scattered and relentless throughout the group process, the group supervisor may ask him to ask questions when the group has run out of ways to examine a situation. The supervisee's curiosity and desire to learn more will be satisfied, and the questions that were perhaps annoying to other group members begin to serve a facilitative purpose in that they further deepen a discussion that would otherwise be winding down.

*Eliminating or minimizing* refers to the act of balancing negative characteristics and occurrences with positive ones. In supervision, this can be as simple as having a supervisee consider what he or she did effectively in the midst of a session that felt like a "total disaster." For instance, a supervisee may present that her work with a client felt clumsy, ineffective, and perhaps even harmful. However, the client at the end of session expressed gratitude and scheduled an appointment for early in the following week, stating, "I look forward to next time." While the supervisee's concerns about her performance will be attended to in great detail, the supervisee will also be instructed to examine why the client seemed to appreciate the session and eagerly anticipates the next one, despite the counselor's shortcomings.

Finally, *reversing or rearranging* refers to the rigid relationship patterns that supervisors and supervisees, and supervisees and their clients may experience, especially when the relationship is not functioning well. Reversal simply means doing the opposite of what has been happening (Gladding & Henderson, 2000). If a supervisor finds herself continually criticizing or expressing concern in a particular manner that the supervisee (or supervisor) does not find effective, the supervisor will simply try to engage in a new way of interacting that may yield more favorable results. Similarly, the supervisee is encouraged to interact with clients or conceptualize cases in a way other than what currently occurs when that way is found to be ineffective. For example, if a supervisee explains that "this is just the way I do therapy with my clients," he may be encouraged to consider doing the opposite or trying a different approach for a discrete period of time to see what the impact is. He will likely find that his willingness to drop the rigid stance is rewarded by a favorable outcome.

The SCAMPER model is simply a launching point for supervisors to consider when engaging creative and flexible approaches in their practice. In supervision, as in counseling, creativity is merely a way to engage in new actions in the hopes of creating favorable or more favorable outcomes. SCAMPER provides a framework in which a supervisor may consider the flexible versus inflexible, routine versus innovative, and fixed versus expansive features of the supervision experience.

Simply thinking differently and expansively about one's practice and acting in accordance with that new thinking is a creative act that requires nothing other than one's willingness. Many creative techniques, similarly, involve just the willingness of the participants. In the next section, creative approaches to supervision are discussed. Each requires no additional technology equipment nor materials other than the participants.

## NO-TECH CREATIVITY: TECHNIQUES USING NO EQUIPMENT NOR MATERIALS

### Metaphor

Several notable theorists in the counseling profession, including Sigmund Freud, Rollo May, Carl Jung, and Milton Erikson, have emphasized the use of metaphor in the therapeutic setting (Guiffrida, Jordan, Saiz, & Barnes, 2007). More recently, the use of metaphor has been explored as a viable and valuable tool in the supervision setting as well (e.g., Bernard & Goodyear, 1998; Guiffrida et al., 2007). *Metaphor*, in this case, refers to a supervisor using seemingly unrelated material as a substitute for directly addressing the actual material of focus or concern. For instance, the supervisor may liken a supervisee's experience to that of a mythical figure or movie character, or may draw comparisons between the supervisee's experience and common phenomenon. For instance, a supervisee may feel depleted and is having signs of burn out, but is very resistant to the idea that she may be susceptible to such an experience. The supervisor may express that the supervisee reminds her of someone happy to be travelling through the desert but physically incapable of continuing without the appropriate nourishment and respite from the sun. The supervisee is then free to explore avenues of respite and replenishment without having to acknowledge the dreaded "burn out" which, for her, is loaded with guilt and self-judgment. Metaphor, in fact, is known to be especially helpful at helping work with client resistance (Lyddon, Clay, & Sparks, 2001); likewise, it has a similar effect on supervisee resistance.

Supervisors may find the use of metaphor particularly beneficial when helping counselors understand and accept the developmental process of becoming a counselor (Guiffrida et al., 2007). Supervisees may be encouraged to view their development in terms of layers of the atmosphere, seedlings growing into full plants, infants growing into maturity, and the like. Supervisors may elect to use metaphors that make sense given their supervisees, unique interests and personality features; a supervisee who is an avid reader may appreciate metaphor that is steeped in literary reference, while a supervisee who is a musician may appreciate a metaphor involving the multiple layers and levels of sound and connection that music has on its listeners. For instance, a supervisor may observe that "the session was structured like a crescendo but the music suddenly stopped without warning" to describe the supervisee's sense that he and the client were working diligently toward an outcome that did not happen, much to the supervisee's dismay.

*Activity: Consider a situation you have encountered recently in your supervision or clinical practice in which you felt uncertain or "stuck," or noticed that dynamic in another person. Create a metaphor for that particular situation. The metaphor may be completely unrelated to the situation, but should ideally help you or another person view the situation in a different or more expansive way. Next, consider your own experience with the use of metaphor in supervision or as a counseling trainee. What kinds of metaphors were you exposed to or have you heard repeatedly in your career? What impact have these metaphors had on your thoughts or beliefs about yourself or your work? (For instance, do you consider yourself a flower that is starting to bloom because of the numerous "seeds of learning" that have been planted since your early training days?)*

## Role Playing

"Role play" refers to the supervisee (or supervisor) espousing the mannerisms, personality, contextual factors, and circumstances of another person, often a client, while another supervisee or supervisor "plays" the counselor (e.g., Browning, Collins, & Nelson, 2005). While role playing is a common activity in counselor training and educational settings (Smith, 2009), many supervisees would rather do most anything else to avoid the feelings of awkwardness or silliness that can accompany such a task. Some supervisors and counselor educators quickly learn that few words evoke more resistance and giddiness in counselor supervisees than the words "role play." One way to avoid such a reaction to the mere suggestion is to simply not suggest the role play. That is, weave role playing into the supervision session spontaneously, at a time when the supervisee is greatly interested in learning about how something might transpire. For instance, if a supervisee wonders aloud how a particular intervention will be received by a client, the supervisor may say, "I'm not sure how he will take it. Let's try it out. You be him and I'll be you. Say whatever you fear he will say. Give me worst case scenario and let's see how it goes." The supervisory dyad is now in a role play without time for nervous anticipation or awkwardness. Further, the supervisee has a chance to approach the problem from the client's perspective and may end up with a greater empathic understanding of the client's circumstance. If the supervisee plays the client in a hostile manner, the supervisor may ask the supervisee what was needed to reduce the hostility. The supervisee quite naturally moves to introspection and insight while recognizing that the client needs validation, respect, acceptance, or simply a better listener. The supervisee now identifies her responsibility in the process, and the supervisor may ask her to use her new insight to play the scene over again, this time as her counselor self (while the supervisor "plays" the client).

Further, it is sometimes useful to have the supervisee switch roles with the supervisor. Again, this is usually well received when it is spontaneous and the supervisor dives in without time for nervous anticipation. The supervisor asks the supervisee to "play supervisor," and the supervisor becomes the supervisee. This is especially useful when the supervisee appears somewhat resistant or hesitant to find brainstorm for solutions or think expansively about a situation, perhaps due to a lack of efficacy or energy. Additionally, this is useful when a supervisee is attached to a solution or conceptualization that may not be useful but is having difficulty thinking expansively. The supervisor initiates the role playing by saying something such as, "You know, I'd like to get a feel for your position here. Let me role play you for a bit, and you be me, and let's see what comes of it." The supervisor, while playing the supervisee, then presents a situation in a manner similar to the supervisee's presentation. While this is a role play, the supervisor is not "playing" or acting, per se. The supervisor presents authentically and is cautious not to mimic or imitate any of the supervisees' mannerisms or speech. The supervisee (playing the supervisor) will typically respond to the supervisor's initial presentation with only a mild amount of commitment. However, the supervisor (playing the supervisee) will continue on with conversation and exploration. After a short while, the supervisee (playing "supervisor") typically becomes energetically involved in the conversation as her investment to the client (and perhaps her prior solution) will motivate her interest in the conversation. The supervisor and supervisee continue to discuss possible solutions or other ways of thinking until the conversation runs its course or until the dyad naturally reverts into their typical roles. At this point, the actual supervisor will ask the supervisee what she gained from the role play. Most times, a supervisee will describe a new way of thinking or new ideas. Oftentimes, the supervisor will also gain a new understanding of a phenomena or concept while engaging in the role play. The supervisor may decide to share that with the supervisee, especially if the supervisor has developed a new empathic understanding of the supervisee's plight. For instance, the supervisor may say, "At first, my intention was to help you think about more ideas here about how to deal with this client. However, during the role play,

I realized how incredibly difficult it is to come up with solutions for this client. I really felt helpless and realized that this client would shoot down all my ideas. I felt discouraged from even trying. You, as the counselor, are really in a tough spot here! I think I get it now."

*Activity: Consider your own reaction or response as you initially read the words "role playing." What was your reaction? Was it positive or negative? Do you experience any avoidance when you think of role playing? If so, why? (Be specific and deconstruct your personal reasons for not wanting to role play). When might you have benefitted from role play as a supervisee?*

## Psychodrama

Psychodrama expands on the concept of simple role playing through a structured, complex experiential approach. Psychodrama refers to utilizing dramatic techniques to explore the "truth" (Moreno, 1946) and most often occurs in a group setting, such as with a group of clients. In supervision, psychodrama may be used to help a supervisee gain a clearer or more expansive understanding of multiple realities and perspectives and may be used with great impact in triadic, or, most optimally, group supervision. Psychodrama involves the reenactment of particular situations, typically, situations of concern to the clinician, and then the active exploration of potential solutions and approaches to resolve those situations (Hinkle, 2008). There are several steps and concepts that need to be understood as one engages in psychodrama techniques. Foremost is the warm-up time (Hinkle, 2008), that is when the supervisees (and supervisor) engage in a case presentation process; supervisors may decide which case will be brought to psychodramatic exploration at this time or the group can decide together through volunteerism or group consensus.

Each psychodramatic event involves a protagonist who is the primary character (in this case, either the client or the supervisee) of concern or interest (Leveton, 2001). The supervisees, including this main character, engage in an enactment. An enactment is a dramatic re-creation of a past or current event, or even a future event (Hinkle, 2008). Through the actions and discussion involved in this re-creation, the supervisee can gain new perspective, insight, or understanding of his original concern or presenting issue. The additional supervisee(s) each play an auxiliary ego. The auxiliary ego is an extension of both the supervisee (and his experience of the situation) and is a professional peer who serves as a guide who moves the protagonist supervisee toward expansive thinking and deepening understanding. Auxiliary egos may use techniques such as mirroring, or mimic the protagonist in a way that draws awareness to their nonverbal or subconscious behaviors, or role reversal where two members of the drama reverse roles with each other for demonstration purposes (Hinkle, 2008). The group may also engage in replaying a scene, which allows the protagonist supervisee to experience the potential solutions or future interactions through enactments repeated until the major possibilities are exhausted (Hinkle, 2008).

The earlier literature on psychodrama is primarily focused on its use in therapy (e.g., Moreno, 1946); however, psychodrama and its core techniques may be adapted to add spontaneity and creativity to triadic or group supervision. Psychodrama may be especially useful at times when supervisees are becoming repetitive in their proposed solutions and approaches, or when a supervisor finds it difficult to keep multiple supervisees fully engaged in the supervision process at once. Psychodrama, by nature, requires the involvement of all supervisees, so disengagement and avoidance is difficult at best. Psychodrama in supervision may be especially useful when issues of parallel process or other countertransference responses arise (Hinkle, 2008). Primarily, the supervisor uses psychodrama to add creative challenge to a supervision experience, which is intended to elicit new, insightful responses and discoveries by the participants.

## LOW-TECH CREATIVITY: TECHNIQUES USING SIMPLE TECHNICAL EQUIPMENT AND/OR SIMPLE MATERIALS

### Bibliosupervision

*Bibliosupervision* is a supervision technique that involves a supervisor selecting a particular story, often a fictional children's story, that corresponds to an identified need in the supervisee (Graham, 2007; Graham & Pehrsson, 2009). The supervisee and supervisor, in the course of a single supervision session, read the piece of literature together (or come prepared to discuss the story if it was preassigned). The supervisory dyad then discuss the story in relation to issues or concerns that arise in the supervisee's experience or caseload. The supervisor may ask questions such as "What themes in this story felt familiar to you?" or "What piece of this story resonated the most with you as you consider your work this week?" The intention is that the literary piece serves a facilitative function in helping the supervisee build efficacy, deepen their understanding of various concepts, and experience a greater depth of understanding of their own work and the experience of others (Graham, 2007).

Supervisors should consider the following when deciding which piece of literature to select: current themes that are emerging for the supervisee in his or her work, the specific goals of the supervision experience, the supervisee's developmental level, and how the material itself relates to counselor development (Graham & Pehrsson, 2009). Some stories that have been useful in bibliosupervision include *The Giving Tree* (Silverstein, 1964), *Stellaluna* (Cannon, 1993), *Oh, the Places You'll Go* (Seuss, 1990), and *Leo the Late Bloomer*

(Kraus, 1971), and each deals with issues specific to counselor development such as trust in oneself, recognition of differences, support, risk taking, validation, and the importance of relationships (Graham & Pehrsson, 2009).

## Metaphoric Drawing and Art

Metaphoric drawing involves a supervisor requesting that a supervisee draw a picture or create a collage that depicts their conceptualization of a client or a specific situation, along with a depiction of how they believe the situation with that client will unfold (e.g., Giuffrida et al., 2007). Supervisees then use the drawing as the launch pad for a discussion with the supervisor or peer supervisees if in a triadic or group setting.

Supervisors, when asking a supervisee to create art or use drawing, should bear in mind that many supervisees become highly anxious or timid about sharing artwork, especially in a group setting with several peers. Supervisors may wish to ask supervisees to use their nondominant hand to create the art, which automatically "allows" an imperfection of sorts and tends to reduce the performance concerns associated with doing art in a professional situation. Supervisors may also purposefully provide limited or childish supplies, again to ease the tension associated with an "acceptable" outcome. For instance, a supervisor may ask supervisees to draw their "ideal counselor self" using only the materials in front of them, and the materials are fluorescent green paper and purple crayons. Typically, the supervisees will giggle as they recognize that the goal is not to create passable art, but instead to create for the sake of the process that accompanies such creation. Finally, supervisors may invite supervisees to draw and then not share the art. Oftentimes, the supervisees will end up sharing the art although they may have initially stated that they would not. The momentum of the process takes over and the supervisees often dismiss their initial guard as they become immersed in the exploration process.

Supervisors may ask their supervisees to draw or create art using a variety of modalities and tools. Supervisees may enjoy using colored chalk on a chalkboard to depict relationships or situations; others like to use crayons or clay. The following ideas involve art media and may be useful to incorporate when a creative avenue is needed to alleviate overly "fixed" thinking, a sense of being stuck or helpless, feelings of boredom or burnout, or a sense of ineffectiveness when using only verbal discussion to work through a situation:

1. Clay sculptures: The supervisee selects playdoh or clay and is instructed to start softening it while describing a client. Once the supervisee reaches the "sticking point" in describing the case, the supervisor will instruct the supervisee to use the clay to sculpt an item of significance to the situation. For instance, the supervisor may

ask the supervisee to sculpt the animal that reminds him most of his client in that session, or, more simply, sculpt the shape of the session itself. Additionally, the supervisor may leave the activity fairly open-ended and may instruct the supervisee to simply play with the clay until he feels inspired to sculpt something and see what happens: Oftentimes, the supervisee will find a natural point in the conversation to turn his attention to the clay and create something that symbolizes a stuck point or unexplored emotion related to the problematic situation he is discussing.

2. Print media image identification: This activity involves the supervisee having access to a selection of print media, usually magazines. The supervisor asks the "stuck" supervisee to briefly glance through the magazines for an image that describes a particular phenomena or dynamic that the supervisee is describing. For instance, the supervisor may say, "Find an image to describe the client during this point of conflict between the two of you." This may be followed by, "Now, find an image that depicts you at that same time." The subsequent discussion involves directed exploration where the supervisor may ask the supervisee to describe the meaning of the image, explain why that particular image was selected, or identify how he felt when discovering the image. The supervisor may make this time limited, such as 1 or 2 minutes, or may assign this as homework in a variety of ways. For instance, the supervisor may ask the supervisee to create a simple image collage of the session as it happened, in the supervisee's view, and then create another collage of that same session from the client's perspective. This is especially useful for supervisees who have difficulty truly understanding that supervisees view similar incidents from different perspectives. The lack of duplicate images in a particular magazine typically forces the supervisee to have to create different images representing different perspectives. The supervisee can address that in the discussion that follows in the next supervision session.

3. Photo prompts: The supervisor presents the supervisee with a small collection of a dozen photos, all quite different in nature, at a strategic point in the supervision session (such as when a supervisee seems unable to express something in words or gain clarity through conversation alone). The supervisor asks the supervisee to select a photo and discuss that photo in relationship to the current discussion or client. The supervisee selects a photo and discusses how and why that photo in particular applies to the situation at hand. The selection process and engagement in a less direct, less confounding discussion helps alleviate the supervisee's feelings of pressure, tension, or "stuckness" with regards to a particular situation and enables more expansive thought and verbal processing to occur.

## MID- AND HIGH-TECH CREATIVITY: TECHNIQUES USING COMPLEX TECHNOLOGY AND/OR MATERIALS

### Sand Tray

*Sand tray* is another metaphoric modality that allows a supervisee to express inter- and intrapersonal processes nonverbally through the use of figurines and objects arranged in a tray of sand (Guiffrida et al., 2007; Homeyer & Sweeney, 1998). The supervisor asks the supervisee to depict a session, a relationship, a conceptualization, or other scenario in the sand tray so that the supervisee may ultimately have a better understanding of his relationships or dynamics with clients in a less defensive, more expansive manner than he may otherwise have (Guiffrida et al., 2007).

Morrison and Homeyer (2008) recommend that supervisors use sand tray when a supervisee needs a better understanding of his clients, specifically children. They assert that using sand tray in supervision helps a supervisee admit to feelings or phenomena that he may not otherwise state verbally, such as disliking a client. Further, sand tray helps make abstract phenomena more concrete and visually palpable. Additionally, Morrison and Homeyer (2008) state that the kinesthetic nature of this activity allows the supervisee to feel an emotional charge that they may otherwise not experience while enjoying the safety of this nonthreatening activity. Supervisees, through sand tray, may discover that they have visually represented concepts that are metaphors and provide a deeper, safe understanding of a concept or experience not otherwise described when verbally discussing a case.

Supervisors who use sand tray should be adequately trained in the practice as a therapeutic modality before applying it to supervision. Sand tray-trained supervisors may use these steps when engaging their supervisee in sand tray during the supervision session (adapted from Homeyer & Sweeney, 1998):

1. Ensure that the room is prepared and there are sufficient miniatures for the supervisee to select from. Prepare the equipment the way it would be prepared for a client, remembering that the supervisor will role model appropriate sand tray preparation and engagement.
2. Inform the supervisee that sand tray is going to be utilized. Discuss any reservations or excitement about this ahead of time.
3. Invite the supervisee to create the sand tray. Step back and observe the process, but do not direct it.
4. Process the sand tray creation. This component is the most meaningful and most expansive part of this process.
5. Clean up the sand tray together. This can occur at the conclusion of processing and will sometimes elicit further discussion (for instance, a supervisee who has discovered that she feels good when her clients become dependent on her may feel hesitant to put the figurines

away, leading to more discovery and process about the difficulty of separation).

6. Document the session. This may occur before cleanup, and the supervisor may invite the supervisee to take a picture of the sand tray or document the sand tray creation before deconstruction.

7. Process the method itself with the supervisee. Discuss how the use of sand tray was beneficial or not beneficial in the supervision process, and invite the supervisee to engage the sand tray again in the future as needed.

## Music Videos

It is likely that most supervisors did not imagine a supervision practice involving music videos as a tool to enhance counselor skill. However, music videos may be an especially useful tool in developing and enhancing counselor empathy (Ohrt, Foster, Hutchinson, & Ieva, 2009). Many counselors and supervisors clearly understand the crucial role that empathy plays in therapeutic relationships. However, supervisors often find empathy-building to be a challenging task. Supervisors may decide to select music videos for use in supervision specifically as an empathy-building exercise.

Supervisors interested in using music videos should follow these steps (Ohrt, Foster, Hutchinson, & Ieva, 2009). First, supervisors will select a music video that they believe the supervisee or supervisees will respond to with affect and thoughtfulness. Oftentimes music videos can be found through a quick internet search of a particular topic (for instance, searching with keywords "music videos, depression" typically yields dozens of options). Supervisors may also simply consider songs and music that has moved them toward greater empathy or compassion, and then may search for those songs on the internet (sites such as YouTube often have a plethora of options). Then, supervisors should follow these steps suggested by Ohrt, Foster, Hutchinson, and Ieva (2009):

Step One: Read the lyrics and provide the supervisee(s) with a transcript of the lyrics (often easily accessible online). The supervisee(s) may have a chance to read the lyrics prior to viewing the video. No discussion happens at this time.

Step Two: View the video together.

Step Three: Allow some time for reflection and introspection. No verbal discussion happens at this time.

Step Four: Discuss and process verbally the thoughts and feelings that the supervisee has about the character(s) in the video or about the lyrics. Supervisees may be asked to consider their initial feelings, thoughts, emotional and physical responses, and whether they identify with any of the characters in the video or song. (Ohrt, Foster, Hutchinson, & Ieva, 2009)

The supervisor then helps move the discussion toward application so that the supervisee may apply any responses and insight to his or her client or clients. This activity is intended to facilitate growth and change for the supervisee; therefore, it is crucial that the supervisor helps the supervisee make meaning of their affective responses and help the supervisee apply that meaning to his work with clients. The supervisor will keep his original intentions in mind. That is, if the activity is intended to help a supervisee build empathy for a specific client (e.g., a person being physically abused by a relational partner), then the supervisor needs to facilitate the links between the supervisee's responses and experience to the client (e.g., Supervisor: "Do you suppose your feelings of helplessness as you watched the video are similar to the client's feelings of helplessness while in this cycle of abuse?")

## Movies

Similar to music videos, movies and documentaries may help a supervisee build empathy, better understand a psychological phenomenon, or have new ideas about relationships or human dynamics. Since they are longer in duration, movies are quite obviously inappropriate for viewing during the supervision session but can easily be assigned as homework. Some long-standing Web sites may provide supervisors with ideas about movies that can be used in supervision, although the Web sites focus specifically on movies for therapeutic purposes (e.g., www.cinematherapy.com, http://www.zurinstitute. com/movietherapy.html). Supervisors may select a movie or provide supervisees with a list of movies to choose from, then the supervisor and supervisee each watch the movie within a specific time frame. Two weeks is usually manageable. Then, the supervisee and supervisor return to supervision to discuss how thematic elements or character features may relate to particular cases or conceptualizations. The supervisor encourages the supervisee to apply any newfound understanding or insight to current cases and helps the supervisee reconceptualize based on these new understandings. For instance, if a supervisee has difficulty understanding the dynamics between a couple in which one member of the couple has alcoholism, the supervisee may be instructed to view the 1994 movie "When A Man Loves A Woman" (Manduki, 1994) that depicts such dynamics. The supervisee returns to session after viewing the movie and the supervisor inquires about how he may be thinking differently about the clients now. The supervisor and supervisee discuss the specific features of the movie that impacted the supervisee's thoughts, and how the supervisee may adjust his conceptualization of the couple with this new information in mind. The supervisee is asked to examine his initial treatment plan to decide whether his treatment plan took into account all of the necessary variables, or perhaps new variables are now clear that may impact treatment decisions. The supervisor highlights that films will not be used to dictate treatment, nor do they necessarily represent an accurate account of any given phenomena, but they are a helpful tool in expanding one's understanding and critical thinking about a particular subject matter.

These benefits are especially useful when working with a supervisee to develop and broaden multicultural understanding and competence. The film "Crash" (Haggis, 2004) may be especially useful in helping supervisees broaden their understanding of race, ethnicity, religious, and class issues (Villalba & Redmond, 2008). In particular, supervisees, after viewing the movie, may be prompted to consider the following questions as they relate to one's multicultural awareness and understanding (adapted from Villalba & Redmond's questions):

1. Of the various cultures depicted in the movie, what was already familiar to you and what was surprising or new to you?
2. What did you notice about the "culture crashes" in the movie? Did this remind you of any "crashes" you have experienced personally or professionally?
3. What did you notice about social, political, economic, or contextual reasons behind the "culture crashes"? How might this enter or relate to your professional work?
4. Which of these characters would you be nervous about working with as a client? Why?
5. Which of these characters would you like to work with? Why?
6. How does all of this (discussion) relate to your work with clients? What are some common themes you are noticing?

# PART III

# CRITICAL COMPONENTS OF CLINICAL SUPERVISION

# TWELVE

# Legal and Ethical Matters

$D$uring a presentation regarding ethics in supervision, a well-respected researcher, clinical supervisor, and counselor educator stated that "supervision is an activity that, for all intents and purposes, is quite stupid for anyone to take on" (R. Miars, personal communication, February 3, 2011). Although the statement elicited a giggle from the crowd, the lecturer was not entirely joking.

Clinical supervision, by nature, is a risky endeavor in that it holds a unique degree of liability for the supervisor (Knapp & VandeCreek, 1997). A client who claims harm may hold a counselor liable for that harm and may hold that counselor's supervisor liable as well (Disney & Stephens, 1994; Knapp & VandeCreek, 1997). In that a clinical supervisor's role is to protect clients, it stands to good reason that a supervisor could be held liable if that protection fails. Because supervisors are responsible for developing and overseeing every aspect of their supervisee's practice, a counselor who demonstrates less than stellar competence in all domains at all times quite naturally poses a risk to his partner in liability, the clinical supervisor.

Clinical supervisors, through their training and experience as counselors, are likely quite aware of the multifaceted influence of ethical and legal matters on their practice. The profession's ethical standards govern one's behavior with clients and describe the epitome of how one should act professionally and interpersonally. Laws, by contrast, are the "acceptable limits of counselor behavior" (Disney & Stephens, 1994, p. 2) and are based on the profession's accepted ethical standards.

Clinical supervisors, like any member of the counseling profession, have a responsibility to maintain current awareness of ethical codes, professional standards, and laws that apply to their specific practice domains and the profession as a whole. Clinical supervisors must maintain intimate awareness of legal and ethical matters related to their supervision practice, their counseling practice, and, perhaps most significantly, matters related to their supervisee's counseling practice.

This chapter discusses legal and ethical issues particular to the practice of supervision and provides information about how supervisors should practice to minimize the negative impact of these issues when they arise. Legal and ethical matters are largely intertwined as laws are often developed from the professional practice standards, which inform and guide behaviors in the profession (Disney & Stephens, 1994). Supervisors are then provided with a model of ethical decision making that can be used with supervisees, followed by a discussion of how to optimally protect oneself while generously serving to protect others.

## ETHICS AND SUPERVISION

Clinical supervisors are charged with training and developing their supervisees in three domains of professional functioning. These domains are ethical knowledge and behavior, competency, and personal functioning (Lamb, Cochran, & Jackson, 1991). This section contends specifically with the ethical knowledge and behavior of the clinical supervisor because an ethically underdeveloped supervisor will certainly not be able to uphold the responsibility of suitably training the next generation of counselors. Supervisors and supervisees alike rely heavily on ethics and codes of ethics to guide and inform their practice.

"Ethics" in the counseling profession refers to the moral decision-making process that counselors engage in as they attempt to protect the rights and welfare of the individuals they serve (Kurpius, Gibson, Lewis, & Corbett, 1991). The codes of ethics related to the counseling profession provide guidelines about how counselors should act, so supervisors must familiarize themselves with all relevant codes of ethics before entering into a supervision arrangement. The Approved Clinical Supervisor credential (ACS; CCE Global) is accompanied by an ethical code that details the expected behaviors of the clinical supervisors who carry that credential. Although the supervisors with the ACS credential are bound to follow this code, it also serves as a concise yet appropriately detailed ethical guide for all clinical supervisors. In addition, the American Counseling Association Code of Ethics (American Counseling Association [ACA], 2005) incorporates the ethical standards for supervision into the core code that governs all counseling practice, thus acknowledging the integral role played by ethical clinical supervision in upholding the counseling profession's mission. Specifically, Section F of the code addresses counseling supervision, training, and teaching. The code provides valuable information and guidance to clinical supervisors about issues such as informed consent, supervisory relationships, endorsing a supervisee, and terminating a supervision relationship. Additional codes of ethics specifically address the practice of clinical supervision, such as the American Association for Marriage and Family Therapy Code of Ethics, the

Commission on Rehabilitation Counselor Certification, and the National Career Development Association. Supervisors are responsible for examining the codes that are relevant to their particular practice. Supervisors hold the responsibility for being familiar with ethical practice whether they are familiar with the codes or not, so the wise supervisors becomes intimately familiar with the codes and refers to them in times of indecision and difficulty.

*Activity: List the codes of ethics that relate to your practice. Include the ACS code whether you plan to carry the credential or not. Now, examine the supervisor sections of those codes. Look for similarities and differences. Which components of the codes are surprising to you? Which components do you believe you will have a difficult time managing autonomously?*

Now, select one item (that pertains to supervision) from the code and discuss why this item may be problematic or troublesome for you in the future (or has been in the past). Be thorough and specific; describe the situation that may occur, the circumstances surrounding that, and how the scenario unfolds from start to finish. Include a brief description of the steps you may need to take in advance to ensure this scenario does not come to fruition. (For instance, you may choose article F.1.c. of the ACA Code of Ethics as you recognize that informed consent may be problematic in your supervision work because your supervisees do not obtain such consent because of current agency practice.) Be certain to fully describe the negative and positive consequences of the ethical violation to all parties involved (you, your supervisee, the agency, and especially the clients).

## COMPETENCE

Competence refers to one's ability to do something with regards to specific standards. In legal terms, someone is competent when they are "duly qualified," "answers all requirements," and has "sufficient ability, capacity, or authority" (Black's Law Dictionary, 1990; Disney & Stephens, 1994). This means that one has the necessary and recognized qualifications to perform the tasks and functions deemed necessary to the practice of a certain discipline in accordance with the standards of that discipline (Cobia & Boes, 2000; Disney & Stephens, 1994; Falvey, 2002).

The issue of competence involves both legal and ethical concerns. Although competence is at the core of the professional code of ethics, issues pertaining to scope of practice and competence have frequently enough appeared in United States courts that legal precedent has been set and favors clients who have been harmed by practitioners (Falvey, 2002). Supervisors hold a dual responsibility in this regard as they monitor their supervisee's scope of practice and competence as well as their own.

## Supervisor Competence

In the case of clinical supervision, supervisors must have appropriate experience in the counseling profession and must have specific training in the practice of clinical supervision (Harrar, VandeCreek, & Knapp, 1990). The Association for Counselor Education and Supervision (Dye & Borders, 1990) provides a standards statement that details 11 core areas of supervisor personal traits, knowledge, and competencies. These standards expect that supervisors are effective counselors who have thorough knowledge of various counseling theories and approaches, as well as thorough knowledge of supervision models, approaches, and techniques. The standards further detail the supervisor's personal traits and characteristics that is consistent with a supervisor's role, including sensitivity to individual differences, a commitment to the role of supervisor, and a sense of humor. The standards further expect supervisors to be knowledgeable purveyors of the many ethical, legal, and regulatory aspects of counseling and supervision and should have strong communication, evaluation, recording, and reporting skills. Clinical supervisors must strive to achieve the highest levels of professional competence, so that they can best help their supervisees reach optimal levels of client service as well. The standards provide supervisors with a thorough list of objectives to work toward in pursuit of such optimal practice.

*Activity:* Review the Standards for Counseling Supervisors document (Appendix A). Highlight the items that you believe you are close to mastering and do not need to focus on. Circle or make a list of five items that you believe you need to pay immediate and careful attention to. Be sure to include an action plan if there are steps you need to take to be able to master those items. (e.g., if you would like to address item 6.5, "Can identify learning needs of the counselor," your action plan may include "read a book about adult learning theory" or "have a conversation with supervisees about how they best learn.")

Clinical supervisors are behaving unethically if their supervisees engage in a practice that they (as supervisors) do not have full competence to practice themselves (Cobia & Boes, 2000). A supervisor simply cannot provide appropriate oversight and guidance to a supervisee who is practicing any techniques or models outside of the supervisor's own range of competence. When this occurs, the supervisor is responsible for arranging appropriate oversight regarding that area of the supervisee's practice (Cobia & Boes, 2000) and, at times, may need to transfer the supervisee to another supervisor whose areas of competence are better aligned with the supervisee's practice interests.

Although many counselor supervisors are fairly clear about their own scope of clinical competence as a counselor (that is, they often know what they are trained in and what they lack training in), they may not have that same clarity about their competence to practice supervision. This occurs for many reasons. First, many supervisors enter supervision practice with no formal training. Instead, they receive supervision from untrained supervisors and assume that they should supervise in a similar manner. They may be unaware that supervision is a specific field of study and practice complete with theories, models, and standards. Next, there is a lack of supervision training in many education programs; so many supervisors enter the supervision practice without a clear understanding of what supervision is "supposed" to be or what it is "supposed" to accomplish (Guest & Dooley, 1999). Finally, many supervisors are unfamiliar with the standards of supervision practice. So as an initial step in becoming a supervisor, supervisors need to become explicitly aware of the standards of practice for supervisors.

In addition to building a strong knowledge base about the models, skills, and techniques of supervision and the supervisory relationship, supervisors should ideally receive supervision-of-supervision from a skilled, experienced supervisor (Borders & Brown, 2005). A supervisor who can review your work in a skilled, constructive fashion can help you to strengthen your own supervisory skills while providing you with needed professional support and feedback. This may be a time-limited experience, perhaps at the beginning of your tenure as a counselor supervisor and intermittently to facilitate ongoing development, or may be integrated as a part of your practice. Integrating supervision-of-supervision into your own practice helps you to continually improve your skill, gain consultative support and feedback, and provides you with an extra measure of legal protection, as someone more knowledgeable can help to oversee your adherence to appropriate and optimal standards of practice.

*Activity: Competent supervisors keep up-to-date on state laws and rules regarding the counseling and supervision profession, as well as relevant codes of ethics. Where can you access the state laws, so that you can keep up-to-date? How will you know when laws have changed?*

### Supervisee Competence

Supervisors, in addition to concerning themselves with their own competence, have to continually evaluate their supervisee's competence. In fact, monitoring for competence is at the core of the supervision experience. Supervisors are specifically charged with the task of ensuring that the counselor (supervisee) is sufficiently able to provide competent service to the client. Supervisors are also tasked with helping supervisees develop their counseling skills to increase their competence in all practice domains. Falender and Shafranske (2004) developed a competency-based approach to psychology supervision that requires the supervisor to critically analyze the skills and functions of psychology trainees through formal, rated processes. Trainees should enter the field only when all competence areas are considered solid enough to warrant greater autonomy. One strength of the approach by Falendar and Shafranskeis is the formalization and standardization of the competency assessment process. Supervisees are not evaluated by arbitrary, purely subjective means. This helps ensure that the supervisor is assessing the supervisee in terms of pure competence; that is, how well the supervisee performs in regards to professional standards. This helps to reduce the impact of personality conflicts or mismatches and other dynamics that may interfere with supervisor objectivity and fair assessment.

*Activity: How will you manage your supervisee's scope of practice? That is, how will you ensure your supervisee is practicing within his scope? What will you do to ensure you have full knowledge of how your supervisee is practicing? How will you manage a situation where you learn that your supervisee is practicing outside of his scope?*

*Imagine you are faced with the following dilemma. How will you respond? Be specific and detailed about your action plan. Include a backup plan in case your supervisee does not respond cooperatively. Dilemma: Your supervisee has attended a weekend workshop on using a form of regression therapy with clients who have experienced childhood trauma. The supervisee would like to start using the technique he learned with his clients beginning this week. You have some concerns because the training was brief, you are not familiar with the techniques, and you are not certain your supervisee fully understands the risks of the techniques. Your supervisee, in supervision, expresses that he intends to use his newly acquired information with at least four of his clients this week and will now be claiming a specialty in "regression therapy."*

- *What are the ethical/legal dilemmas in this scenario?*
- *How will you help the supervisee find and consider the legal and ethical dilemmas?*
- *Be specific about the scope of practice issues in this scenario. Which issues pertain to supervisor scope of practice and which issues are about the supervisee's scope of practice?*
- *How will you respond to the scope of practice issues?*

## Evaluation of Competence

Supervisors should have a clearly articulated method by which they will evaluate supervisee's competence. Supervisors who are working with trainees in a graduate or technical program will likely have an instrument provided by the training program based on the professional standards and program expectations. Supervisors working with prelicensure supervisees may have an instrument that is provided by the state and is submitted at various intervals, but that instrument may be brief and too truncated to fully encompass all relevant standards of the profession. Supervisors working with postlicensure supervisees might not have a formal tool for competence assessment at all. The literature provides supervisors with several tools to select from, all of which are in accordance with field standards. Although multiple measures of assessment are typically more useful in gaining a clear picture of counselor performance, supervisors are well served to have at least one assessment tool that assists their evaluation process (Perosa & Perosa, 2010). Supervisors may use a tool that is relevant to all standards or, with more competent practitioners, may use a tool that focuses on a specific domain. Some tools that measure counselor's competence include the Skilled Counseling Scale (Urbani et al., 2002), the Skilled Group Counselor Training Model (Smaby, Maddux, Torres-Rivera, & Zimmick, 1999), the Counseling Skills Scale (Eriksen & McAuliffe, 2003), and the Postgraduate Competency Document (Storm, York, Vincent, McDowell, & Lewis, 1997). Some examples of domain-specific tools are the Sexual Orientation Counselor Competency Scale (Bidell, 2005), the Multicultural Awareness/Knowledge/Skills Survey (D'Andrea, Daniels, & Heck, 1991), and the Multicultural Counseling Inventory (Sodowsky, Taffe, Gutkin, & Wise, 1994).

Supervisees should clearly know when and how they are being evaluated, and the instrument of choice should be noted in the supervision contract, along with a clear statement about practicing within one's scope of training and practice (see Chapter 3 for further discussion about the supervision contract). The purpose here is twofold: first, to provide the supervisee with useful and constructive feedback that will help further his skill development for the betterment of client service. Second, to provide the supervisee with a fair understanding of the appropriately objective manner in which his competence will be measured.

Evaluation processes and concerns are described in much more explicit detail in Chapter 14. However, the legal and ethical concerns associated with evaluation are of particular importance to clinical supervisors. Supervisors hold evaluative power in the supervision relationship. Supervisors provide evaluative assessment of the supervisee's competence in both informal and formal ways. Typically, supervisors provide formal assessments to supervisees who are in training programs or are early in their career. Once supervisees are postlicensure, however, the tendency to receive formal evaluation is limited to employment reviews, which may not be based on counselor performance standards. Supervisors are keenly aware that their evaluations may affect a supervisee's status in a training program or employment setting; therefore, supervisors may shy away from providing evaluation and taking corrective or protective measures when necessary (Falvey, 2002).

Clinical supervisors are, by definition, gatekeepers to the profession (Bernard & Goodyear, 2009), and after a supervisee enters the profession, the supervisor serves as a gatekeeper to the client or ongoing practice as a whole. That is, if a supervisee is a threat to client harm, the supervisor is tasked with preventing the counselor from being positioned to do such harm.

Supervisors may be fearful of carrying out the gate keeping function for a number of reasons. First, a supervisor may feel as if he will be doing harm to the supervisee by prohibiting practice or career advancement. In that supervisors have been well trained to avoid harm, the thought of limiting one's freedom to pursue his vocation of choice may create internal conflict and dissonance for the supervisor. Next, a supervisor may question his or her evaluative judgment. Although it is recommended that supervisors have access to collegial consultation or supervision-of-supervision, a supervisor who works in the absence of such support may feel doubtful and concerned about taking protective measures. In addition, supervisors may feel concerned that they have not been appropriately engaged in feedback and evaluation up to the point of concern. A supervisor who is concerned that he has been negligent of his own oversight responsibilities may be hesitant to take protective measures, even when such measures are needed for the client's protection. The supervisor may recognize that he has not provided the supervisee with fair, objective evaluation and is concerned about the ramifications of "surprising" a supervisee with new and impactful evaluative feedback.

## DUE PROCESS

Fairness and competence are ethical matters that, in combination, introduce the legal issue of due process (Cobia & Boes, 2000). Due process is a constitutional right, granted under the United States Constitution's 14th Amendment, and asserts that no state shall "deprive any person of life, liberty, or property, without due process of law." This means that a person should first have the chance to defend themselves and challenge a proposed corrective or punitive action before that action being implemented (Disney & Stephens, 1994). There are two types of due process: procedural and substantive (Cobia & Boes, 2000), and a clinical supervisor's main concern is on procedural due process. The procedural due process refers to the fundamental fairness of the process surrounding a situation where an individual may be deprived of life, liberty, or property. The procedural due process requires that the individual be entitled to a hearing and a chance to defend oneself before a neutral party before any freedom can be removed, even temporarily (Falvey, 2002).

Clinical supervisors should recognize that supervisees must be given honest, evaluative feedback and adequate time to demonstrate improvement on the specific areas of concern. Supervisees should be given specific information about what performance changes are required or expected of them, and the evaluation and feedback schedule should be regular and clearly documented (Cobia & Boes, 2000). If a clinical supervisor sees an immediate need to intervene suddenly, the supervisor should concern himself with client protection first in accordance with ethical standards of the profession. The supervisor should consult with a colleague or supervisor and should be able to clearly articulate (and document) the concerns and rationale for prohibiting practice. Supervisors should recognize that their ability and commitment to provide supervisees with effective, honest feedback through the course of supervision will help to protect them in the event that a supervisee is unfit to practice. Supervisors who provide supervisees with appropriate and timely evaluation, even in the case of minor concerns, are well positioned to defend their adherence to due process if major concerns later arise.

## INFORMED CONSENT

Informed consent is an ethical and legal concept that refers to a client's right to make decisions about whether to enter counseling based on clear, transparent information about the process (Nystul, 2011). This concept arises from the principle of respect for one's autonomy and freedom to willingly enter into a treatment arrangement. Supervisors are concerned with informed consent on two levels: (1) whether the supervisee is following appropriate informed consent practices in his work with clients and (2) whether the supervisor is following appropriate informed consent practices with the supervisee.

Informed consent in the counseling process is imperative in that clients have a right to know about the treatment they are electing to receive, including the associated risks and benefits, and have a right to know the qualifications of the individual providing such treatment (Haas & Malouf, 2005). Legal features that pertain to informed consent include the following:

1. That the client is capable of understanding the information provided and has the capacity to make autonomous choices.
2. The client's consent must be willing and voluntary without coercion.
3. The client must be given all necessary information to make a fully informed decision (Knapp & VandeCreek, 2006).

All three conditions must be met for informed consent to be fulfilled. The process should also be documented as a part of the client's records (Bernard & Goodyear, 2009) to demonstrate concordance with practice standards and legal mandates.

Further, if that treatment provider is under supervision, the client should be aware of the nature of that supervision and ought to be given information about how treatment and confidentiality are impacted by the supervision process. A supervisor has the responsibility to ensure that their supervisee is engaging in an appropriate informed consent process and is clear with clients that he is receiving supervision. Further, supervisors teach supervisees that informed consent is an ongoing process that occurs each time the treatment plan changes. For example, if a supervisee decides to move from cognitive techniques to a family-of-origin based approach, that supervisee should explain the new treatment to the client and should obtain consent before engaging in the new treatment. The supervisor is responsible for ensuring that the supervisee takes such measures and may be liable for the supervisee who fails to obtain informed consent from each client before engaging in treatment.

Informed consent in the supervision process is qualitatively different than in the counseling process. Supervisees do not always have the luxury of selecting their supervisor; oftentimes, a supervisor is assigned or paired with them without viable alternatives. Supervisees also do not have the choice about whether or not they would like to receive supervision, as it is often a mandatory experience for counselors in training and for counselors who are unfit for autonomous practice. Counselors can elect to leave the training program or the profession if they would prefer not to engage in supervision when mandated.

Supervisors should inform supervisees of the parameters of supervision, including evaluative processes, supervisor qualifications, expectations, cost, methods, and due process procedures (Bernard & Goodyear, 2009; McCarthy et al., 1995). Informed consent is often covered through the supervision professional disclosure statement and the supervision contract. If these two tools are comprehensive in nature, informed consent between the supervisor and the supervisee is likely satisfied.

## CONFIDENTIALITY AND PRIVILEGE

Confidentiality is an ethical standard that prevents a counselor from being obligated to share information that a client discloses during a counseling session, except with the client's specific permission to share such information (Disney & Stephens, 1994). Counselors rely on the promise of confidentiality to create a trusting, open environment in which the client can share anything he desires. Clients rely on confidentiality, so that they can share openly and honestly the information they may prefer others not to hear. When confidentiality is violated for any reason, there is often a negative impact on the therapeutic relationship. The act of breeching confidentiality has both ethical and legal implications. At the very least, a breech in confidentiality can be harmful to a client. At its worst, breeches in confidentiality can have devastating impacts on every aspect of a client's life.

### Confidentiality to the Client

Confidential materials in counseling include conversations between the counselor and the client (both in and out of sessions), written documents, video or audio recordings, assessment records, and progress notes. A clinical supervisor has the duty to maintain client confidentiality as well. That is, the client's confidentiality extends into the supervision relationship. In honoring the principle of "fidelity," counselors must honestly represent and disclose the nature of the supervision relationship and process (Sherry, 1991). Clients are to be informed of the supervision relationship at the onset of counseling through the counselor's professional disclosure statement and the informed consent form in which the client accepts the supervisee's participation in supervision (see Chapter 4, Supervision Consent, for further discussion). The client should be well aware of what that participation entails and should know the identity of the supervisor and how to reach the supervisor in case he has questions or concerns (Borders & Brown, 2005; Cobia & Boes, 2000; Sherry, 1991).

Because supervisors hold the responsibility to maintain client confidentiality, supervisors use the same privacy precautions with supervision materials that they would with client records and conversations. Supervision happens only in private places with appropriate confidentiality measures taken, and supervision records are kept secure with the same measures that one uses for client records.

Bernard and O'Laughlin (1990) encourage supervisors to keep the following seven components in mind when establishing an environment that will optimally protect client confidentiality. These elements are as follows:

1. Discuss ethical standards and confidentiality standards and laws with each supervisee
2. Maintain strict confidentiality of all client materials
3. Secure client materials ongoingly and carefully
4. Prohibit unprofessional discussions
5. Prohibit inappropriate disclosure of client identity or identifying features
6. Ensure clients are informed of practice policies regarding confidentiality and privacy
7. Make certain to clearly discuss exceptions to confidentiality, both at the start of treatment and at sensible intervals as needed

### Confidentiality to the Supervisee

Although client confidentiality extends into the supervision experience, supervisees are not entitled to the same tenets of confidentiality that clients are entitled to. Clinical supervisors have, in this order, a responsibility to protect the client, the public, the profession, and the supervisee (Sherry, 1991). Therefore, supervisors have a duty to provide evaluative information to parties in addition to the supervisee, sometimes without express permission of the supervisee. Supervisees should be informed both verbally and in the supervision contract that information provided and gathered during the course of supervision can be shared as needed to fulfill protective responsibilities. The supervisor will not freely share private supervision information but will instead share only the information that is directly relevant to the supervisee's functioning and competence (Sherry, 1991).

Clinical supervisors are keenly aware that the supervision relationship will likely be impaired when private information from supervision sessions is revealed. However, supervisors may engage in the following steps in an effort to minimize the negative impact of such actions when necessary:

1. Supervisors should make certain that supervisees are clear about the unique limitations of confidentiality in the supervision relationship. A statement reflecting these limitations may be included in the supervision contract and may be discussed during the Pre-Supervision Interview and Initial Session.

2. Supervisors should make their order of responsibility clear to the supervisee, both verbally and on the supervision contract (i.e., to protect the client, the public, the profession, and then the supervisee). Implications of this order of responsibility should be discussed in terms of confidentiality and potential impact on the supervisory relationship.

3. Supervisors should provide honest, clear feedback to supervisees when concerns are beginning to arise, and ongoingly thereafter. Supervisors should use terms such as "this is a concern about client care," so that supervisees are clear that the concern extends beyond the supervision dyad into the "external" world.

4. When a supervisor believes that evaluative information from supervision needs to be shared, the supervisor should privately consult with his own supervisor or a colleague who is also skilled in supervision to obtain objective feedback and affirmation or disaffirmation that information should indeed be shared.

5. The supervisor should, when possible, discuss the matter with the supervisee first before sharing with an outside source (with the exception of the consultation described in the previous step).

6. The supervisor should speak with the supervisee directly about the impact of these actions on the supervisory relationship and subsequent client care. Supervisors should recognize that there may be a strain in the supervision relationship and should engage the supervisee in a discussion about how to mend that strain for the betterment of the supervisee's performance. (Note: This conversation may be introduced early in the process but is probably more suitable after the supervisee has had time to fully understand the performance problem and implications of the evaluative report.)

7.  If the supervisee determines that the supervisory alliance is broken beyond repair, the supervisor should help to facilitate the acquisition of a new supervisor, when feasible.

In addition, the private rather than purely confidential nature of the supervision relationship may further motivate supervisors to steer clear of therapy-esque conversations that may arise from time to time. Instead, examine psychological concerns only inasmuch as they impact client relationships and client care. This is an appropriate use of supervision energy and is impactful in developing competent counselors (as the ability to understand how one's own features impacts the therapy process is important). However, supervisors are responsible for helping supervisees remember that what they share in supervision may not be kept confidential if concerns about competence or client care arise. Supervisors may ask their supervisees to have a personal counselor available, as it is fair practice for a supervisor to refer a supervisee to a personal counselor to discuss issues that are beyond the scope of appropriate supervision discussion. This is especially relevant if a supervisee is in enough distress or turmoil that the emotional or psychological distress could cause malpractice or negligence, in which case supervision material would almost inevitably have to be revealed to some degree if client protection is needed.

## MALPRACTICE

Malpractice, or incompetent practice, is professional negligence and occurs when the supervisor is acting below acceptable professional standards (Falvey, 2002). There are four criteria that have to be evidentially shown for malpractice to be established legally:

1.  Duty: Duty is the fiduciary (trust-related) responsibility the supervisor maintains to care for the welfare of another person (the supervisee) over which the supervisor has direct control and has knowledge of their actions.
2.  Breach: Breach refers to a break in the aforementioned duty, where the supervisor's actions or inactions were foreseeable and unreasonable given the supervisor's fiduciary responsibility.
3.  Causation: The breach of duty causes (either directly or proximately) injury.
4.  Damage: There is evidence of physical, financial, or emotional injury (Falvey, 2002).

Malpractice can involve a supervisor's direct liability or indirect (vicarious) liability.

## DIRECT LIABILITY

Direct liability involves the actions or inactions of the clinical supervisor in providing clinical supervision service (Falvey, 2002; Harrar et al., 1990). A supervisor is responsible for his performance and actions when providing supervision and is responsible when he fails to act in a manner that meets professional expectations and standards.

Supervisors should be especially cognizant of the following ways they could be directly liable for malpractice in supervision:

1. Inappropriate advice: If a supervisor gives a supervisee inappropriate advice and the supervisee carries out that advice that then harms the client, the supervisor may be liable for harm to the client.
2. Dereliction: Dereliction refers to a supervisor neglecting to fulfill supervisory responsibilities "for the planning, course, and outcome of the supervisee's work" (Harrar et al., 1990, p. 39).
3. Failure to listen appropriately: Supervisors need to listen to a supervisee's concerns and comments about their clients to better understand the clients' needs. A supervisor who fails to listen to a supervisee's reports may hold direct liability if a client is harmed.
4. Inappropriate assignments: The supervisor is responsible for knowing the skill and competence level of the supervisee. So, if a supervisor assigns a task or intervention that is outside of the supervisee's range of competence or training, he may be directly liable for harm (Harrar et al., 1990).

Supervisors who are practicing in strong accordance with the professional standards for clinical supervisors are probably not going to have many difficulties with matters of direct liability. However, supervisors are in the uniquely risky position of holding vicarious liability for the work of their supervisees. Vicarious liability is often more concerning for supervisors as they have much less control over their supervisee's practice than they do over their own. However, because of their position of power and authority, supervisors hold liability for each and every one of their supervisees and every action or failed action of those supervisees (Harrar et al., 1990).

### Vicarious Liability

*Respondeat superior*, or *vicarious liability*, is a legal term that literally means "Let the master respond" (Harrar et al., 1990). This term refers to the legal doctrine that states that one person who has authority or control over another (the supervisor) can be legally liable for any damages that a client suffers because of the negligence of the subordinate (the supervisee) (Disney & Stephens, 1994).

A supervisor can be held liable for the supervisee's actions if the following criteria are met:

1.  The supervisee has voluntarily consented to work under the direction and control of the supervisor and act in ways that are beneficial to the supervisor. It does not matter whether the supervisee is a paid or volunteer service provider, and it does not matter whether the supervisor is paid for providing supervision. Liability exists nonetheless.
2.  The supervisee has acted within the scope of tasks allowable by the supervisor.
3.  The supervisor has the power to direct and control the supervisee's work (Harrar et al., 1990).

Supervisors are typically only held liable for a supervisee's negligence if the negligent acts happen in the course and scope of the supervision relationship (Disney & Stephens, 1994). According to Disney and Stephens (1994), the scope and course of the relationship are typically determined by these factors:

1.  The supervisor's power to control the supervisee (a university faculty member or managerial supervisor often has more power to control the supervisee than a site supervisor or offsite private supervisor does)
2.  Whether the supervisee has the duty to perform the act (whether the harmful act was clearly part of the supervisee's duty as a counselor)
3.  The time, place, and purpose of the action (whether the act occurred as a part of the counseling process versus occurring outside of the counseling setting, such as by coincidental meeting or in public)
4.  The supervisee's motivation in committing the act (if the supervisee thought the act would help the client, the act was within the scope of counseling; if the supervisee acts out of self-interest without concern for the client's welfare, the act is likely not within the course and scope of the supervisory relationship)
5.  If the supervisor could have reasonably foreseen the act

The supervisor can be held vicariously liable for any harm caused by the supervisee's negligence if the courts decide that the problematic act falls within the course and scope of the supervision relationship as determined by a combination of the above factors. It is important to recognize that the majority of problematic acts that result in harm to the client are likely within the scope and course of the supervision relationship (Disney & Stephens, 1994).

Because the main concern legally focuses on who has administrative control over the supervisee, it does not matter whether the supervisor is an employee of the supervisee's agency as they do if they are an external consultant or private practitioner. The supervisor is held to the same ethical and legal standards, regardless (Harrar et al., 1990).

## MULTIPLE RELATIONSHIPS

Multiple relationships are discussed in detail throughout this book. At this point, the ethical and legal issues regarding multiple relationships are examined. Above all, supervisors should disengage from any multiple relationships that impair their ability to be objective and provide honest evaluative feedback or are exploitative to the supervisee (Borders & Brown, 2005; Cormier & Bernard, 1982; Disney & Stephens, 2004; Falvey, 2002).

According to Disney and Stephens (1994), multiple relationships can cause difficulties in the supervision experience in several ways. First, because a supervisor holds more power than a supervisee, there is a diminished consent. That is, the supervisee cannot easily agree or disagree to engage in any dynamic, as the supervisor holds the power to create difficulties if the supervisee is not amenable or cooperative. An example of this is a clinical supervisor who asks the supervisee to meet with one of the supervisor's family members for "just one session." The supervisee knows that this is unethical, but the supervisor assures her that it is acceptable because it is a one-time occurrence. The supervisee feels compelled to comply; after all, the supervisor is supposed to be the more knowledgeable party.

Second, the supervisor has the power to exploit the supervisee. Imagine a supervisor who asks a supervisee to buy cookies from his daughter's school fundraiser. The supervisee may not have the funds nor desire to purchase cookies but feels obligated to agree to this small "favor." Another example is the supervisor who rents out a portion of her office suite to a supervisee. The supervisor recognizes that the supervisee's practice has grown and decides to raise the supervisee's rent. The supervisee believes the rent is too expensive, but feels powerless to engage the supervisor in such a discussion.

Next, engaging in multiple relationships creates role conflict at times, typically for both parties. In the ACES Ethical Guidelines for Counseling Supervisors (ACES, 1993), supervisors are instructed to minimize potential conflicts between multiple roles and to divide the roles among several supervisors when possible. This means that someone who serves as both a managerial and a clinical supervisor may attempt to divide the roles by delegating one role to another supervisor. In some instances, mental health agencies will contract supervisors to come into the agency and provide clinical supervision, so that the manager does not serve both functions. If a separation of roles is impossible, supervisees should, according to the code of ethics, be made aware of the expectations and responsibilities that pertain to each of the intermingled roles. Further, this should be documented in full on the supervision contract and updated when expectations or roles change.

On a more concerning level, research indicates that supervisors and supervisees engage in alarmingly high rates of dual relationships of a romantic or sexual nature. These relationships are to be avoided entirely. Although it is plausible that romantic or sexual feelings may develop in a supervisory relationship, the supervisor has the responsibility to seek consultation or supervision around such issues and must prohibit romantic or sexual behaviors from occurring at all cost (Borders & Brown, 2005).

## Self-Protection While Protecting Others

Inevitably, many potential supervisors question their decision to engage in supervision once they are fully aware of the ethical and legal contingencies involved with such an endeavor. However, there are a number of measures supervisors can take to minimize the risk involved. First, the supervisory relationship can serve as a tool of prevention. That is, a strong alliance that allows for mutual respect and trust will help reduce a supervisor's chance of being brought into a lawsuit (Snider, 1985). Next, supervisors should remain current on all issues related to ethical and legal aspects of their profession (Disney & Stephens, 1994; Snider, 1985). This includes national standards, state laws and regulations, and other shifting entities. Third, have an attorney on retainer who is well-versed in malpractice issues, particularly those related to the helping professions (Snider, 1985). If working for an agency, make certain that the supervisor will have access to the attorney's services if and when needed. Fourth, make certain all parties are adequately insured with liability insurance that is specific to their practice (Snider, 1985). Fifth, maintain and role model appropriate boundaries with the supervisee at all times (Recupero & Rainey, 2007). Sixth, supervisors should familiarize themselves with the areas of practice that tend to pose the most common legal and ethical problems and be certain to work preventatively with supervisees to address those problems (Recupero & Rainey, 2007). Next, review client charts regularly and ensure that progress note content appears to be congruent with the supervisee's case reports and audio or video records. Finally, make certain that the supervisor has the appropriate amount of power and authority to protect clients when needed (Disney & Stephens, 1994).

When a clinical supervisor is considering working with a supervisee who is employed by an agency, the supervisor should consider carefully how he or she will be able to exercise appropriate power and authority when necessary for the protection of clients (Disney & Stephens, 1994). Supervisors should work in conjunction with the supervisee's agency to determine how control will be shared. For instance, imagine that a supervisee is emotionally distraught about a traumatic life event. The supervisee does not want to miss work as she cannot afford the days off and believes that she will be harmful to clients if she does not hold her sessions as planned. However, after careful assessment, the supervisor determines that the supervisee is too distraught and distracted to see clients, will likely be ineffective and may possibly cause harm, and will do more harm than good by holding her sessions as planned. The supervisor makes the difficult decision that the supervisee should take at least a few days off from engaging directly with clients and plans to reassess the supervisee before her return to direct care. However, the supervisee refuses and states that seeing her clients would be "therapeutic to us all." If the supervisor is a private practice supervisor without a direct relationship to the agency, she will likely not be able to enforce this request. In this case, the harm to clients is foreseeable, but the supervisor does not have the power to exercise the necessary precautions to protect client welfare. By contrast, if the supervisor has an arrangement with the agency that she may require a break in service to protect client welfare, then the supervisee has arranged to have the appropriate authority to protect clients if the need arises.

In addition to arranging to have appropriate authority, supervisors may be wise to follow the model provided by Vesper and Brock 1991, in (Disney & Stephens, 1994):

1. Be certain that the frequency of supervision is clearly defined and followed (e.g., weekly, every other week).
2. Have a clearly defined method to identify client concerns.
3. Carefully detail and conceptualize the treatment plan.
4. Be certain to thoroughly discuss implementation of the treatment plan.
5. Review potential outcomes, both the intended outcomes and potential, unexpected outcomes, plus the risks and benefits of the treatment choices.

Following a model such as this helps the supervisor reduce the potential of negligence on the part of the supervisee. If the supervisee is attentive and nonnegligent in her practice, the supervisor is less likely to encounter a situation where he is held vicariously liable. If the supervisor is involved in a suit and is held liable for the supervisee's negligence, the supervisor has the option to sue the supervisee to recover any monetary penalties. The supervisor, to recovery monies lost in a vicarious liability lawsuit, has to show clear evidence that he, as a supervisor, was not negligent and fully upheld his responsibilities in providing appropriate supervisory oversight (Disney & Stephens, 2004). Thorough case reviews performed in a regular, systematic manner could help a supervisor establish nonnegligence when appropriate.

Supervisors are also wise to carefully examine their malpractice insurance when they decided to become supervisors. It is a good idea to use the same insurance provider as your supervisees (Disney & Stephens, 1994), as that may motivate greater concern and advocacy on the insurance company's part if two of their insured patrons are facing the same legal issue. Further, it is crucial that you find out from your provider whether your malpractice insurance covers supervision specifically. Make certain that the policy includes a stipulation for supervision practice or that there is written documentation of any assurances the carrier provides. Supervisors should maintain a copy of the supervisee's current insurance policy as part of the supervision record.

Finally, supervisors must be dutiful about appropriate and thorough documentation of their supervision activities, so that, in times of legal issues, evidence can be produced to demonstrate appropriately responsible, nonnegligent actions (supervision documentation is discussed further in Chapter 13).

## ETHICAL DECISION-MAKING MODEL

The American Counseling Association endorses Forester-Miller and Davis' (1996) seven-step ethical decision-making model. This model stems from the counseling profession's five foundational moral principles, identified by Kitchener (1984): autonomy (independence and freedom of choice), nonmaleficence (not causing harm to others), beneficence (adding to the client's welfare), justice (treating people fairly), and fidelity (honoring one's commitments).

The model's seven steps are as follows (Forester-Miller & Davis, 1996):

1. Identify the problem. Gain as much clarity as possible and be specific, objective, and thorough.
2. Apply the ACA Code of Ethics (ACA, 2005). Examine relevant codes of ethics to see whether the problem is addressed by the code.
3. Determine the nature and dimensions of the dilemma.
   a. Consider the aforementioned moral principles
   b. Review current professional literature
   c. Consult with colleagues or supervisors
   d. Consult with state or national organizations
5. Generate potential courses of action. Brainstorm and come up with as many solutions as possible.
6. Consider the potential consequences of all options and determine a course of action.
7. Evaluate the selected course of action. Evaluate the plan in terms of justice, fairness, and publicity. Would the solution stand up to public scrutiny? (Stadler, 1986)
8. Implement the course of action.

*Activity: Consider an ethical dilemma that you have encountered as a counselor while you were receiving supervision. Describe the incident as it occurred, including who was involved, what happened, and the effect the dilemma had on you.*

*Next, describe how you brought the dilemma to supervision. Did you approach your supervisor with the dilemma, or did your supervisor elicit the information from you somehow? Did you initially know you were dealing with an ethical dilemma? If not, how did you figure that out?*

*Now, describe what happened in the supervision session as you processed the dilemma. Try to delineate the steps your supervisor and you used to find a solution. Who generated the solution? How was it generated? Did you feel prepared to implement the solution?*

*Finally, practice your ethical problem-solving skills by using that same example and following the seven steps outlined above. You will need to access your relevant codes of ethics to do so. Write down as much information as you can generate for each of the steps. If you feel unfamiliar and unconfident using this model, repeat the above exercise two or three times until it feels more natural to you. If you feel fairly masterful of this process, you may wish to continue this activity with a volunteer who can role play a supervisee and will bring a dilemma to you.*

*For an added layer of complexity, envision a supervision dilemma that may occur during the supervision process and work through the seven steps with the supervisor's code of ethics on hand to help find solutions and resolution.*

# THIRTEEN

# Evaluation, Documentation, and Risk Management

*E*valuation is an inherent and critical component of an effective, impactful supervision experience. Without evaluation, supervisees are not readily able to determine their strengths, weaknesses, and areas of needed attention (Hahn & Molnar, 1991). Evaluation in clinical supervision is the process or product of providing a supervisee with professional analysis and opinion of the quality of his work. This opinion is based on a comparison of the supervisee's performance with professional practice standards and supervisor expectations. A clinical supervisor is concerned with two types of evaluation: *formative*, which is feedback that is interwoven throughout the supervision experience in an ongoing manner, and *summative* evaluation, which is an evaluation of the counselors' overall performance and is typically provided at specific points of time (Osborn & Kelly, 2010). The first type of evaluation, formative, is typically delivered to the supervisee in the form of ongoing, informal or formal *feedback*. *Feedback* refers to the act of providing information to a supervisee about the activities he is engaged in. It may be reflective information that holds no judgment or value and is intended to prompt further reflection, or it may be evaluative, or judging, in nature. The latter type, summative feedback, is more formal and is typically presented as a professional performance assessment. The professional performance assessment is the primary focus of this chapter, as this type of evaluation has performance, relational, legal, and ethical implications. Feedback practices are covered in great detail in the next chapter of this book so are not addressed here. This chapter further examines documentation in clinical supervision and concludes with a discussion of risk management practices.

## FORMAL EVALUATION: PROFESSIONAL PERFORMANCE ASSESSMENT

### The Purpose of Performance Assessment

Performance assessment in the form of a formal evaluation has several key functions in counselor development and supervision. Primarily, performance assessments help a supervisor to verify objectively that a counselor is capable of working effectively with clients and then provides the tool by which the supervisor documents that verification.

A counselor in training is typically assessed at many points in his graduate program, at the time he is first selected for entry into the program and typically at several additional points while in the training program. Once a counselor demonstrates competence to enter the field and is approved for graduation, he typically becomes involved with the state licensing board. During that involvement, the counselor usually experiences additional formal assessment at prescribed intervals and a supervisor or other representative of the field confirms that the counselor is demonstrating the capability and skill necessary to work autonomously with clients. Although some counselors may not experience formal performance assessment beyond licensure, informal assessment and evaluation are constantly being conducted by a counselor's clients who undoubtedly hold some evaluative opinion about their counselor's performance.

Performance assessment allows a counselor and supervisor to regularly examine and measure growth and development in specific areas of counselor competence and professional functioning. Further, a formal performance assessment allows a counselor to examine his supervisor's (and perhaps others') view of his work from a fairly objective stance. This is particularly useful in helping a supervisee relate feedback to formal performance categories and practice standards, thus reducing the notion that feedback and evaluation may be based on the supervisor's personal or arbitrary opinion of the counselor's work (Welfare, 2010). Performance assessments may also help a supervisee to understand and clarify his areas of needed growth, which can help when setting new or additional supervision goals. Finally, formal performance assessment is necessary, so that if, at some point, a supervisee shows any degree of underperformance (performance under the acceptable level of practice), the supervisor is engaging in appropriate *due process* should the need for gate keeping arise.

Supervisors should keep in mind that there is no such thing as a supervisee who is free from the threat of error, harm, or underperformance. Even the most generally competent, well-functioning supervisees may experience changes in their personal or professional life that will impair their performance, either temporarily or permanently. Maintaining an ongoing practice of formal performance assessment gives supervisors a platform from which to speak with the supervisee about concerns in a manner that relates to practice standards and performance changes. The performance concerns can be tracked over time through formal evaluation. These evaluations provide the supervisee with a clear view of his areas of underperformance, so that he can focus on the specific areas of concern, rather than terming himself (or his supervisor) as "generally incompetent" without a clear sense of the specific problem that needs to be improved upon. In addition, supervisors should conceptualize "competence" in terms of specific practice domains rather than an overall characterization of one's general abilities. Competence refers to one's ability to perform a task, duty, or role (Roe, 2002), with different tasks inevitably carrying different levels of capability. Competence may also be conceptualized on a continuum: that is, there are degrees of competence that fluctuate over time. Although one counselor may be quite competent and skilled at providing group supervision, then spends 10 years engaging solely in individual therapy, he might expect to return to group work with slightly diminished competence as a result of the 10-year hiatus.

Assessment and evaluation is a process of determining how a supervisee is performing in relation to a specific competency domain or feature. Supervisees may respond to this evaluative process with some anxiety and trepidation in the same way many humans experience nervousness with evaluative processes. Supervisors understand this phenomenon and honor the importance of transparency, trust, and professionalism in the formal assessment process. This allows the supervisory relationship to remain intact through some of the necessary disruption or discord that evaluation sometimes causes. Eventually, the supervisory relationship is strengthened if the supervisor can provide honest, helpful, and transparent assessment for the betterment of counselor development and client care.

### Practice Standards

Transparency, in terms of evaluation and assessment, refers to clear understanding that supervisees have about the evaluation process and the standards against which their performance is being measured (Foster & McAdams, 2009). Supervisees should know at the start of supervision what the formal evaluation process will be and should be given a blank copy of whatever assessment tool will be used for the formal evaluation. If the supervisee is a student in a training program, the supervisor and supervisee should review the assessment tool early in the supervision process, so that both parties are clear about what is expected and how progress will be tracked over time. If the supervisee is a prelicensure candidate and the supervisor is required to submit a performance update to the state licensing board, that report should be similarly reviewed and discussed. Oftentimes, licensure reports do not contain specific information pertaining to most counselor competencies. In this case, the supervisor should create their own assessment tool or access one of the counselor assessment tools that were created specifically for this purpose.

Some tools that are appropriate for post-Masters counselors are the Skilled Counseling Scale (Urbani et al., 2002), the Skilled Group Counselor Training Model (Smaby, Maddux, Torres-Rivera, & Zimmick, 1999), the Counseling Skills Scale (Eriksen & McAuliffe, 2003), and the Postgraduate Competency Document (Storm, York, Vincent, McDowell, & Lewis, 1997).

These tools all address the key areas of counselor performance. Supervisors who do not elect to use a formal tool may decide to create their own tool that is congruent with the standards of practice specific to that supervisee's field. For instance, Frame and Stevens-Smith (1995) list nine essential functions of effective professional counselor development. The identified elements are as follows (Frames & Stevens-Smith, 1995):

1. Openness (to new information, ideas)
2. Flexibility
3. Positivity
4. Cooperativeness
5. Willingness to accept and incorporate feedback
6. Awareness of one's impact on others
7. Ability to effectively manage and deal with conflict
8. Ability to accept personal responsibility
9. Ability to appropriately and effectively express feelings

A supervisor may present a supervisee with this list and score the supervisee based on these elements, perhaps on a scale of 1–5 or 1–10, with the goal of the supervisee developing these dispositions further over time (n.b., the initial creators of this list used the list as part of a training program evaluation instrument where items were scored on a 1–5 Likert scale). The list may be reexamined at specific intervals, such as every 3 months, to assess for improvement and discuss areas that have not improved.

An additional list is presented by Welfare (2010) and can also be used for evaluation purposes. This list incorporates the following primary competencies addressed by professional organizations and accrediting bodies (Welfare, 2010):

1. Assessment and conceptualization
2. Treatment planning
3. Intervention skills
4. Therapeutic alliance skills
5. Professional, ethical, and legal behavior
6. Multicultural competence
7. Interpersonal attributes

Regardless of which evaluation instrument a supervisor uses, it is imperative that a supervisor knows and understands the performance standards to which the supervisee is expected to adhere. The supervisor should make certain that the supervisee understands the standards of practice in the field. Although most counselors are exposed to this information repeatedly in their preparation program, supervisors should recognize that the information makes better sense to most counselors once they are actually in practice.

Supervisors should also make certain that their supervisees understand how the standards of practice provide the supervisor with the point of reference from which to assess supervisee performance.

Supervisors will often select evaluation tools based on the supervisee's training, licensing, or employment requirements. However, supervisors may elect to implement additional evaluative measures, so that they can comprehensively assess one's overall competence across multiple domains of practice. In that a supervisor ultimately holds the responsibility and liability for his supervisee's competence, it is necessary for supervisors to thoroughly understand how the supervisee functions in each and every practice domain. This specific understanding is especially useful when a supervisee is showing underperformance; that is, the supervisor who has specific knowledge of multiple areas of functioning can determine whether the supervisee is having problematic behaviors, which warrant specific remediation, or if the supervisee is generally unfit to be working directly with clients at all.

## Supervisor Competence and Responsibility

Supervisors have an ethical responsibility to engage in ongoing formal and informal evaluations (American Counseling Association, 2005; Supervision Interest Network, Association for Counselor Education and Supervision [ACES], 1993). The Ethical Guidelines for Educators and Supervisors (ACES, 1993) clearly states that "Supervisors, through ongoing supervisee assessment and evaluation, should be aware of any personal or professional limitations of supervisees which are likely to impede future professional performance." (Section 2.12). Clinical supervisors are evaluators by definition and are constantly assessing the supervisee's performance in terms of professional competence and ability to serve clients safely and well. Although this can be admittedly quite stressful and difficult, it is simply too central a function to be overlooked or minimized (Benson & Holloway, 2005). A supervisor who diminishes or ignores his responsibility as an evaluator is not practicing competent, ethical counselor supervision.

Even when a supervisor is able and willing to accurately and honestly assess a counselor's performance, the process of sharing one's assessment formally or even informally can be a cause of anxiety or concern. Many supervisors feel hesitant to engage in evaluative processes for a number of reasons. For instance, supervisors may simply not know how to evaluate or assess a supervisee in a manner appropriate to his development and experience level, especially if he did not experience evaluative assessment from his own supervisor. Further, supervisors may feel inept at delivering feedback in a supportive manner. Supervisors are counselors who are well practiced in providing unconditional positive regard and nonjudgmental objectivity to their clients, and the role shift from counselor to supervisor impedes their ability to bring professional judgment into a helping relationship

(Powell, 2004). Supervisors are used to exercise their power with great caution and often seek to empower others; thus, they may feel uncomfortable providing verbal or written evaluation that requires them to acknowledge the power that is inherent to their position (Borders & Brown, 2005; Holloway, 1995). Supervisors may experience guilt or concern about the consequences of critical evaluative feedback on a supervisee's well-being; that is, a supervisee may experience emotional distress, shame, increased anxiety, and other factors that supervisors are typically used to reducing, not inducing, in others. Further, supervisors may fear the repercussions of negative evaluations on several levels: on client care, on job performance, on the supervisee's willingness to disclose in supervision, and on the quality of the supervisory working alliance.

Positive supervisory alliances rely on trust and emotional safety, amongst other factors. Supervisors honor that trust by providing honest, accurate evaluation of a supervisee's work in an ongoing, professional manner. According to Hahn and Molnar (1991, p. 419), "good supervisory relationships are based on several factors, none of which is incompatible with accurate evaluations." In fact, research reveals that effective supervisors provide regular, ongoing, critical feedback in a respectful and professional manner (Chur-Hansen & McLean, 2007). On the other hand, supervisors who are not able or willing to provide ongoing critical feedback or who provide only praise are often viewed as ineffective and undesirable (Chur-Hansen & McLean, 2007; Magnuson, Wilcoxon, & Norem, 2000). The absence of honest, accurate evaluation places a supervisor on shaky legal and ethical ground, so supervisors are well advised to accept and embrace this component of their practice for the best interest and protection of all parties.

### Evaluation and Due Process

Supervisors are the professionals charged with the task of monitoring and evaluating a supervisees' ability to practice at any given time (ACES, 1993). However, supervisors may feel trapped as they balance the desire to protect clients from harm with their own desire to stay out of complicated legal matters or, at the very least, conflictual situations. Supervisors and counselor educators are concerned with lawsuits if they remove a supervisee from practice or, in more extreme circumstances, the counseling field entirely. However, supervisors who make regular and accurate evaluation a part of their practice can comfortably take the necessary actions to remove a counselor from practice when needed for client protection.

As discussed in Chapter 12, due process is a constitutional right that affords supervisees a chance to learn of concerns and remediate their work before being denied the right to practice counseling. Supervisors working with supervisees from training programs will likely be the most concerned with issues of due process, as due process must be followed in many cases to remove a student from a training program. The following are some steps that an internship supervisor may take that will help ensure due process is followed if a problem arises:

1. Clearly communicate the training experience expectations with specific focus on the assessment or evaluation criteria.
2. Specify how and when formal evaluation will occur (if the university provides an assessment tool, indicate that on the contract as well).
3. Specify how and when remedial efforts will occur when necessary. (The aforementioned items are all included in the supervision contract and discussed during the first supervision session.)
4. Develop an initial relationship with the university supervisor/professor/internship liaison; share the expectations and evaluation criteria with that person.
5. Ask the university liaison to make site visits or conduct phone check-ins regularly, during which time progress is accurately and transparently reported (in the presence of the supervisee).
6. Document clearly the goals of supervision and make certain the goals align with the areas of noted concern.
7. Maintain supervision notes where progress and feedback is clearly documented.
8. Assign homework to the supervisee that addresses the areas of concern; keep copies of these assignments.
9. If the supervisor has any concerns about the supervisee making adequate progress, contact the university immediately and express these concerns. Ask for feedback about your conceptualization of the problem to learn whether any additional contextual variables may be affecting performance.
10. Ask the university to be part of the remedial plan. Do not work in isolation or as a separate entity to the university.

Supervisors, at times, feel hesitant to contact a university for fear of getting a supervisee "in trouble" or straining the supervisory relationship. At times, supervisors are not sure whether the supervisee is truly underperforming or if the problem is external to the supervisee. Supervisors should make early contact with the training program to elicit help in these situations, and the supervisor should be transparent with the supervisee about this process. Although this may cause some initial stress or anxiety for the supervisee, the supervisor is wise to ensure there is open communication and ongoing cooperation between all parties. The supervisor may get some assistance from trained counselor educators and may learn that the problems the supervisee is demonstrating preceded this particular internship experience, unbeknownst to the field supervisor. Supervisors should recognize that universities need a great deal of documentation to adequately demonstrate due process;

that is, supervisees need formal evaluation describing the deficiencies and a chance to remediate such deficiencies. A supervisor who waits until the end of a placement to discuss concerns with the program has hindered the program from having adequate time to help a supervisee remediate. Thus, the university does not have the chance to follow due process and will have great difficulty justifying holding a supervisee back from progressing into the field.

## Is It Time to Enact the Gate Keeping Function?

Supervisors have the difficult evaluative task of discerning which problematic behaviors can be corrected and which problems indicate that the supervisee should not be practicing at this time (the gate keeping function of supervision). Problematic behaviors are behaviors, attitudes, or characteristics that are fairly typical for a professional at that supervisee's training level or in that particular context (Lamb, Cochran, & Jackson, 1991). On the contrary, *impairment* refers to the supervisee who is not competent to practice and will usually demonstrate many of the following characteristics (Lamb et al., 1987; Lamb, Cochran, & Jackson, 1991):

1. The supervisee does not appear to acknowledge or understand the problematic behavior when presented with feedback about it.
2. The problematic behavior is not a simple skill deficit (training alone will not resolve the deficiency).
3. The supervisee consistently provides service that is negatively affected by the problem areas.
4. The problematic behavior spans across several areas of professional functioning.
5. The problem area has potential for ethical or legal consequence if not addressed.
6. The supervisor or training personnel spend a disproportionate or unusual amount of time addressing the supervisee.
7. The supervisee does not improve with feedback, remedial efforts, or time.
8. The supervisee's behavior negatively affects the public image of the agency or institution.

These features help a supervisor to determine whether the supervisee can be effectively worked with to remediate the problematic areas. Remediation is the term used to describe the supervisor's actions that are taken to correct or improve a specific supervisee problem or skill deficit. Although a supervisor has the responsibility to assist a supervisee to the fullest extent of his abilities, many supervisors recognize that, occasionally, a supervisee's deficits or problems are simply irreparable enough to warrant ongoing contact with clients.

Lamb, Cochran, and Jackson (1991) present a four-process plan to identify and respond to supervisee impairment. Although their plan was intended for supervisees in a training program, this plan could be quite easily adopted by professional organizations and private practice supervisors for use with any counseling supervisee. The plan is described below.

## Reconnaissance and Identification

This step involves the supervisor engaging in an ongoing assessment process in which he gathers information about the supervisees' initial performance. The evaluation loop begins: the supervisor provides corrective and evaluative feedback, the supervisee has the opportunity to incorporate the feedback, and the supervisor continues to assess how the supervisee performs. The supervisor provides written and verbal feedback that is consistent in content along with skill development and training recommendations.

The supervisor describes areas of concerns in terms of hypothesis that will be either confirmed or disconfirmed. For instance, a supervisor might say, "I have an initial hunch that you are finding it difficult to challenge clients for fear of causing discomfort to one or both of you. This may negatively impact your work in time. Let's keep an eye on this."

## Discussion and Consultation

This step involves ongoing review of the supervisee's development with special attention paid to the areas in which the supervisee has received feedback. This phase may include discussion of alternatives and may include measures like additional oversight if concerns are continuing to grow.

## Implementation and Review

This phase addresses the supervisee's ability to change and continue to develop based on ongoing feedback. In some cases, supervisees are still not making appropriate changes to bring their demonstrated skills to acceptable professional standards. In these instances, supervisors will meet with the supervisee and other relevant parties to address the problems. This may be an employment supervisor, human resource personnel, licensing board representative, or other key person who has a vested interest in the supervisee's underperformance. In this phase, the vested parties may decide that the supervisee should be suspended from practice because an imminent possibility of harm to a client or clients. Supervisees are an integral part of this process, and discussions happen in their presence with transparency and honesty. The supervisee is given a clear explanation, in writing and verbally, of what needs to improve before returning to practice.

## Anticipating and Responding to Organizational Reaction

After the probation or suspension that occurred in the prior phase, all involved parties typically brace themselves for the necessary fallout from the decision. Supervisees may lose their job or practice, their license, or both. Sometimes, supervisees are transferred to a position that does not involve seeing clients directly. In these cases, there are consequences to the clients, the colleagues, and the supervisee. There may be vicarious impact as well; because these situations are necessarily kept discrete and confidential, colleagues or peers may experience heightened anxiety or concern, especially if they receive distorted or inaccurate information about the supervisee's plight.

Although these steps may seem cumbersome and challenging, supervisors will find that these difficult situations are not likely to be common in their practice. Further, they will likely feel quite satisfied in knowing that they effectively protected the clients and the integrity of the profession by taking appropriate, impactful steps to help a supervisee avoid harm to clients.

## Risk Management When Gate Keeping

Asking or requiring a supervisee to step away from practice is often a painful and stressful task for all involved. Supervisors are often concerned about whether they have acted appropriately, objectively, professionally, and in the best interest of all parties. Self-doubt and second guessing are common. Supervisors will find that consultation and supervision-of-supervision are useful tools in making sure that objectivity remains intact, all necessary due process steps are thoroughly followed, and the best interests of the clients, the profession, and the supervisee are adequately addressed. Further, supervisors typically need emotional, psychological, and perhaps legal support when engaging in a process of this nature. However, with ample support, consultation, and diligent documentation, supervisors will find themselves on fairly certain legal and ethical footing.

When a supervisor determines the need to prohibit a supervisee from direct client care, an ample trail of documentation is necessary. Specifically, documents should include any and all assessments or formal evaluations that were provided to the supervisee, as well as any plans or contracts that specify how the supervisee may make the needed improvements. The supervisor needs to demonstrate that the supervisee had been given enough warning and chance to remediate performance concerns. This is especially important to an employer, training program, or state regulatory board because, without such documentation, there is not sufficient evidence to prove that due process has been honored.

Further, a supervisor should not hesitate to elicit the assistance of the state licensing board when problems arise. Supervisors can contact the board to present a hypothetical situation or may need the board to help remove a supervisee from client contact. The licensing boards are intended to protect the consumers and are typically quite concerned when a report of supervisee malpractice has been made.

## DOCUMENTATION IN SUPERVISION

### To Document or Not to Document?

Documentation is a critical and effective risk management activity that all supervisors should faithfully and diligently attend to (Falvey, 2002: Harrar, VandeCreek, & Knapp, 1990). As counselors, supervisors likely fully understand the importance and relevance of accurate, timely documentation in the context of client care. In clinical supervision, documentation is especially significant on two levels: first, to document appropriate oversight of client care, and second, to provide documentation and record of supervisee evaluation. Surprisingly, many supervisors neglect to document their work (Falvey, 2002). However, Falvey (2002, p. 117) reminds supervisors of the legal doctrine stating that "an absent or inadequate record will itself be viewed as evidence of substandard care, no matter what care was actually provided."

Documentation in supervision is not optional (Falvey, 2002). Written supervision documentation provides evidence of ethical and comprehensive client care, thus providing additional legal protection for the supervisor and supervisee similar to the protection provided by progress notes that counselors write about therapy sessions (Glenn & Serovich, 1994). Supervisors have the responsibility to be familiar with each and every one of the client cases their supervisees are working with (Huber & Baruth, 1987). This may seem like an impossible task to supervisors whose supervisees have tremendous caseloads. However, oversight of all cases is necessary to avoid negligence on the part of the counseling supervisee and the supervisor. Supervisors need to ensure that supervisees are not losing track of their clients, forgetting to attend to particular client needs, or allowing clients to slip through the cracks inadvertently or, in some instances, intentionally.

Falvey, Caldwell, and Cohen (2002) provide a comprehensive system called "The Focused Risk Management Supervision System (FORMSS)." This system is a collection of documents that are designed to provide supervisors with a concise yet comprehensive method of supervision documentation. Although some of the forms are available in the appendices of this text, the collection in its entirety may be quite useful to supervisors as they prepare their supervision charts.

## THE SUPERVISION CHART

The Supervision Chart or Supervisee File is the tool that the supervisor creates to organize the many documents that are pertinent to the work with each supervisee. This chart, initially introduced in Chapter 5 of this text, is brought into each supervision session, so that the documents therein are easily accessible. The "chart" may be a simple file folder with the supervisee's name on it or may be a small three-ring binder divided into sections for optimal organization. Regardless of format, the chart should include the following documents:

Supervisee information/contact information form (refer to Chapter 5 for the specific details of the form, or see Appendix B)
The supervision contract
Additional contracts relating to the supervision relationship (e.g., contracts with the agency, with another third party payer, with the university or training program)
A copy of the supervisee's job description or, if a student trainee, the program requirements
A copy of the supervisee's malpractice insurance
The supervisee's resume
The supervisor's professional disclosure form
The supervisee's informed consent document
Copies of the supervisee's license/prelicensure information
Copies of all relevant Codes of Ethics
All evaluations or assessments of the supervisee's work
Attendance and payment log to track actual time spent in supervision and related payment or invoice information
Supervision session notes

### Session Notes

Supervision session notes are kept diligently and regularly by the supervisor. Supervisors should create a form specific to their work setting or may use one of the forms provided in this text (see Appendix F for a sample Supervision Session Report). Regardless of format, the supervision session note should include the following:

Session date
Methods of supervision (live, verbal report, audio/video review)
Duration of session
Initial risk management concerns presented by the supervisee
Names or identifying initials of clients who were reviewed and any relevant treatment planning information or diagnostic information
Clearly specify any guidance or directives given to the supervisee

Risk management items such as duty to warn, abuse, suicidality, and the plans to address such concerns; include any follow-up or resolution notes as well

Skill development feedback and recommendations

Skill or competence issues that were addressed

Supervision homework or reflection assignments

Notes to oneself (the supervisor) about items in need of follow-up

Notes about cancelled or missed supervision appointments

Supervision notes should clearly reflect any evaluative feedback the supervisor provides to the supervisee or self-evaluation the supervisee reveals in session. For instance, if a supervisee notices while watching a video that she avoids skillful interruption for fear of being "rude" to a client, the supervisor will make a note of that insight. The supervisor can then use the supervision records to track patterns of supervisee skills or behaviors and can notice whether behaviors improve or worsen over time. In addition to noting the feedback provided to the supervisee, the supervisor should note the supervisee's reactions or responses to that feedback if it is unusual or noteworthy. For example, a supervisee may seem particularly upset or distressed by an observation the supervisor makes or may seem resistant to an improvement strategy described by the supervisor. Although that may be an isolated response, it is often useful to make a note of anything that may contribute to a better contextual understanding later on.

Session notes are to be written in clear, objective language, similar to the manner in which one writes a progress note about a client. These session notes are effective memory aids and should be used to refresh the supervisor's memory about clients and skill development. Supervisors should review the prior session's notes directly before session and should keep those notes accessible for reference throughout the supervision session.

Supervisors also need to develop a way to ensure they are familiar with every client on the supervisee's caseload. In organizations where caseloads are large, supervisees usually can gain access to an electronic list of his or her clients. Supervisors can ask the supervisee to bring that list into session. Although it may not be possible to review every case, the supervisor can highlight the names of the cases that were reviewed and keep that list until the following session when the remainder of the clients can be reviewed. In smaller practices, supervisees might be asked to bring a current client list each week. Some supervisors ask the supervisees to discuss any new clients that enter their practice. In this situation, it is usually quite easy for a supervisor to begin with a list of the supervisee's clients, then add names as they are introduced and cross names off as they terminate. This process serves two purposes: it documents the supervisor's oversight of the entire caseload and it helps to ensure that the supervisee is not neglecting any of his or her clients.

In addition, supervisors will notice that supervisees actively avoid speaking of certain clients. This may be for a number of reasons, but the avoidance itself is indicative of a dynamic that needs to be addressed in supervision.

## THE CASE REVIEW FORM

An alternative to comprehensive session notes is the Case Review Form introduced by Glenn and Serovich (1994). Although supervisors may engage in a similar process without using this particular form, this form is illustrative of an effective approach to supervision documentation, so is presented here in detail. The Case Review Form allows the supervisor to track and document supervision activities (Glenn & Serovich, 1994). Specifically, cases should be reviewed in depth at each major milestone in the counseling process: from the time of initial contact, through the assessment and treatment planning processes, and completing with termination and follow-up. It does not replace supervision and the conversation therein; instead, it provides a logical method to track and document supervision discussions and the important content of those discussions.

The Case Review Form is a one-page form that is intended to be placed into client charts every time a supervisee gets assigned a new client (Glenn & Serovich, 1994). However, this form can also be effectively used as a record kept separate from the client chart by the supervisor or supervisee or, ideally, the form can be printed on carbonless copy paper, so that the supervisee and supervisor both have access to the same information and each can keep the record in their own supervision charts or portfolios.

The Case Review Form has several components that can be slightly adjusted to fit the particular practice context:

Client(s) name
Counselor name
Date assigned (or initial session date)
Case Milestones and the date the review was completed (including a list of the major case milestones: initial contact, first appointment, assessment completion, treatment plan completion, therapy completed, termination date, and follow-up)
Legal and ethical issues to evaluate and monitor (with a note to document any and all actions pertaining to legal or ethical issues)
A note-taking portion where the date, supervisor's comments, and signatures of both the supervisor and supervisee can be included

The Case Review Form is intended to document the facts relevant to a case and positive reinforcement of the supervisee's skillful behaviors (Glenn & Serovich, 1994). This form is also the place where supervisors should document specific directives when given, and additional questions that arise for the supervisor and supervisee as they discuss a case.

The initial authors of the form invite supervisors to adjust the form to align with one's theoretical orientation and practice setting (Glenn & Serovich, 1994). However, the form is not intended to replace any part of the supervision process; instead, it is to be used as a documentation and communication tool that facilitates record keeping and clarifies the content of the supervision discussions.

## Record Retention

Although some recommend keeping supervision records for the same length of time as client records should be kept (Falender & Shafranske, 2004; Falvey, 2002), supervisors may wish to keep certain parts of the supervision record indefinitely. Supervisors might determine the length of time client records are saved in their state and will clear their charts of client-related information in accordance with that timeline. However, they may wish to save performance assessments and supervisee profiles indefinitely. This is useful if a supervisee wishes to return for supervision much later in the future, or if the supervisee later in his or her career finds himself mandated to supervision or having difficulties with his practice. The performance assessment notes from earlier in one's career may be quite useful later in practice.

## Additional Risk Management for Supervisors

Accurate, transparent evaluation processes and dedicated documentation practices are two examples of effective risk management practices in supervision. Supervisors have additional measures they can take to reduce the impact of legal or ethical issues as they arise.

## Be Familiar With Practice Materials

Supervisors must be familiar with all forms and documents that the supervisee presents to clients (Disney & Stephens, 1994). This includes informed consent and professional disclosure statements. In addition, supervisors should carefully review all marketing materials, websites, electronic advertisements, and business cards. One of the more common and subtle infractions pertains to scope of practice issues. New counselors may indicate on promotional materials that they have certain areas of specialty. However, unless that supervisee has truly engaged fully enough in learning that specialty, it may be that the area of "specialty" is actually just an area of interest and should be marketed as such. The supervisor can help the supervisee make determinations about specialty areas and will consult with colleagues who practice that specialty to ensure boundaries are not being violated. For instance, imagine a supervisee who claims art therapy as a specialty area. Board certified art therapists are usually familiar with the accreditation and training requirements necessary to claim art therapy as a specialty; however, the well-meaning new counselor who enjoys using art therapy in practice may not be aware that an art therapy credentialing board exists (ATCB; http://www.atcb.org/) and that particular credentials are necessary to claim that specialty (http://www.atcb.org/board_certification/). The supervisor is responsible for ensuring that a supervisee does not mislead consumers to believe that he or she is more specialized or skilled than what is appropriate given his background and training.

## Be Familiar With Online Communities and Marketing Activities

Supervisees have a plethora of technology-based networking tools and communities to become involved in to market their practice or build referral sources. Supervisors must be aware of the supervisee's involvement in such communities. Networking sites such as LinkedIn, Facebook, and Twitter may all be useful and enjoyable for the supervisee, but the supervisor should help the supervisee to determine that appropriate professional boundaries and liability issues are addressed. Most counselors understand that privacy settings must be kept high to ensure appropriate separation of professional and personal information. However, many supervisors will find it helpful to sit with their supervisee at a computer and do an "electronic hunt" for information in the same manner a client might. Perform a Google search, log onto Facebook or MySpace and find the supervisee, view their information on Twitter or LinkedIn, or any of the other sources available. Supervisees are often surprised to find that supervisors can easily access information that the supervisee believes was fairly well protected.

In addition, there are liability concerns in instances when supervisees have blogs or open sites where their clients may be the audience. Supervisees should be advised to be cautious about the information they disseminate. Liability issues or relationship strains may arise when misunderstandings or unintended interpretations occur. Imagine a case of a client who reads his counselor's blog, complete with examples, stories, and guidance. The client believes that the story was written specifically about him and believes the counselor has betrayed his confidence. Supervisors can imagine a number of variations to this situation, but the underlying principles are the same: use discretion and maintain the illusion of confidentiality and actual confidentiality, consider the impact of the written words on the client and the therapeutic relationship, and determine whether the particular mode of communication is worth the inherent risks involved.

## Check Credentials

A supervisor must ensure that the supervisee is using titles and credentials appropriately. If a supervisee is not licensed, he or she should follow the designation allowable by the state regulatory board for prelicensed counselors. This supervisee may not imply that he or she is licensed or practicing autonomously.

*Activity: Check with the state regulatory board to see how prelicensed supervisees should be representing themselves to clients. Carefully review all laws and rules related to prelicensed marketing, representation, and scope of practice issues. Share these rules with the supervisees to ensure compliance.*

Although it is fairly easy for a supervisor to look over paper documents, it is often more challenging to fully understand how a supervisee is presenting himself in person and how thoroughly and accurately he is providing and obtaining informed consent. It is useful for a supervisor to request audio or video recordings of a first session, which can be carefully reviewed for such information.

## Use Technology

Next, it is practically impossible for a modern supervisor to justify complete reliance on verbal report in supervision practice. Although some agencies continue to disallow audio or video recordings, supervisors who wish to well protect themselves from being held liable should only conduct supervision when access to raw session material is possible. Supervisors who engage in regular audio or video review are protecting themselves from being held responsible if a client is damaged by a supervisee (Disney & Stephens, 1994), and with the inexpensive and accessible nature of technology, it is simply negligent to rely on self-report alone. Further, Disney and Stephens (1994) recommend that every session is recorded. This practice takes a minimal amount of time and provides a more optimal level of protection for all parties; the supervisor, supervisee, and especially the clients.

## Direct Client Contact

Another important risk management tool is direct client contact or live supervision. Supervisors may need to enter a counseling session or meet with a client if the supervisor has concerns that the client is not being appropriately treated (Disney & Stephens, 1994). This is a complicated matter as the presence of the supervisor inevitably has an impact on the therapeutic relationship, so this should only happen after careful forethought and planning.

## Time

Supervisors need to be certain that they are spending adequate time with their supervisee. Sometimes, supervisors believe that they need to spend whatever amount of time is required by the agency, licensing board, or training program. However, those time requirements are typically stated as minimums. Instead, supervisors need to determine when a supervisee needs additional time and the supervisor needs to be available to provide that time. Oftentimes, supervisees may express resistance to spending more time in supervision, especially if they are contending with difficult work load issues. However, supervisors hold the liability for that supervisee's work and may have to help the supervisee find a way to receive extra oversight and supervision when either party determines that need.

## Be Selective

Supervisors may be selective about who they supervise, where they supervise, and how they supervise. Supervisors are agents of change; as such, they should not accept the idea that they must do supervision a particular way because the agency or organization's history dictates the practice. Instead, supervisors should recognize that they are hired or promoted into the role because of their value and expertise. They should share their expertise with the parties who may assist the supervisee in aligning the supervision practices to current professional standards. Most agencies will allow changes to the status quo if they understand the positive impact such change will have on client care and cost. If clients are better served and supervisees are better supported, there will likely be fewer threats of lawsuit and less employee turnover (which agencies will recognize as costly endeavors). Supervisors have an ethical responsibility to not accept more supervisees than they can adequately supervise and should resist the urge to supervise someone who is beyond their scope of supervisory capability. Use the Pre-Supervision Interview (discussed in Chapter 4) as a time to screen potential supervisees thoroughly and make decisions based on objective, rational criteria.

## Back-Up Plan

Supervisors should have a back-up plan for their supervisees to follow when they will be unavailable for a significant length of time (more than 24 hours). This back-up person should be a colleague who is also skilled in supervision. Supervisees should be informed in advance of the need to use the back-up supervisor at a particular time, and it is helpful to let the supervisees know how and when to access the back-up supervisor when needed. Supervisees may be instructed to use the back-up supervisor for issues concerning client safety, mandatory reporting, suicide and homicide concerns, and similar topics. The back-up supervisor should be asked to keep detailed notes of any situation that arises, and a plan should be made to check in with the back-up supervisor directly upon return to practice.

## Consult, Consult, Consult

Supervisors must have a roster of available professionals to consult with when in need. Supervisors, like counselors, should not work in isolation and should call upon others for help as soon as there is a hint that it is needed.

*Activity: Develop your roster of professionals to consult with. Complete the form below. When you discover some items are blank, contact some of your colleagues or check with your state counseling organizations to learn about additional support people or venues available if the need arises. Do not stop working on this form until it is complete; once it is complete, it should be stored in an easily accessible, prominent place where you can quickly reference it as needed.*

*My Consultation Roster:*

> Include the name, position or title, agency or practice setting, and phone number or email address for each of the following:
> Your clinical supervisor
> Your administrative supervisor
> Three colleagues who are trained in clinical supervision (be sure they are trained to provide supervision; remember that experience alone does not imply adequate training)
> A local expert on clinical supervision (typically a counselor educator from a local university's counseling or psychology department) or the person from whom you took a supervision class or workshop
> Your attorney or your agency's legal liaison
> Your malpractice insurance's advice or consultation contact information
> Your state licensing board legal representative or investigator
> Your state counseling organization legal representative or consultant
> Your national organization legal representative or advice line

# FOURTEEN

# The Fine Art of Feedback

*O*ne definition of *art* is a "method, facility, or knack" (Collins English Dictionary, n.d.). To get something *down to a fine art* is to become especially skilled through education and practice. This seems especially applicable when one considers the role of feedback in clinical supervision. Feedback in its finest form is beneficial, impactful, and meets its core intentions: to protect clients, shape supervisee skills, and influence future actions. At its worst, feedback is ineffective, damaging, and far reaching in its toxicity. Supervisors who have mastered the art of feedback know how to tailor the delivery, method, and techniques of their feedback so that the supervisee can best hear, understand, and utilize the information. Supervisors without this knack may find the feedback process to be the most unsatisfying and ineffective task of supervision, much to the detriment of all involved. Where the supervisory relationship is the heart of supervision, the feedback process is undoubtedly the soul.

This chapter examines many dimensions of feedback so that supervisors may develop consistent, intentional methods to guide their feedback practices. First, the chapter examines the multiple layers of feedback and feedback loops surrounding the supervisee. Second, this chapter discusses the characteristics of effective and ineffective feedback, with a significant focus on creating a feedback-friendly climate. Next follows some specific instruction about how to deliver feedback in an effective, impactful manner, as well as a consideration of how to negotiate the feedback cycle with the supervisee. Following that is an examination of feedback pitfalls to be avoided, and the chapter concludes with some specific examples of feedback in action.

## THE NATURE OF FEEDBACK

Clinical supervision is, at its very core, the opportunity for a supervisee to develop clinical skills and improve clinical competence through a thoughtful examination and discussion of how others experience his work. This examination focuses on the *feedback*, or responses, a supervisee receives from multiple sources about his clinical performance and the effectiveness of that performance. Feedback is an integral component of human behavior and is foundational in how humans learn and develop. Humans receive feedback about their actions or words, decide how they would like to interpret and make meaning of that feedback, and use that feedback to determine how they will act in the future. This process is particularly daunting in clinical supervision as supervisees receive feedback, determine which feedback to attend to, attempt to make sense of feedback, and use feedback to better their clinical skills, improve clinical relationships, and determine their clinical effectiveness.

The process of receiving and making meaning of feedback can be professionally and personally impactful. Supervisees and supervisors understand the emotional and psychological impact of the feedback process, so oftentimes times there is an approach-avoidance relationship with feedback. Many counselors feel a strong desire for feedback and would like to know how others experience their work. At the same time, they sometimes brace themselves for the inevitable sting that certain feedback may cause. While research reveals that supervisees are eager for feedback (e.g., Dowling & Wittkopp, 1982; Heckman-Stone, 2003), supervisees will at times withhold important information from a supervisor, effectively avoiding the negative feedback that would inevitably follow (Ladany et al., 1996). Supervisors experience a similar approach-avoidance struggle. Oftentimes, supervisors would like to share their evaluative opinion of the supervisee's actions with the supervisee but are concerned about the impact of such information. Supervisors feel concern that critical feedback may crush the supervisee's ego or efficacy, or may impact their clinical performance negatively. Further, supervisors are concerned with maintaining a positive supervisory working alliance and worry that providing the supervisee with difficult feedback may strain or tear that alliance.

Supervisors may also feel uncomfortable or incompetent at providing effective, impactful feedback, so may feel a temptation to avoid the process altogether. In spite of the wide range of feelings and behaviors the feedback process elicits, most agree that feedback is a critical, formative component of the counselor development experience and is a central and crucial function of clinical supervision (e.g., Claiborn & Goodyear, 2005).

*Activity:* Consider a time when you received particularly memorable professional feedback as a counselor. Who was the feedback from? How was the feedback delivered? What was the content of the feedback? How did you feel as you received the feedback? How did you feel following the delivery of the feedback? What was the consequence of the feedback? (How did it affect your relationship with the person providing the feedback? How did it impact your work?) What do you suppose made this feedback so memorable?

## CONTENT AND PROCESS

Feedback is comprised of two intertwining features: *content*, or the actual words and information being conveyed, and *process*, or the contextual occurrences that accompany that information. Content refers to the information that is delivered to the supervisee either verbally or, at times, nonverbally, that sends an evaluative or reflective message to the supervisee. *Process* includes variables such as the supervisor's delivery and communication style and technique, the affective tone that accompanies a message, the interpersonal communication that occurs between the supervisor and supervisee, and the manner in which the supervisee attends to the information being discussed. Supervisors who want to make sure their supervisees attend to and utilize feedback are going to be as concerned with the feedback process as they are with content.

While these two components are necessarily intertwined, supervisors need to be thoughtful and competent with each. If a supervisor has insightful, beneficial information to impart but is not skillful at delivering the message, it is likely that the feedback will not be listened to, understood, or incorporated. If a supervisor has a marvelous delivery style but unimpactful or irrelevant content, a similar negative result occurs.

## CONTENT VARIABLES

### Evaluation

Clinical supervision without evaluative feedback is little more than a conversation among colleagues. Feedback is a form of evaluative communication in supervision. Feedback is information that is intended to improve the supervisee's performance by comparing the supervisee's actions to a standard or expectation (van de Ridder, Stokking, McGaghie, & ten Cate, 2008). Feedback is a tool intended to shape and adjust future behaviors so that a supervisee is better aligned with strong practice standards (Claiborn & Goodyear, 2004) or is providing more impactful service to a client. While evaluation may be formative or summative, feedback may best be conceptualized as *formative* evaluation, or evaluation that guides one's behavior in an ongoing manner. This is different from *summative* feedback, which is a distinct, cumulative evaluation of prior work up to the point of evaluation.

### The Positive or Negative Continuum

Feedback is often termed "positive" or "negative." Positive feedback is typically feedback that reassures or confirms a supervisee that his behavior aligns with an appropriate standard of practice. Positive feedback reinforces a choice, typically in the hopes of strengthening the supervisee's resolve to make the same type of decision again in the future, should a similar situation arise. Negative feedback is often called constructive, critical, or corrective feedback and indicates that the supervisee's behavior does not meet the expected standard (Claiborn & Goodyear, 2004). "Positive" and "negative" are terms that refer only to the supervisee's performance in relationship to a standard or measure of practice. This has nothing to do with how the message is received or any of the emotional accompaniments; the terms are merely descriptors of where the supervisee's actions fall in relation to practice standards or expectations (Claiborn & Goodyear, 2004).

## The Question at Hand

According to Osborn and Kelly (2010), formative feedback answers the question "How am I doing?" Supervisors provide feedback that responds to this question, as feedback is intended to help a supervisee improve his performance. Supervisors avoid providing feedback that addresses a supervisee's character, personality, or contextual variables except as they relate to and impact counseling performance.

## Feedback is Facilitative

Feedback should be direct and honest, while being respectful and constructive (Chur-Hansen & McLean, 2006). Supervisors should be specific, behaviorally focused, and clear about the item of discussion. Supervisors should present feedback that elicits a response and will motivate a change. For instance, a supervisor who says "I didn't like the way you spoke with that client. I wouldn't want to be spoken to like that" is probably going to cause some amount of distress in the supervisee, which could motivate change, but the supervisee is left wondering exactly what to change and how. Instead, the supervisor may say, "When your voice got louder and stronger, the client seemed to disengage. I don't know that he actually heard your words." Feedback may be followed by a question designed to elicit thoughtfulness from the supervisee about what behavior he needs to change and how he may change it. To further the example, the supervisor may ask, "What could you do differently so that the client can stay completely present in the session and really hear your words to him?" Next, the supervisor may help the supervisee examine and consider any skill deficits by asking a question like, "Is there anything that may stop you from using a softer voice and checking in with the client? That sounds like it would be effective, but something got in the way of doing that this time. What do you suppose it was?" The supervisee then needs to consider what impaired his performance in that moment so as to avoid that same impediment the next time.

## Declutter

Supervisors provide clear, concise feedback so that supervisees know what to attend to without added clutter. Additionally, this models the clear, concise interjections that a counselor should be using in session with clients. For instance, "I noticed that you praised that client" may elicit more focused thoughtfulness than "I noticed that you complimented the client on his shoes and then later told him he did a great job scaling his depression." Follow-up inquiry should be concise as well. "What did you hope for when you used praise?" is more favorable than "When you gave him that praise, what were you thinking that would accomplish?"

## Proceed With Caution

Select words and sentence structures that reflect tentativeness (Borders & Leddick, 1987). For instance, "Is it that...?" or "Do you imagine...?" present a challenge to the supervisee and require a thoughtful response, whereas "I think it's..." or "You should see that..." do not elicit the same thoughtful contemplation.

## PROCESS VARIABLES

Heckman-Stone (2003) provides a multistep plan that supervisors can follow to prepare and engage a supervisee in the feedback process. The steps are as follows:

- At the beginning of supervision, clearly describe the nature of the supervision process and the centrality of feedback and evaluation in the supervision process.
- Clarify the performance criteria that will be used for evaluation purposes (e.g., standards of practice for the field, a certain list of criteria).
- Provide reliable observation of the supervisee's work. This means that the supervisor is gaining access to video or audio recordings or engaging in some form of live supervision or observation.
- Compare the observed performance with the goals and standards originally presented to the supervisee.
- Facilitate supervisee self-evaluation.
- Provide feedback to the supervisee.
- Discuss the feedback.
- Monitor the supervisee's performance to determine whether feedback was utilized.

This plan is a thorough one and may appear cumbersome, but with practice becomes second nature to many supervisors and supervisees alike.

Additionally, there are several process-related components that clinical supervisors must consider as they develop and hone their art. While feedback may seem like a relatively simple endeavor to some, its many layers of complexity and intricacy paired with its critical importance make its many components worthy of further examination.

## Ethics and Feedback

It is an ethical imperative that supervisors clearly explain the criteria or standards against their performance will be measured. Supervisors must also provide information about how that performance will be measured and how that evaluative information will be communicated to the supervisee (and other parties as appropriate) (Stoltenberg & McNeill, 2010). It is ethically unsound to evaluate supervisees formally on criteria they have not been made familiar with, and it will feel unjust to provide even informal feedback to supervisees in that same manner. While the mere act of providing feedback will not typically strain a supervisory alliance, providing surprising feedback with reference to unbeknownst standards undoubtedly will.

## Source Credibility

Supervisees receive feedback from multiple sources and accept feedback more readily from some sources than others. Supervisees receive informal and/or formal feedback from their clients, their clinical and managerial supervisors, colleagues, and others. They typically assign weight to that feedback based on their perceived credibility and importance of the feedback source. A supervisee is more likely to willingly accept feedback when that source is viewed by the supervisee as credible or relevant. Credibility means that the source is both expert and trustworthy (Claiborn & Goodyear, 2004). The supervisee will determine who is well positioned to provide feedback and will respond to feedback in accordance with his perception of that source's credibility. To this end, it is crucial that supervisors pay attention to the credibility they hold with their supervisees; without credibility as a supervisor and a clinician, the supervisor will have a difficult time encouraging the supervisee to accept and consider his feedback.

Further, supervisors consider the implications of conflicting feedback from different sources. When a supervisor's feedback appears to conflict with the feedback a counselor receives from a client, the supervisee will likely feel some pull to select one feedback item as more credible than the other. Further, multiple sources of feedback may enhance the feedback process if the supervisee has multiple pieces of congruent information, or may cause some angst when the supervisee has seemingly incongruent feedback to contend with.

*Activity:* *Think of two sources of feedback in your professional life: one credible, one not credible. What made the credible person credible enough to provide you with feedback, in your view? What made the other person noncredible? What happened or would have happened if the person without credibility attempted to provide you with feedback?*

*What makes or will make you a credible source of feedback to your supervisees? What do you suppose will hurt your credibility as a source of feedback? Consult with a colleague or friend who readily accepts feedback from you. Ask that colleague or friend what makes them willing to accept feedback from you. Their answers will help you determine what makes you credible to them. While these answers are useful in determining your general credibility, you will also need to learn what makes you credible to your particular supervisee. How will you find this out?*

### Reliability

Similar to credibility, supervisees must determine whether the person providing feedback is providing information based on reliable data. If a supervisor is providing feedback based on verbal report, that supervisor may not be viewed as operating from a reliable viewing platform. That is, the supervisor has not been privy to actual raw data from a session, so is not well equipped to provide reliable feedback about a supervisee's performance in that session. Supervisors may provide feedback about what they experience in the moment with the supervisee, but feedback based on anything less than direct observation may be suspect in the supervisee's view.

### Timing

Research indicates that someone who is learning clinical tasks or is processing and making sense of a simple clinical experience benefits from more immediate feedback (Hattie & Timperley, 2007). For those who are processing more complex matters, some delay may be useful so that the clinician has time to fully engage in the multiple levels of complexity (Clariana, Wagner, & Roher Murphy, 2000). Supervisees can often help a supervisor understand their most receptive and beneficial feedback times as well. Some supervisees know that they work best with more frequent supervision or debriefing. Others recognize that they appreciate time after sessions to absorb and fully integrate the session material before processing that material with another. This is an important topic of conversation that should be covered as the supervisor and supervisee set up their initial supervision contract and determine the frequency and timing of supervision sessions.

## Intent

Supervisors should explain the nature and intent of evaluative feedback at the start of supervision, and perhaps at additional times in the supervision process. A supervisor provides feedback to help a supervisee align with performance standards for the purposes of client care, skill development, and performance improvement. Feedback is not intended to create a clone or soldier for the supervisor, nor is it based on the supervisor's like or dislike for the supervisee's personality or contextual variables.

## Affective Accompaniments

Feedback may elicit an emotional response, as can the absence of feedback. Supervisees may receive feedback that upsets them or causes them distress. They may interpret the feedback as a reflection of their overall competence as a counselor or as a person. They may feel angry, ashamed, frustrated, unfairly judged, or betrayed. Additionally, they may feel supported, bolstered, validated, affirmed, and proud as the result of feedback that they hold in a positive regard. The absence of feedback can cause a wide range of affective experiences as well. Supervisees who believe they are not receiving adequate feedback may feel paranoid, concerned, or insecure about their clinical performance. In the absence of specific feedback, they have little to do but speculate about the quality of their work. On the contrary, some supervisees may feel relieved, confident, and unencumbered in the absence of feedback and view this absence as confirmation that they are indeed performing to standard. Claiborn and Goodyear (2004) remind supervisors that the emotional accompaniments of feedback are important but separate from the evaluative content.

## Volume

Supervisors are not helping the supervisee if they withhold feedback; further, they are not helpful when they provide a barrage of feedback that is too voluminous to be absorbed. Supervisors will consider many variables when considering how much feedback to provide. Supervisors consider the supervisee's openness to feedback at a particular point in time, the usefulness of providing many items of feedback rather than exploring one item in depth.

## Utilization

Providing feedback to a supervisee does not imply that the supervisee will use that feedback. In fact, a supervisee may not actually even receive or notice the feedback that was provided. Further, if a supervisee does not know how to make sense of the feedback or how to apply the feedback to future behaviors, the information may not be translated into action. For feedback to be impactful, the information conveyed must be followed by an outcome or response as shown in the supervisee's future behaviors.

## Delivery Method

There are various methods in which feedback can be provided. Feedback may be verbal, written formally or informally, or administered through electronic modes of communication (e.g., email, discussion boards). Further, supervisors have a myriad of styles and techniques to select from when delivering feedback. One's delivery method, style, and skill largely influence the supervisee's absorption and utilization of the feedback. To provide useful, effective feedback, the supervisor must hone his delivery skills and techniques.

## THE TECHNICAL ASPECTS OF FEEDBACK IN SUPERVISION

### The Spirit of Collaboration

Many supervisors and supervisees alike can probably recall instances of painful feedback in their professional or personal lives. Many can recall tales of woe where feedback resulted in hurt feelings, a broken heart, embarrassment or fear. Skillful humans have developed useful defenses to protect themselves against similar painful feedback and painful emotional experiences. These defenses inevitably are carried into the sensitive and anxiety-provoking supervision experience.

In Chapter 7, supervisee games were described as a somewhat light-hearted way to conceptualize supervisee defenses. Supervisors should keep in mind that defensive strategies, or games, will be accessed at times of perceived threat, and times of feedback are naturally going to be viewed as potentially threatening. This is especially the case when a supervisee is aware that the feedback should be negative if it is to be accurate.

Typically, a supervisor prefers that a supervisee spends his or her energy on self-evaluation and performance improvement rather than on ego protection and defensive strategy. To ensure that real and perceived threats are kept to a minimum, a supervisor should conceptualize the feedback process as a collaborative process in a shared experience. Millar (2009) recommends that supervisors conceptualize feedback as a "meeting point" rather than a uni-directional activity where one person "gives something" to another. Instead, supervision is an interactive, ongoing process with both members equally involved. This approach helps diminish the power imbalance that is inherent in the supervision relationship and reduces the opportunity for misuse or abuse of power (Millar, 2009; Page & Wosket, 2001).

A spirit of collaboration in supervision involves a number of key components. First, the supervisor remembers that while he may have more technical or clinical expertise in the helping profession, he and his supervisee have equal expertise in the business of being human. Supervision is a time and a place for humanness above all else. Supervisors must send a clear message that imperfection is the norm and perfection is useless in the supervision enterprise. If supervisees are performing perfectly, supervision is a boring and useless experience. Thus, supervisees who bring their imperfect choices and behaviors to supervision are performing quite well in their capacity as a supervisee.

Second, the collaborative spirit by definition involves the engagement of both parties: the supervisor is committed to doing his job by providing feedback regularly and effectively, and the supervisee is committed to his job by engaging in discussion of such feedback. Further, the supervisee joins the supervisor in the feedback process by engaging in self-evaluation of his work and by actively evaluating the effectiveness of his supervisor and the supervision experience. Thus, the collaborative spirit is one of reciprocal feedback. The supervisor and supervisee provide feedback to one another in a spirit of mutual evaluation, and each agrees to evaluate their own performances in the spirit of ongoing improvement as well. Finally, a collaborative spirit means that the supervisor and supervisee remind one another constantly of the mutuality of their mission: That is, they both wish to serve clients well, develop their respective skills, and have an effective, mutually satisfying supervision experience together.

## WORKING WITH INTENTION

When counselors provide feedback to a client, they should first consider their therapeutic intention in providing such feedback. Similarly, when a supervisor is providing feedback to a supervisee, he should consider his supervisory intention in providing such feedback.

To provide intentional, impactful feedback, supervisors have many decisions to make internally. First, supervisors have to determine specifically which behavior or skill they would like to provide feedback about. Next, they have to consider how to provide feedback so that it can be well received by the supervisee. This means they consider both the content of the feedback and the emotional experience that coincides with that feedback. Claiborn and Goodyear (2004) state that "the extent to which feedback, whether negative or positive, is accompanied by particular emotions in the sender and receiver is primarily a matter of technique" (p. 211). So, supervisors carefully and intentionally plan their technical delivery based on what they know about the technical aspects of feedback and the personality and contextual experiences of their supervisee.

Supervisors are cautious not to provide feedback callously or impulsively. Instead, they use supervision as an opportunity to model appropriate and clinically intentional feedback and information sharing in the same manner the supervisor wishes the supervisee to use with his clients.

## EARNING THE RIGHT TO CHALLENGE

When a supervisor provides feedback, the supervisee is immediately challenged to do something with that feedback simply by the nature of the feedback process. The supervisee may accept the feedback and use it as a catalyst for change, or he may dismiss the feedback or cast it aside for later consideration. However, before a supervisor can issue challenging feedback, the supervisor needs to earn the right to provide such feedback. Earning the right to provide feedback is not a difficult process, but it can certainly be a complex one. The right to challenge is based on several dynamic features: the supervisor's credibility in the supervisee's view, the supervisor's skill in creating an emotionally safe and accepting environment, and the supervisee's willingness to be supervised. Supervisors should remember that they are continually earning the right to challenge the supervisee; when a supervisor is working diligently and regularly to earn that right, the supervisee will often reciprocate with a willing and open stance.

Earning the right to challenge does not imply that supervisors wait for a supervisee's permission to provide feedback. In some cases, permission will simply never be granted. Supervisors accept their evaluative role as part of the supervision process and readily embrace the usefulness and necessity of feedback as a core component of skill development. Supervisors provide feedback readily, but ensure that they are working hard to deliver that feedback in an impactful way that honors the supervisee's experience, knowledge, and competence.

## THE THREE CONSTITUENTS

In dyadic (individual) supervision, there are three constituents of feedback that all need to be present for the feedback cycle to be fully complete: the supervisor, the feedback message itself, and the supervisee. The primary job of the message is to influence the supervisee to make change; so, the supervisor has to consider carefully how to make the message as influential as possible and deliver it in the most effective way possible. Each constituent needs to be committed to the process for the feedback loop to be complete. If the supervisee appears distracted or otherwise struggling, the supervisor should take care to ensure that distracting issues are settled before proceeding. Additionally, the supervisor has the responsibility to ensure that the feedback is well intentioned, well timed, and thoughtful. If the supervisor is having an emotional reaction or simply a bad day, the supervisor needs to make certain that his distracters or interfering variables are minimized enough to engage in objective, effective.

Supervisors should also consider the following guidelines as they consider the feedback process and related contextual factors:

*Familiarize your supervisee with your feedback style* during the presupervision interview and subsequent sessions.

*Create a culture of mutual feedback.* Supervisors and supervisees share feedback with each other. Supervisors engage supervisees in a process of evaluating the effectiveness of their supervision sessions and their supervisor, and through this process, a common bond of vulnerability and acceptance is formed.

*Integrate feedback* into all sessions, regularly. Formative feedback is woven into the session and is not an isolated or discrete event. Do not save feedback for the end of session or provide it as an afterthought a week or two later. Feedback is provided in the here and now and is timely, thus giving the supervisee a chance to reflect upon what has recently occurred. It is difficult to make improvements on actions that are merely a vague memory.

*Do not ask for permission* to provide feedback. Feedback is an expected and central part of the supervision process. Asking for feedback is analogous to asking for permission to practice supervision competently.

*Do not apologize* or cringe when sharing feedback. An apology implies that feedback is inherently painful or wrong. Instead, it is welcome, helpful, and necessary.

*Notice nonverbal signals* that the feedback is not being received or listened to. Move from feedback content to feedback process if any barriers to reception are detected.

*Be specific and descriptive.* Use language that clearly compares the behavior to the standard or criteria it is being measured against.

## EFFECTIVE AND INEFFECTIVE FEEDBACK

Supervisors and supervisees typically share similar wishes of the feedback process; that is, they would like feedback to be effective, relevant, impactful, and relatively painless. The following lists of effective and ineffective feedback characteristics are by no means comprehensive; rather, they are a compilation of items from the literature (Claiborn & Goodyear, 2004; Holloway, 1995) as well as anecdotal and personal experience. Supervisors should add to the list and might consider these lists to be a set of standards by which their own performance as a "feedback provider" is measured.

Effective feedback is:

Accurate
Supportive
Challenging
Clear
Specific
Timely
Intentional
Immediate
Credible
Objective
Constructive
Contextually appropriate
Culturally appropriate
Matter-of-fact
Consistent
Ongoing
Behaviorally oriented
Relevant
Meaningful
Linked to standards of practice
Based on direct observation
Well balanced between positive and negative
Well intentioned: for the good of client care or skill improvement

Ineffective feedback is:

Erroneous
Inadequate
Vague
Nonspecific
Inaccurate
Late: past the point of relevance
Conflicting or inconsistent
Culturally inappropriate
Biased or distorted
Voluminous and overwhelming
Mal intentioned
Mean spirited
"Out of the Blue"

Character based
Personally attacking
Territorial in nature
Seemingly arbitrary
Based on assumptions or faulty guesses

*Activity:* Consider your experience receiving feedback as a supervisee and consider the ineffective and effective feedback lists above. In your opinion, what are the top five qualities of effective feedback? Ineffective feedback?

# Appendix A

**ASSOCIATION FOR COUNSELOR EDUCATION AND SUPERVISION**
Adopted by ACES Executive Counsel and Delegate Assembly March, 1993

Preamble:

The Association for Counselor Education and Supervision (ACES) is composed of people engaged in the professional preparation of counselors and people responsible for the ongoing supervision of counselors. ACES is a founding division of the American Counseling Association (ACA) and as such adheres to ACA's current ethical standards and to general codes of competence adopted throughout the mental health community.

ACES believes that counselor educators and counseling supervisors in universities and in applied counseling settings, including the range of education and mental health delivery systems, carry responsibilities unique to their job roles. Such responsibilities may include administrative supervision, clinical supervision, or both. Administrative supervision refers to those supervisory activities that increase the efficiency of the delivery of counseling services; whereas, clinical supervision includes the supportive and educative activities of the supervisor designed to improve the application of counseling theory and technique directly to clients.

Counselor educators and counseling supervisors encounter situations that challenge the help given by general professional ethical standards. These situations require more specific guidelines that provide appropriate guidance in everyday practice.

The Ethical Guidelines for Counseling Supervisors are intended to assist professionals by helping them:

1. Observe ethical and legal protection of clients' and supervisees' rights;
2. Meet supervisees' training and professional development needs in ways consistent with clients' welfare and programmatic requirements; and
3. Establish policies, procedures, and standards for implementing programs.

The specification of ethical guidelines enables ACES members to focus on and to clarify the ethical nature of responsibilities held in common. Such guidelines should be reviewed formally every five years, or more often if needed, to meet the needs of ACES members for guidance.

The Ethical Guidelines for Counselor Educators and Counseling Supervisors are meant to help ACES members in conducting supervision. ACES is not currently in a position to hear complaints about alleged non-compliance with these guidelines. Any complaints about the ethical behavior of any ACA member should be measured against the ACA Ethical Standards and a complaint lodged with ACA in accordance with its procedures for doing so.

One overriding assumption underlying this document is that supervision should be ongoing throughout a counselor's career and not stop when a particular level of education, certification, or membership in a professional organization is attained.

### DEFINITIONS OF TERMS:

**Applied Counseling Settings** - Public or private organizations of counselors such as community mental health centers, hospitals, schools, and group or individual private practice settings.

**Supervisees** - Counselors-in-training in university programs at any level who work with clients in applied settings as part of their university training program, and counselors who have completed their formal education and are employed in an applied counseling setting.

**Supervisors** - Counselors who have been designated within their university or agency to directly oversee the professional clinical work of counselors. Supervisors also may be persons who offer supervision to counselors seeking state licensure and so provide supervision outside of the administrative aegis of an applied counseling setting.

1. Client Welfare and Rights
    1.01 The Primary obligation of supervisors is to train counselors so that they respect the integrity and promote the welfare of their clients. Supervisors should have supervisees inform clients that they are being supervised and that observation and/or recordings of the session may be reviewed by the supervisor.
    1.02 Supervisors who are licensed counselors and are conducting supervision to aid a supervisee to become licensed should instruct the supervisee not to communicate or in any way convey to the supervisee's clients or to other parties that the supervisee is himself/herself licensed.
    1.03 Supervisors should make supervisees aware of clients' rights, including protecting clients' right to privacy and confidentiality in the counseling relationship and the information resulting from it. Clients also should be informed that their right to privacy and confidentiality will not be violated by the supervisory relationship.

**1.04**  Records of the counseling relationship, including interview notes, test data, correspondence, the electronic storage of these documents, and audio and video recordings are considered to be confidential professional information. Supervisors should see that these materials are used in counseling, research, and training and supervision of counselors with the full knowledge of the clients and that permission to use these materials is granted by the applied counseling setting offering service to the client. This professional information is to be used for full protection of the client. Written consent from the client (or legal guardian, if a minor) should be secured prior to the use of such information for instructional, supervisory, and/or research purposes. Policies of the applied counseling setting regarding client records also should be followed.

**1.05**  Supervisors shall adhere to current professional and legal guidelines, such as Section D-1 of the ACA Ethical Standards, when conducting research with human participants.

**1.06**  Counseling supervisors are responsible for making every effort to monitor both the professional actions, and failures to take action, of their supervisees.

2.  Supervisory Role

Inherent and integral to the role of supervisor are responsibilities for:

  **a.**  Monitoring client welfare;
  **b.**  Encouraging compliance with relevant legal, ethical, and professional standards for clinical practice;
  **c.**  Monitoring clinical performance and professional development of supervisees; and
  **d.**  Evaluating and certifying current performance and potential of supervisees for academic, screening, selection, placement, employment, and credentialing purposes.

**2.01**  Supervisors should have had training in supervision prior to initiating their role as supervisors.

**2.02**  Supervisors should pursue professional and personal continuing education activities such as advanced courses, seminars, and professional conferences on a regular and ongoing basis. These activities should include both counseling and supervision topics and skills.

**2.03**  Supervisors should make their supervisees aware of professional and ethical standards and legal responsibilities of the counseling profession.

**2.04**  Supervisors of post-degree counselors who are seeking state licensure should encourage these counselors to adhere to the standards for practice established by the state licensure board of the state in which they practice.

2.05   Procedures for contacting the supervisor, or an alternative supervisor, to assist in handling crisis situations should be established and communicated to supervisees.

2.06   Actual work samples via audio and/or video or live observation in addition to case notes should be reviewed by the supervisor as a regular part of the ongoing supervisory process.

2.07   Supervisors of counselors should be meeting regularly in face-to-face sessions with their supervisees.

2.08   Supervisors should provide supervisees with ongoing feedback on their performance. This feedback should take a variety of forms, both formal and informal, and should include verbal and written evaluations. It should be formative during the supervisory experience and summative at the conclusion of the experience.

2.09   Supervisors who have multiple roles (e.g., teacher, clinical supervisor, administrative supervisor, etc.) with supervisees should minimize potential conflicts. Where possible, the roles should be divided among several supervisors. Where this is not possible, careful explanation should be conveyed to the supervisee as to the expectations and responsibilities associated with each supervisory role.

2.10   Supervisors should not participate in any form of sexual contact with supervisees. Supervisors should not engage in any form of social contact or interaction that would compromise the supervisor-supervisee relationship. Dual relationships with supervisees that might impair the supervisor's objectivity and professional judgment should be avoided and/or the supervisory relationship terminated.

2.11   Supervisors should not establish a psychotherapeutic relationship as a substitute for supervision. Personal issues should be addressed in supervision only in terms of the impact of these issues on clients and on professional functioning.

2.12   Supervisors, through ongoing supervisee assessment and evaluation, should be aware of any personal or professional limitations of supervisees that are likely to impede future professional performance. Supervisors have the responsibility of recommending remedial assistance to the supervisee and of screening from the training program, applied counseling setting, or state licensure those supervisees who are unable to provide competent professional services. These recommendations should be clearly and professionally explained in writing to the supervisees who are so evaluated.

2.13   Supervisors should not endorse a supervisee for certification, licensure, completion of an academic training program, or continued employment if the supervisor believes the supervisee is impaired in any way that would interfere with the performance of counseling duties. The presence of any such impairment should begin a process of feedback and remediation wherever possible so that the supervisee understands the nature of the impairment and has the opportunity to remedy the problem and continue with his/her professional development.

**2.14** Supervisors should incorporate the principles of informed consent and participation; clarity of requirements, expectations, roles and rules; and due process and appeal into the establishment of policies and procedures of their institutions, program, courses, and individual supervisory relationships. Mechanisms for due process appeal of individual supervisory actions should be established and made available to all supervisees.

3. Program Administration Role

**3.01** Supervisors should ensure that the programs conducted and experiences provided are in keeping with current guidelines and standards of ACA and its divisions.

**3.02** Supervisors should teach courses and/or supervise clinical work only in areas where they are fully competent and experienced.

**3.03** To achieve the highest quality of training and supervision, supervisors should be active participants in peer review and peer supervision procedures.

**3.04** Supervisors should provide experiences that integrate theoretical knowledge and practical application. Supervisors also should provide opportunities in which supervisees are able to apply the knowledge they have learned and understand the rationale for the skills they have acquired. The knowledge and skills conveyed should reflect current practice, research findings, and available resources.

**3.05** Professional competencies, specific courses, and/or required experiences expected of supervisees should be communicated to them in writing prior to admission to the training program or placement/employment by the applied counseling setting, and, in case of continued employment, in a timely manner.

**3.06** Supervisors should accept only those persons as supervisees who meet identified entry level requirements for admission to a program of counselor training or for placement in an applied counseling setting. In the case of private supervision in search of state licensure, supervisees should have completed all necessary prerequisites as determined by the state licensure board.

3.07 Supervisors should inform supervisees of the goals, policies, theoretical orientations toward counseling, training, and supervision model or approach on which the supervision is based.

3.08 Supervisees should be encouraged and assisted to define their own theoretical orientation toward counseling, to establish supervision goals for themselves, and to monitor and evaluate their progress toward meeting these goals.

3.09 Supervisors should assess supervisees' skills and experience in order to establish standards for competent professional behavior. Supervisors should restrict supervisees' activities to those that are commensurate with their current level of skills and experiences.

3.10 Supervisors should obtain practicum and fieldwork sites that meet minimum standards for preparing students to become effective counselors. No practicum or fieldwork setting should be approved unless it truly replicates a counseling work setting.

3.11 Practicum and fieldwork classes should be limited in size according to established professional standards to ensure that each student has ample opportunity for individual supervision and feedback. Supervisors in applied counseling settings should have a limited number of supervisees.

3.12 Supervisors in university settings should establish and communicate specific policies and procedures regarding field placement of students. The respective roles of the student counselor, the university supervisor, and the field supervisor should be clearly differentiated in areas such as evaluation, requirements, and confidentiality.

3.13 Supervisors in training programs should communicate regularly with supervisors in agencies used as practicum and/or fieldwork sites regarding current professional practices, expectations of students, and preferred models and modalities of supervision.

3.14 Supervisors at the university should establish clear lines of communication among themselves, the field supervisors, and the students/supervisees.

3.15 Supervisors should establish and communicate to supervisees and to field supervisors specific procedures regarding consultation, performance review, and evaluation of supervisees.

3.16 Evaluations of supervisee performance in universities and in applied counseling settings should be available to supervisees in ways consistent with the Family Rights and Privacy Act and the Buckley Amendment.

**3.17** Forms of training that focus primarily on self understanding and problem resolution (e.g., personal growth groups or individual counseling) should be voluntary. Those who conduct these forms of training should not serve simultaneously as supervisors of the supervisees involved in the training.

**3.18** A supervisor may recommend participation in activities such as personal growth groups or personal counseling when it has been determined that a supervisee has deficits in the areas of self understanding and problem resolution that impede his/her professional functioning. The supervisors should not be the direct provider of these activities for the supervisee.

**3.19** When a training program conducts a personal growth or counseling experience involving relatively intimate self disclosure, care should be taken to eliminate or minimize potential role conflicts for faculty and/or agency supervisors who may conduct these experiences and who also serve as teachers, group leaders, and clinical directors.

**3.20** Supervisors should use the following prioritized sequence in resolving conflicts among the needs of the client, the needs of the supervisee, and the needs of the program or agency. Insofar as the client much be protected, it should be understood that client welfare is usually subsumed in federal and state laws such that these statutes should be the first point of reference. Where laws and ethical standards are not present or are unclear, the good judgment of the supervisor should be guided by the following list.

    **a.** Relevant legal and ethical standards (e.g., duty to warn, state child abuse laws, etc.);

    **b.** Client welfare;

    **c.** Supervisee welfare;

    **d.** Supervisor welfare; and

    **e.** Program and/or agency service and administrative needs.

*Source:* Reproduced with permission from the American Counseling Association.

# Appendix B

## Supervisee Information Form

Date: _____

Name (include any prior names): _____

Phone number(s): (Work) _____ (Cell) _____

(Home) _____ Email address: _____

Mailing address: _____

*Employment/training site information:*

Place of practice: _____

Type of setting (agency, private) _____

Position title and duties (or attach a job description): _____

_____

Physical address: _____

Mailing address: _____

Administrative supervisor or employer's name: _____

Phone number: _____ Email address: _____

If private practice, name of back-up counselor or any other person(s) with access to clients/records:

Name(s) and phone number(s) _____

Name of office partners/practice partners (if any): _____

*Education/credentials:*

Degrees (degree type and academic institution): _____
Completion year: _____

Credentials/licenses (license name, date of issue, and whether current):

_____

Currently working toward additional licenses/certifications? Indicate what supervision is required and who will be providing such supervision:

_____

Use the back of this form to describe any history of complaints, grievances, or ethical violations, as well as the outcome of each of those situations (both in training programs and through career).

Attach a resume or employment history.

**Emergency contact person** (Name and Phone number): _____
_____

# Appendix C

## I. COUNSELOR AWARENESS OF OWN CULTURAL VALUES AND BIASES

### A. Attitudes and Beliefs

1. Culturally skilled counselors believe that cultural self-awareness and sensitivity to one's own cultural heritage is essential.
2. Culturally skilled counselors are aware of how their own cultural background and experiences have influenced attitudes, values, and biases about psychological processes.
3. Culturally skilled counselors are able to recognize the limits of their multicultural competency and expertise.
4. Culturally skilled counselors recognize their sources of discomfort with differences that exist between themselves and clients in terms of race, ethnicity, and culture.

### B. Knowledge

1. Culturally skilled counselors have specific knowledge about their own racial and cultural heritage and how it personally and professionally affects their definitions and biases of normality/abnormality and the process of counseling.
2. Culturally skilled counselors possess knowledge and understanding about how oppression, racism, discrimination, and stereotyping affect them personally and in their work. This allows individuals to acknowledge their own racist attitudes, beliefs, and feelings. Although this standard applies to all groups, for White counselors, it may mean that they understand how they may have directly or indirectly benefited from individual, institutional, and cultural racism as outlined in White identity development models.
3. Culturally skilled counselors possess knowledge about their social impact upon others. They are knowledgeable about communication style differences, how their style may clash with or foster the counseling process with persons of color or others different from themselves based on the A, B, and C Dimensions,and how to anticipate the impact it may have on others.

## C. Skills

1.   Culturally skilled counselors seek out educational, consultative, and training experiences to improve their understanding and effectiveness in working with culturally different populations. Being able to recognize the limits of their competencies, they (a) seek consultation, (b) seek further training or education, (c) refer out to more qualified individuals or resources, or (d) engage in a combination of these.
2.   Culturally skilled counselors are constantly seeking to understand themselves as racial and cultural beings and are actively seeking a non-racist identity.

## II. COUNSELOR AWARENESS OF CLIENT'S WORLDVIEW

### A. Attitudes and Beliefs

1.   Culturally skilled counselors are aware of their negative and positive emotional reactions toward other racial and ethnic groups that may prove detrimental to the counseling relationship. They are willing to contrast their own beliefs and attitudes with those of their culturally different clients in a nonjudgmental fashion.
2.   Culturally skilled counselors are aware of their stereotypes and preconceived notions that they may hold toward other racial and ethnic minority groups.

### B. Knowledge

1.   Culturally skilled counselors possess specific knowledge and information about the particular group with which they are working. They are aware of the life experiences, cultural heritage, and historical background of their culturally different clients. This particular competency is strongly linked to the "minority identity development models" available in the literature.
2.   Culturally skilled counselors understand how race, culture, ethnicity, and so forth may affect personality formation, vocational choices, manifestation of psychological disorders, help seeking behavior, and the appropriateness or inappropriateness of counseling approaches.
3.   Culturally skilled counselors understand and have knowledge about sociopolitical influences that impinge on the life of racial and ethnic minorities. Immigration issues, poverty, racism, stereotyping, and powerlessness may impact self-esteem and self-concept in the counseling process.

## C. Skills

1.  Culturally skilled counselors should familiarize themselves with relevant research and the latest findings regarding mental health and mental disorders that affect various ethnic and racial groups. They should actively seek out educational experiences that enrich their knowledge, understanding, and cross-cultural skills for more effective counseling behavior.
2.  Culturally skilled counselors become actively involved with minority individuals outside the counseling setting (e.g., community events, social and political functions, celebrations, friendships, neighborhood groups, and so forth), so that their perspective of minorities is more than an academic or helping exercise.

## III. CULTURALLY APPROPRIATE INTERVENTION STRATEGIES

### A. Beliefs and Attitudes

1.  Culturally skilled counselors respect clients' religious and spiritual beliefs and values, including attributions and taboos, because they affect worldview, psychosocial functioning, and expressions of distress.
2.  Culturally skilled counselors respect indigenous helping practices and respect helping networks among communities of color.
3.  Culturally skilled counselors value bilingualism and do not view another language as an impediment to counseling (monolingualism may be the culprit).

### B. Knowledge

1.  Culturally skilled counselors have a clear and explicit knowledge and understanding of the generic characteristics of counseling and therapy (culture bound, class bound, and monolingual) and how they may clash with the cultural values of various cultural groups.
2.  Culturally skilled counselors are aware of institutional barriers that prevent minorities from using mental health services.
3.  Culturally skilled counselors have knowledge of the potential bias in assessment instruments and use procedures and interpret findings, keeping in mind the cultural and linguistic characteristics of the clients.
4.  Culturally skilled counselors have knowledge of family structures, hierarchies, values, and beliefs from various cultural perspectives. They are knowledgeable about the community where a particular cultural group may reside and the resources in the community.

5. Culturally skilled counselors should be aware of relevant discriminatory practices at the social and community level that may be affecting the psychological welfare of the population being served.

## C. Skills

1. Culturally skilled counselors are able to engage in a variety of verbal and nonverbal helping responses. They are able to send and receive both verbal and nonverbal messages accurately and appropriately. They are not tied down to only one method or approach to helping but recognize that helping styles and approaches may be culture bound. When they sense that their helping style is limited and potentially inappropriate, they can anticipate and modify it.

2. Culturally skilled counselors are able to exercise institutional intervention skills on behalf of their clients. They can help clients to determine whether a "problem" stems from racism or bias in others (the concept of healthy paranoia), so that clients do not inappropriately personalize problems.

3. Culturally skilled counselors are not averse to seeking consultation with traditional healers or religious and spiritual leaders and practitioners in the treatment of culturally different clients when appropriate.

4. Culturally skilled counselors take responsibility for interacting in the language requested by the client and, if not feasible, make appropriate referrals. A serious problem arises when the linguistic skills of the counselor do not match the language of the client. This being the case, counselors should (a) seek a translator with cultural knowledge and appropriate professional background or (b) refer to a knowledgeable and competent bilingual counselor.

5. Culturally skilled counselors have training and expertise in the use of traditional assessment and testing instruments. They not only understand the technical aspects of the instruments but are also aware of the cultural limitations. This allows them to use test instruments for the welfare of culturally different clients.

6. Culturally skilled counselors should attend and work to eliminate biases, prejudices, and discriminatory contexts in conducting evaluations and providing interventions, and should develop sensitivity to issues of oppression, sexism, heterosexism, elitism, and racism.

7. Culturally skilled counselors take responsibility for educating their clients to the processes of psychological intervention, such as goals, expectations, legal rights, and the counselor's orientation.

Arredondo, P., Toporek, M. S., Brown, S., Jones, J., Locke, D. C., Sanchez, J., & Stadler, H. (1996). *Operationalization of the multicultural counseling competencies*. Alexandria, VA: AMCD. Reproduced with permission from the American Counseling Association.

# Appendix D

### Counseling Supervision Contract
Provided by Cynthia J. Osborn, PhD, LPCC-S, Counseling and Human Development Services Program, Kent State University

This contract serves as verification and a description of the counseling supervision provided by Cynthia J. Osborn, PhD, LPCC-S ("Supervisor"), to _____ ("Supervisee"), Counseling Practicum Student enrolled in Practicum I in the CHDS Program at Kent State University for Spring Semester 2010.

## I. PURPOSE, GOALS, AND OBJECTIVES:

a. Monitor and ensure welfare of clients seen by Supervisee
b. Promote development of Supervisee's professional counselor identity and competence
c. Fulfill academic requirement for Supervisee's Practicum
d. Fulfill requirements in preparation for Supervisee's pursuit of counselor licensure

## II. CONTEXT OF SERVICES:

a. One (1) clock hour of individual supervision weekly
b. Individual supervision will be conducted in the Counseling and Human Development Center (CHDC; 310 White Hall), Kent State University, on _____ [day of week], from _____ to _____ [exact time], where monitor/DVD player is available to review video recordings
c. Motivational interviewing style, interpersonal process recall, and role plays will be used in supervision
d. Regular review of counseling video recordings in weekly individual supervision

## III. METHOD OF EVALUATION:

a. Feedback will be provided by the Supervisor during each session, and a formal evaluation, using the CHDS standard evaluation of student clinical skills, will be conducted at mid-semester and at the conclusion of the Spring Semester. A narrative evaluation will also be provided at mid-semester and at the conclusion of the semester as an addendum to the objective evaluations completed.

**293**

b. Specific feedback provided by Supervisor will focus on Supervisee's demonstrated counseling skills and clinical documentation, which will be based on Supervisor's regular observation of Supervisee's counseling sessions (via video recording and live), as well as review of clinical documentation.

c. Supervisee will evaluate Supervisor at mid-semester and at the close of Spring Semester, using the CHDS standard evaluation form for evaluating supervisors. A narrative evaluation will also accompany the objective evaluations.

d. Supervision notes will be shared with Supervisee at Supervisor's discretion and at the request of the Supervisee.


## IV. DUTIES AND RESPONSIBILITIES OF SUPERVISOR AND SUPERVISEE:

1. Supervisor:
   a. Examine client clinical information (e.g., assessment) and determine appropriate services
   b. Review on a regular basis Supervisee's video recorded counseling sessions
   c. Sign off on all client documentation
   d. Challenge Supervisee to justify approach and techniques used
   e. Monitor Supervisee's basic attending skills, specifically those consistent with a motivational interviewing style
   f. Present and model appropriate directives
   g. Intervene when client welfare is at risk
   h. Model and ensure American Counseling Association (ACA; 2005) *ACA Code of Ethics* are upheld
   i. Maintain professional liability insurance coverage
   j. Maintain weekly supervision notes
   k. Assist Supervisee in reviewing various counseling theories, with goal of gaining an appreciation for an integrative practice approach
   l. Assist Supervisee in developing an appreciation for and demonstrating the "spirit" of motivational interviewing
   m. Assist Supervisee in gaining greater self-awareness during counseling and supervision sessions
2. Supervisee:
   a. Uphold ACA Code of Ethics (2005)
   b. Maintain professional liability insurance coverage
   c. View counseling session video recordings in preparation for weekly supervision

    d. Complete "Counselor Trainee Self-Critique and Reflection Form" as a result of having viewed counseling session video recordings and have these ready to discuss in Supervision

    e. Be prepared to discuss all client cases—have client files, current, and completed client case notes, and counseling session video recordings ready to review in weekly supervision sessions

    f. Justify client case conceptualizations made and approach and techniques used

    g. Complete client case notes and supervision notes in a timely fashion and place in appropriate client files

    h. Consult with Counseling Center staff and Supervisor in cases of emergency

    i. Implement supervisory directives in subsequent sessions

    j. Practice skills consistent with a motivational interviewing style with the goal of developing and demonstrating the "spirit" of motivational interviewing

    k. Practice working from a variety of and appropriate counseling theories

    l. Demonstrate willingness to discuss in supervision her experiences of professional development

3. Supervisee's Expressed Learning Objectives for Practicum I:

    a.

    b.

    c.

    d.

    e.

## V. PROCEDURAL CONSIDERATIONS:

    a. Supervisee's written case notes, treatment plans, and video recordings will be reviewed and evaluated in each session.

    b. Issues related to Supervisee's professional development will be discussed in each supervision session.

    c. Sessions will be used to discuss issues of conflict and failure of either party to abide by directives outlined here in contract. If concerns of either party are not resolved in supervision, _____, CHDS Community Counseling program coordinator, will be consulted.

    d. In event of emergency, Supervisee is to contact Supervisor at the office, (000) 000-0000, or at home, (000) 000-0000, or on her cell phone, (000) 000-0000.

## VI. SUPERVISOR'S SCOPE OF COMPETENCE:

Dr. Osborn earned her PhD in counselor education from Ohio University in 1996. She is licensed as a Professional Clinical Counselor, with supervisory endorsement (PCC-S; #E2428) by the state of Ohio, and is also licensed in Ohio as a Chemical Dependency Counselor (LCDC-III). She is currently a Professor in the CHDS Program at Kent State University. She has received formal academic training in clinical supervision, has supervised both CHDS doctoral student supervisors and Community Counseling Master's students during the course of either their supervision or Practica training at Kent State University, and teaches a section of the doctoral level supervision course in the CHDS program at KSU. She has received training and has practiced as an LPCC in the areas of substance abuse counseling and utilizes primarily a solution-focused counseling approach and a motivational interviewing style.

## VII. TERMS OF THE CONTRACT:

This contract is subject to revision at any time, upon the request of either the Supervisor or Supervisee. A formal review of the contract will be made at the mid-term of Spring Semester 2010, and revisions will be made only with consent of Supervisee and approval of the Supervisor.

We agree, to the best of our ability, to uphold the directives specified in this supervision contract and to conduct our professional behavior according to the ethical principles of our professional association.

_____/_____          _____/_____
Supervisor     Date                Supervisee     Date

Counseling and Human Development Center
325 White Hall - Third Floor
Kent State University
Kent, Ohio 44242
(330) 672-2208

This contract is effective from _____ to _____.
(start date)                    (finish date)

(Date of revision or termination) _____

*Source:* Based on Osborn & Davis (1996).

# Appendix E

Lisa Aasheim, PhD, LPC, LMHC, NCC, ACS

Clinical Supervisor

(Business Address)

(Phone Number)

## PROFESSIONAL QUALIFICATIONS

I currently work as an assistant professor in the Counselor Education Department at Portland State University. I am the Director of the Community Counseling Training Clinic and the Coordinator of the School Counseling Program.

I specialized in couples, marriage, and family and community mental health at the Masters level (MS from Portland State University, Counselor Education Program), then returned for a doctoral degree after several years of field work as an addictions specialist, and couples and family counselor. I earned a PhD from Oregon State University and specialize in Counselor Education and Supervision. My education and training has prepared me to supervise student interns and prelicensure and postlicensure counselors, and I am skilled at providing supervision-of-supervision for clinical supervisors. For several years, I have taught a 30-hour course in clinical supervision that is required by the State of Oregon to supervise prelicensure registered interns. I am an Licensed Professional Counselor in Oregon and a Licensed Mental Health Counselor in Washington.

## SCOPE OF PRACTICE/AREAS OF COMPETENCE

I am qualified to supervise counselors who are using most common therapeutic modalities and treatment methods including group, couples, family, individual, and addiction-focused treatment methods. Some areas of practice are outside of my scope of competence, and I will not provide supervision in such cases (e.g., Eye Movement Desensitization and Reprocessing, hypnosis and related techniques).

## APPROACH TO SUPERVISION/METHODS

I approach supervision from a systems perspective and select an approach to supervision that best suits the supervisee's personality, philosophy, work setting, systemic context, competence level, and experiential history. I most frequently select an Integrated Development Model, Discrimination Model, or Systems Approach. I most typically integrate a developmental approach to supervision and primarily use a teaching and coaching role with novice supervisees and a consultation role with more experienced professionals.

Regardless of the approach, the underlying beliefs remain consistent. First, my role as a supervisor is always to protect client welfare, improve your skills and competence, and provide professional guidance and support, so that my supervisees can reach their fullest and most enjoyable potential. I am a facilitator and supporter whose primary purpose is to improve the competence of the counselor for the benefit of the clients, counselor, and the profession. Second, regardless of approach, a variety of supervision modalities and techniques will be used to best reach the core goals. We will use raw data review (video or audio recordings), dramatic techniques, art, journaling, sand tray, and other modalities that will further our work together. In addition, sometimes there are independent assignments ("homework") that are intended to assist the supervisee with dilemmas or areas of needed growth. "Homework" will not usually add strain to an already heavy workload and oftentimes will help a supervisee in alleviating stress or burden.

## EVALUATION

Evaluative feedback is a fundamental component of supervision and is interwoven into every supervision encounter. Informal evaluative feedback is provided in an ongoing manner in each session, and formal evaluative feedback is provided at regular intervals (based on supervisee needs and external requirements). All evaluation criteria are introduced at the beginning of the supervisory relationship, serve as training objectives, and are used throughout the process as a basis for ongoing feedback. The evaluation criteria include your developmental goals, professional and ethical standards of practice, and school or agency goals as appropriate. In addition to the feedback and evaluations I provide, supervises are asked to self-evaluate their performance and development regularly. This is to aid in the development of self-supervision and will allow me to gain further insight into your level of self-efficacy and professional needs.

## CONFIDENTIALITY AND PRIVILEGED COMMUNICATION

Confidentiality is a cornerstone of our profession, and we will guard client confidentiality with great caution and diligence. Due to the nature of clinical supervision, confidentiality extends to the client, but supervision itself should be considered private but not confidential. Supervisors are often asked to report to regulatory boards and other entities, and, at times, a supervisor needs to put concern for client welfare above a supervisee's desire for privacy. Confidentiality is not upheld if there is concerning evidence that the supervisee is unable to perform counseling at appropriate levels of competence and safety. Client records, audio and video recordings, and other materials with identifying features must be transported, stored, and reviewed in accordance with the highest level of diligence and concern for client confidentiality.

## SUPERVISION-OF-SUPERVISION

I understand the benefit and importance of maintaining and enhancing professional skills, and I am a firm believer in the value of ongoing supervision. Therefore, I participate in supervision of my supervision and consultation with well-respected, knowledgeable colleagues regarding my clinical and supervisory work. I may discuss my work and interactions with supervisees as part of such work, although names and identifying details will not typically be disclosed.

## FEES

No fees are charged to any supervisee if supervision occurs within the academic setting and as part of the supervisee's training (such as if I am their internship or practicum supervisor or I am the site supervisor at an agency). Other supervisees pay the agreed-upon rate at the start of each session as outlined in the supervision contract.

## EMERGENCY CONTACT

Supervisees should contact me by cell phone and send a text message indicating that there is an emergency. I typically return calls within the hour. If there is a medical or mental health emergency, do not await a return call. Supervisees are to follow the emergency protocol procedures set forth by their employer or as we discuss in the initial supervision session.

## ETHICAL ADHERENCE

I follow the Association for Counselor Education and Supervision Code of Ethics (now embedded in the American Counseling Association Code of Ethics) and National Board for Certified Counselors Code of Ethics and the Standards for the Ethical Practice of Clinical Supervision. I provide a copy of these documents to all supervisees, along with codes of ethics that apply to the supervisee's specific field of counseling (e.g., Addictions, Social Work, Marriage and Family Therapy).

# Appendix F

## Supervision Session Report

Date: _____

Supervisee name: _____

Others present in session: _____

Session location: _____ Duration (minutes): _____

### Supervision method(s):

Self-report _____ Audio review _____

Video review _____ Live observation _____

### Follow-up from prior session(s) or between session issues:

*List item(s)/outcome(s)*                                **Follow-up needed:**




### Current concerns/case reviews:

*List clients and relevant treatment*

*progress/concerns/plans*                                **Follow-up needed:**




### Professional development needs/concerns/plans:        **Follow-up needed:**




### Administrative items:                                **Follow-up needed:**

# References

Abbott, J. M., Klein, B., & Ciechomski, L. (2008). Best practices in online therapy. *Journal of Technology in Human Services, 26*(2/4), 360–375.

Ainsworth, M. S., & Bowlby, J. (1991). An ethological approach to personality development. *American Psychologist, 46*(4), 333–341.

Allen, G., Szollos, S., & Williams, B. (1986). Doctoral students' comparative evaluations of best and worst psychotherapy supervision. *Professional Psychology: Research and Practice, 17*(2), 91–99.

Altfeld, D., & Bernard, H. (1997). An experiential group model for group psychotherapy supervision. In C. E. Watkins, Jr. (Ed.), *Handbook of psychotherapy supervision* (pp. 381–399). New York, NY: John Wiley & Sons.

American Association for Marriage and Family Therapy. (1993). *Approved supervisor designation: Standards and responsibilities.* Washington, DC: Author.

American Association of State Counseling Boards (AASCB). (2011). *AASCB approved supervisor model.* Retrieved from http://www.aascb.org/displaycommon.cfm?an=8.

American Counseling Association. (1995). *ACA code of ethics and standards of practice.* Alexandria, VA: Author.

American Counseling Association. (2005). *Ethical standards.* Alexandria, VA: Author.

Association for Counselor Education and Supervision. (1990). *Standards for counseling supervisors.* Alexandria, VA: Author.

Association for Counselor Education and Supervision. (1993). Ethical guidelines for counseling supervisors. *ACES Spectrum, 53,* 1–4.

American Psychiatric Association. (2000). *Diagnostic and statistical manual of mental disorders* (Revised 4th ed.). Washington, DC: Author.

Association for Counselor Education and Supervision. (1993). *Ethical guidelines for counseling supervisors.* Alexandria, VA: Author.

Baird, B. N. (2008). *The internship, practicum, and field placement handbook: A guide for the helping professions.* Upper Saddle River, NJ: Pearson/Prentice Hall.

Bandura, A. (1982). Self-efficacy mechanism in human agency. *American Psychologist, 37*(2), 122–147.

Bandura, A., & Adams, N. E. (1977). Analysis of self-efficacy theory of behavioral change. *Cognitive Therapy and Research, 1*(4), 287–308.

Benson, K. P., & Holloway, E. (2005). Achieving influence: A grounded theory of how clinical supervisors evaluate trainees. *Qualitative Research in Psychology, 2*(2), 117–140.

Bernard, J. M. (1979). Supervisor training: A discrimination model. *Counselor Education and Supervision, 19,* 60–68.

Bernard, J. L., & O'Laughlin, D. L. (1990). Confidentiality: Do training clinics take it seriously? *Law & Psychology Review, 14*(59), 59–69.

Bernard, J. M. (1997). The discrimination model. In C. E. Watkins (Ed.), *Handbook of psychotherapy supervision* (pp. 310–327). New York, NY: Wiley.

Bernard, J. M., & Goodyear, R. G. (1998). *Fundamentals of clinical supervision* (2nd. ed.). Needham Heights, MA: Allyn & Bacon.

Bernard, J. M., & Goodyear, R. K. (2004). *Fundamentals of clinical supervision* (3rd ed.). Needham Heights, MA: Allyn & Bacon.

Bernard, J. M., & Goodyear, R. K. (2009). *Fundamentals of clinical supervision* (4th ed.). Upper Saddle River, NJ: Merrill/Pearson.

Berne, E. (1964). *Games people play.* New York: Grove.

Bhat, C. S., & Davis, T. E. (2007). Counseling supervisors' assessment of race, racial identity, and working alliance in supervisory dyads. *Journal of Multicultural Counseling and Development, 35*(2), 80.

Bidell, M. P. (2005). The sexual orientation counselor competency scale: Assessing attitudes, skills, and knowledge of counselors working with lesbian, gay, and bisexual clients. *Counselor Education and Supervision, 44*(4), 267–279.

Black, B. (1988). Components of effective and ineffective psychotherapy supervision as perceived by supervisees with different levels of clinical experience (Doctoral dissertation, Columbia University, 1987). *Dissertation Abstracts International, 48,* 3105B.

Black, H. C. (1990). *Black's law dictionary* (6th ed.). St. Paul, Minnesota: West Publishing.

Blume, A. W. (2005). *Treating drug problems.* New Jersey: Wiley.

Boethius, S. B., Sundin, E., & Ogren, M. -L. (2006). Group supervision from a small group perspective. *Nordic Psychology, 58*(1), 22.

Bond, M., & Holland, S. (1998). *Skills of clinical supervision for nurses: A practical guide for supervisees, clinical supervisors and managers.* Buckingham/Philadelphia, PA: Open University Press.

Borders, L. D. (1992). Learning to think like a supervisor. *The Clinical Supervisor, 10*(2), 135–148.

Borders, L. D., Cashwell, C. S., & Rotter, J. S. (1995). Supervision of counselor licensure applicants: A comparative study. *Counselor Education and Supervision, 35,* 54–69.

Borders, L. D., & Leddick, G. R. (1987). *Handbook of clinical supervision.* Alexandria, VA: American Association for Counseling and Development.

Borders, L. D., & Leddick, G. R. (1988). A nationwide survey of supervision training. *Counselor Education and Supervision, 27,* 271–283.

Borders, L. D. (1991). Supervisors' in-session behaviors and cognitions. *Counselor Education and Supervision, 31*(1), 32–47.

Borders, L. D., & Brown, L. L. (2005). *The new handbook of counseling supervision.* Mahwah, NJ: Lawrence Erlbaum Associates.

Bordin, E. S. (1979). The generalizability of the psychoanalytic concept of the working alliance. *Psychotherapy: Theory, Research, and Practice, 16*, 252–260.

Bordin, E. S. (1983). Supervision in counseling: II. Contemporary models of supervision: A working alliance based model of supervision. *Counseling Psychologist, 11*, 35–42.

Bowlby, J. (1988). *A secure base: Clinical applications of attachment theory.* London, England: Routledge.

Bradley, L. J., & Gould, L. J. (2001). Psychotherapy-based models of supervision. In L. J. Bradley & N. Ladany (Eds.) *Counselor supervision; principles, process and practice* (3rd ed., pp. 147–180). New York, NY: Brunner-Routledge.

Bradley, L. J., & Ladany, N. (2001). *Counselor supervision: Principles, process, and practice* (3rd ed.). New York, NY: Routledge.

Bradley, L. J., & Ladany, N. (2010). *Counselor supervision* (4th ed.). New York, NY: Routledge.

Bradshaw, T., Butterworth, A., & Mairs, H. (2007). Does workplace-based clinical supervisions during psychological intervention education enhance outcome for mental health nurses and the service users they work with? *Journal of Psychiatric and Mental Health Nursing, 14*, 4–12.

Breunlin, D. C., Karrer, B. M., McGuire, D. E., & Cimmarusti, R. A. (1988). Cybernetics of videotape supervision. In H. A. Liddle, D. C. Breunlin, & R. C. Schwartz (Eds.), *Handbook of family therapy supervision* (pp. 194–206). New York, NY: Guilford.

Bronson, M. K. (2010). Supervision of career counseling. In L. Ladany & L. J. Bradley (Eds.), *Counselor supervision* (4th ed., pp. 261–286). New York, NY: Routledge.

Browning, S., Collins, J. S., & Nelson, B. (2005). Creating families: A teaching technique for clinical training through role-playing. *Marriage & Family Review, 38*, 1–19.

Bubenzer, D. L., West, J. D., & Gold, J. M. (1991). Use of live supervision in counselor preparation. *Counselor Education and Supervision, 30*(4), 301–309.

Burkard, A., Johnson, A. J., Madson, M. B., Pruitt, N., & Contreras-Tadych, D. A. (2006). Supervisor cultural responsiveness and unresponsiveness in cross-cultural supervision. *Journal of Counseling Psychology, 53*(3), 288–301.

Campbell, J. (2006). *Essentials of clinical supervision.* New Jersey, NJ: Wiley & Sons.

Cannon, J. (1993). *Stellaluna.* Orlando, FL: Harcourt Brace.

Carifio, M., & Hess, A. (1987). Who is the ideal supervisor? *Professional Psychology: Research and Practice, 18*(3), 244–250.

Cashwell, C. S. (1994). *Interpersonal process recall. ERIC Clearinghouse on Counseling and Student Services, Greensboro, NC.* Washington, DC: Office of Educational Research and Improvement (ED).

Center for Credentialing and Education. (2009). *The approved clinical supervisor (ACS) code of ethics.* Retrieved from http://www.cce-global.org/extras/cce-global/pdfs/acs_codeofethics.pdf

Chur-Hansen, A., & McLean, S. (2006). Trainee psychiatrists' views about their supervisors and supervision. *Australian Psychiatry, 15*(4), 269–272.

Chur-Hansen, A., & McLean, S. (2007). Supervisors' views about their trainees and supervision. *Australasian Psychiatry, 15*(4), 273–275.

Claiborn, C. D., & Goodyear, R. K. (2005). Feedback in psychotherapy. *Journal of Clinical Psychology, 61*(2), 209–217.

Clariana, R. B., Wagner, D., & Roher Murphy, L. C. (2000). Applying a connectionist description of feedback timing. *Educational Technology Research and Development, 48*(3), 5–21.

Cobia, D. C., & Boes, S. R. (2000). Professional disclosure statements and formal plans for supervision: Two strategies for minimizing the risk of ethical conflicts in post-master's supervision. *Journal of Counseling and Development, 78,* 293–296.

Cobia, D. C., & Pipes, R. B. (2002). Mandated supervision: An invention for disciplined professionals. *Journal of Counseling and Development, 80*(2), 140–146.

Constantine, M. G. (1997). Facilitating multicultural competency in counseling supervision: Operationalizing a practical framework. In D. B. Pope-Davis & H. L. K. Coleman (Eds.), *Multicultural counseling competencies: Assessment, education and training, and supervision* (pp. 310–324), Thousand Oaks, CA: Sage Publications.

Constantine, M. G., & Sue, D. W. (2007). Perceptions of racial microaggressions among black supervisees in cross-racial dyads. *Journal of Counseling Psychology, 54*(2), 142–153.

Cook, D. A. (1994). Racial identity in supervision. *Counselor Education and Supervision, 34*(2), 132–141.

Cooper, J. B., & Ng, K. M. (2010). On becoming an emotionally intelligent counseling supervisor. In J. Culbreth & L. Brown (Eds.), *State of the art in clinical supervision* (pp. 207–234). New York, NY: Routledge.

Cormier, L. S., & Bernard, J. M. (1982). Ethical and legal responsibilities of clinical supervisors. *The Personnel and Guidance Journal, 60*(8), 486–491.

Corsini, R. J. (2002). *The dictionary of psychology.* London: Brunner-Routledge.

Costa, L. (1994). Reducing anxiety in live supervision. *Counselor Education and Supervision, 31*(1), 30–40.

Council for Accreditation of Counseling and Related Educational Programs. (2001). *2001 standards*. Retrieved from http://www.cacrep.org/doc/2001%20Standards.pdf

Council for Accreditation of Counseling and Related Educational Programs. (2008). *2009 standards*. Retrieved from http://www.cacrep.org/2009standards.html.

Crimando, W. (2004). Administration, management, and supervision. In T. F. Riggar & D. R. Maki (Eds.), *Handbook of rehabilitation counseling* (pp. 305–317). New York, NY: Springer.

Cross, E. G., & Brown, D. (1983). Counselor supervision as a function of trainee experience: Analysis of specific behaviors. *Counselor Education and Supervision, 22*, 333–341.

D'Andrea, M., Daniels, J., & Heck, R. (1991). Evaluating the impact of multicultural counseling training. *Journal of Counseling and Development, 70*, 143–150.

DeLucia-Waak, J. L., & Kalodner, C. R. (2005). Contemporary issues in group practice. In S. Wheelan (Ed.), *The handbook of group research and practice* (pp. 65–84). London, England: Sage Publications.

Dewald, P. A. (1997). The process of supervision in psychoanalysis. In C. E. Watkins (Ed.) *Handbook of psychotherapy supervision* (pp. 31–43). New York, NY: Wiley.

Disney, M. J., & Stephens, A. M. (1994). *Legal issues in clinical supervision* (10th ed.). Alexandria, VA: American Counseling Association.

Dowling, S., & Wittkopp, J. (1982). Students' perceived supervisory needs. *Journal of Communication Disorders, 15*, 319–328.

Drapela, V. J. (1983). *Counselor as consultant and supervisor* (211 p.). Springfield, IL: Thomas Publishing.

Duan, C., & Roehlke H. (2001). A descriptive "snapshot" of cross-racial supervision in university counseling center internships. *Journal of Non-White Concerns in Personnel and Guidance, 29*(2), 131–146.

Dudding, C. C., & Justice, L. M. (2004). An E-Supervision model: Videoconferencing as a clinical training tool. *Communication Disorders Quarterly, 25*(3), 145–151.

Duncan, B. L., Miller, S. D., Reynolds, L., Sparks, J., Claud, D., Brown, J., & Johnson, L. D. (2003). The session rating scale: Psychometric properties of a "working" alliance scale. *Journal of Brief Therapy, 3*(1), 3–12.

Dye, H. A., & Borders, L. D. (1990). Counseling supervisors: Standards for preparation and practice. *Journal of Counseling and Development, 69*, 27–32.

Eberle, R. F. (1971). *SCAMPER: Games for imagination development*. Buffalo, NY: D.O.K. Publishers.

Edwards, D., Cooper, L., Burnard, P., Hanningan, B., Adams, J., Fothergill, A., & Coyle, D. (2005). Factors influencing the effectiveness of clinical supervision. *Journal of Psychiatric and Mental Health Nursing, 12*, 405–414.

Edwards, T. M., & Heshmati, A. (2003). A guide for beginning family therapy group supervisors. *The American Journal of Family Therapy, 31*, 295–304.

Efstation, J. F., Patton, M. J., & Kardash, C. M. (1990). Measuring the working alliance in counselor supervision. *Journal of Counseling Psychology, 37*(3), 322–329.

Ekstein R., & Wallerstein, R. S. (1972). *The teaching and learning of psychotherapy* (2nd ed.). New York, NY: International University Press.

Elizur, J. (1990). "Stuckness" in live supervision: Expanding the therapist's style. *Journal of Family Therapy, 12*, 267–280.

Ellis, M. V. (2001). Harmful supervision, a cause for alarm: Comment on Gray et al. (2001) and Nelson and Friedlander (2001). *Journal of Counseling Psychology, 48*, 401–406.

English, R. W., Oberle, J. B., & Byrne, A. R. (1979). Rehabilitation counselor supervision: A national perspective. *Rehabilitation Counseling Bulletin Special Issue, 22*(3), 179–304.

Enyedy, K. C. (2003). Hindering phenomena in group supervision: Implications for practice. *Professional Psychology, Research and Practice (0735-7028), 34*(3), 312.

Eriksen, K., & McAuliffe, G. (2003). A measure of counselor competency. *Counselor Education and Supervision, 43*(2), 120–133.

Falender, C. A., & Shafranske, E. P. (2004). *Clinical supervision: A competency-based approach*. Washington, DC: American Psychological Association.

Falvey, J. (2001). Clinical judgment in case conceptualization and treatment planning across mental health disciplines. *Journal of Counseling and Development, 79*, 292–303.

Falvey, J. E. (2002). *Managing clinical supervision: Ethical practice and legal risk management*. Pacific Grove, CA: Brooks/Cole.

Falvey, J. E., Caldwell, C. F., & Cohen, C. R. (2002). *Documentation in supervision: The focused risk management supervision system FoRMSS*. Pacific Grove, CA: Brooks/Cole.

Faugier, B. (1994). Thin on the ground. *Nursing Times, 90*, 64–67.

Feltham, C., & Dryden, W. (1994). *Developing counselor supervision*. Thousand Oaks, CA: Sage Publications.

Fisher, B. (1989). Differences between supervision of beginning and advanced therapists: Hogan's hypothesis empirically revisited. *The Clinical Supervisor, 7*(1), 57–74.

Forester-Miller, H., & Davis, T. (1996). *A practitioner's guide to ethical decision-making*. Alexandria, VA: American Counseling Association.

Foster, V. A., & McAdams, C. R. (2009). A framework for creating a climate of transparency for professional performance assessment: Fostering student investment in gatekeeping. *Counselor Education and Supervision, 48*(4), 271–284.

Frame, M. W., & Stevens-Smith, P. (1995). Out of harm's way: Enhancing monitoring and dismissal processes in counselor education programs. *Counselor Education and Supervision, 35*, 118–129.

Frawley-O'Dea, M. G., & Sarnat, J. E. (2001). *The supervisory relationship: A contemporary psychodynamic approach.* New York, NY: Guilford Press.

Friedlander, M. L., & Ward, L. G. (1984). The name assigned to the document by the author. This field may also contain sub-titles, series names, and report numbers. Development and Validation of the Supervisory Styles Inventory. *Journal of Counseling Psychology, 31*(4), 541–557.

Gatmon, D., Jackson, D., Koshkarian, L., Martos-Perry, N., Molina, A., Patel, N., & Rodolfa, E. (2001). Exploring ethnic, gender, and sexual orientation variables in supervision: Do they really matter? *Journal of Multicultural Counseling and Development, 29*, 102–113.

Gelso, C. J., & Carter, J. A. (1985). The relationship in counseling and psychotherapy: Components, consequences, and theoretical antecedents. *Counseling Psychologist, 13*(2), 155–194.

Gladding, S. T. (2009). *Counseling: A comprehensive profession.* Upper Saddle River, NJ: Merrill/Pearson.

Gladding, S. T., & Henderson, D. A. (2000). Creativity and family counseling: The SCAMPER model as a template for promoting creative processes. *The Family Journal, 8*(3), 245–249.

Glaser, R. D., & Thorpe, J. S. (1986). Unethical intimacy. *American Psychologist, 41*, 43–51.

Glenn, E., & Serovich, J. M. (1994). Documentation of family therapy supervision: A rationale and method. *American Journal of Family Therapy, 22*, 345–355.

Goodyear, R. K., & Bradley, F. O. (1983). Part three: Integration and evaluation, theories of counselor supervision: Points of convergence and divergence. *The Counseling Psychologist, 11*(1), 59–67.

Goodyear, R. K., & Guzzardo, C. R. (2000). Psychotherapy supervision and training. In S. D. Brown & R. W. Lent (Eds.), *Handbook of counseling psychology* (3rd ed., pp. 83–108). New York, NY: Wiley.

Goodyear, R., Abadie, P., & Efros, F. (1984). Supervisory theory into practice: Differential perception of supervision by Ekstein, Ellis, Polster, and Rogers. *Journal of Counseling Psychology, 31*(2), 228–237.

Goodyear, R. K., & Nelson, M. L. (1997). The major formats of psychotherapy supervision. In C. E. Watkins, Jr. (Ed.), *Handbook of psychotherapy supervision* (pp. 328–344). New York: Wiley.

Gottlieb, M. C. (1993). Avoiding exploitive dual relationships: A decision-making model. *Psychotherapy: Theory, Research, Practice, and Training, 30,* 41–48.

Graham, M. A. (2007). *The Graham model of bibliosupervison: A multiple baseline analysis.* Unpublished doctoral dissertation, Oregon State University, Corvallis, OR.

Graham, M., & Pehrsson, D. (2009). Bibliosupervision: A creative supervision technique. *Journal of Creativity in Mental Health, 4*(4), 366–374.

Grant, B. (1995). Supervisory power as an asset. *AAMFT Supervision Bulletin, 8*(1), 63.

Gray, L. A., Ladany, N., Walker, J. A., & Ancis, J. R. (2001). Psychotherapy trainees' experience of counterproductive events in supervision. *Journal of Counseling Psychology, 48,* 371–383.

Greer, J. A. (2002). Where to turn for help: Responses to inadequate clinical supervision. *Clinical Supervisor, 21,* 135–143.

Griffith, B., & Frieden, J. (2000). Facilitating reflective thinking in counselor education. *Counselor Education and Supervision, 40,* 82–93.

Guest, C. L. J., & Dooley, K. (1999). Supervisor malpractice: Liability to the supervisee in clinical supervision. *Counselor Education and Supervision, 38*(4), 269–279.

Guiffrida, D. A., Jordan, R., Saiz, S., & Barnes, K. L. (2007). The use of metaphor in clinical supervision. *Journal of Counseling & Development, 85,* 393–400.

Guindon, M. (2011). *A counseling primer.* New York: Routledge.

Haas, L., & Malouf, J. L. (2005). *Keeping up the good work: A practitioner's guide to mental health ethics.* Sarasota, FL: Professional Resource Press.

Haggis, P. (Director). (2004). *Crash* [Motion picture]. United States: Bob Yari Productions-Dej Productions-Lions Gate Films.

Hahn, W. K., & Molnar, S. (1991). Intern evaluation in university counseling centers. *The Counseling Psychologist, 19,* 414–430.

Hansen, J. C., Pound, R., & Petro, C. (1976). Review of research on practicum supervision. *Counselor Education and Supervision, 16,* 107–116.

Hantoot, M. S. (2000). Lying in psychotherapy supervision: Why residents say one thing and do another. *Academic Psychiatry, 24*(4), 179–187.

Harrar, W. R., VandeCreek, L., & Knapp, S. (1990). Ethical and legal aspects of clinical supervision. *Professional Psychology: Research and Practice, 21,* 37–41.

Hart, G., Borders, L., Nance, D., & Paradise, L. (1995). Ethical guidelines for counseling supervisors. *Counselor Education and Supervision, 34,* 270–276.

Hattie, J., & Timperley, H. (2007). The power of feedback. *Review of Educational Research, 77*(1), 81–112.

Hayes, R. (1989). Group supervision. In L. Bradley (Ed.), *Counselor supervision: Principles, process and practice* (pp. 399–422). Muncie, IN: Accelerated Development.

Hayes, S. C., Wilson, K. G., Gifford, E. V., Follette, V. M., & Strosahl, K. (1996). Experiential avoidance and behavioral disorders: A functional dimensional approach to diagnosis and treatment. *Journal of Counseling and Clinical Psychology, 64*(6), 1152–1168.

Haynes, R., Corey, G., & Moulton, P. (2003). *Clinical supervision in the helping professions: A practical guide.* Pacific Grove, CA: Brooks Cole.

Heckman-Stone, H. C. (2003). Trainee preferences for feedback and evaluation in clinical supervision. *The Clinical Supervisor, 22*(1), 21–33.

Hein, S., & Lawson, G. (2008). Triadic supervision and its impact on the role of the supervisor: A qualitative examination of supervisors' perspectives. *Counselor Education & Supervision, 48*(1), 16–31.

Heine, S. H., Lehman, D. R., Markus, H. R., & Kitayama, S. (1999). Is there a universal need for positive self-regard? *Psychological Review, 106,* 766–794.

Heppner, M. J., O'Brien, K. M., Hinkelman, J. M., & Flores, L. Y. (1996). Training counseling psychologists in career development: Are we our own worst enemies? *The Counseling Psychologist, 24*(1), 105.

Heppner, P., & Handley, P. G. (1981). A study of the interpersonal influence process in supervision. *Journal of Counseling Psychology, 28*(5), 437–444.

Herbert, J. T. (1997). Quality assurance: Administration and supervision. In D. R. Maki & T. F. Riggar (Eds.), *Rehabilitation counseling profession and practice* (pp. 246–258). New York: Springer.

Herbert, J. T., & Trusty, J. (2006). Clinical supervision practices and satisfaction within the public vocational rehabilitation program. *Rehabilitation Counseling Bulletin, 49,* 66–80.

Herlihy, B. (2006). Ethical and legal issues in supervision. In J. Campbell, *Essentials of supervision* (pp. 18–34). New York: Wiley.

Hernandez-Wolfe, P. (2010). Family counseling supervision. In L. Ladany & L. J. Bradley (Eds.), *Counselor supervision* (4th ed., pp. 287–308). New York, NY: Routledge.

Hess, A. K. (1986). Growth in supervision: Stages of supervisee and supervisor development. *The Clinical Supervisor, 4*(1–2), 51–67.

Hinkle, M. G. (2008). "Psychodrama: A creative approach for addressing parallel process in group supervision." *Journal of Creativit in Mental Health, 3*(4), 15–23.

Holloway, E. L. (1987). Developmental models of supervision: Is it development? *Professional Psychology: Research and Practice, 19,* 138–140.

Holloway, E. L. (1992). Supervision: A way of teaching and learning. In S. D. Brown & R. W. Lent (Eds.), *Handbook of counseling psychology* (2nd ed., pp. 177–214). New York, NY: Wiley.

Holloway, E. L. (1994). Overseeing the overseer: Contextualizing training in supervision. *Journal of Counseling and Development, 72,* 526–530.

Holloway, E., & Carroll, M. (Eds.). (1999). *Training counselling supervisors: Strategies, methods and techniques.* London, England: Sage Ltd.

Holloway, E. L., Freund, R. D., Gardner, S. L., Nelson, M. L., & Walker, B. R. (1989). Relation of power and involvement to theoretical orientation in supervision: An analysis of discourse. *Journal of Counseling Psychology, 36,* 88–102.

Holloway, E. L., & Johnston, R. (1985). Group supervision: Widely practiced but poorly understood. *Counselor Education and Supervision, 24,* 332–340.

Holloway, E. L., & Neufeldt, S. A. (1995). Supervision: Its contributions to treatment efficacy. *Journal of Consulting and Clinical Psychology, 63,* 207–213.

Holloway, E. L., & Wampold, B. E. (1986). Relation between conceptual level and counseling-related tasks: A meta-analysis. *Journal of Counseling Psychology, 33,* 310–319.

Holloway, E. L. (1995). *Clinical supervision: A systems approach.* Thousand Oaks, CA: Sage Publications.

Holloway, E., & Wolleat, P. (1994). Supervision: The pragmatics of empowerment. *Journal of Education and Psychological Consultation, 5*(1), 23–43.

Homeyer, L. A., & Sweeney, D. S. (1998). *Sandtray: A practical manual.* Royal Oak, MI: Self-Esteem Shop.

Hubble, M. A., Duncan, B. L., & Miller, S. D. (1999). *The heart and soul of change: What works in therapy.* Washington, D.C.: APA Press.

Huber, C. H., & Baruth, L. G. (1987). *Ethical, legal, and professional issues in the practice of marriage and family therapy.* Columbus, OH: Merrill Publication Company.

Huhra, R. L., Yamokoski-Maynhart, C. A., & Prieto, L. R. (2008). Reviewing videotape in supervision: A developmental approach. *Journal of Counseling & Development, 86,* 412–418.

Hutt, C. H., Scott, J., & King, M. (1983). A phenomenological study of supervisees' positive and negative experiences in supervision. *Psychotherapy: Theory, Research & Practice, 20*(1), 118–123.

Inman, A. G. (2006). Supervisor multicultural competence and its relation to supervisory process and outcome. *Journal of Marital and Family Therapy, 32*(1), 73–85.

Inskipp, F., & Proctor, B. (1993). *Art, craft & tasks of counseling supervision (part 1).* Twinckenham: Cascade Publications.

Kadushin, A. (1968). Games people play in supervision. *Social Work, 13,* 23–32.

Kadushin, A., & Harkness, D. (2002). *Supervision in social work* (4th ed.). New York, NY: Columbia University Press.

Kagan, N. (1980). Influencing human interaction—Eighteen years with IPR. In A. K. Hess (Ed.), *Psychotherapysupervision: Theory, research, and practice* (pp. 262–283). New York: Wiley.

Kagan, N. I., & Kagan, H. (1997). Interpersonal process recall. In P. W. Dowrick (Ed.), *Practical guide to using video in the behavioral sciences* (pp. 221–230). New York: Wiley.

Kaiser, T. L. (1997). *Supervisory relationships: Exploring the human element.* Pacific Grove, CA: Brooks Cole Publishing.

Kerr, M., & Bowen, M. (1988). *Family evaluation: An approach based on Bowen theory.* New York: Norton.

Killian, K. D. (2001). Reconstructing racial histories and identities: The narratives of interracial couples. *Journal of Marital and Family Therapy, 27*(1), 27–42.

Kindsvatter, A., Granello, D. H., & Duba, J. (2008). Cognitive techniques as a means for facilitating supervisee development. *Counselor Education and Supervision, 47*(3), 179–192.

Kitchener, K. S. (1984). Intuition, critical evaluation and ethical principles: The foundation for ethical decisions in counseling psychology. *Counseling Psychologist, 12*(3), 43–55.

Klitzke, M. J., & Lombardo, T. W. (1991). A "Bug-in-the-Eye" can be better than a "Bug-in-the-Ear": A teleprompter technique for on-line therapy skills training. *Behavior Modification, 15*(1), 113–117.

Knapp, S., & Vandecreek, L. (1997). Ethical and legal aspects of clinical supervision. In C. E. Watkins (Ed.) *Handbook of psychotherapy supervision* (pp. 589–602). New York, NY: Wiley.

Knapp, S., VandeCreek, L. (2006). *Practical ethics for psychologists: A positive approach.* Washington, DC: American Psychological Association.

Kraus, R. (1971). *Leo the Late Bloomer.* Illustrations by Jose Aruego. New York: Windmill Books, HarperCollins.

Kurpius, D., Gibson, G., Lewis, J., & Corbett, M. (1991). Ethical issues in supervising counseling practitioners. *Counselor Education and Supervision, 31*, 48–55.

Ladany, N., Constantine, M. G., Miller, K., Erickson, C., & Muse-Burke, J. (2000). Supervisor countertransference: A qualitative investigation into its identification and description. *Journal of Counseling Psychology, 47*, 102–115.

Ladany, N., & Melincoff, D. S. (1999). The nature of counselor supervision nondisclosure. *Counselor Education & Supervision, 38*(3), 161–177.

Ladany, N., & Bradley, L. J. (2010). *Counselor supervision.* London, England: Routledge.

Ladany, N., & Friedlander, M. L. (1995). The relationship between the supervisory working alliance and supervisee role conflict and role ambiguity. *Counselor Education and Supervision, 34*, 220–231.

Ladany, N., & Walker, J. A. (2003). Supervisor self-disclosure: Balancing the uncontrollable narcissist with the indomitable altruist. *Journal of Clinical Psychology, 59*(5), 611–621.

Ladany, N., Friedlander, M. L., & Nelson, M. L. (2005). *Critical events in psychotherapy supervision: An interpersonal approach.* Washington, DC: American Psychological Association.

Ladany, N., Hill, C. E., Corbett, M. M., & Nutt, E. A. (1996). Nature, extent, and importance of what psychotherapy trainees do not disclose to supervisors. *Journal of Counseling Psychology, 43*, 10–24.

Ladany, N., Hofheinz, E. W., Inman, A. G., Constantine, M. G. (1997). Supervisee multicultural case conceptualization ability and self-reported multicultural competence as functions of supervisee racial identity and supervisor focus. *Journal of Counseling Psychology, 44*(3), 284–293.

Ladany, N., Lehrman-Waterman, D., Molinaro, M., & Wolgast, B. (1999). Psychotherapy supervisor ethical practices: Adherence to guidelines, the supervisory working alliance, and supervisee satisfaction. *The Counseling Psychologist, 27*(3), 443–475.

Ladany, N., Marotta, S., & Muse-Burke, J. L. (2001). Counselor experience related to complexity of case conceptualization and supervision preference. *Counselor Education and Supervision, 40*(3), 203–219.

Ladany, N., Walker, J. A., & Melincoff, D. S. (2001). Supervisory style: Its relationship to the supervisory working alliance and supervisor self-disclosure. *Counselor Education and Supervision, 40*, 263–275.

Lamb, D. H., Cochran, D. J., & Jackson, V. R. (1991). Training and organizational issues associated with identifying responding to intern impairment. Professional impairment during the internship: Identification, due process, and remediation. *Professional Psychology: Research and Practice, 18*, 597–603.

Lamb, D., Presser, N., Pfost, K., Baum, M., Jackson, R., & Jarvis, P. (1987). Confronting professional impairment during the internship: Identification, due process, and remediation. *Professional Psychology: Research and Practice, 18*, 597–603.

Lambert, M. J., & Barley, D. E. (2001). Introduction—Research summary on the therapeutic relationship and psychotherapy outcome. *Psychotherapy, 38*(4), 357.

Lambert, M. J. (1980). Research and the supervisory process. In A. K. Hess (Ed.), *Psychotherapy supervision: Theory, research, and practice* (pp. 423–452). New York, NY: Wiley.

Lambert, M. J., & Ogles, B. M. (1997). The effectiveness of psychotherapy supervision. In C. E. Watkins, Jr. (Ed.), *Handbook of psychotherapy supervision* (pp. 421–446). New York, NY: Wiley.

Larson, L. M., & Daniels, J. A. (1998). Review of the counseling self-efficacy literature. *The Counseling Psychologist, 26*(2), 179–218.

Lawson, G., Hein, H., & Getz, S. F. (2009). A model for using triadic supervision in counselor preparation programs. *Counselor Education and Supervision, 48*(4), 257–270.

Lawson, G., Hein, H., & Stuart, C. L. (2009). A qualitative investigation of supervisees experiences of triadic supervision. *Journal of Counseling and Development, 87*(4), 449–457.

Leddick, G., (1994). Developmental Models. In *Models of clinical supervision. ERIC digests.* Retrieved September 21, 2010 from http://www.ericdigests.org/1995-1/models.htm

Lee, R. E., & Everett, C. A. (2004). *The integrative family therapy supervisor: A primer.* New York, NY: Brunner-Routledge.

Leveton, E. (2001). *A clinician's guide to psychodrama* (3rd Ed.). New York, NY: Springer.

Levitt, D. H., & Alissa, B. (2010). Theories of counseling. In B. T. Erford (Ed.). *Orientation to the counseling profession: Advocacy, ethics, and essential professional foundations* (pp. 95–123). Boston, MA: Pearson.

Levitt, D. H., & Bray, A. (2010). Theories of counseling. In B. T. Erford (Ed.), *Orientation to the counseling profession: Advocacy, ethics, and essential professional foundations* (pp. 95–123). New Jersey: Merrill.

Liddle, H. A. (1988). Systematic supervision: Conceptual overlays and pragmatic guidelines. In H. A. Liddle, D. C. Breunlin, & R. C. Schwartz (Eds.), *Handbook of family therapy training and supervision* (pp. 153–171). New York, NY: Guilford.

Liddle, H. A., & Schwartz, R. (1983). Live supervision/consultation: Conceptual and pragmatic guidelines for family therapy training. *Family Process, 22,* 477–490.

Little, C., Packman, J., Smaby, M. H., & Maddux, C. D. (2005). The skilled counselor training model: Skills acquisition, self-assessment, and cognitive complexity. *Counselor Education & Supervision, 44*(3), 189–200.

Loganbill, C., Hardy, E., & Delworth, U. (1982). Supervision: A conceptual model. *The Counseling Psychologist, 10,* 3–42.

Luke, M, & Bernard, J. M. (2006). The school counseling supervision model: An extension of the discrimination model. *Counselor Education and Supervision, 45,* 282–295.

Lyddon, W. J., Clay, A. L., & Sparks, C. L. (2001). Metaphor and change in counseling. *Journal of Counseling & Development, 79*(3), 269–274.

Lyth, G. (2000). Clinical supervision: A concept analysis. *Journal of Advanced Nursing, 31*(3), 722–729.

Magnuson, S., Norem, K., & Wilcoxon, S. A. (2002). Clinical supervision for licensure: A consumer's guide. *Journal of Humanistic Counseling, Education and Development, 41*(1), 52–60.

Magnuson, S., & Shaw, H. (2003). Adaptations of the multifaceted genogram in counseling, training, and supervision. *The Family Journal, 11,* 45–54.

Magnuson, S., Wilcoxon, S. A., & Norem, K. (1999). A profile of lousy supervision: Experienced counselors' perspectives. *Counselor Education and Supervision, 39*(3), 189–203.

Magnuson, S., Wilcoxon, S. A., & Norem, K. (2000). A profile of lousy supervision: Experienced counselors' perspectives. *Counselor Education and Supervision, 39*, 189–202.

Maggs, C. (1994). Mentorship in nursing and midwifery education: Issues for research. *Nurse Education Today, 14*, 22–29.

Maki, D. R., & Bernard, J. M. (2003). The ethics of clinical supervision. In R. R. Cottone & V. M. Tarvydas (Eds.). *Ethical and professional issues in counseling*. Upper Saddle River, NJ: Merrill Publishers.

Mandoki, L. (Director). (1994). When a man loves a woman [Motion picture]. United States: Touchstone Pictures.

McAdams C. R., III, & Wyatt, K. L. (2010). The regulation of technology-assisted distance counseling and supervision in the United States: An analysis of current extent, trends, and implications. *Counselor Education and Supervision, 49*, 179–192.

McCarthy, P., Sugden, S., Koker, M., Lamendola, F., Maurer, S., & Renninger, S. (1995). A practical guide to informed consent in clinical supervision. *Counselor Education and Supervision, 35*, 130–138.

McCollum, E. E., & Wetchler, J. L. (1995). In defense of case consultation: Maybe "dead" supervision isn't dead after all. *Journal of Marital and Family Therapy, 21*(2), 155–166.

McNeill, B. W., & Worthen, V. (1989). The parallel process in psychotherapy supervision. *Professional Psychology: Research and Practice, 20*(5), 329–333.

Melchert, T. P., Hays, V. L., Wiljanen, L. M., & Kolocek, A. K. (1996). Testing models of counselor development with a measure of counseling self-efficacy. *Journal of Counseling & Development, 74*, 640–644.

Miars, R. D., Tracey, T. J., Ray, P. B., Cornfeld, J. L., O'Farrell, M., & Gelso, C. J. (1983). Variation in supervision process across trainees experience levels. *Journal of Counseling Psychology, 30*(3), 403–412.

Middleman, R. R., & Rhodes, G. B. (1985). *Competent supervision: Making imaginative judgments*. Englewood Cliffs, NJ: Prentice-Hall.

Miles, M., & Morse, J. (1995) Using the concepts of transference and counter-transference in the consultation process. *Journal of the American Psychiatric Nurses Association, 1*(2), 42–47.

Millar, A. (2009). Develping skills: Practice, observation, and feedback. In: P. Henderson (Ed.), *Supervisor training: Issues and approaches* (2nd ed., pp. 107–122). London, England: Karnac Books.

Miller, C. D., & Oetting, E. R. (1966). Students react to supervision. *Counselor Education and Supervision, 6*(1), 73–74.

Milne, D. (2009). Evidence-based clinical supervision: Principles and practice. Chichester, UK: BPS/Blackwell.

Milne, D., James, I., Keegan, D., & Dudley, M. (2002). Teacher's PETS: A new observational measure of experiential training interactions. *Clinical Psychology & Psychotherapy, 9,* 187–199.

Milne, D. L., Leck, C., & Choudhri, N. Z. (2009). Collusion in clinical supervision: Literature review and case study in self-reflection. *The Cognitive Behaviour Therapist, 2,* 106–114.

Milne, D. L., Pilkington, J., Gracie, J., & James, I. A. (2003). Transferring skills from supervision to therapy: A qualitative and quantitative N=1 analysis. *Behavourial and Cognitive Psychotherapy, 31,* 193–202.

Milne, D., & Westerman, C. (2001). Evidence-based clinical supervision: Rationale and illustration. *Clinical Psychology & Psychotherapy, 8*(6), 444–457.

Milne, D., Aylott, H., Fitzpatrick, H., & Ellis, M. V. (2008). How does clinical supervision work? Using a "best evidence synthesis" approach to construct a basic model of supervision. *The Clinical Supervisor, 27*(2), 170–190.

Montalvo, B. (1973). Aspects of live supervision. *Family Process, 12,* 343–359.

Moreno, J. L. (1946). *Psychodrama: Volume I.* New York: Beacon House.

Morrissey, J., & Tribe, R. (2001). Parallel process in supervision. *Counselling Psychology Quarterly, 14*(2), 103–110.

Morrison, M., & Homeyer, L. (2008). Supervision in the sand. In A. Drews & J. Mullen (Eds.), *Supervision can be playful: Techniques for child and play therapist supervisors.* Lanham, MD: Rowman and Littlefield.

Moskowitz, S. A., & Rupert, P. A. (1983). Conflict resolution within the supervisory relationship. *Professional Psychology: Research and Practice, 14*(5), 632–641.

National Board for Certified Counselors. (2005). *Code of ethics.* Greensboro, NC: Author.

Nelson, M. L., & Holloway, E. L. (1990). The relation of gender to power and involvement in supervision. *Journal of Counseling Psychology, 37,* 473–481.

Nelson, M. L., & Friedlander, M. L. (2001). A close look at conflictual supervisory relationships: The trainee's perspective. *Journal of Counseling Psychology, 48,* 384–395.

Nelson, M. L., Barnes, K. L., Evans, A. L., & Triggiano, P. J. (2008). Working with conflict in clinical supervision: Wise supervisors' perspectives. *Journal of Counseling Psychology, 55*(2), 172–184.

Nelson, M. L., & Neufeldt, M. A. (1998). The pedagogy of counseling: A critical examination. *Counselor Education & Supervision, 38,* 70–88.

Neswald-McCalip, R. (2001). Development of the secure counselor: Case examples supporting Pistole & Watkins's (1995) discussion of attachment theory in counseling supervision. *Counselor Education and Supervision, 41*(1), 18–27.

Neufeldt, S. A. (1999). *Supervision strategies for the first practicum* (2nd ed.). Alexandria, VA: American Counseling Association.

Newgent, R. A., Davis, H., Jr., & Farley, R. C. (2005). Perceptions of individual, triadic, and group models of supervision: A pilot study. *Clinical Supervisor, 23*, 65–79.

Noelle, M. (2002). Self-report in supervision: Positive and negative slants. *The Clinical Supervisor, 21*, 125–134.

Nordentoft, H. M. (2008). Changes in emotion work at interdisciplinary conferences following clinical supervision in a palliative outpatient ward. *Qualitative Health Research, 18*(7), 913–927.

Nystul, M. S. (2011). *Introduction to counseling: An art and science perspective* (4th ed.). Upper Saddle River, New Jersey: Pearson.

Ohrt, J. H., Foster, J. M., Hutchinson, T. S., & Ieva, K. P. (2009). Using music videos to enhance empathy in counselors-in-training. *Journal of Creativity in Mental Health, 4*(4), 320–333.

Oliver, M., Nelson, K., & Ybanez, K. Systemic processes in triadic supervision. *Clinical Supervisor, 29*(1), 51–67.

Orchowski, L., Evangelista, N. M., & Probst, D. R. (2010). Enhancing supervisee reflectivity in clinical supervision: A case study illustration. *Psychotherapy: Theory, Research, Practice, Training, 47*(1), 51–67.

Osborn, C. J., & Davis, T. E. (1996). The supervision contract: Making it perfectly clear. *The Clinical Supervisor, 14*(2), 121–134.

Osborn, C. J., & Kelly, B. L. (2010). No surprises: Practices for conducting supervisee evaluations. In J. R. Culbreth & L. L. Brown (Eds.), *State of the art in clinical supervision* (pp. 19–44). New York: Routledge/Taylor & Francis.

Overholser, J. C. (1993). Elements of the Socratic method: I. Systematic questioning. *Psychotherapy: Theory, Research, Practice, Training, 30*(1), 67–74.

Page, S., & Wosket, V. (2001). *Supervising the counsellor: A Cyclical model.* London: Brunner-Routledge.

Patterson, C. H. (1974). *Relationship counseling and psychotherapy.* New York: Harper & Row.

Patton, M. J., & Kivlighan, D. M. J. (1997). Relevance of the supervisory alliance to the counseling alliance and to treatment adherence in counselor training. *Journal of Counseling Psychology, 44*, 108–111.

Pearson, Q. M. (2000). Opportunities and challenges in the supervisory relationship: Implications for counselor supervision. *Journal of Mental Health Counseling, 22*, 283–294.

Pearson, B., & Piazza, N. (1997). Classification of dual relationships in the helping professions. *Counselor Education and Supervision, 37*(2), 89–99.

Pederson, P. B. (1991). Multiculturalism as a generic approach to counseling. *Journal of Counseling and Development, 70*, 6–12.

Peterson, F. K. (1991). Issues of race and ethnicity in supervision: Emphasizing who you are, not what you know. *The Clinical Supervisor, 9*(1), 15–31.

Perosa, L. M., & Perosa, S. L. (2010). Assessing competencies in couples and family therapy/counseling: A Call to the profession. *Journal of Marital and Family Therapy, 36*, 126–143.

Pfeffer, J., & Salancik, G. R. (1975). Determinants of supervisory behavior: A role set analysis. *Human Relations, 28*(2), 139–154.

Pierce, R., Carkhuff, R. R., & Berenson, B. G. (1967). The differential effects of high and low functioning counselors upon counselors-in-training. *Journal of Clinical Psychology, 23*, 212–215.

Pistole, M. C., & Watkins, C. E. J. (1995). Attachment theory, counseling process, and supervision. *Counseling Psychologist, 23*(3), 457–478.

Powell, D. J. (2004). *Clinical supervision in alcohol and drug abuse counseling: Principles, models, methods.* New Jersey, NJ: Jossey-Bass.

Prest, L. A., Schindler-Zimmerman, T., & Sporakowski, M. J. (1992). The initial supervision session checklist (ISSC): A guide for the MFT supervision process. *The Clinical Supervisor, 10*, 117–133.

Priest, R. (1994). Minority supervisor and majority supervisee: Another perspective of clinical reality. *Counselor Education and Supervision, 32* (2), 152–158.

Prieto, L. R., & Scheel, K. R. (2002). Using case documentation to strengthen counselor trainees' case conceptualization skills. *Journal of Counseling and Development, 81*, 455–461.

Proctor, B. (2006). Contracting in supervision. In C. Sills (Ed.), *Contracts in counseling and psychotherapy* (pp. 161–174).Thousand Oaks, CA: Sage Publications.

Quarto, C. J. (2002). Supervisors and supervisees perceptions of control and conflict in counseling supervision. *The Clinical Supervisor, 21*(2), 21–37.

Ramos-Sanchez, L., Esnil, E., Goodwin, A., Riggs, S., Osachy, T. L., Wright, L. K., Ratanasiripong, P. & Rodolfa, E. (2002). Negative supervisory events: Effects on supervision and supervisory alliance. *Professional Psychology: Research and Practice, 33*(2), 197–202.

Rak, C. F., & Britton, P. J. (1997). Common counselor struggles with supervision. *The Journal for the Professional Counselor, 12*, 55–66.

Ray, D., & Altekruse, M. (2000). Effectiveness of group supervision versus combined group and individual supervision. *Counselor Education & Supervision, 40*(1), 19–30.

Recupero, P. R., & Rainey S. E. (2007). Liability and risk management in outpatient psychotherapy supervision. *Journal American Academy of Psychiatry Law, 35*, 188–195.

Rigazio-DiGilio, S. A., Daniels, T. G., & Ivey, A. E. (1997). Systematic cognitive developmental supervision: A developmental-integrative approach to psychotherapy supervision. In C. E. Watkins (Ed.) *Handbook of psychotherapy supervision* (pp. 233–248). New York, NY: Wiley.

Ringel, S. (2001). In the shadow of death: Relational paradigms in clinical supervision. *Clinical Social Work Journal, 29*(2), 171.

Roe, R. A. (2002). What makes a competent psychologist? *European Psychologist, 7*(3), 192–202.

Rogers, C. R. (1957). The necessary and sufficient conditions of therapeutic personality change. *Journal of Counseling Psychoogy, 21*, 95–103.

Romans, J. S. C., Boswell, D. L., Carlozzi, A. F., & Ferguson, D. B. (1995). Training and supervision practices in clinical, counseling, and school psychology programs. *Professional Psychology: Research and Practice, 26*, 407–412.

Ronnestad, M. H., & Skovholt, T. M. (1993). Supervision of beginning and advanced graduate students of counseling and psychotherapy. *Journal of Counseling and Development, 71*, 396–405.

Rose Burke, W., Goodyear, R. K., & Guzzard, C. R. (1998). Weakenings and repairs in supervisory alliances. *American Journal of Psychotherapy, 52*(4), 450–462.

Rosenblatt, A., & Mayer, J. (1975). Objectionable supervising styles: Students' views. *Social Work, 18*, 184–189.

Rosenbaum, M., & Ronen, T. (1998). Clinical supervision from the standpoint of cognitive-behavior therapy. *Cognitive-Behavior Therapy (CBT) Supervision, 35*(2), 220–230.

Rowell, P. C. (2010). Group supervision of individual counseling. In N. Ladany & L. J. Bradley (Eds.). *Counselor supervision* (pp. 197–214). New York: Taylor & Francis.

Roulx, K. R. (1969). Some physiological effects of tape recording on supervised counselors. *Counselor Education and Supervision, 8*, 201–205.

Rubel, D. J., & Kline, W. B. (2008). An exploratory study of expert group leadership. *The Journal for Specialists in Group Work, 33*(2), 138–160.

Safran, J. D., & Muran, J. C. (2000). *Negotiating the therapeutic alliance: A relational treatment guide*. New York: Guilford Press.

Scherl, C., & Haley, J. (2000). Computer monitor supervision: A clinical note. *American Journal of Family Therapy, 28*(3), 275–282.

Schmidt, J. P. (1979). Psychotherapy supervision: A cognitive-behavioral model. *Professional Psychology, 10*(3), 278–284.

Scott, K. J., Ingram, K. M., Vitanza, S. A., & Smith, N. G. (2000). Training in supervision: A survey of current practices. *The Counseling Psychologist, 28*(3), 403–422.

Searles, H. F. (1955). The informational value of the supervisor's emotional experiences. *Psychiatry, 18*, 135–146.

Seuss, T. (1990). *Oh, the places you'll go*. New York: Random House Books.

Sexton, T. L., Whiston, S. C., Bluer, J. C., & Walz, G. R. (1997). *Integrating outcome research into counseling practice and training*. Alexandria, VA: American Counseling Association.

Sherry, P. (1991). Ethical issues in the conduct of supervision. *The Counseling Psychologist, 19*(4), 566–584.

Shellenberger, S. (2007). Use of the genogram with families for assessment and treatment. In F. Shapiro, F. W. Kaslow, & L. Maxfield (Eds.), *Handbook of EMDR and family therapy processes* (pp. 76–94). New York: Wiley.

Shulman, L. (2006). The clinical supervisor-practitioner working alliance: A parallel process. *The Clinical Supervisor, 24*, 23–47.

Silverstein, S. (1964). *The giving tree*. New York: Harper & Row.

Snider, P. D. (1985). The duty to warn: A potential issue of litigation for the counseling supervisor. *Counselor Education and Supervision, 25*(1), 66–73.

Smaby, M., Maddux, C., Torres-Rivera, E., & Zimmick, R. (1999). A study of the effects of a skills-based versus a conventional group counseling training program. *Journalists for Specialists in Group Work, 24*, 152–163.

Smith, A. L. (2009). Role play in counselor education and supervision: Innovative ideas, gaps, and future direction. *Journal of Creativity in Mental Health, 4*, 124–138.

Smith, R. C., Mead, D. E., & Kinsella, J. A. (1998). Direct supervision: Adding computer- assisted feedback and data capture to live supervision. *Journal of Marital and Family Therapy, 24*(1), 113–126.

Sodowsky, G. R., Taffe, R. C., Gutkin, T. B., & Wise, S. L. (1994). Development of the multicultural counseling inventory: A self-report measure of multicultural competencies. *Journal of Counseling Psychology, 41*, 137–148.

Spence, S. H., Wilson, J., Kavanagh, D., Strong, J., & Worrall, L. (2001). Clinical supervision in four mental health professions: A review of the evidence. *Behaviour Change, 18*(3), 135–155.

Stadler, H. A. (1986). Making hard choices: Clarifying controversial ethical issues. *Counseling & Human Development, 19*, 1–10.

Stevens, D. T., Goodyear, R. K., & Robertson, P. (1997). Supervisor development: An exploratory study in changes in stance and emphasis. *The Clinical Supervisor, 16*, 73–88.

Stinchfield, T. A., Hill, N. R., & Kleist, D. M. (2007). The reflective model of traidic supervision: Defining an emerging modality. *Counselor Education and Supervision, 46*(3), 172–183.

Stoltenberg, C. (2005). Enhancing professional competence through developmental approaches to supervision. *American Psychologist, 60*, 857–864.

Stoltenberg, C. D., & Delworth, U. (1987). *Supervising counselors and therapists: A developmental approach*. San Francisco, CA: Jossey-Bass.

Stoltenberg, C. D., & McNeill, B. W. (1997). Clinical supervision from a developmental perspective: Research and practice. In E. Watkins, Jr. (Ed.), *Handbook of psychotherapy supervision* (pp. 184–202). New York, NY: Wiley.

Stoltenberg, C. D., & McNeill, B. W. (2010). *IDM supervision: An integrative developmental model for supervision counselors and therapists.* New York, NY: Routledge.

Stoltenberg, C. D., McNeill, B. W., & Delworth, U. (1998). *IDM supervision: An integrated developmental model for supervising counselors and therapists.* San Francisco, CA: Jossey-Bass.

Stoltenberg, C., McNeill, B., & Crethar, H. (1994). Changes in supervision as counselors and therapists gain experience: A review. *Professional Psychology: Research and Practice, 25*(4), 416–449.

Storm, C., York, C., Vincent, R., McDowell, T., & Lewis, R. (1997). The Postgraduate Competency Document (PGCD). In C. Storm & T. Todd (Eds.), *The reasonably complete systemic supervisor resource guide* (pp. 195–202). Needham Heights, MA: Allyn & Bacon.

Sue, D. W. (2004). Whiteness and ethnocentric monoculturalism: Making the "invisible" visible. *American Psychologist, 59,* 759–769.

Supervision Interest Network, Association for Counselor Education and Supervision. (1993, Summer). ACES ethical guidelines for counseling supervisors. *ACES Spectrum, 53*(4), 5–8.

Tanenbaum, R. L., & Berman, M. A. (1990). Ethical and legal issues in psychotherapy supervision. *Psychotherapy in Private Practice, 8,* 65–77.

Teitelbaum, S. H. (1990). Supertransference: The role of the supervisor's blind spots. *Psychoanalytic Psychology, 7,* 243–258.

Tobin, D. J., & McCurdy, K. G. (2006). Adlerian-Focused supervision for countertransference work with counselors-in-training. *The Journal of Individual Psychology, 62*(2), 154–167.

Townend, M. (2008). Clinical supervision in cognitive behavioral psychotherapy: development of a model for mental health nursing through ground theory. *Journal of Psychiatric and Mental Health Nursing, 15,* 328–339.

Tummala-Narra, P. (2004). Dynamics of race and culture in the supervisory encounter. *Psychoanalytic Psychology, 21*(2), 200–311.

Urbani, S., Smith, M., Maddux, C., Smaby, M., Torres-Rivera, E., & Crews, J. (2002). Skills-based training and counselor self-efficacy. *Counselor Education and Supervision, 42,* 92–106.

Usher, C. H., & Borders, L. D. (1993). Practicing counselors' preference for supervisory style and supervisory emphasis. *Counselor Education and Supervision, 33*(2), 66–79.

van de Ridder, J., Stokking, K. M., McGaghie, W. C., & ten Cate, O. J. (2008). What is feedback in clinical education? *Medical Education, 42*(2), 189–197.

Vesper, J. H., & Brock, G. W. (1991). Ethics, legalities, and professional practice issues in marriage and family therapy. Boston, MA: Allyn & Bacon.

Villalba, J. A., & Redmond, R. E. (2008). Crash: Using a popular film as an experiential learning activity in a multicultural counseling course. *Counselor Education & Supervision, 47*(4), 264–276.

Wampold, B. E., & Hollway, E. L. (1997). Methodology, design and evaluation in psychotherapy supervision research. In C. E. Watkins (Ed.) *Handbook of psychotherapy supervision* (pp. 233–248). New York, NY: Wiley.

Ward, L. G., Friedlander, M. L., Schoen, L. G., & Klein, J. C. (1985). Strategic self-presentation in supervision. *Journal of Counseling Psychology, 32*, 111–118.

Watkins, C. E., Jr. (1990). The separation-individuation process in psychotherapy supervision. *Psychotherapy, 27*, 202–209.

Watkins, C. E., Jr. (1992). Reflections on the preparation of psychotherapy supervisors. *Journal of Clinical Psychology, 48*, 145–147.

Watkins, C. E., Jr. (1993). Development of the psychotherapy supervisor: Concepts, assumptions, and hypotheses of the Supervisor Complexity Model. *American Journal of Psychotherapy, 47*, 58–74.

Watkins, C. E., Jr. (1995). Psychotherapy supervision in the 1990s: Some observations and reflections. *American Journal of Psychotherapy, 49*(4), 568–581.

Watkins, C. E., Jr. (Ed.). (1997). *Handbook of psychotherapy supervision*. New York, NY: Wiley.

Watson, J. C. (2003). Computer-based supervision: Implementing computer technology into the delivery of counseling supervision. *Journal of Technology and Counseling*. Retrieved from http://jtc.colstate.edu/vol3_1/Watson/Watson.htm.

Welfare, L. E. (2010). Evaluation in supervision. In L. Ladany & L. J. Bradley (Eds.), *Counselor supervision* (4th ed., pp. 337–351). New York, NY: Routledge.

West, J. D., Bubenzer, D. L., Pinsoneault, T., & Holeman, V. (1993). Three supervision modalities for training marital and family counselors. *Counselor Education and Supervision, 33*, 127–138.

Westfield, J. S. (2009). Supervision of psychotherapy models, issues, and recommendations. *The Counseling Psychologist, 37*(2), 296–316.

Whitman, S. M., & Jacobs, E. G. (1998). Responsibilities of the psychotherapy supervisor. *American Journal of Psychotherapy, 52*(2), 166–175.

Wiley, M., & Ray, P. (1986). Counseling supervision by developmental level. *Journal of Counseling Psychology, 33*, 439–445.

Wolpe, J. (1973). *The Practice of Behavior Therapy* (2nd ed.). New York: Pergamon Press.

Wood, J. A., Hargrove, D. S., & Miller, T. W. (2005). Clinical supervision in rural settings: A Telehealth model. *Professional Psychology: Research and Practice, 36*(2), 173–179.

Wood, J. A. V., Miller, T. W., & Hargrove, D. S. (2005). Clinical supervision in rural settings: A telehealth model. *Professional Psychology: Research and Practice, 36*, 173–179.

Worthen, V., & McNeill, B. W. (1996). A phenomenological investigation of "good" supervision events. *Journal of Counseling Psychology, 43*, 25–34.

Worthington, E. L., Jr. (1987). Changes in supervision as counselors and supervisors gain experience: A review. *Professional Psychology: Research and Practice, 18*, 189–208.

Wulf, J., & Nelson, M. L. (2000). Experienced psychologists' recollections of predoctoral internship supervision, and its contributions to their development. *Clinical Supervisor, 19*(2), 123–145.

Ybarra, M., & Eaton, W. (2005). Internet-based mental health interventions. *Mental Health Services Research, 7*(2), 75–87.

Zinkin, L., (1989). The group as a container and contained. *Group Analysis, 22*(3), 227–234.

# Index

Made in the USA
Middletown, DE
15 January 2019